Unlocking God's Secrets

Past, Present, and Future

Bob Morley

Unlocking God's Secrets

Past, Present, and Future

Bob Morley

Ambassador International
GREENVILLE, SOUTH CAROLINA & BELFAST, NORTHERN IRELAND

Unlocking God's Secrets: Past, Present, and Future
© 2008 Bob Morley
All rights reserved
Printed in the United States of America

Cover design and page layout by David Siglin of A&E Media

ISBN 978-1-932307-95-5
Published by the Ambassador Group

Ambassador International
427 Wade Hampton Blvd.
Greenville, SC 29609
USA
www.emeraldhouse.com

and

Ambassador Publications Ltd.
Providence House
Ardenlee Street
Belfast BT6 8QJ
Northern Ireland
www.ambassador-productions.com

The colophon is a trademark of Ambassador

Copyright: November 8, 2007
U.S. Library of Congress

TXu 1-569-861

DEDICATION

This book is dedicated to every person who passes the information contained on these pages to others who need to know.

PART ONE

PART ONE

CHAPTER ONE

This past week I was watching a debate on TV between two heralds of the atheistic corner versus two die hard believers. The score was tied zero to zero, and I kept waiting for the knock out punch to be thrown. Unfortunately, like a heavyweight boxing match between two over the hill has beens who had spent the majority of their training time at the dinner table, the match ended with arms hanging limp in both corners. All the old worn out punches had been thrown, and neither side had been moved. The tiresome effort expended by both sides was the only indicator that the match had even occurred. Both were weary, but nothing was accomplished. Neither side could prove whether there was or was not a God.

Sound familiar? For generations the greatest debate has continued, sometimes heated, but often reduced to merely a hum drum philosophical discussion. Almost everyone is resigned to the "fact" that there is no definitive answer. One side ends up using the "it must be taken on faith" ploy, while the other side is reduced to the weak "since He can't be proven, God must not exist" catch all. The most monumental and important question that can be answered has become the biggest stalemate of all time.

It's time for all the debaters to hit the showers. The secret truth is that there is no debate at all. The dramatic answer has been given. The problem is that virtually no one was paying attention. The definitive proof was masterfully spelled out very simply, but the world was asleep at the switch. This book is the alarm clock. Once you read the absolute truth outlined in these pages, you, too, will be ready to hand a shower towel to every person you ever meet who thinks there is still anything to debate. You, too, will be able to say with authority, "Hit the showers. It is finished."

Additionally, for maybe the very first time in your life, you will understand what the entire history of the whole world is all about, from beginning to end, and what your particular role in it actually is. By the last sentence of this book you will finally know the answer to the age old question, "What is the true meaning of life?"

But first, let's take an exciting journey that will put an absolute end to the debate about the existence of God. We are about to explore something that was in plain sight all along, and we are going to be in complete shock at what we see.

CHAPTER TWO

I can hear you now. "So, Bob, what is this simple truth that can end this debate once and for all?"

There is a straightforward statement in Isaiah 46:10 that says, *"I am God, and there is none like me. I make known the end from the beginning, from ancient times, what is still to come."*

That is it. That is the simple truth that ends all debate. God proves His existence by foretelling things to come, long before they happen. No mortal could tell twenty five hundred years in advance the exact date that something will occur. But God did. No mortal could string together thousands of predictions and not miss on a single one. Never. But God did. And He based the proof of His existence on doing exactly that.

He even went so far as to name the names of unsuspecting participants in future events, hundreds of years before they were even born. Talk about audacity. Only a fool would do something that absurd, unless He really was the God who knew everything. To name names and set dates hundreds or thousands of years in advance, as proof of who He is, is utterly preposterous, unless . . . unless he truly, and irrefutably, is God. Unless He wanted to stop the debate once and forever. Unless He wanted to send the debaters to the showers, cold showers at that.

God knew that everyone would want to know for sure if He existed. The problem is that virtually no one has taken the time to look at the undisputable proof He gave us. It was right before our eyes, but if it wasn't on prime time TV, or on the front page of the local newspaper, our society surely wasn't going to search for it. And that's where the problem lies. Proverbs 25:2 says, *"It is the glory of God to conceal a matter; to search out a matter is the glory of kings."* Unfortunately the word "search" brings to mind thoughts of hard work and much time spent. We think we spend more than enough time at work as it is, and any spare time at all should be given to our inalienable right of chasing pleasure and rest. Who wants to actually "search" out something?

Fortunately the hard work of searching out the hidden things has been done for us. Now, you and I are going to look at the evidence. The shower towels are in the drier. By the end of these pages we will be able to start passing them out.

Let's start with one of His proofs that I mentioned in which He even boldly told the name of one of the future prophetic participants, more than a hundred years before he was even born, even before his parents knew what they would name him, or even existed themselves. This fulfilled prophecy obviously caused the knees to wobble of the man it happened to, when he found that He had been singled out by name by God. I'll bet he shuddered at night for quite a few months to come.

We need to go back twenty six hundred years to find a fellow named Cyrus. His father, Cambyses, was king of Persia, while his mother, Mandane, was the daughter of the Median King Astgag. When Cambyses died in 559 BC, Cyrus took over the throne and became the Persian king. Not satisfied with that, he revolted against his Median grandfather and took over the Medes as well, thus uniting the Persian Mede Empire.

Conquest seemed to be Cyrus's long suit, so he fairly quickly set out to conquer Asia Minor and Lydia. By 540 BC Cyrus decided that about the only thing left to add to his trophy case was Babylon. As long as Nebuchadnezzar was the king of the Assyrians, Cyrus stayed put, but by 539 BC the feared king Nebuchadnezzar was dead and buried, and the likelihood of victory seemed much more sure. Nebuchadnezzar's son, Belshazzar, was in his second year at the Assyrian helm, so Cyrus marched his army straight to the Babylonia stronghold. Without us looking into the phenomenal "writing on the wall" episode here, we'll just shorten the story by saying that without a single Medo-Persian loss of life, Cyrus put an end to the Assyrian Empire.

One of the things Cyrus did as king of pretty much the entire known world was free the Jewish slaves he found in Babylon. He did this in the spring of 536 BC. We know this not only because the Bible tells us, but because in 1880 an archaeologist named

Hormuad Rassam excavated a cylinder which is now known as the Cyrus Cylinder, on which is written his conquests, as well as his policy to let the Israelite slave nation go home and rebuild their destroyed city of Jerusalem, as well as the temple to their God. This entire era is well documented in secular history. And the tomb of Cyrus, by the way, is still on the siteseeing 'things to see' list in the town of Pasargadae, Iran.

Before we get into the really juicy part, let me mention that the reason the Jews were being held in captivity in the first place was that Nebuchadnezzar and his ferocious Assyrians had pretty much wiped out the nations of Israel and Judah back in the spring of 606 BC. We might mention that it was at that time that Daniel, of the later 'lion den' fame, was taken into captivity. By the time Cyrus showed up, Daniel was an old man of 83 and was on hand to witness his takeover.

Over a hundred years before Cyrus was even born, about 700 BC, God was telling a man by the name of Isaiah some things He wanted written down for posterity, primarily so that you and I could send the debaters to the showers.

In Isaiah 45:1-5, God said, "*This is what the Lord says to His anointed, to Cyrus, whose right hand I take hold of to subdue nations before him and to strip kings of their armor, to open doors before him so that gates will not be shut: I will go before you and will level the mountains; I will break down the gates of bronze and cut through the bars of iron. I will give you the treasures of darkness, riches stored in secret places, so that you may know that I am the Lord, the God of Israel, who summons you by name. For the sake of Jacob my servant, of Israel my chosen, I summon you by name and bestow on you a title of honor, though you do not acknowledge me. I am the Lord, and there is no other; apart from me there is no God.*"

In the chapter preceding that, God had said, "*This is what the Lord says - your redeemer, who formed you in the womb: . . . who says of Cyrus, 'He is my shepherd and I will accomplish all I please; he will say of Jerusalem, "Let it be rebuilt," and of the temple, "let its foundations be laid."'*" Isaiah 44:24-28

Think long and hard about what we just read. Well over a hundred years before Cyrus was even born, and almost a hundred years before the Jewish people were even overthrown by the Assyrians, God wrote a message to tell you and me that He would form a baby in its mother's womb who would be named Cyrus. This child would later, by God's design, become a mighty enough king to take over the fierce Assyrians, during a future Israelite captivity that had not even begun. God then foretold that Cyrus would also free the enslaved Jews and let them rebuild their capital city and its temple, both of which at that time were still standing.

Only someone outside of our time and space could predict such a series of events that would come true a hundred and fifty years later. Obviously no human could do something like that. Remember, this is the type of prophecy God told us would be the proof of His existence.

As an aside, the famous historian, Josephus, tells us that Cyrus was actually handed the scroll of Isaiah in which God had written His letter to him. We can be confident that the fact that the Jewish God had talked directly to him so many years in advance was the reason that Cyrus readily freed the Jewish slaves and allowed them to return to Jerusalem and rebuild their city and temple. Interestingly, however, Cyrus never stopped his pagan worship, also just like God had foretold in Isaiah, when He said to the then unborn Cyrus, *"though you do not acknowledge me."*

Let's examine this historic episode deeper. In 700 BC the nations of Israel and Judah were doing fine. They were in such good shape that they had totally thrown God out of their society and were head over heels into the worship of idols. They thought that they were invincible. They thought that they had no need for the God of their forefathers, a God they could not see.

God foretold in numerous books of the Bible that He had had enough of their idol worship. He told them in several prophecies that they were going into captivity for their refusal to acknowledge him. In fact, through His prophet Jeremiah, God had told them, *"And this land shall be a desolation and astonishment and these nations shall serve the king of Babylon seventy years."* Jeremiah 25:11

Did you notice that not only did God tell them that they were going into captivity, but He also told them what country would defeat them, and for how long the captivity would last? That in itself is an astonishing prophecy that was fulfilled exactly as He said it would be.

Obviously He was right about the defeating king being the Assyrian king who reigned from Babylon. Now, let's add up the years and see about the seventy year part. From the spring of 606 BC to the spring of 536 BC is seventy years. We can be confident that the date of the captivity and the date of freedom were the very same date. When God says seventy years, He always hits it on the head, to the day. In fact, we will look at some other even more astounding examples in which He did foretell exact dates, and not surprisingly He was always correct.

One of them was fulfilled just recently, and quite honestly is one of my two very favorite prophecies.

Keep on reading. We are just beginning to scratch the surface of the proof that the debate has long since been over. The participants were just too busy listening to the sound of their own voices to hear the news. As we will see, with one fulfilled prophecy after another, God gave us the definitive proof of His existence.

CHAPTER THREE

Before we leave the period of the Israelite bondage in Babylon, we will take a look at what may be one of the strangest and most complicated proofs that God gave us of His existence. It also took one of the longest periods of time to fulfill. Additionally, it is one of His most exact foretellings, ending exactly on the prescribed date. As a result of all of this, it is one of the most awesome stories you will ever hear. And it is one of my very favorite examples of the extraordinary way God has proven to us that the debate about His existence is completely ridiculous.

One of the people who lived during the period of captivity that we have been discussing was Ezekiel. God spoke many of His prophecies through him, but strangely, God often made poor Ezekiel act them out in order to have a more dramatic effect on the Jews who were around him.

For instance, God once told Ezekiel to lie on his left side for 390 days, and then on his right side for an additional 40 days. He told Ezekiel that this was to represent punishment for Israel's disobedience. We can't be sure if God made poor Ezekiel lie that way all day long or just for a few hours a day, but whatever the case, it surely must have caused his friends to take notice.

God's exact instruction to Ezekiel was, *"I have assigned you the same number of days as the years of their sin. So for 390 days you will bear the sin of the house of Israel. After you have finished this, lie down again, this time on your right side, and bear the sin of the house of Judah. I have assigned you 40 days, a day for each year."* Ezekiel 4:5-6 God goes on to tell the people of Israel through His prophet, Ezekiel, that He is extremely angry with them because they've been worshiping idols instead of Him. That is the reason for their current bondage. He then explains His future punishment by saying, *"I will inflict punishment on you and will scatter your survivors to the winds."* Ezekiel 5:10

So, what we know at this point is that because of the Jewish infidelity to God, He is going to punish them for a total period of 430 years (390 years for the sins of Israel, plus 40 years for the sins of Judah), and that their 430 year punishment will include a period of captivity, plus a period of being scattered to the winds.

We also know from the last chapter that the captivity lasted seventy years, exactly as God also had predicted. Logic tells us that the Jews were going to be in for a period of 360 years of being scattered after the slavery in Babylon was over. That is the total of 430 years minus the 70 years of captive punishment already served. On top of that, we know that the captivity ended in 536 BC when Cyrus released the Jews to return to their promised land to rebuild Jerusalem and their temple.

We need to also know, though, that history tells us that only about 42,000 of the half million population of Jews in Babylon actually made the 600 mile journey back to Jerusalem. Most of the rest decided to just stick around in Babylon. We must realize that after 70 years in captivity the vast majority of released Jews did not even remember their parents' old land. It stands to reason when we consider that after the Civil War very few released slaves made any effort to return to Africa either. By that time, America was home. It was the only home they really knew.

Other than the 42,000 Jews who headed back to Jerusalem, the ones who did want to pick up their few belongings and start life anew decided to go north to lands they had heard about that sounded like more prosperous territory. Additionally, I will mention that of the 42,000 who did return to their parents' homeland, very few could be called true children of God. Most of those had been long since indoctrinated to the worship of pagan Babylonian idols, and they continued to do it.

Getting back to our prophecy, it should be obvious that since God had said that the total period of punishment would be 430 years, and since the 70 years in captivity had been served, we should now see the nation of Israel come back together 360 years later, or 176 BC. That was the predicted year for the end of the total punishment, the end of the scattering to the winds.

This is where the story really gets fun. In 176 BC nothing happened. Oops. Did I just say that nothing happened? Can the debaters return from the showers and take the platform again? Did God miss on that one? It sure seems like it.

The fact is, that as scholars came and went through the centuries trying to make some sense of this one prophecy gone awry, the only answer that seemed to fit was a type of debaters' answer that there "really was no answer." People needed to either just "keep the faith and believe" in the face of this doubt, or jump up and down and say, "We've got you, there is no God." Century after century dragged on this way. No one could figure out why the "scattering of Israel" did not end in 176 BC. The Jews kept getting scattered farther and farther apart. They were constantly thrown out of nations, or persecuted unmercifully in places like Russia and Hitler's Germany.

The ingathering never occurred. They even lost their native language, Hebrew, which became for all intent and purposes a dead language like Latin. The scattered Jewish people found themselves in 70 different nations, hated by almost everyone.

It seemed like God had really goofed up this time. There was even the famous prophecy of God showing Ezekiel the valley of dry bones, symbolizing the nation of Israel. In that story God asked, *"Can these bones live?"* He then told Ezekiel, *"Prophesy to these bones and say to them, 'dry bones, hear the word of the Lord! This is what the sovereign Lord says to these bones: I will make breath enter you, and you will come to life.*

I will attach tendons to you and make flesh come upon you and cover you with skin; I will put breath in you and you will come to life. Then you will know that I am the Lord." Ezekiel 37:3

God even boldly went on to say in verse 20, *"I will take the Israelites out of the nations where they have gone. I will gather them from all around and bring them back into their own land.*

I will make them one nation in the land, on the mountains of Israel."

Later, to another one of His favorite people, God had the audacity to tell the whole world, including us, that this rebirth would happen in only one day. He told Isaiah to write down, *"Who has ever heard such a thing? Who has ever seen such a thing? Can a country be born in one day or a nation be brought forth in a moment? ...Rejoice with Jerusalem and be glad for her, all you who love her, rejoice greatly with her, all you who mourn over her."* Isaiah 66:8-9

After time seemed to drag endlessly on, scholars began to write books about how the Jews would be reunited again as prophesied, but that it would happen in heaven. And as the books were published the debaters gradually started taking to the stage. "There is no all knowing God," they said.

Poor Ezekiel's having to lie on his sides for a total of 430 days was brushed aside and tried to be forgotten as the blunder that it obviously was. No one wanted to talk about it at all. It was a mystery sent to the closet of "faith".

Then, like a whirlwind, events took place almost in an instant on the historical stage and on May 15, 1948, Israel once again became a nation, in one day. Everything happened as predicted. God was given more credence. Everything happened the way He said it would happen.

The problem for everyone "in the know" was that everything really didn't happen the way God said it would. The astute Bible scholars deep down inside knew that God had said it would happen in 176 BC. A day or two off would have been one thing, but a prophetic miss of over two thousand years is a stretch by anybody's rules. If this prophetic date was wrong, the very existence of an all knowing God could well be in question.

Enter now an extremely smart student of the Bible named Dr. Grant Jeffrey. For some reason he happened to notice a neglected fact that in Leviticus 26 God repeated a principle four separate times. In verse 18 He said, *"If after all this you will not listen to me, I will punish you for your sins seven times over."* God went on to reiterate the point in verse 21 by saying, *"If you remain hostile to me and refuse to listen to me, I will multiply your afflictions seven times over, as your sins deserve."*

God knew the Israelites were like children and had to be warned over and over, so in the same chapter, verses 23 & 24, God reworded the fact again by saying, *"If in spite of these things you do not accept my correction but continue to be hostile toward me, I myself will be hostile to you and will inflict you for your sins seven times over.* And just for good measure God drove home the point in verse 28 with, *"Then in my anger I will be hostile toward you, and I myself will punish you for your sins seven times over."*

All right, it now seems fairly clear that if God pronounced a punishment, and the attitude adjustment He required did not occur, His children were going to sit in the corner seven times longer than He originally had specified.

So let's review what had happened. God had told the Jewish people that because they did not acknowledge Him as God, they were going to have 430 years of punishment, including 70 years as slaves to the Babylonians, plus 360 years of being scattered to the wind. That should have all occurred from 606 BC to 176 BC. The rub was that after the first seventy years the Jews were supposed to realize that He was their God and repent. Unfortunately that didn't happen. Even the few who returned to Jerusalem snubbed the majority of their 42,000 noses at Him. They either continued worshiping the idols they had worshiped in Babylon, or they worshiped nothing.

Now, though, knowing the seven times rule, we can look back and see if God's prophecy of time was correct after all. The first thing we need to do is multiply the remaining 360 years of punishment left after the captivity by seven. That gives us 2,520 years. Next we need to convert from the 360 day years of the Hebrew lunar calendar to our years which contain 365 1/4 days. That means that the new punishment period of scattering for the Jews should last 2,484 of our solar years. Hang in there. We are just about finished doing math.

So, counting 2,484 years from 536 BC forward, we come up to the year 1948. Even more astonishing than the year is the fact that if we take the total number of days involved, 907,200, and move forward from the date of Cyrus's decree, which we do know, we end up at May 15, 1948. That is the exact date that Israel declared itself as a nation and was accepted by the UN, the only time in the history of the world that a nation actually became a nation in only one day, exactly as God said would happen in Isaiah 66:8, to the exact day. Over 2,500 years in advance God predicted the exact date that Israel would again become a nation, and on May 15,1948, it happened as He said.

I think you can understand why this entire prophecy is one that I rank in my top two favorites. Surely only God, outside of our time dimension, could have pulled this one off. Can any man or woman alive actually debate with a straight face the fact that there is a God in the face of such an astonishing plethora of amazing predictions? It would be unfathomable, but there is even more, as we shall soon see.

Chapter Four

We have already seen in just a few illustrations that are startling to say the least, that the existence of God is undeniable. If you haven't come to that conclusion yet, I'm convinced that you will see the door nailed shut as we examine many more and diverse examples of God's complete infallibility.

Before we do that, though, I would like to take a moment to exercise some kindness toward the four debaters who drove me to the computer to write these pages.

On one side we had two non believers who I am sure are totally convinced of their stand, and in ways I can understand their position. When I was a young lad there was a lot of talk about Sasquatch. Countless articles were written, putting forth the idea that Bigfoot did indeed exist in the far northwest wilds. Every other magazine seemed to pose some pretty good notions that made thinking people wonder about the possibility of his existence. As time went on, though, no concrete proof ever materialized. The end result for most of us was the realization, "since he can't be proven, he must not exist." That is exactly what the non believing debater hung his hat on, just as thousands before him had done. In fact, having been a staunch non believer myself for thirty years of my life, I did exactly the same thing. Of course, just as with all the other non believers, my problem stemmed from the fact that I had never been told the information we are exploring right now. I did not know that there was irrefutable proof of the existence of God.

On the other side of the platform were the two believers. As I said, their final response was basically that some things must be "taken on faith." Now, I have no problem with some things being taken on faith. Obviously as a believer there are some things that I, too, take on faith. But the existence of God is way too important for you and me, and the entire human race, to take on faith. All of our decisions are altered by our belief that God is, or is not, real.

The faith issue normally boils down to an illustration of sitting in a chair. We are told that the act of sitting is an act of faith, and it is. We have faith that the chair will hold us up. Without that faith we would sit down very gingerly. The problem with that analogy is that some people sit down in their chair and unexpectedly find themselves in a heap on the floor. Granted, it doesn't happen often, but it does happen. Therefore, faith is actually just a form of hope. Admittedly, it is the highest form of hope there is, but it still is hope. In a way, the book of Hebrews alluded to that when we are told that *"faith is the substance of things hoped for."*

Now, before all of you believers start throwing rocks in my direction I will complete the writer of Hebrews statement, which I believe to be God's statement as well, that faith is also the *"evidence of things not seen."* And as I said, there are many things that I as a believer do take on faith, and I believe that my unwavering faith in those things occurring in the future are the evidence that they will indeed happen. Expounding on that statement would fill a book, and if I were writing it you would see how much I truly believe in living by faith; however, that discourse is not relevant to what needs to be accomplished in these pages.

What needs to be done here is to prove without a shadow of a doubt to anyone reading these pages that the existence of God is not a matter of faith. The existence of God is even a more solid fact than the existence of the law of gravity. We can have faith that the chair won't fall down, but if it should, we undeniably *know* that we will hit the floor. The law of gravity is far beyond a faith act. It is fact. Irrefutable fact. In the same manner, God gave us undebatable fact that He exists, and is who He says He is, the sovereign God over everything. And everything includes everything, which by the way, includes you and me.

One of the most important ways that God accomplished this *knowing* for us was with His prophecies that come true every single time. As we saw in the beginning of this book, God said, *"I am God and there is none like me, I make known the end from the beginning, from ancient times, what is still to come."* Isaiah 46:10

So important to God was prophecy in proving His existence to mankind that to date we know that 8,352 verses in the Bible are prophetic. That is almost a third of the entire Bible. We can be one hundred percent convinced, though, that every year we will find more and more verses that contain prophecies. It may in fact be that on some level every single verse in the Bible is actually prophetic. We are all still babies when it comes to God's Word.

With such an overpowering proof of God's being real staring us in the face, it is amazing to me that the newspapers don't print about it on the front page of the paper every day. Unfortunately, though, even the average churches of today don't seem to want to talk about it. It could be because the ministers themselves don't really want to take the time necessary to "search out the matter", or it could be that most believers have just come to associate the word prophecy with the end times, and they would rather not think about that subject. That whole "end times" thing gets too close to home to their own mortality, and that, of course, is a forbidden topic in our society.

End time prophecy does exist, and it is fascinating, but as we have already seen, it is not the end time prophecies that prove today that God is as real as the law of gravity. It is the prophecy that has already come to pass so dramatically, the way God said that it would, that nails the door shut on any doubt about Him. And as we have already glimpsed, God's prophecy is so awesome as to often make us say WOW.

One such case for me has to do with one of my boyhood heroes, Alexander the Great. For those of us who studied hard at the last minute for our high school and junior high history tests, and then promptly forgot every name and date the minute we laid our pencils down, it might be a good idea to first take a look at this young man who accomplished more in fifteen years than any other figure in history. In fact, he changed the world for the future more than anyone else who ever lived, with the exception, of course, of Jesus.

When Alexander was born in 356 BC, Greece was still just a geographical grouping of five different tribes who hated and were constantly at battle with each other. It was the Hatfields and McCoys times four. Skirmishes and outright battles were daily occurrences, and had been since long before anyone could remember. Each tribe had their own warrior king, and Alexander's father, Phillip, was the king of the tribal state of Macedonia.

Talk about an education, Alexander's teacher as a young lad was non other than the great Greek philosopher, Aristotle.

If you have ever read works by Aristotle, you can appreciate why the young Alexander often would sneak away and run off to watch his father train his men for battle. That obviously was a lot more fun for a boy than listening to Aristotle hour after hour. And with these training exercises as a class room, Alexander was to become one of the military geniuses of all time.

At age eighteen Alexander's life, and the life of our planet, changed dramatically with the thrust of a knife by a lunatic assassin. Phillip was killed on the steps of the temple of Zeus and instantly our young hero became the king of Macedonia. Alexander, who was with his father at the time, did jump in and kill the assassin, but there has always been some speculation that possibly he had some part in the plot.

While watching his father train his army, Alexander had been formulating battle tactics in his mind. Now that he was king he quickly trained his inherited army in these revolutionary strategies, including a brand new battle formation he came up with known as the phalanx, which along with other ingenious new tactics, introduced the speed of a leopard to his fighting forces. Within just months he had indoctrinated his charges in these new maneuvers and he set out to conquer all four of the other Grecian tribes.

Not only did Alexander succeed with lightning fast speed to defeat the other armies, which no other Greek had ever been able to do, but he convinced the other tribes to unite and form one nation. His men loved him, partially because he never told them what to do in battle, but instead said only, "Follow me." His bravery and courage were never questioned. It is interesting that through the years literally thousands of arrows, lances, and swords came flying in his direction, but he did not die on the battle field. As we read on we will get a clue as to why.

One of the problems the brilliant young Alexander could immediately see with this new Greek nation was that each of the five former tribes spoke a different language. He understood that this would cause a gigantic communication problem, especially in battle, since his army would now be a combination of the previous five tribal armies. Having studied at Aristotle's feet, who himself was a master linguist, Alexander sat down and created, by himself, a new language from the different dialects. It was called Koine Greek, or common Greek, and he demanded that all his soldiers learn it.

In only two years Alexander felt that his new combined army was ready for conquest, and he personally hungered for it. As we saw a few chapters back, a few hundred years earlier Cyrus had united the Medes and the Persians and this new Medo-Persian empire, now led by King Darius, was in total control of most of the known world. Alexander wanted what Darius had. The problem was that his army, and brand new baby nation, did not share his confidence that the forces of Darius could be defeated.

Secretly Alexander decided to change that. Under the pretext of liberating the oppressed Greeks living in Troy, on the western coast of what is now Turkey, Alexander led his superiorly trained army against a few Medo-Persian outposts. He advertised it to his subjects as a quick in and out liberation raid. Unknown to all his advisers and generals, Alexander had two underlying motives.

He knew that he could raise his army's confidence with rapid victories, and he also knew that he would infuriate King Darius who would bring his entire might against him. That was what Alexander really wanted. He alone in Greece knew that his army could defeat Darius if it was forced to fight.

Like lightning the new Grecian army obliterated several smaller Medo-Persian outposts, which did indeed raise his army's spirits; and at the same time he positioned his own forces so that there would be no way for them to escape, should Darius join the fray with his whole force. His army would have to fight.

As planned, Darius was enraged and mobilized his formidable forces to teach this upstart Greek king a lesson. But Alexander had been planning for this for years as he would lie in his bed at night. The strategy he devised was to quickly demoralize the Persian army. And his plan to accomplish that was to immediately destroy their most elite battalion. With the cunning of a leopard Alexander actually stalked this battalion, and when he felt the terrain was perfect he led his entire force straight at them with his new phalanx maneuver, tearing them to shreds so quickly that even his own army didn't realize what had happened. The rest of the Medo-Persian army was completely stunned. They had never seen anything like this, and inside each of Darius's men was fear. The confidence now in the hearts of the Greeks was at an all time high.

Alexander did not stop to rest on his laurels. He immediately kept up the offensive, picking and choosing his lightning swift attacks. The Medo-Persian army was in total disarray. The solders of Darius panicked and fled, leaving their king unprotected. In fact, two of those soldiers, seeking to gain favor with Alexander, killed King Darius and rushed to tell him. Alexander's response was that only a king could kill a king, and he immediately slew both of the traitors himself.

Alexander had done the impossible. He had defeated the army that supposedly could not be defeated. And he had done it almost effortlessly. His own army was delirious. This upstart nation that had been created almost overnight from a band of five rival tribes, that didn't even speak the same language, had demolished the greatest power in the world. The year was 331 BC, and Alexander was only 25 years old. From then on his soldiers would follow him to the gates of hell if he said, "Follow me."

Even though Alexander now was king over not only Greece, but the entire Medo-Persian empire, he was not satisfied. He wanted the whole world. And basically that is what he got. His army headed south and took control of the land bridge that united the three continents of Asia, Africa, and Europe. This land bridge extended from Egypt in the south all the way north to what is now Istanbul, Turkey. They then even conquered land all the way eastward to India and the gateway to China.

Alexander was not just a military genius, though, because his ideas of winning over the conquered people were equally as effective as his military strategies. Once an empire or nation was under his control he did not enslave them. Instead, he allowed them to pretty much do things they way they wanted. His only real passion was that they embrace the Greek culture and his new "Common Greek" language. This practice endeared him to his subjects worldwide.

In 323 BC Alexander the Great died at the young age of 33. In fifteen short years he had conquered the known world. In the process he united the world in language in a way that even the Roman Empire that would come later could not change. Even the Israelites who were scattered around the world found that they needed to have their scriptures that we now call the Old Testament translated from Hebrew into Greek, in what is referred to as the Septuagint, or LXX. As an aside, the name Septuagint comes from the fact that it took seventy translators seven months to complete. And interestingly, the translation was done in the city that bears our hero's name, Alexandria, Egypt.

When Alexander died his son was at his side. This boy would normally have been given the scepter; however, when asked, "To whom do you will your kingdom?", he replied, "Give it to the strong." As a result, his four generals divided up the empire. Lysimachus took Greece. Cassander got Asia Minor. Seleucus took Syria and east to old Persia. And Ptolemy took Egypt and a big part of North Africa.

In fifteen short years Alexander had completely changed the face of the world and much of its future. Though many have tried, never before or after has there been anyone like him. He truly was "the Great."

So why in the world did we spend so much time in a history lesson on Alexander the Great? Because God told his story hundreds of years in advance through His prophet Daniel. In fact, when Alexander and his army headed south to conquer Egypt he naturally took over Jerusalem and the rest of Israel as well. History tells us that the high priest at the time requested an audience with Alexander and showed him the second, seventh, and eighth chapters of Daniel, in which God had foretold his life. Alexander is reputed to have fallen down and declared the God of Israel the God of gods. He then took with him many of the Jewish royal family of Judah and made them administrators of the conquered lands. This had much to do with the further scattering of the Jews and the need for the Septuagint to be printed in Alexander's own language.

Let's see exactly what God had said back during the time when Nebuchadnezzar's Assyrian Empire was at its zenith, before Cyrus had even united the Medes and Persians and created the empire that Alexander would later destroy. At the time these prophecies were made there was no nation of Greece, and the smartest people of the time would have wagered all they had on the probability that those five warring tribes that lived there could never be united, no less ever become world conquerors. But even hundreds of years in advance, God could see everything that would happen in the future.

The book of Daniel is one of the most phenomenal books in the Bible. The prophecies contained in it are so detailed that only someone outside our time limitations could have uttered them. The fulfilling of many of them occurred with our hero, Alexander, and his four generals, and you are going to be awe struck as you read them in the next chapter.

To give you just a taste, though, I will tell you that through Daniel, God was to outline a bit of future that we now can look at as history. In these remarkable prophecies God outlined the four world empires; the Assyrians, the Persia-Medes, the Greeks, and the Romans; but let's take a quick glance at what God showed Daniel in two separate visions about Alexander.

About his first vision, Daniel said in chapter 8, *"Suddenly a goat with a prominent horn between his eyes came from the west, crossing the whole earth without touching the ground. He came toward the two horned ram I had seen standing beside the canal and charged at him in great rage. I saw him attack the ram furiously, striking the ram and shattering his two horns. The ram was powerless to stand against him; the goat knocked him to the ground and trampled on him, and none could rescue the ram from his power. The goat became very great, but at the height of his power his large horn was broken off, and in its place four prominent horns grew up toward the four winds of heaven,"*

God, being all wise, knew that debaters would come along who scoffed at this and said that it could have represented several people in history, or none at all. So, leaving nothing to chance, God sent an angel to Daniel to interpret the vision for him, and for us. Here is what the angel had to say in verses 20 through 22, *"The two horned ram that you saw represents the kings of Media and Persia. The shaggy goat is the king of Greece* (Remember, Greece was hundreds of years away from even becoming a nation at that time), *and the large horn between his eye is the first king* (The first king of Greece was Alexander). *The four horns that replaced the one that was broken off represent four kingdoms that will emerge from his nation but will never have the same power* (As we saw, Greece was divided among Alexander's four generals)."

To clarify it even more, God gave Daniel another dream and interpreted it as well through an angel in chapter 11. In the interpretation the angel says (speaking of Darius), *"When he has gained power by his wealth, he will stir up everyone against the kingdom of Greece. Then a mighty king will appear, who will rule with great power and do as he pleases. After he has appeared, his empire will be broken up and parceled out toward the four winds of heaven. It will not go to his descendants, nor will it have the power he exercised because his empire will be uprooted and given to others."*

Lest we forget, when Daniel was given these dreams, and these interpretations, the Assyrians under Nebuchadnezzar were the dominant world empire and Daniel was in captivity in the capital of Babylon, along with another Israelite we mentioned earlier by the name of Ezekiel. The thought of Greece becoming a united nation in the future would have been considered the ramblings of a lunatic. But God, of course, sees the whole future, and He showed Daniel what was going to happen, which fortunately provided us in the 21st century with unquestionable proof that He exists. He did not want that fact to become a "faith" issue. He knew that between then and now we humans would finally understand that gravity is a fact, and He wanted His existence to be able to be proven just as conclusively.

In the next chapter you will see the minutest details God would provide to make His point an unchallengeable one.

CHAPTER FIVE

Later on you and I are going to be looking at beautiful and exciting prophecies that have come to fulfillment in just the past few years, about things having to do with flowers and lakes and highways and vegetables and all sorts of things: foretellings that have just recently come true that will excite us as to how they are impacting our daily lives today. But for right now it is important that we continue to look at things that God predicted that have been fulfilled in the past in phenomenal detail. It is exciting because they prove to us that He exists, and that He is who He says He is.

Therefore, I am going to stay with Daniel for a little while. Daniel, by the way, is my very favorite person in the Old Testament. When we examine virtually every other hero that was written about, we are met with plenty of character flaws, and that includes the big names like Abraham, Jacob, Isaac, David, Samson, and the rest. Daniel stands apart. While all the others occasionally lied, cheated, murdered, stole, or were cowardly, Daniel's entire life was one of unswerving righteousness and bravery. There is not a single blemish in his biography.

It is even interesting to note that the angel who came to Daniel to explain his visions to him, over and over told him that he was highly esteemed. I have a feeling that it was because he was so obedient to the true nature of God that God gave Daniel some of the most monumental prophecies to write down for posterity. In fact, the two most important prophecies in the Bible are found in Daniel. These are prophecies that affect us and our futures the most emphatically.

It could also be that since those two very major prophecies were given to Daniel to preserve, he was additionally given the most incredibly detailed foretelling of less important events, for the primary purpose of proving that God's prophecies always come true. I believe He did this so that we would be more inclined to pay heed to the two truly monumental ones that we will discuss later.

I said that the events of the prophecies we are now going to discuss were not all that important, and they truly aren't to us, other than as historical record. They dealt primarily with the generals Alexander left in charge of his empire on his deathbed, and their offspring. Obviously if they had done things a little bit differently the world today might be slightly different, but I think you will see as we explore these minute predictions, that the big reason for God going to the trouble of even having Daniel write them down could primarily have been to establish His credentials. And that they undeniably do.

For now, I am just going to relate event by event as found in Daniel eleven. I think the best way to do that will be to quote a verse that foretold something, and then immediately tell you what actually happened. You will be fascinated as you read these comparisons. And, as you read them, remember to stay focused on the fact that each verse was written hundreds of years before the people involved were even born. Otherwise you will be trapped into thinking that what you are reading is a reporter's account of an event that happened the day before he wrote it. These fulfilled prophecies are that close to the way history actually played out. As I begin to write these comparisons I am absolutely convinced that you are going to be flabbergasted.

As you recall, when we left Alexander on his deathbed he had given his empire to the strong, which turned out to be his four generals. Again, Lysimachus took over the northern part, Cassander took Asia Minor, Seleucus took what is now Syria, and Ptolemy took the southern part of Egypt and parts of Africa.

We already read what the angel told Daniel in chapter eleven, would happen at Alexanders death, *"his empire will be broken up and parceled out toward the four winds. It will not go to his descendants, nor will it have the power he exercised, because the empire will be uprooted and given to others."*

Now we will continue in verse 5 of chapter eleven as the angel is describing what is going to happen afterwards. *"The king of the South will become strong, but one of his commanders will become stronger than he and will rule his own kingdom with great power."*

The king of the South was Ptolemy I, who took Egypt. Seleucus, who took Syria had originally been a commander under Ptolemy in Alexander's army. Seleucus became the most powerful of the four new kings.

In verse 6 the angel continues, *"After some years they will become allies. The daughter of the king of the South will go to the king of the North to make an alliance, but she will not retain her power, and he and his power will not last. In those days she will be handed over with her royal escort and her father and the one who supported her."*

In that verse the phrase "after some years" is a term usually referring to the passing of a generation, which was the case here as well. In the next generation Ptolemy II is the king of the South and Antiochus II is the king of the North. Ptolemy II, in order to form an alliance, took his daughter, Berenice, to Syria to marry Antiochus II. Unfortunately they did not count on the wrath of a woman scorned, for Laodice, a former wife of Antiochus II had both Berenice and Antiochus II murdered. At the same time her father, Ptolemy II died somewhat mysteriously. For fun, go back and reread that verse. The detail is phenomenal.

Verses 7 through 9 tell us, *"One of her family line will arise to take her place. He will attack the forces of the king of the North and enter his fortress; he will fight against them and be victorious. He will also seize their gods, their metal images, and their valuable articles of silver and gold and carry them off to Egypt. For some years he will leave the king of the North alone. Then the king of the north will invade the realm of the king of the South but will retreat to his own country."*

Berenice's brother, Ptolemy III, invaded the North and won a great victory. With the spoils he brought back, he erected a big monument, called Marmor Adulitanum, in celebration of his victory. After that he left the North alone. In 240 BC the North invaded the South, led by Seleucus II, but the attack failed and the northern army went home like a dog with its tail between its legs. Once again, every detail came true. Reread it and see for yourself. Each verse is a WOW verse.

God's prophecy continues in verse 10 with, *"His sons will prepare for war and assemble a great army, which will sweep on like an irresistible flood and carry the battle as far as his fortress."*

Sure enough, the sons of Seleucus II, created a gigantic army. The older son, Seleucus III, was killed in battle in Asia Minor, but the younger son, Antiochus III, took the army like a flood all the way to the gates of Egypt and had some success before returning home.

In verse 11 we find prophetically, *"Then the king of the South will march out in rage and fight against the king of the North, who will raise a large army, but it will be defeated. When the army is carried off, the king of the South will be filled with pride and will slaughter many thousands,"*

Egypt's Ptolemy IV soundly defeated Antiochus III's 70,000 man army at the gigantic battle of Raphia. It was a complete destruction of the northern forces. God was 100% correct again, as always.

The prophecy goes on, *"yet he will not remain triumphant. For the king of the North will muster another army, larger than the first, and after several years, he will advance with a huge army fully equipped."*

Antiochus III could not get the Raphia defeat out of his mind, so fourteen years later he returned to Egypt with an even more massive army.

Verse 14 continues, *"In those times many will rise against the king of the South. The violent men among your own people will rebel in fulfillment of the vision, but without success."*

This is the first time in the eleventh chapter that the Hebrews are even mentioned, and as the above verse predicts, many Jews at this time did help Antiochus III against Egypt.

Hopefully you are keeping your focus where it needs to be in these verses. The events that are being described really happened about 200 BC, which is about three and a half centuries <u>after</u> the verses were actually written by Daniel.

Other than naming names as we saw He did with Cyrus, or prophesying the dates as He did with Israel's rebirth on May 15, 1948, what more could God have done to prove to us that He does exist, and that He exists without our time constraints? These verses are utterly awesome, so let's continue with the next verse, number 15.

"Then the king of the North will come and build up siege ramps and will capture a fortified city. The forces of the South will be powerless to resist; even their best troops will not have the strength to stand."

At this time Antiochus III captured the fortified city of Sidon in 198 BC. The Egyptians attempted to conquer Syria, but they were not able to do anything against the growing power of Antiochus III. The actual events and the prophesying verses continue to be startlingly identical.

In verse 16 we read, *"The invader will do as he pleases; no one will be able to stand against him. He will establish himself in the Beautiful Land and will have power to destroy it."*

As you can guess, by "Beautiful Land" God is referring to His holy land of Israel, and sure enough, Antiochus III next conquered Palestine.

The angel tells Daniel in the next verse, *"He will determine to come with the might of his entire kingdom and will make an alliance with the king of the South. And he will give him a daughter in marriage in order to overthrow the kingdom, but his plans will not succeed or help him."*

Antiochus now concocts a plan to have his daughter, Cleopatra marry Ptolemy V, hoping to take over a united kingdom. Cleopatra, however, had a mind of her own, and once married, sided with her new husband. This put the kibosh on poor old Antiochus's carefully planned out plot. If he had read God's Word in Daniel he would have known it would not work.

God's prophecy continues in verse 18, *"Then he will turn his attention to the coastlands and will take many of them, but a commander will put an end to his insolence and will turn his insolence back upon him. After this, he will turn back toward the fortresses of his own country but will stumble and fall, to be seen no more."*

Finally, Antiochus III decided to try to take control of Greece, but he was defeated in 191 BC at Thermopylae, and again two years later at Magnesia, southwest of Ephesus. The latter defeat was at the hands of the Romans. This last defeat crushed his spirit and he headed home, only to be killed along the way as he tried to plunder a temple at Elam.

Can you imagine being a Hebrew student of scripture at that time? You would not have needed to watch the evening news on TV, except to check off the events foretold in Daniel eleven as they occurred in the world around you. I'm confident that the reason God did not prophesy the exact dates, as He did elsewhere, was because He did not want the prophecies to interfere with the future events. He foretold them solely to prove to his people, and to us, that He was who He said He was, the God of all creation.

So let's explore the rest of this remarkable chapter, which in reality is an encapsulated history of the Grecian and Roman empires. I will mention before we go on that the Book of Daniel was actually a look at all of world history up to and including the time that we know as the "end times". But the purpose of these pages is not an examination of the fascinating end time prophecies, but the ones already fulfilled.

Chapter eleven of Daniel continues after the death of Antiochus III with verse 20 stating, *"His successor will send out a tax collector to maintain the royal splendor. In a few years, however, he will be destroyed, yet not in anger or in battle."*

As we have seen, Rome now came on the scene, and the successor to Antiochus III, Seleucus IV, had to come up with a way to pay the new Roman Empire a thousand talents each and every year. In order not to harm *"the royal splendor,"* Seleucus IV appointed a man named Heliodorus to collect taxes. Within a few years Seleucus IV was killed with poison, by his own tax collector no less, *"not in anger or in battle."* I am very tempted, but I won't type any tax collector jokes here. But wouldn't this be the perfect time for one?

The angel of God goes on to describe future events to Daniel by saying, *"He will be succeeded by a contemptible person who has not been given the honor of royalty. He will invade the kingdom when its people feel secure, and he will seize it through intrigue."*

When God said intrigue, He meant it. You may need a score card here. Seleucus IV's son, Demetrius, was the logical successor to the throne, but he was in Rome in prison when his father overdosed on poison given to him by the tax man. (I'm still dying to tell some tax man jokes) The younger son was still a baby. Enter on the scene the brother of Seleucus IV, the conniving Antiochus IV.

Antiochus IV was in Athens when he heard of his brother's sudden departure. As God said, he was *"contemptible."* He got a friend of his in Antioch by the name of Andronicus to murder the young baby son of his brother Seleucus. After that terrible deed was done, Antiochus IV had Andronicus murdered.

He then succeeded in taking over his brother's business. As I said, talk about intrigue, this episode had plenty of it. And as usual, God hit the nail on the head every step of the way, hundreds of years in advance.

The adventures of Antiochus IV are the final ones we will look at in chapter eleven. Daniel's writing continues about him, *"Then an overwhelming army will be swept away before him."*

Almost immediately after Antiochus IV took power, Egypt sent a gigantic army to defeat him, but somehow the forces of Antiochus were able to repel them. At this point there are several more verses dealing with different back and forth battles with Egypt that did occur exactly as predicted.

Skipping down to verse 27, though, we read, *"The two kings, with their hearts bent on evil, will sit at the same table and lie to each other, but to no avail, because an end will still come at the appointed time."*

This attempted peace meeting did occur; however, in the end it was futile.

Verse 28 states, *"The king of the North will return to his own country with great wealth, but his heart will be set against the holy covenant. He will take action against it and then return to his own country."*

On his way back home from the failed peace talks with Egypt, Antiochus IV decided to plunder Jerusalem, which he did. In the process he killed 80,000 Hebrews and took another 40,000 into slavery.

The prophecy continues in verse 28 with, *"At the appointed time he will invade the South again, but this time the outcome will be different from what it was before. Ships from the western coastlands will oppose him and he will lose heart."*

Still obsessed with the desire to finally defeat Egypt once and for all, Antiochus IV heads back south with his army. This time, though, the Roman fleet *"from the western coastlands"* comes into the picture and he wisely decides that he had better give up his quest for good.

The final verses we will look at are verses 30 through 32, in which God lets Daniel see, *"Then he will turn back and vent his fury against the holy covenant. He will return and show favor to those who forsake the holy covenant. His armed forces will rise up to desecrate the temple fortress and will abolish the daily sacrifice. Then they will set up the abomination that causes desolation. But the people who know their God will firmly resist him."*

Antiochus IV took the loss of his goal to conquer Egypt out on the Israelites, partly because he blamed them for not fully supporting his endeavor, and partly because he simply hated the Jewish religion. He and his troops went into Jerusalem and completely desecrated the temple. He then even sacrificed a sow on the alter, which was a complete abomination, and even set up a statue of a Greek god in the holy place. This started a revolt that we know of as the Maccabean Revolt by thousands of religious Jews, which resulted in terrible slaughter.

The rest of the eleventh chapter deals with prophecies that will occur in the end times that we won't discuss here. I will say that the last part we looked at is in actuality a dual prophecy in that it, too, will be duplicated in the end times.

As I said before we started this study, the eleventh chapter of Daniel is one of the most remarkable in the entire Bible. And the purpose of it is probably primarily to show anyone that there is no debate about God's existence. Obviously it is a human impossibility to see into the future at all, much less in such startling and awesome detail like what we just looked at.

There can not even be any discussion about the fact that God exists. It is not a matter of faith. It is real. It has been proven. And just the same as the fact that whether we know about the law of gravity or not, it is still fact, the same is true of God. Whether man is knowledgeable about the conclusive proof that God exists or is totally in the dark, does not change the fact. God is real. He was at the beginning of creation. He is now. And he will be forever. Our little beliefs one way or the other have no impact on that fact. The debates have always been ridiculous.

Remember, in Isaiah 46 God told us, *"I am God and there is non like me. I make known the end from the beginning, from ancient times, what is still to come."*

CHAPTER SIX

It should be quite obvious by now that God never intended His existence to be something that had to be taken on faith. The proof that He exists virtually screams from every chapter of the Bible. As we have so far, we will be focusing in these pages on the proof He gave us by foretelling very detailed events long in advance of them actually happening.

I will, however, mention very briefly that God also proved His point very dramatically by stating medical and scientific truths long before any human could have possibly known about them. The examples of these startling statements could easily fill several books, but I thought it might be interesting to bring up just a few of them here, to give us a little idea of the sort of prophecies He used to make any thinking person know, without reservation, that God is God, and that He is all knowing.

Let's look first in the area of medicine. One of my favorites in this area is found in Genesis 17:12, when God said, *"For the generations to come every male among you who is eight days old must be circumcised."*

The eight days mentioned is the interesting part. Only recently in modern medicine have doctors found that when a baby is born, they have no bacteria in their intestines for the first few days. By the seventh day, the bacteria multiply and produce vitamin K. Without vitamin K and prothrombin protein (which is produced by the liver using vitamin K), the blood will not clot properly and the possibility of severe bleeding as well as infection would make circumcision very dangerous in the early Jewish communities. It is quite obvious that only God would have known such a thing back then.

Actually, God gave the Israelites a lot of instruction over three thousand years ago that no one at that time could have possibly known the reason for. For instance, the existence of germs was not discovered until 1890; however, God obviously knew about them and gave the Jews a whole lot of instruction about hygiene and sanitation. I could literally list dozens of verses on those subjects, but as a way of example we can read God's instruction in Leviticus 6:28 about cooking meat in a pot, *"the pot is to be scoured and rinsed with water."* God had these words written down before 1450 BC.

It is hard for us to believe, but it was only in the mid 1800's that any doctors at all thought that any diseases could be transmitted by anything that we could not see. One of the first was a Hungarian doctor by the name of Ignaz Semmelweis. He noticed that young mothers who gave birth in hospitals were more likely to die than the ones who gave birth in their homes. In fact, the staggering death rate among new hospital birth mothers was between fifteen and thirty percent in 1845 in the hospital where Dr. Semmelweis was practicing. Extremely observant, he noticed that the young interns would examine dead bodies in the morning and immediately go and examine expectant mothers in another ward, without washing their hands. This was the normal practice up to the late 1800's because the concept of germs was unknown.

Dr. Semmelweis began insisting that the interns under him wash vigorously before touching expectant mothers. The mortality rate dropped almost overnight down to two percent.

The striking thing is that the medical staff continued to think his ideas were ridiculous and they fired him. He went to another hospital and instituted the same hand washing procedures with the same results, dropping that hospital's mortality rate from fifteen percent to less than one percent. It still took decades, though, to convince the medical community to change their habits, and even when they did they normally washed in a bowl, where the germs could stay, rather than washing in running water.

This all happened very recently by historical calendars, but God was giving the Israelites instruction to wash with running water thirty five hundred years ago. There are quite a few verses that talk about this, but to take just one example, we can look at Leviticus 15:13, *"And when he who has a discharge is cleansed of his discharge, then he shall count for himself seven days for his cleansing, wash his clothes, and bathe his body in running water; then he shall be clean."*

It actually took one of God's medical instructions to stop the terrible black plague that devastated a third of the European population, including some entire villages. No one had ever heard of the notion of quarantine. Doctors gave advice such as to stop eating pepper or garlic. Many thought the problem was caused by the position of the planets. The nightmare was a total mystery to everyone.

Finally, after what seemed like an endless hell on earth, some ministers in Vienna started pouring over the scriptures. The answer was found in Leviticus 13:46, in which God introduced the idea of quarantine. In talking about people who had leprosy or plaguelike symptoms, God said, *"He shall be unclean. All the days he has the sore he shall be unclean. He is unclean, and he shall dwell alone; his habitation shall be outside the camp."*

The dreaded black plague was finally stopped with the instruction given by God. There is even a statue in the center of Vienna dedicated to the countless black plague victims, and to the church leaders who found the way to end the nightmare in the instructions of the all knowing God.

Medical science is not God's only strong suit. His words have foretold truth in all areas of science. In astronomy, for example, God asked Job in chapter 38, verse 31, *"Can you bind the beautiful Pleiades?"* Only recently have scientists come to realize that the stars that make up Pleiades are the gravitational center of the Milky Way.

In the next verse Job is asked, *"Can you guide Arcturus?"* We now know that Arcturus is the fastest star in the heavens, traveling at a phenomenal 125,000 miles per second. Can you imagine trying to guide that? Arcturus has, in fact, become known as the "Runaway Star." God obviously knows everything.

Statements like these that God made are scattered throughout the entire Bible. People sometimes say, though, that God did not go into enough detail about such things as the creation for modern man to believe in it. Now, let's be serious, can you imagine if God had tried to explain cosmic proper time, $E=MC2$, gravitational pull, time dilation, and the like, to the readers of His Word prior to today. None of it would have made any sense to them at all.

We need to realize that although everything God said was fact, His Bible is not meant to be a complete encyclopedia of everything He knows. If it were, there would not be room enough for it on planet earth, and no mortal could ever read it in a lifetime. That was not the purpose of His Word. The purpose was to prove to us that He exists and to lay out His plan for you and I to be able to spend eternity with Him. Interspersed in that, we also find out some of the characteristics of who He is.

That being said, though, it is awesomely amazing to see how God proves His existence with ultra simple phrases that eventually become meaningful as mankind learns a smattering more about the marvelous universe He created. Some of those little phrases are complete mysteries to the human finite brain for hundreds and thousands of years.

One such phrase that mystified me is found in Hebrews 1:10-12, which says, *"In the beginning, O Lord, you laid the foundations of the earth, and the heavens are the work of your hands. They will perish, but you remain; they will all wear out like a garment. You will roll them up like a robe; like a garment they will be changed. But You remain the same, and your years will never end."*

What struck me so odd was the phrase, *"You will roll them up like a robe."* It just didn't make sense to me at all.

I knew there was universe in every direction from the earth.

To me the entire universe must be like a ball. How in the world could God roll up the universe like a garment if it was a ball?

It would have to be flat to do that. Can you see the problem I struggled with?

Now comes the hottest thing in science, string theory.

It is only about fifteen years old and every new physicist and mathematician wants to specialize in it. Many string theory scientists believe it holds the answers to everything in the universe. It is the basis for all the popular Matrix movies, so it must be important stuff.

The basic thought of string theory is that everything taken to its base form is made up of energy that is in the shape of a string. The latest discovery in string theory physics is that these "strings" make up membranes, cleverly called "branes". These branes can be infinitesimally small, or they can be gigantic. The newest suggestion coming out of "brane" physics is that all of the universe exists on one "brane", a relatively flat surface, kind of like a piece of cloth, or would you believe, a "robe". If this theory is true, and scientists all seem to agree that it is, then God could truly roll the universe up like a robe. Some of the simplest statements in God's Word are turning out to be the most awesome.

As a total aside, string theory also says that our universe, our spacial dimension, is like a slice of bread in a loaf. It claims that there are parallel universes, the other slices in the loaf.

We may not know that this is indeed true until we cross the line we call death, but it may be that heaven is a parallel dimension to what we currently live on. Many verses in the Bible allude to something like that.

String theory even talks about something it calls "worm holes", which are actually tunnel like holes that exist between the parallel dimensions. In other words, these are tunnel like openings between the universes in which something could travel back and forth between the two. Does that sound to you like the tunnels constantly described by people who have had near death experiences. It does to me. It also sounds a lot like descriptions of things mentioned in the Bible, such as Jacob's ladder. This has nothing to do with the purpose of this book, but I personally believe it all makes sense, and I also believe that there could well be the main "worm hole" over Jerusalem. If so, that would explain so much that is in the Bible.

As I said, I obviously have gotten off track of our purpose, but I think this entire concept can become food for a lot of pondering for all of us. For now, though, let's return to things that God told us in advance that are totally provable. Things that leave no doubt about His existence, and more.

CHAPTER SEVEN

String theory, at this point in time, must be taken on faith. As we have said over and over, God did not want His existence to have to be taken on faith. That was the reason for His prophecies. He even threw out the gauntlet to anyone that thought they could predict future events like He could. God even said to those who thought they could, *"Present your case,' the Lord God says. 'Bring forth your strong arguments,' the King of Jacob says. 'Let them declare to us what is going to take place; as for the former events, declare what they were, that we may consider them, and know their outcome; or announce to us what is coming. Declare the things that are going to come afterward, so that we may know that you are gods."* (Isaiah 41:21-23 NASB)

An interesting note in the above challenge is that God says that if others could do it He would admit that they were gods. Obviously, He knows, as we do, that no one but He Himself could tell the future 100%. And, of course, no one has ever even come close.

There was a big deal made of the scribblings of Nostradamus, and some are still trying to sell some books about him, but it is now widely known that all his predictions were rubbish. The widely circulated news that he had written about Hitler has now been laid to rest. The only word that the original junkies thought came close was the word "Ister". We know for a fact that he used that word for the River Danube.

Edgar Cayce's prophecies were so often wrong that it is almost pathetic that he was ever thought of as having any prophetic ability. In fact, it is even humorous to read about the scores of times he predicted that oil or mineral deposits would be found in such and such location, and his relatives would waste their money in a search that ended only in dust.

And then there is Jean Dixon and the scores of others like her. An interesting study was done by *Readers Digest* recently that

concluded that the modern top ten so called psychics and prophets were wrong 98% of the time. When we consider that many
of their predictions revolved around such things as the future
divorces of Hollywood stars, I am actually amazed that they
couldn't have guessed better than 2% of the time.

Only God knows the future from the beginning, or as He
Himself said, *"I am God, and there is none like me. I make known
the end from the beginning, from ancient times, what is still to come."*
Isaiah 46: 9-10

In speaking of God, Psalm 119:160 says, *"All your words are
true."* And that refers to all His words; the things He foretells,
His statements, and His promises. If God said it, we can be totally sure it is true. And interestingly, we have seen more of His
prophecies fulfilled in our lifetime than just about any other time
in history.

We discussed in chapter three the phenomenal prophecy that
told the exact date that Israel would be revived as a nation, in only
one day. To get the full impact of that event, though, we really
need to consider the fact that Israel's rebirth alone was an incredible prediction. No other nation in history has ever been destroyed
and scattered, and then come back together to form a nation.

Additionally as we mentioned, no other dead language has
ever come alive again like we have seen happen with the Hebrew
language. No one speaks the ancient languages of the dissolved
empires. Latin is not even spoken anywhere in every day life.
But when Israel became a nation in 1948 and the people began to
come back from the seventy nations they had been scattered in, a
common language had to be found.

God had prophesied in Zephaniah 3:9, *"For then will I turn to the
people a pure language, that they may call upon the name of the Lord, to
serve Him with one consent."* In order for the Hebrew language to
come alive again new words even had to be added. Remember,
when it died there were no words for automobile or bicycle or
computer. Now, after two thousand years as an extinct language,
Hebrew is again taught to school children and about seven million Jews use it as their common language. What an incredible
story that is.

There is a lot more to the rebirth of Israel that God foretold, such as where the Jews would come from. For instance, in the next verse in Zephaniah God said, *"From beyond the rivers of Ethiopia my suppliants, even the daughter of my dispersed, shall bring mine offering."* Only God could know that His "dispersed" would even end up in Ethiopia, no less return from there, but about 1990 twenty five thousand black Jews returned to their homeland, Israel.

God also said in Isaiah 43:6, *"I will say to the north, Give up; and to the south, Keep not back: bring my sons from afar, and my daughters from the ends of the earth."* The north obviously is a reference to Russia, where Jews to this day are coming from in mass to their promised land. And they are arriving daily from the ends of the earth by boat, plane, and car. We are witnessing the fulfillment of prophecy.   •

Other predictions for this renewed Israel are coming true right before our eyes. It is almost like May 15, 1948, was a magic date on God's calendar. For example, speaking of the time after the return, God said, *"Be glad then, Children of Zion, and rejoice in the Lord your God: for He hath given you the former rain moderately, and He will cause for you to come down rain, the former rain and the latter rain in the first month."* Joel 2:23

We need to remember what the land that we now know as Israel was like. It was an arid desert. Rain was a very seldomly seen commodity for centuries and centuries. When Mark Twian traveled there he stated that it was the most barren land he had ever seen, with nothing growing at all. He called it a complete wasteland. In <u>Innocents Abroad</u>, written in 1867, Twain called it "desolate and unlovely. It is a hopeless, dreary, heartbroken land." And what normally happens to deserts? They continue to expand and take over more land each year, such as the case with the Sahara. Unusual as it is, however, the rainfall in Israel keeps increasing at a rate of 10% per year. Is God doing something behind the scenes? That is the only logical answer.

He told His people twenty seven hundred years ago, *"Water will gush forth in the wilderness and streams in the desert. The burning sand will become a pool, the thirsty ground bubbling springs. In the*

haunts where jackals once lay, grass and reeds and papyrus will grow."
Isaiah 35:6-7

Today, that is exactly what is happening. One of the most deso-late areas on earth was the land from south of the Dead Sea to the Gulf of Acaba. Springs are literally gushing forth from rocks. There is now one of the most beautiful crystal clear, spring fed pools in the entire world. It did not exist at all only fifteen years ago. All around it grows lush grass and *"reeds and papyrus."* And this pool, called Sapphire, which really is a small lake, is being used to irrigate the land around it to grow some of the most beau-tiful vegetables and flowers imaginable. Mark Twain would not believe his eyes.

Actually, in Isaiah 27:6, God said, *"In the days to come Jacob will take root, Israel will bud and blossom and fill all the world with fruit."* We are seeing that happening today in incredible ways. The United Nations says that Israel is now the most agriculturally efficient land in the world. Ninety percent of their flowers are now exported, primarily to Europe. Speaking of Europe, ninety percent of the citrus eaten there comes from Israel, which only a few years ago was totally barren desert.

God had said this all would happen, and it did. In Isaiah 35:2 He had foretold, *"The desert and the parched land will be glad; the wilderness will rejoice and blossom. Like the crocus, it will burst into bloom; it will rejoice greatly and shout for joy. The glory of Lebanon will be given to it, the splendor of Carmel and Sharon; they will see the glory of the lord, the splendor of our God."*

An ironic side note is that one of the largest packing compa-nies of the fruits, vegetables, and flowers that now are exported worldwide is the Carmel Packing Company in Israel.

I have to smile when I see *"Carmel"* in the above Isaiah quote.

God even got very specific as to locations in Israel that would produce different things in this time. For example, in Hosea 2:15 He prophesied, *"There I will give her back her vineyards, and will make the Valley of Achor a door of hope."* We need to understand that the Valley of Achor, which lies between Jericho and Qumran, where the famous Dead Sea scrolls were found, was one of the least likely places in the world to see vineyards less than twenty years ago. To understate it, there was no water. It was sand and rock, and nothing else. The only thing that could grow there was your thirst.

Today it is literally mile after mile of the most beautiful grape vineyards you could ever hope to see. The entire area is a place of beauty. And the grapes are some of the most luscious on earth. But on top of the lush grape vineyards, a traveler will also see quite a few herds of healthy sheep in the area. That shouldn't be surprising, however, because in Isaiah 65:10 God told us it would happen. In that verse He said, *"Sharon will become a pasture for flocks, and the Valley of Achor a resting place for herds."*

I find it extremely interesting that for centuries Biblical scholars thought that these prophecies about Israel being reborn as a nation, its language being restored, and the land dramatically changing from desert wasteland to a lush, productive garden, would come true, but only in heaven. They naturally supposed that these things were beyond the possible. The debaters that spoke against the existence of God even pointed to these prophecies as places where the Bible obviously was in error. The chances of them being fulfilled seemed outlandish at best. They just didn't understand that, *"Nothing is impossible with God."* Luke 1:37

I also find it intriguing that all of these foretellings are indeed part of what is classified as "end time" prophecies.

That might shock most people, since the normal notion of people who have never really studied God's Word is that "end time" prophecies only entail the prophecies about the seven year period of time known as the tribulation, the seven year period that ends in the often mentioned battle of Armageddon.

In reality, though, there are quite a few end time prophecies that describe events immediately preceding the tribulation period. One of those deals with the Dead Sea separating, one part coming to life and the other part remaining salt. This was one of those "impossible" predictions only a dozen years ago.

In Ezekiel 47:11, speaking of the Dead Sea separating in the "end times", God said, *"But the swamps and marshes will not become fresh; they will be left for salt."* In the past twelve years a land mass has incredibly popped up that has divided the Dead Sea into two separate bodies, and the southern part is drying up at a rate of three feet per year, leaving behind big boulders of pure salt. There are now trees growing in the area where the southern part of the Dead Sea was only ten years ago, trees surrounded by the salt piles that were left. These are truly phenomenal times to be alive.

Another one of those "end time" events that has my attention is a two chapter prophecy found in Ezekiel 38 and 39 which describes in detail the coming war of "Gog and Magog." Since it is not a fulfilled prophecy as yet, I will not spend any time on the details of it. I will say, however, that it is actually one of the very few prophecies that must occur that as yet has not come to pass. And I will tell you that the participants in this future war are specifically named, and include Russia aligning with Iran and other Islamic nations against Israel. Politicians and world affairs scholars of the past would have said that such a confederacy of nations was improbable at best, but think of what we are seeing on the TV news right now. Such an alliance of former enemies is not such an unheard of possibility any more. In fact, I believe that partnership is already a certainty. Of God we can say as the Psalmist says, *"All your words are true."*

In the first part of this book we have already seen how the existence of God is provable and does not need to be taken on faith. Incredibly, we have only scratched the surface. In Part Two we will be completely astounded as we begin to look at what I firmly believe to be the two most phenomenal prophecies God gave us. Prepare to be spellbound. You may never be the same.

PART TWO

CHAPTER EIGHT

When we consider prophecies, we need to be aware of the fact that of the thousands of "holy books" of the thousands of religions that exist on earth, not one of them contains a single fulfilled prophecy, with the glaring exception of the Bible.

That in itself is a startling statement, and even more so since we know that every one of the thousands of biblical predictions that were suppose to have happened by now have indeed taken place, often very dramatically.

Without knowing the facts, some would think that what I just wrote about other holy books could not possibly be true, but it is. Recently an e-mail circulated so continuously in cyberspace that I would estimate that I received it myself no less than a dozen times. At the end of that e-mail, which listed a lot of interesting facts about Iraq, was a purported quote from the Koran which talked about the events of 9/11 and issued a warning to the planners. This quote was a complete hoax. There is no such verse in the Koran. And, as is true with all other "holy books", absolutely none of the very few prophecies found in that Islamic book have ever been fulfilled.

It bears repeating, there has never been a single fulfilled prophecy in any "holy book" of the thousands that exist, other than the Bible. And every prophecy in the Bible that should have been fulfilled by now has indeed come true. Additionally the number of such fulfilled foretellings in the Bible is staggering, numbering into the several thousands.

Not only do these fulfilled prophecies prove conclusively that God exists, but they also prove that the Bible was in fact written by God. Should that be at all surprising? Obviously God, who created everything, is more than intelligent enough to be able to communicate with His creation. It is only natural that He would. Hopefully that is becoming as obvious as the fact of God's existence. If not, read on and it will.

The fulfilled prophecies that we have examined thus far all were made prior to 400 BC, and we will be astounded as we read even more of them in pages to come. Many, however, were predicted after the calendars changed to AD, and we will be studying some of them as well.

At this time, though, let's take a trip back again to the time of the Babylonian captivity and see a prophecy in the book of Daniel that is by far the most amazing foretelling ever made. This is one of the two prophecies that I catagorize as the two most important ever made. This one, in my opinion, should be the leader in the all time hall of fame for prophecies. If there is still a dry debater in the house, he can hit the showers for sure when he finds out about this one, and those related to it.

As we noted earlier, Daniel's life was the epitome of righteousness. In fact, as an aside, I find it very interesting that God Himself mentioned Daniel as one of His top three examples of righteousness. I make that statement due to a passage in which God is talking to Ezekiel about sending judgement on Israel. In those verses Ezekiel says, *"The word of the Lord came to me: 'Son of man, if a country sins against me by being unfaithful and I stretch out my hand against it to cut off its food supply and send a famine upon it and kill its men and their animals, even if these three - Noah, Daniel, and Job -were in it, they could save only themselves by their righteousness, declares the Sovereign Lord."* Ezekiel 14:12-14. I firmly believe that it is because of his righteousness and continual obedience that Daniel was given the most important prophecies in the Bible.

As you recall, God sent angels to actually talk to Daniel and tell him what to write down. This was the case in the amazing foretelling of the four world empires that were to come, Assyria, Medo/Persia, Greece, and Rome. An angel also told Daniel about the future life of Alexander the Great, and the completely awesome verse by verse detailed description in the eleventh chapter of Daniel we studied of the lives of the four heirs to the Greek empire and their offspring.

An angel, Gabriel, also brought these words in Daniel 9:25, *"Know and understand this: From the issuing of the decree to restore and rebuild Jerusalem until the Anointed One, the ruler, comes, there will be seven sevens, and sixty two sevens."*

I will say it again for emphasis, this is one of the two most important prophecies that God ever made. It is worth our total attention. And it does not disappoint.

We need to first of all understand that the Hebrew word for "sevens" in this scripture was "shabuwa", which was an idiom like our words decade and score. We all understand that decade means ten years and score means twenty years. In the same way Shabuwa meant seven years. Therefore, Gabriel is telling Daniel that sixty nine seven year periods (seven shabuwa and sixty two shabuwa) will pass between the decree to rebuild Jerusalem and the coming of the Anointed One.

If we now do the math we find that 69 times 7 years is 483 years. The years referred to in this case were obviously Jewish years which each contained 360 days. Therefore, 483 times 360 days equals 173,880 days. This number of days will become very important to us so please make a mental note.

Since we now know our history from previous chapters, it is interesting to note that Gabriel gave this prophecy to Daniel two years before Cyrus and his Medo/Persian army took over Babylon. As we learned earlier, the Jews were then treated much nicer, and many were allowed to return to their homeland. Jerusalem, however, remained in ruins.

Next we need to look at another character who enters the scene about eighty five years after Gabriel told Daniel the prophecy. His name was Nehemiah.

Although, as we have seen, about 42,000 of the Israelites returned to their homeland after Cyrus demolished the Assyrian Empire that had kept them captive for seventy years, most of the Jewish people remained in Babylon where they felt at home, or headed north for better opportunities. One of those who did not go to his ancestors' home of Jerusalem was Nehemiah. He worked his way up to holding the important job as the cup bearer to the king of Persia, Artaxerxes. Obviously Nehemiah was well liked by Artaxerxes to hold such an intimate job.

At this point we will need to know about an event that happened that became pivotal in one of the two most important prophecies that exists. We will read Nehemiah's own account.

"In the month of Kislev in the twentieth year, while I was in the citadel of Susa, Hanani, one of my brothers, came from Judah with some other men, and I questioned them about the Jewish remnant that survived the exile, and also about Jerusalem.

They said to me, 'Those who survived the exile and are back in the province are in great trouble and disgrace. The wall of Jerusalem is broken down, and its gates have been burned with fire.'

When I heard these things, I sat down and wept. For some days I mourned and fasted and prayed before the God of heaven." Nehemiah 1:1-4

He continues in chapter 2, *"In the month of Nisan in the twentieth year of King Artaxerxes, when wine was brought for him, I took the wine and gave it to the king. I had not been sad in his presence before; so the king asked me, 'Why does your face look so sad when you are not ill? This can be nothing but sadness of heart.'*

I was very much afraid, but I said to the king, 'May the king live forever! Why should my face not look sad when the city where my fathers are buried lies in ruins, and its gates have been destroyed by fire.'

Then the king said to me, 'What is it you want?'

Then I prayed to the God of heaven, and I answered the king, 'If it pleases the king and your servant has found favor in his sight, let him send me to the city in Judah where my fathers are buried so that I can rebuild it." Nehemiah 2:1-5

Artaxerxes agrees to the request and writes a decree to that effect, including letters to different governors to give Nehemiah safe passage, and even provide the lumber needed for the rebuilding. Secular history tells us that this decree was made on March 14, 445 BC.

Let's refresh our memory and look once again at the phenomenal prophecy in Daniel 9:25, *"Know and understand this: From the issuing of the decree to restore and rebuild Jerusalem until the Anointed One, the ruler, comes, there will be seven sevens, and sixty two sevens."*

We know that there were three other decrees made, but they all dealt exclusively with rebuilding the temple. The decree described in Nehemiah that was made on March 14, 445 BC, was the only decree made to rebuild Jerusalem.

We also learned that to see what was fulfilled we must count forward 173,880 days on the Jewish calendar. When we do, we end up at April 6, 32 AD, which we know was the fourth Feast of Passover in Jerusalem under the reign of Tiberius. Now, hold on to your hat. We also know for a certainty that April 6, 32 AD was the exact day that Jesus rode into Jerusalem on a donkey and let the crowds praise Him as King. God foretold over 500 years in advance, to the exact day, the day that His *"Anointed One"* would come.

Let's pause and let this sink in. If we only had one prophecy to look at, this one by itself would prove not only that God exists, but that He communicates to us through the Bible, and additionally that Jesus is the Anointed One.

But wait a minute. If I were John Doe debater who had already been sent to the showers, I would come rushing out at this point, soaking wet, with a towel draped around me and yell,

"I've got you now, Bob. I admit that you proved to me conclusively in Part One with the scores of examples of fulfilled prophecy that God does exist, and by the same token that He does in fact communicate to us with the Bible. But the thought that Jesus is proven to be the Messiah by this prophecy doesn't hold water. We all know that Jesus was a rabbi, so it stands to reason that He knew the scriptures backward and forward and just arranged it so that He could appear on that specific date. You've opened up a whole new debate, and I am ready for you."

My response is a simple, you are exactly correct. Jesus did know that date, and He did arrange to come into Jerusalem as the Anointed One. Furthermore, He also arranged at the same time to ride in on a donkey, fulfilling another prophecy in Zechariah 9:9. *"Rejoice greatly, O Daughter of Zion! Shout, Daughter of Jerusalem! See, your king comes to you, righteous and having salvation, gentile and riding on a donkey, on a colt, the foal of a donkey."*

On top of that, I will admit further that the Pharisees in all likelihood knew that day as well, for they said in Luke 19:39,

"Teacher, rebuke your disciples." To this Jesus replied in the next verse, *"I tell you, if they keep quiet the stones will cry out."*, a refer-

ence to a prediction in Joshua 24:27, *"This stone will be a witness against us. It has heard all the words the Lord has said to us. It will be a witness against you if you are untrue to your God."*

The fact is that Jesus had hoped that all the people would have studied the Word of God enough to know the exact day that was foretold in Daniel 9:25. Unfortunately the people had not studied. They had not "searched out the matter", which we learned early on from Proverbs 25 *"is the glory of kings."*

And since they did not know, the scripture tells us just one verse later in Luke 19:41, *"As He approached Jerusalem and saw the city, He wept over it and said, 'If you, even you, had only known on this day what would bring you peace - but now it is hidden from your eyes."* He went on to declare a prophecy,*"The days will come upon you when your enemies will build an embankment against you and encircle you and hem you in on every side. They will dash you to the ground, you and the children within your walls. They will not leave one stone on another, because you did not recognize the time of God's coming to you."*

That prophecy was fulfilled in detail in 70 AD when the Romans destroyed the city again and even tore the Temple apart stone by stone to get the gold that had melted down the walls when the temple was accidentally torched.

Yes, you are right, John Doe debater, Jesus did indeed know the date that prophecy was to be fulfilled. And He did arrange to ride in on a donkey. Therefore, the all knowing God, knowing of your skepticism, proved irrefutably that Jesus was the anointed One with about three hundred other very specific prophecies about the life of Jesus. Wrap that wet towel tighter around you because you are about to be sent back to the showers. Fantastic proof is coming. This debate is over, too.

CHAPTER NINE

The coming of Jesus as the Messiah is the second most prophesied event in God's Word. In fact, the primary purpose of the Old Testament was to alert the people that He was coming, plus to explain the purpose of His earthly visit. As stated earlier, there are about three hundred separate prophecies pertaining to Jesus that were all fulfilled in His life.

The phenomenal prophecy looked at in the last chapter was given over five hundred years in advance, and was meant to be studied to the point that the Israelites would be expecting their Messiah on that day. Jesus even arranged it so that they would not miss it. Unfortunately, the only ones who had searched the scriptures and were expecting the event were the rabbis, and they were expecting someone entirely different. They were expecting an earthly king who would save them from the tyranny of the Romans. The mission of Jesus, however, was much greater than just that, and could only be accomplished by a humble servant who was willing to shed his blood for mankind. It was a higher calling, and the Jewish population missed it. As a result, as Jesus foretold when He wept over Jerusalem, their spiritual eyes would be blinded, *"but now it is hidden from your eyes."* And it will remain hidden from God's "chosen people" until a time in the future, again prophesied in the Bible.

It is intriguing that they missed it, since there are so many other prophecies that foretold it. But the fact that they missed it was to be to the advantage of the rest of the world. It gave us the chance to become part of God's chosen people in a totally different way than by just being born Jewish. It gave us time to open our own eyes and *"search out a matter"*, which is *"the glory of kings."* It gave us the opportunity to make up our own minds.

Let's now take a look at just a few of the 332 other prophecies in the Old Testament that dealt with the coming of the "Anointed one". We'll start at His earthly beginning.

In Micah 5:2 we read, *"But you, Bethlehem Ephrathah, though you are small among the clans of Judah, out of you will come for me one who will be ruler over Israel, whose origins are from old, from ancient times."*

As every five year old child in our culture knows from Christmas stories, Jesus was born in Bethlehem. The familiar story in Matthew 2:1 relates, *"After Jesus was born in Bethlehem in Judea, during the time of King Herod, Magi from the east came to Jerusalem and asked, 'Where is the one who has been born king of the Jews? We saw his star in the east and have come to worship Him."*

John Doe debater could continue with his weak debate that Jesus arranged His birth, too. The problem with that is that He could have only arranged it if He were divine. The more plausible words out of John Doe's mouth would be that it was just coincidence. God foresaw that logic, and tore it to shreds with so many similar prophecies that have been proven mathematically to be galaxies beyond the realm of random chance.

For instance, God foresaw that King Herod, when he heard from the Magi that a king had been born, would decide to kill all the baby boys in Bethlehem that were two or under. Since God knew this would happen, He prophesied that He would help Jesus's parents get him to Egypt as a means of escape.

In Hosea 11:1 we read, *"When Israel was a child, I loved him, and out of Egypt I called my son."*

In talking about the slaughter of the baby male children by King Herod, God had foretold in the old Testament book of Jeremiah in verse 15, *"A voice is heard in Ramah, mourning and weeping, Rachel weeping for her children and refusing to be comforted because they are no more."* Four hundred years later we read what actually happened in Matthew 2:16, *"When Herod realized that he had been outwitted by the magi, he was furious, and he gave orders to kill all the boys in Bethlehem and its vicinity who were two years old and under, in accordance with the time he had learned from the Magi."*

Baby Jesus, however was saved as predicted, for in Matthew 2:13, *"An angel of the Lord appeared to Joseph in a dream. 'Get up,' he said, 'take the child and his mother and escape to Egypt. Stay there until I tell you, for Herod is going to search for the child to kill Him."*

After everything appeared safe, God did indeed call the family back in Matthew 2:19-20, *"After Herod died, an angel of the Lord appeared in a dream to Joseph in Egypt and said, 'Get up, take the child and his mother and go to the land of Israel, for those who are trying to take the child's life are dead."*

Interestingly, in the next verse we learn, *"So he got up, took the child and his mother and went to the land of Israel. But when he heard that Archelaus was reigning in Judea in place of his father, Herod, he was afraid to go there. Having been warned in a dream, he withdrew to the district of Galilee, and he went there to live in a town called Nazareth. So was fulfilled what was said through the prophets: He will be called a Nazarene."* Matthew 2:21-22

We might mention at this point that there were several prophecies that foretold the lineage of Jesus. Starting back in Genesis 49:10, written over 1,500 years before Jesus walked the earth, we find the words of the patriarch, Jacob, *"The scepter will not depart from Judah, nor the ruler's staff from between his feet, until it comes to whom it belongs and the obedience of the nations is his."* In both Matthew 1:16 and Luke 3:23 the ancestry of Jesus is traced back to the tribe of Judah. Jesus is even called the Lion of Judah.

Continuing on, we can witness God's foretelling of John the Baptist's preaching preceding Jesus in Isaiah 40:3, *"A voice of one calling: 'In the desert prepare the way for the Lord; make straight in the wilderness a highway for our God."*

Of course, seven hundred years later, John the Baptist, on seeing Jesus, said. *"Look, The Lamb of God, who takes away the sin of the world! This is the one I meant when I said, 'A man who comes after me has surpassed me because he was before me.' I myself did not know him, but the reason I came baptizing in water was that he might be revealed to Israel."* John 1:29-31

I find the rest of that testimony by John the Baptist interesting because Isaiah, writing some seven hundred years earlier had foretold of the Messiah, *"The spirit of the Lord will rest on him."* Isaiah 11:2.

And in John 1:32, John the Baptists continues, *"Then John gave this testimony: 'I saw the Spirit come down from heaven as a dove and remain on Him. I would not have known him, except that the one who sent me to baptize with water told me, 'The man on whom you see the Spirit come down and remain is He who will baptize with the Holy Spirit.' I have seen and I testify that this is the Son of God."*

I must admit that after typing John's closing sentence I had to pause. It was like, what more could be said to add to, *"I have seen and I testify that this is the Son of God."* But then I thought of John Doe debater, who has not seen in person what John the Baptist saw. He may need more proof, so we'll continue to give him the proof he needs for this debate about Jesus through God's way of proving things. *"I am God, and there is none like me, I make known the end from the beginning, from ancient times, what is still to come."* Isaiah 46:9-10

In fact, we will get into even much more detailed prophetic statements than we have up to now. The way Jesus began His ministry was quite telling, in that His first act of public speaking was to read the scroll of Isaiah 61 in the temple. It, in itself was a foretelling of the ministry of Jesus, and He read, *"The Sprit of the Sovereign Lord is on me, because the Lord has anointed me to preach good news to the poor. He has sent me to bind up the brokenhearted, to proclaim freedom for the captives, and release from darkness the prisoners,"*

Seven hundred years in advance God prophesied first about John the Baptist and then about the well known event of Jesus driving the money changers out of the temple. In Malachi 3:1-4 we read, *"I will send my messenger, who will prepare the way before me. Then suddenly the Lord you are seeking will come to his temple; the messenger of the covenant, whom you desire, will come,' says the Lord Almighty. 'But who can endure the day of his coming? Who can stand when he appears? For he will be like a refiner's fire or a launderer's soap. He will sit as a refiner and purifier of silver; he will purify the Levites and refine them like gold and silver. Then the Lord will have men who will bring offerings in righteousness."*

The temple, of course, was run by the Levites, as they were the only tribe of Israel who could be priests. In Matthew 21:12 the actual story is told, *"Jesus entered the temple area and drove out all who were buying and selling there; He overturned the tables of the money changers and the benches of those selling doves. 'It is written' He said to* them, 'My house will be called a house of prayer, but you are making it a den of robbers." Jesus cleansed the temple like "launderer's soap."

The Levites should have known because in Jeremiah 7:11 God said, about 585 BC,"Has this house, which bears my Name, become a den of robbers to you? But I have been watching! Declares the Lord." The prophecies predicted the disciple Judas's roll in history in Psalm 41:9, "Even my close friend, whom I trusted, he who shared my bread, has lifted up his heel against me." And God got even more specific over 400 years in advance of his betrayal in Zechariah 11:12, "I told them,'If you think it best, give me my pay; but if not, keep it.' So they paid me thirty pieces of silver."

Of course, the actual event was recorded in the New Testament in Matthew 26:14-15, "Then one of the twelve - the one called Judas Escariot - went to the chief priests and asked, 'What are you willing to give me if I hand Him over to you?' So they counted out for him thirty pieces of silver."

We might have thought that Judas, being a disciple, would have known that he wasn't going to get to keep the silver pieces, though, because God foretold exactly what would happen to the blood money in the next verse of Zechariah. Evidently Judas was too busy embezzling as the keeper of the purse to take the time to, "search out a matter."

The actual prophecy stated, "And the Lord said to me, 'Throw it to the potter' - the handsome price at which they priced me! So I took the thirty pieces of silver and threw them into the house of the Lord to the potter."

The actual event played out in Matthew 26:3-7,

"When Judas, who had betrayed Him, saw that Jesus was condemned, he was seized with remorse and returned the thirty silver coins to the chief priests and the elders. 'I have sinned,' he said, 'for I have betrayed innocent blood.'

'What is that to us', they replied. 'That's your responsibility.'

So Judas threw the money into the temple and left. Then he went away and hanged himself.

The chief priests picked up the coins and said, 'It is against the law to put this into the treasury, since it is blood money.' so they decided to use the money to buy the potter's field, as a burial place for foreigners."

God had even mentioned *"potter."*

In the next chapter we are going to be examining more and more minutely detailed prophecies that God made that were fulfilled, but it dawned on me that John Doe debater might be a mathematician. If so, taking a quick break to see what his mathematical cronies have to say about what we have been looking at might be an eye opening experience.

A few years back *Science Speaks* published an article in which that revered secular publication looked at the probability of one person's life fulfilling eight of the prophecies that the life of Jesus fulfilled. The article was carefully reviewed by an independent committee of the American Scientific affiliation, and then by the Executive Council of the same organization.

Their findings stated, "The study has been found to be dependable and sound in regard to scientific material. The mathematical analysis included is based upon principles of possibility which are thoroughly sound."

The finding they reviewed and found to be true was that the chances of any one man's life fulfilling just eight of the over 300 prophecies is one in ten to the seventeen power. Written out numerically that is: 1 in 100,000,000,000,000,000.

I'm not a mathematician but I think that would be one in a hundred zillion, if zillion is in fact the correct term. What I do know is that we have already explored fourteen fulfilled prophecies in the life of Jesus, and we are just beginning. We obviously are way past one in a hundred zillion already.

Did I just hear the shower water running again? Come back, John Doe, there is a lot of really exciting stuff yet to cover.

CHAPTER TEN

One would think that if the day Jesus was crucified was as monumental as His followers say, God would have put a lot of emphasis on that day in prophecy. As we will learn, He did.

In fact, the very next verse in Daniel after the foretelling of the exact day that Jesus would ride into Jerusalem, by use of the seven sevens and sixty two sevens, we read, "After the sixty two sevens the Anointed One will be cut off." Cut off is obviously a reference to His being killed. And throughout the entire Old Testament there is verse after prophetic verse about the very smallest detail of that day of all days.

The first thing that happened to Jesus after Judas betrayed Him was a sham of a trial before the high priest, Caiaphus. Over 700 years earlier God had foretold what would happen next. "He was oppressed and afflicted, yet he did not open his mouth; he was led like a lamb to the slaughter, and as a sheep before her shearers is silent, so he did not open his mouth." Isaiah 53:7

As we might expect from the above prophecy, that is exactly what happened. Then the high priest stood up and said to Jesus, 'Are you not going to answer? What is this testimony that these men are bringing against you?' But Jesus remained silent." Matthew 26:62

In fact, after the sham of the mock trial with Caiaphus, Jesus was taken to Pilate and the same foretold results occurred. "When He was accused by the chief priests and the elders, He gave no answer. Then Pilate asked Him, 'Don't you hear the testimony they are bringing against you?' But Jesus made no reply, not even to a single charge - to the great amazement of the Governor," Matthew 27:12

Once again we can look back more than 700 hundred years earlier and read, "I offered my back to those who beat me, my cheeks to those who pulled out my beard; I did not hide my face from mocking and spitting." Isaiah 50:6

Additionally, in Micah 5:1 we find, "They will strike Israel's ruler on the cheek with a rod."

Of course, after the ridiculous trial, Matthew 26:67 says, *"Then they spit in His face and struck Him with their fists. Others slapped him and said, 'Prophesy to us, Christ. Who hit you?"*

We all know that, *"Two robbers were crucified with him, one on His right and one on his left."* Matthew 27:38, but we should realize that God foretold that fact also, *"he poured out his life unto death, and was numbered with the transgressors."* Isaiah 53:12

The painful spikes driven in His hands and feet were explained hundreds of years earlier in places like Zechariah 12:10, *"they will look on me, the One they have pierced,"* and Isaiah 53:5, *"But he was pierced for our transgressions."*

Even the vinegar was foretold that we read about in Luke 23:36, which says, *"The soldiers also came up and mocked Him. They offered him wine vinegar."* We know from Psalm 69:21, written centuries before, *"They put gall in my food and gave me vinegar for my thirst."* The *"gall"* part even came true for we read, *"There they offered Jesus wine to drink, mixed with gall."* Matthew27:34

Dozens and dozens of very detailed accounts of that day were told in prophetic verses hundreds of years in advance.

God, the Father, did want us to pay attention to that day, even down to the part that is spoken of in Psalm 22:18, *"They divide my garments among them and cast lots for my clothing."*

That prophecy was indeed fulfilled. *"When the soldiers crucified Jesus, they took His clothes, divided them into four shares, one for each of them, with the undergarment remaining. This garment was seamless, woven in one piece from top to bottom. 'Let's not tear it,' they said to one another. 'Let's decide by lot who will get it."* John 19:23-24

As an aside, Roman crucifiction, which had not even been invented until about 500 years after most of the many prophecies were given that described the death of Jesus in so much detail, could take several days to result in death. It was a slow, agonizing death.

There were times, however, that the Roman soldiers needed to speed up the death. This was the case with Jesus, since they wanted it all to be finished prior to the next day's Jewish Sabbath. In order to speed up the process the soldiers normally broke the legs of the victims with a club, since the only way to breathe on a cross was to push the body up with the legs. In the prophetic Psalm 34:20, God relates in advance about Jesus,

"He protects all his bones, not one of them will be broken."

The disciple John, who was there throughout the entire ordeal reports to us, *"But when they came to Jesus they found that He was already dead, they did not break His legs."*

Through Isaiah, God showed what would happen when the crucifiction was over, *"He was assigned a grave with the wicked, and with the rich in his death, though he had done no violence, nor was any deceit in his mouth."* Isaiah 53:9

This prophecy, too, was fulfilled. *"As evening approached, there came a rich man from Arimathea, named Joseph, who had himself become a disciple of Jesus. Going to Pilate, he asked for Jesus' body, and Pilate ordered that it be given to him. Joseph took the body, wrapped it in clean linen cloth, and placed it in his own new tomb that he had cut out of a rock. He rolled a big rock in front of the entrance and went away."* Matthew 27:57-60

In this chapter we looked at eleven more of the prophecies about that infamous day in history, and there are others. For the moment, though, let's stop and consider once and for all the probabilities of one man fulfilling the twenty five that we have mentioned so far. In the last chapter we learned that the chances were one in a hundred zillion that one man could have fulfilled just eight of the fourteen we had covered. Can you wrap your mind around the number that would come up for the chance of any one man fulfilling twenty five of these prophecies.

Dr. Grant Jeffrey, who is extremely brilliant, in his truly wonderful book, The Signature of God, which I wholeheartedly recommend, did come up with the answer for the chance of one man's life fulfilling seventeen of such prophecies. The startling figure is one in 480,000,000,000,000,000,000,000,000,000,000.

That is one in 480 billion, times a billion, times a trillion. And that is only seventeen prophecies. We have studied twenty five.

Jesus fulfilled over three hundred. There never was a debate.

As we have already discussed, God is outside our time and space constraints. The Word of God, like Him, was written outside our time and space constraints as well. It was given to normal men to write, but the words came from outside our time.

Second Timothy 3:16 says, *"All scripture is God breathed."*

I mention this, before we leave this chapter dealing with the day of the crucifiction of Jesus, because I think you will find it sobering to read a Psalm, written many centuries earlier, that was so obviously written by Jesus Himself describing that day. Hebrews 2:11-12 even tells us that these are the words of Jesus. I am convinced you will never read the 22nd Psalm the same way again. You will be stunned as you actually discover what was going through the mind of the man, Jesus, as He hung on the cross for those excruciating hours on that day of all days.

"My God, my God, why have you forsaken me? Why are you so far from saving me, so far from the words of my groaning? O my God, I cry out by day, but you do not answer, by night, and am not silent. Yet you are enthroned as the Holy One.

I am poured out like water, and all my bones are out of joint. My heart has turned to wax; it has melted away within me. My strength is dried up like a potsherd, and my tongue sticks to the roof of my mouth; you lay me in the dust of death.

Dogs have surrounded me; a band of evil men has encircled me, they have pierced my hands and feet. I can count all my bones; people stare and gloat over me.

They divide my garments among them and cast lots for my clothing.

But you, O Lord, be not far off, O my Strength, come quickly to help me. Deliver my life from the sword, my precious life from the power of the dogs.

I will declare your name to my brothers; in the congregation I will praise you.

You who fear the Lord, praise him! All you descendants of Jacob, honor him! Revere him, all you descendants of Israel! For he has not despised or disdained the suffering of the afflicted one, he has not hidden his face from him but has listened to his cry for help.

From you comes the theme of my praise in the great assembly; before those who fear you will I fulfill my vows.

The poor will eat and be satisfied; they who seek the Lord will praise him - may your hearts live forever!

All the ends of the earth will remember and turn to the Lord, and all the families of the nations will bow down before him, for dominion belongs to the Lord and he rules over the nations.

All the rich of the earth will feast and worship; all who go down to the dust will kneel before him -those who cannot keep themselves alive.

Posterity will serve him; future generations will be told about the Lord. They will proclaim his righteousness to the people yet unborn - for he has done it."

CHAPTER ELEVEN

So far we have been looking at actual prophetic verses to prove undeniably that God exists, and also to prove that Jesus was the Anointed One sent by God. Some of those prophecies were so very clear and detailed, such as chapter eleven in Daniel that predicted step by step what would happen to Alexander's kingdom after he died. Others took a little more digging, such as the one that predicted the exact date Israel would become a nation. There actually are many other ways that God used to predict the future or explain things.

One of the more fascinating to me was with the use of names throughout His Word. To start with we need to be aware that Hebrew names all had a meaning, kind of like the native American Indian names. For example, let's look at ten biblical names and their meanings:

> 1 - Adam means "man"
> 2 - Enoch means "teaching"
> 3 - Enosh means "mortal"
> 4 - Jared means "shall come down"
> 5 - Kenan means "sorrow"
> 6 - Lamech means "despairing"
> 7 - Mahalalel means "blessed God"
> 8 - Methuselah means "his death shall bring"
> 9 - Noah means "comfort"
> 10 - Seth means "is appointed"

These ten names were not taken at random. They actually comprise the first genealogy given in the Bible in Genesis 5.

We listed those names in alphabetical order, but in Genesis five they are obviously listed in chronological order; Adam, Seth, Enosh, Kenan, Mahalalel, Jared, Enoch, Methuselah, Lamech, and finally Noah.

Maybe you should be sitting down for this. When we read the meanings of those names a sentence is formed, which reads: "Man is appointed mortal sorrow, (but) blessed God shall come down, teaching (that) His death shall bring the despairing comfort."

In the fifth chapter of the very first book in the Bible God spelled out what was going to happen. Mankind was, in fact, appointed mortal sorrow since God had said that if man ate of the tree of the knowledge of good and evil, he would surely die. That is truly mortal sorrow. But Jesus did come to earth, teaching that His death would bring life. What a phenomenal prophecy, and it was couched in a simple genealogy.

Sometimes just one name could tell an entire story. For instance, the name Barabbas means child of God. We all know the story, Barabbas was set free and Jesus was crucified. The truth was that Jesus died on the cross so that the "children of God" could be set free. All of theology was summed up in the simple reference to Barabbas. Ponder it and you will realize how totally incredible that is.

Besides names, one other way that God prophesied was through what is termed "types and shadows." These are the events or things in the Old Testament that pointed to Jesus.

And the Old Testament is chock full of them. Scofield defined one hundred and twenty eight of these in his Bible, but there are actually many more. Let's look at an obvious one first, the Passover Lamb.

I'm sure you know the story of the first Passover. It occurred when the Israelites were still in Egypt. The final plague that God sent on the Egyptians to force Pharaoh to let His people go was the death of all the firstborn sons throughout Egypt. God told his people that they were to slaughter a lamb and put its blood on the top and sides of their door posts so that the angel of death would know which house belonged to a Jew and "pass over" that house. Within that entire story are several "types and shadows" of Jesus. For example, the blood on the door post, of course, forms the shape of a cross. Additionally, Exodus 12:5 says the Lamb was to be spotless, as Jesus was when He came 2,000 years later. There are too many to discuss here, but the one that I think you will find the most interesting, after reading our last chapter, is mentioned in Exodus 12:46,

"Do not break any of the bones" of the lamb.

Isn't it interesting to consider that the last meal Jesus ate, which we know as 'The Last Supper," was in fact Passover.

I am totally convinced that if a person spent twelve hours a day studying God's Word, from the time he or she could read, until death at the ripe old age of 105, that person would say "Wow" out loud more times on the very last day than on any previous day. The more we study, and the deeper we dig, the more we realize how utterly fantastic and intricate the Bible is.

No other book even comes close to the genius of it. We are barely scratching the surface of that genius in this book. Professor Harold Gans, a noted mathematician with over 180 technical papers to his credit, and a senior U.S. Army codes consultant, started studying the Bible as a complete skeptic. After several years he concluded that the Bible had to have been written by God, and He had to have written it in a single second. The intricate weaving of an unknown myriad of things throughout the entire 66 books of the Bible, both on the surface, and underlying it, according to Gans, is far beyond human scope, even with the help of the most sophisticated computers.

Now, though, we will just keep looking at the surface phenomenona in God's Word. Some of them in the Old Testament are extremely easy to spot because we are actually told what they are in the New Testament. One that comes to mind is the "brazen Serpent."

The story is told in Numbers 21:4-9 that the children of Israel started complaining during their journey in the desert, *"they spoke against God and Moses, and said, 'Why have you brought us up out of Egypt to die in the desert? There is no bread! There is no water! And we detest this miserable food!"*

Then the Lord sent venomous snakes among them, they bit the people and many of them died. The people came to Moses and said, 'We sinned when we spoke against the Lord and you. Pray that the Lord will take the snakes away from us.' So Moses prayed for the people.

The Lord said to Moses, 'Make a snake and put it up on a pole; anyone who is bitten can look at it and live.' So Moses made a bronze snake

and put it up on a pole. Then when anyone was bitten by the snake and looked at the bronze snake, he lived."

There are so many words that are used throughout the Bible that we know represent specific things. Egypt, for example always represents the world and its sinful ways. A snake, of course, is sin itself or Satan. In this story, mankind is bitten by sin, but isn't it kind of a quandary why God would want them to look at sin on a pole? Not at all, for we find in 1 Peter 2:24, in speaking of Jesus, *"He Himself bore our sins on the tree."*

Jesus himself cleared up any mystery that could have existed about this story when He said in John 3:14, *"Just as Moses lifted up the snake in the desert, so the Son of Man must be lifted up, that everyone that believes in Him may have eternal life."*

Actually, the entire forty year wilderness experience was filled with "types and shadows" of Jesus. An example is in Exodus 16:6 when the Israelites were thirsty, God told Moses, *"I will stand there before you by the rock at Horeb. Strike the rock, and water will come out of it for the people to drink."*

Once again, this "type" takes no real searching on our part, for we are told in 1 Corinthians 10:3-4, in talking about the Israelites in the wilderness, *"They all ate the same spiritual food and drank the same spiritual drink; for they drank from the spiritual rock that accompanied them, and that rock was Christ."*

Another "type" of Jesus that is actually explained to us so that we wouldn't miss it was the well known story of the manna. In Exodus 16:11-15 God supplied the answer to the Hebrews' complaints about food when He told Moses, *"I have heard the grumbling of the Israelites. Tell them, 'At twilight you will eat meat, and in the morning you will be filled with bread. Then you will know that I am the Lord your God."*

That evening quail came and covered the camp, and in the morning there was a layer of dew around the camp. When the dew was gone, thin flakes like frost on the ground appeared on the desert floor. When the Israelites saw it, they said to each other, 'what is it?' For they did not know what it was."

Moses said to them, ' It is the bread the Lord has given you to eat."

Jesus again explained this "type," two thousand years later for the Jews of His time, as well as for any of us who reads John 6:32, *"I tell you the truth, it is not Moses who has given you the bread from heaven, but it is my Father who gives you the true bread from heaven. For the bread of God is He who comes down from heaven and gives life to the world."*

It is said that "the Old Testament is the New Testament concealed, and the New Testament is the Old Testament revealed," which is surely the case. For this reason I think it is wise for people to read and learn the New Testament before they go to the Old Testament. By doing that their eyes are more open to spot the incredible "types and shadows" that it contains.

The story of Noah's Ark is also a fascinating "shadow" of what was to come. If we think about it, the Ark carried the only eight righteous people of that time over the flood, and spared them from the wrath of God. Interestingly, in the story in Genesis 6:14, God told Noah, *"So make yourself an ark of cypress wood; make rooms in it and coat it with pitch inside and out."* What is interesting is that the Hebrew word for pitch is kafar, which also is used a total of seventy times in the Bible and normally is used to mean atonement.

In instituting the act of sacrifice, God told the Israelites in Leviticus 17:11, *"it is the blood that makes atonement for one's life."* The word for atonement used here was kafar, the same word as for pitch to cover Noah's Ark, which was used to save the righteous.

After Jesus shed his blood, we read Paul speaking about Him in Romans 3:25, *"God presented him as a sacrifice of atonement, through faith in His blood."* Also in Hebrews 2:17 it is stated, *"For this reason He had to be made like His brothers in every way, in order that He might become a merciful and faithful high priest in service to God, and that He might make atonement for the sins of the people."* Once again, the pitch, kafar, that covered the Ark is the same word used as atonement in describing what Jesus accomplished on Calvary.

Additionally, it is noteworthy, to look at Genesis 7:11, which tells us, *"on the seventeenth day of the second month - on that day all the springs of the great deep burst forth, and the floodgates of heaven were opened."* We know from Jewish calendars that the seventeenth day of the second month was the exact same day of the year that Jesus arose from the dead.

Chapter Twelve

We have studied some of the over three hundred actual prophecies that God put in the Old Testament that came true hundreds and thousands of years later in the life of Jesus of Nazareth. He did this not only to make sure there could be no debate about His own existence, but also to make it crystal clear to anyone who might question if Jesus truly was the Messiah that He was to send. Additionally, we have already scratched the surface of how God used names and "types and shadows" to foretell the future Anointed One and the reason He would come.

God wants all mankind to be able to see for a certainty that there could be no one other than Jesus to fulfill the roll of Savior. Being outside our time and space God could see that false religions by the scores would spring up, offering hope in a false messiah. Probably the most well known today is the Islamic teaching that a Mahdi will arise that will be mankind's answer. Moslems worldwide, of course, believe Islam to be true. And unfortunately, many uninformed onlookers think that the Moslem Allah, which really came from an ancient moon god, is the same as the God of the Bible. As we mentioned in passing, the Koran contains not one fulfilled prophecy from their false god, Allah. In the Koran's Sura 3:19, though, we can read that Allah says, "The only true faith in Allah's sight is Islam."

I find it interesting that the "coming" Islamic Mahdi looks very much like the person in the end time prophetic statements by God that He refers to as the beast, the antichrist. I could go into scores of uncanny comparisons, but I'll just mention the white horse.

In Revelation 6:2 the Apostle John writes of his vision of the end time days, *"I looked and there before me was a white horse! Its rider held a bow, and he was given a crown, and he rode out as a conqueror bent on conquest,"* This is the first thing that will occur when Jesus, The Lamb of God, opens the first of seven seals.

One of the big traditions in Islam is that the Mahdi will ride a white horse. With that in mind, Saddam Hussein of Iraq had his special white stallion always at the ready just in case Allah might tap him on the shoulder. Moamar Qaddafi of Lybia has his own white stallion, constantly brushed and ready to be mounted. It wouldn't surprise me in the least to learn that President Mahmoud Ahmadinejad of Iran has a white pony.

We can see why God wanted there to be no doubt about who the true Christ really is. In the world of false impostors, it could be a challenge to pick the real Messiah, unless the proven God of over 8,000 prophecies pointed Him out for us in such unmistakable fashion. Three hundred fulfilled prophecies in His life obviously should end any debate, but God continued to pile on proof upon proof with His other ingenious devises such as the types and shadows we have been looking at.

Often God used actual people as types of the Christ that was to come. Volumes have been written showing Joseph and Moses as such types, and most assuredly they were. One of Jesus's own favorites was Jonah for we read his own words,

"A wicked and adulterous generation asks for a miraculous sign! But none will be given it except the sign of the prophet Jonah. For as Jonah was three days and three nights in the belly of a huge fish, so the son of Man will be three days and three nights in the heart of the earth." Matthew 12:39-40

The most intriguing to me, however, is the mysterious person found only three places in the Bible by the name of Melchizedek. We read about him first in Genesis 14:18-20 when Abram meets him on his return from a military victory, *"Then Melchizedek king of Salem brought out bread and wine. He was priest of God Most High, and he blessed Abram, saying, 'Blessed be Abram by God Most high, creator of heaven and earth. And blessed be God Most High, who delivered your enemies into your hand.' Then Abram gave him a tenth of everything."*

Notice that Melchizedek offered Abram bread and wine, which are the same two items Jesus offered His disciples at the last supper, and the same that are still partaken of today by Christians around the world. And note also that Abram paid him a tenth of everything, a tithe.

We see the name Melchizedek show up very briefly again in Psalm 110:4, which talks about the coming Messiah, *"The Lord has sworn and will not change his mind: 'You are a priest forever, in the order of Melchizedek."*

Finally the pieces are put together even more clearly in the New Testament in Hebrews 6:19-20 and 7:1, written about 35 years after the crucifiction and resurrection of Jesus, *"We have this hope as an anchor for the soul, firm and secure. It enters the inner sanctuary behind the curtain, where Jesus, who went before us, has entered on our behalf. He has become a priest forever, in the order of Melchizedek.*

This Melchizedek was a king of Salem and priest of God Most High. He met Abraham returning from the defeat of the kings and blessed him, and Abraham gave him a tenth of everything. First, his name means 'king of righteousness'; then also , 'king of Salem' means 'king of peace.' Without father or mother, without genealogy, without beginning of days or end of life, like the Son of God he remains a priest forever."

The next 24 verses in Hebrews 7 go on to talk in even more detail about Jesus now being the priest in the heavenlies, in the order of Melchizedek. There is still a lot of mystery surrounding who Melchizedek really was, but we do know for sure that he may be one of the closest "types" of Jesus that God gave us. As I said, he is very intriguing.

Before we look into my very favorite shadow, I want to mention that throughout the Bible Jesus is depicted as having four distinct natures, those of a servant, a king, a man, and God.

Those four aspects are said to be the defining difference between the four Gospels: Matthew, Mark, Luke, and John, which study the life of Christ from four different perspectives. Matthew, the tax collector, looks at the humanity of Jesus.

Mark, the one to write the first and shortest gospel written, observes His kingship. Luke, the doctor who wrote the longest of the gospels sees the servant nature of Jesus. And John, the "beloved disciple", focuses on His divinity. Often throughout the Bible those four distinctions are displayed as an ox (servant), a lion (king), the face of a man (humanity), and an eagle (God).

An example is found in a vision that Ezekiel had about 593 BC. You remember him. He was the man who God instructed to lie on his left side for 390 days and then on his right side for 40 days, to represent the length in years of Israel's punishment for their disobedience. Of course, as we saw, that punishment was multiplied times seven since they did not repent, and culminated on the exact date that Israel became a nation in 1948. At any rate, prior to his horizontal display, he had a vision in which he saw four mysterious living creatures.

The description of these four living creatures is found in Ezekiel 1:10, *"Their faces looked like this: Each of the four had the face of a man, and on the right side each had the face of a lion, and on the left the face of an ox; each also had the face of an eagle. Such were their faces."*

The same type of reference is found in Revelation 4:7 in a verse describing what John saw around God's throne in his vision that tells of the things yet to come. In this vision, which occurred about 650 years after the vision Ezekiel had, once again John describes seeing four living creatures. He writes about them in that verse, *"The first living creature was like a lion, the second was like an ox, the third had a face like a man, the fourth was like a flying eagle."*

This shadow of the four descriptions of Jesus shows up in some of the least expected places. My favorite place, in fact my very favorite of all the shadows, is found ingeniously hidden in one of the most boring sections of the entire Bible. It is one of those places that is hard to read through without having your mind wander. It seems to be a wonderful place to insert your book mark, turn off the light, and go to sleep, if you happen to be reading the Bible in bed. But remember, *"It is to the glory of God to conceal a matter; to search out a matter is the glory of kings."* Proverbs 25:2

The utterly boring passage I am referring to is the second chapter of Numbers, the fourth book in the Old Testament. The author was none other than Moses, the leader of the Israelites, who had started as a Hebrew baby in a basket in the bulrushes, but was brought up by Egypt's royal family. In 1446 BC he led his true people out of Egyptian captivity.

Before we go further with this phenomenal shadow it is important to mention that when God freed His people through Moses, He also did it on the exact day that he had predicted hundreds of years earlier that He would. He had told Abram in a dream, before he had even had his first son, *"Know for certain that your descendants will be strangers in a country not of their own, and they will be enslaved and mistreated four hundred years. But I will punish the nation they serve as slaves, and afterward they will come out with great possessions."* Genesis 15:13-14

Much later, Abram's grandson, Jacob, and his eleven sons with their families, went to Egypt to escape a famine in 1876 BC, during a time when his twelfth son, Joseph, was heading up the food distribution for the Pharaoh. Thirty years later the next Pharaoh enslaved all the Jews in Egypt. They remained in bondage for four hundred years. The end of the captivity is chronicled in Exodus 12:40-41, *"Now the length of the time the Israelite people lived in Egypt was 430 years. At the end of the 430 years, to the very day, all the Lord's divisions left Egypt."* Just as God foretold the date the Israelites' slavery in Babylon would end, as well as the exact date the Israelites would become a nation again in 1948, He had earlier foretold the number of years they would be in bondage to the Egyptians, as the above verse says, *"to the very day."* God's predictions are almost monotonously exact in their fulfillment. Of course, He told us that was how to know without doubt that He was real.

Getting back to my very favorite shadow, which is cleverly concealed in the boring book of Numbers, let me set the stage for you. In the book of Numbers the Hebrew people have passed the Red Sea and are in their forty year wilderness journey to the promised land. God gives exact instructions as to how the trip is to unfold, down to the minutest details. In the second chapter God actually tells them very specifically how to arrange the twelve tribes of Israel as they travel.

If you are reading this in bed, do not turn the light out and go to sleep. This is not the time. Bear with me and read this chapter and I promise you that you will say "Wow" when you see the concealed message. It is absolutely incredible.

The chapter reads, *"The Lord said to Moses and Aaron: The Israelites are to camp around the Tent of Meeting some distance from it, each man under his standard with the banners of his family.*

On the east, toward the sunrise the division of the camp of Judah are to encamp under their standard. The leader of the people of Judah is Nahshon son of Amminadab. His division numbers 74,600.

The tribe of Issachar will camp next to them. The leader of the people of Issachar is Nethaniel son of Zuar. His division numbers 54,400.

The tribe of Zebulun will be next. The leader of the people of Zebulon is Eliab son of Helon. His division numbers 57,400.

All the men assigned to the camp of Judah, according to their divisions, number 186,400. They will set out first."

I am typing this with my one typing finger so surely you can keep reading with your two eyes. I promise you it will be well worth it. The chapter continues:

"On the south will be the division of the camp of Rueben under their standard. The leader of the people of Reuben is Elizur son of Shedeur. His division numbers 46,500.

The tribe of Simeon will camp next to them. The leader of the people of Simeon is Shelumiel son of Zurishaddai. His division numbers 59,300.

The tribe of Gad will be next. The leader of the people of Gad is Eliasaph son of Deuel. His division numbers 45,650.

All the men assigned to the camp of Reuben, according to their divisions, numbers 151,450. They will set out second.

Then the Tent of Meeting and the camp of the Levites will set out in the middle of the camps. They will set out in the same order as they encamp, each in his own place under his standard.

On the west will be the divisions of the camp of Ephraim under their standard. The leader of the people of Ephraim is Elishama son of Ammihud. His division numbers 40,500.

The tribe of Manasseh will be next to them. The leader of the people of Manasseh is Gamaliel son of Pedahzur. His division numbers 32,200."

I guarantee you that you will never forget this shadow, so hang in there as we continue:

"The tribe of Benjamin will be next. The leader of the people of Benjamin is Abidan son of Gideoni. His division numbers 35,400.

All the men assigned to the camp of Ephraim, according to their divisions, number 108,100. They will set out third.

On the north will be the divisions of the camp of Dan, under their standard. The leader of the people of Dan is Ahiezer son of Ammishaddai. His division numbers 62,700.

The tribe of Asher will camp next to them. The leader of the people of Asher is Pagiel son of Ocran. His division numbers 41,500.

The tribe of Naphtali will be next. The leader of the people of Naphtali is Ahira son of Enan. His division numbers 53,400.

All the men assigned to the camp of Dan number 157,600. They will set out last, under their standards."

OK, we read it. Of course, we knew that God had concealed something very important in all of that. Can you imagine the poor Jewish scribes who had to tediously copy this exactly, through the hundreds of years that followed? I'm sure they wondered what in the world the reason for having to copy all of this was. I imagine a thousand years later some tired scribe thought, "Who really cares?" The answer is you and me. Thank you poor tired scribe. Without knowing it, you were being used by God to give twenty first century man a powerful message.

Allow me to recap. In the center of the tribes of Israel as they crossed the desert was the tribe of Levites who were the priests, and the Tent of Meeting, which housed the Ark of the Covenant. To the west, toward the Mediterranean Sea, were the tribes of Ephraim, Manasseh, and Benjamin, totaling 108,100 men. To the east, toward what is now Jordan, were the tribes of Judah, Issachar, and Zebulun, totaling 186,400 men. To the south, toward Egypt were the tribes of Reuben, Simeon, and Gad, with a total of 151,450 men. And finally, to the north, toward what is now Jerusalem, were the tribes of Dan Asher, and Naphtali, with 157,600 men.

If you haven't envisioned it already, God's arrangement of the tribes of Israel forms an almost perfect cross, probably exactly to the scale of the one Jesus was nailed to on Calvary, about fifteen hundred years later. We have a scale of 108 on the top, 186 on the bottom, and 151 and 157 on the sides.

Close your eyes and imagine the site at night, from a distance to the north, with the camp fires burning. A lighted cross marching toward what was to become the City of God.

Or better yet, picture that burning cross on a dark night, as seen from the heavens. Jesus Himself was witnessing that forty year march toward the city He later wept over. A very slow, human cross, moving across the wilderness for forty years. And forty is

God's number for a trial. A trial it would surely become for the Son of God, as we can see by the sweat on His brow turning to drops of blood as He prayed in the Garden of Gethsemane the night before the actual sacrifice; praying, *"Father, if you are willing, take this cup from me, yet not my will, but yours be done."* Luke 22:42

The shadow, however, does not end with this powerful picture of the gigantic cross of Christ, moving toward the city that would turn that cross of humanity into the rough wooden cross, a cross that would be described across time limitations in the lamenting words of Jesus that we read earlier in Psalm 22.

No, the picture is even more dramatic, for the emblems on the standards of the outside tribes of Benjamin, Zebulun, Gad, and Naphtali, were an ox, a lion, a face of a man, and an eagle.

From the heavenlies Jesus watched that cross move slowly onward to Jerusalem, the place of the sacrifice. But He was also there as it traveled; the Servant, the King of Kings, fully man, and fully God.

The wilderness journey, as well as the Bible in its entirety, from Genesis to Revelation, is all about Jesus. It is all one story. A love story. You and I are the recipients of that love.

PART THREE

CHAPTER THIRTEEN

Obviously it would be impossible in any single book to examine all of the 8,352 verses in the Bible that are currently listed as prophetic verses. God overwhelmed us with so many prophecies to be completely sure that anyone who endeavored to get any Biblical knowledge would have no doubt at all about His existence, or the fact that He did indeed communicate to us through His Word. We have already seen a small number of His prophecies that have been fulfilled exactly the way He said they would, to the exact date and even with people such as Cyrus who had not even been born when the prophecy was given.

On top of that, the uses of "types and shadows" and names throughout the Bible to foretell things are almost breathtaking in their genius. Additionally, we have mentioned just a few of the amazing scriptures that predicted future knowledge in areas of medicine and science.

One example in the modern scientific arena is virtually never given the publicity it deserves. That in itself should give us cause to wonder because it involves the most recognizable name in science, and his most recognizable theory. The person I am referring to is none other than Albert Einstein himself, and the theory is his Theory of Relativity which produced the common formula, E= MC squared.

Although Einstein was not a religious man, he was Jewish and had a fundamental knowledge of the Jewish Torah, the first five books of the Bible. There came a time when Einstein was stumped as to the characteristics of light. Almost as a last ditch effort he picked up the book of Genesis to see what it had to say about light in the very first chapter. Something caused him to do more than just a cursory reading of the chapter. In fact, he studied the chapter in the original Hebrew in which it had been written. He first studied verse 3, which reads, *"And God said, 'Let there be light,' and there was light. And God saw the light was good, and He separated the light from the darkness."*

Einstein noticed that the Hebrew word used for light was "ohr." He then went to verse 14 and read, *"And God said, 'Let there be lights in the expanse of the sky."* Instantly, Einstein noticed that the original word used for light in that verse was not "ohr." In verse 14 the word for light was "maohr." This was the key Einstein's brilliance needed to unlock the secret of light. He knew that maohr actually meant "from light". This led him to the knowledge that the light spoken of in verse three was Divine light, whereas the light in verse 14 was of a different kind. He knew that ohr was also used in the Torah to refer to the shekinah glory of God, or the primal light. That was the very first light.

Einstein then studied the Hebrew language more closely and by doing what he called "grammatical divisions and substitutions" arrived at the word for mass being ma, the word for light was ohr, the word for raised was rum, and the word for squared was rebah. This led his phenomenal mind to discover that energy (E) could be derived from mass (M) multiplied by the square of the mathematical constant which is the speed of light (C2). Obviously, this is E=MC2. Einstein even gave credit to God and the book of Genesis in an address he made to a group of rabbis in New York City. Isn't it interesting that the source of the key is never mentioned in our school books today?

Speaking of men like Albert Einstein, the greatest scientist of all time, Sir Isaac Newton, was an avid devotee of the Bible. He was a Biblical fundamentalist who studied the Bible daily and wrote over a million words of notes on it. Newton, born on Christmas day, 1642, not only discovered the Law of Gravity, but he also invented such things as calculus, the science of mechanics, and the science of optics. He was the greatest mathematician of modern times and held the honored Chair of Mathematics at Cambridge for 33 years. His interest in numbers led him on a life long study of Biblical numerology, being convinced that God had hidden meanings in numbers. Through the centuries other brilliant thinkers, such as Augustine and Leonardo DiVinci, had held the same view, and they were right.

God used numbers in some cases to actually tell stories, much like He did with names in the genealogy in Genesis 5 that we studied earlier that actually wrote out the prophetic sentence, "Man is appointed mortal sorrow but blessed God shall come down, teaching that his death shall bring the despairing comfort."

We will look at one example of His use of a number like that in a moment, and I am convinced you will be flabbergasted when you read about it. Before we do, though, let's see what numbers in general mean in the Bible. Each number is almost constantly used throughout all of the 66 books in the Bible to represent a specific thing. And phenomenally, God actually arranged in real life Biblical history that the numbers of things or people would normally match up with the meaning associated with the numbers.

Biblical scholars generally agree on the meanings that God assigned to most of the numbers. In fact, several books have been written covering the meanings of well over a hundred different numbers. For brevity sake, however, we'll just take a brief look at the most common ones:

Number	Meaning
1	God the Father, or a beginning
2	Fullness of testimony, or truth
3	Divinity, or trinity
4	God's creative work
5	God's grace
6	Man
7	Perfection (God's favorite number)
8	Jesus, or new beginning
9	Finality
10	Redemption, or responsibility
11	Disorder
12	Completeness
13	Satan
40	Testing, or trial
120	Holy spirit
666	Antichrist

We mentioned above that the number 7 seems to be God's favorite number. It is actually used in the Bible over 600 times.

His second most favorite number is the number 3. This is not the place for an in depth study of these numbers in the Bible, but I can assure you that it is a fascinating one. I will just encourage you to keep these meanings handy as you read your Bible.

Before we leave this list of numbers and their meanings, though, I will try to very briefly explain why scholars agree with the meanings. Obviously the number obtains its meaning by the seemingly endless times it may be used in situations in which the same thing occurs. As we are aware, 40 is very often used in events of testing and trial, such as the 40 days and nights of the flood, the 40 year wilderness experience of the Israelites' journey to the promised land, and the 40 days in the wilderness that Jesus spent being tested by Satan. It is easy to see the theme unfolding whenever we see a 40. God also seems to multiply and divide to make His point. For instance, 400 (40 X 10) is looked at as a period of punishment such as the 400 years of slavery in Egypt that was preordained by God.

Whenever the number 120 is used in the Bible the presence of the Holy Spirit seems to follow. For example, after King Solomon built the temple he naturally had a dedication ceremony. We find in the story in 2 Chronicles 5:12, *"they were accompanied by 120 priests sounding trumpets."* Afterwards Solomon prayed his dedication prayer.

"When Solomon finished praying, fire came down from heaven and consumed the burnt offering and the sacrifices, and the glory of the Lord filled the temple. The priests could not enter the temple of the Lord because the glory of the Lord filled the temple." 2 Chronicles 7:1-2

Because of this supernatural presence, Solomon offered a whopping big sacrifice in verse 5 of, *"a hundred and twenty thousand sheep and goats,"* In this, of course, we see 120 times a thousand. If ten is redemption, what must a thousand be?

The most well known use of 120 occurred on the day of Pentecost in the New Testament. As you probably know, Jesus was with His disciples for 40 days after his resurrection until His ascension into heaven. There's that 40 number again. Before Jesus ascended to heaven He told His disciples in Acts 1:4,

"Do not leave Jerusalem, but wait for the gift my Father promised, which you have heard me speak about. For John baptized with water, but in a few days you will be baptized with the Holy Spirit."

The followers of Jesus did exactly as He said, and in verse 15 we read, *"In those days Peter stood up among the believers (a group numbering about a hundred and twenty)."*

Ten days after Jesus left, *"When the day of Pentecost came, they were all together in one place. Suddenly a sound like the blowing of a violent wind came from heaven and filled the whole house where they were sitting. They saw what seemed to be tongues of fire that separated and came to rest on each of them. All of them were filled with the Holy Spirit..."*

As I said, it seems that whenever the number 120 is used the Holy Spirit shows up.

Often we see a similar thing with Jesus and the number 8. As you recall, we saw that Noah's Ark was covered in pitch, the same word used for atonement, and the Ark was a "shadow" of Jesus's saving work. Inside the Ark were 8 people being saved.

But the numbers are not just used with situations. We need to understand that in both Greek and Hebrew there are no numbers as such. Numbers are actually letters, such as we are use to in the Latin language. We all know that in Latin V is 5, X is 10, I is 1, L is 50, C is 100, M is 1,000, etc. The same is true in the two main Biblical languages. If MIX were a word in Latin, it would also be the number 1,009, and likewise the same is true with the Hebrew and Greek languages.

As an aside, isn't it interesting that Alexander's life was so miraculously spared from the thousands and thousands of arrows, lances, and swords that were aimed at him during his fifteen years on the battlefield? It is worth pondering that God would need a language like the Koine Greek that Alexander developed, which is one of the most precise ever invented. It was used to quickly spread His Gospel throughout the world.

Speaking of that common Greek language that spread so fast on the heels of Alexander's army, about 260 BC, the king of Egypt was Ptolemy Philadelphus, who was one of the characters God foretold would come on the scene in that marvelous chapter eleven of Daniel that we studied. Ptolemy was living in the Alexandria, Egypt, named obviously after our old hero, Alexander. He was building a library that he wanted to be the best in the world, and he decided to have a Greek translation done of the Hebrew Holy Book to put in it. He contracted 72 Hebrew scholars to do the translation, six from each of the twelve tribes. The 72 translators completed the work in exactly 72 days, inspiring the name of it, the LXX (70), or the Septuagint, since 70 was the closest whole number to 72.

The Septuagint was the book that Jesus read from about three hundred years later, and today it comprises the oldest complete manuscripts we have to work from. Do you see God's number 7 times 10 in that real life situation? Interesting, isn't it?

Getting back to our original discussion, sometimes the searching into the numbers themselves for God's hidden meanings led scholars into how the letters that made up numbers would occasionally actually spell out words. Such is the case with the number 8 being representative of Jesus. Astonishingly, not only are there situations like Noah's ark that deal with 8 and point to Jesus, but all of His names do as well. That's right, every name in the Greek New Testament used for Jesus forms a number that is divisible by 8. Ask any mathematician and you will find that this is extremely incredible. The list of names translated into numbers is: Emmanuel = 25,600, which is 3,200 times 8, Christ =1,480, or 185 times 8, Savior = 1,408 or 176 times 8, Messiah = 656, or 82 times 8, Son = 880, which is 110 times 8, and Lord = 800, which is exactly 100 times 8.

In contrast, let's look at the names for Satan; and since Satan was present in the Old Testament times we will first look at his Old Testament names that were written in Hebrew, which also uses letters for numbers: The piercing serpent = 1,170, or 28 times 13, Beelzebub = 598, or 46 times 13, Belial = 78, which is 6 times 13, and Satan = 364, or 28 times 13. Of course, Satan was around in New testament times as well, so let's now look at his Greek New Testament names: Satan = 2,197, which is 169 times 13, dragon = 975, or 75 times 13, and Serpent = 780, or 60 times 13.

Also interesting is the fact that when we look at the person Satan will inhabit during the tribulation we find him called the man of sin =1963, or 151 times 13, as well as the son of perdition = 1,807, which is 139 times 13.

Lest we think that there is anything coincidental in all of this, not a single one of those names listed for Jesus is divisible by 13. Likewise, not a single one of those names listed for Satan is divisible by 8. God obviously is very interested in numbers and puts hidden meanings in them, many of the meanings we have yet to search out. But remember, *"to search out a matter is the glory of kings."* As an aside, we will "search out" that phrase in chapters to come in a way that will be unforgettable.

Now, though, I want to go over the use of a specific number in the Bible that I told you would flabbergast you.

The story occurs in the very last chapter of the four Gospels; Matthew, Mark, Luke, and John. I find it intriguing that it is located there, at the very end of the only four Biblical accounts of the life, death, and resurrection of Jesus. You will, too.

To set the stage, the resurrection of Jesus after His crucifiction had already taken place. Jesus had even appeared to His disciples twice. The second time evidently occurred several days earlier. The disciples were at the Sea of Galilee and Peter, being a fisherman, decided to go fishing while he was waiting for something else to happen. The rest of the disciples decided to go along, too. The story takes up in John 21:4, *"Early in the morning Jesus stood on the shore, but the disciples did not realize it was Jesus.*

He called out to them, 'Friends, haven't you any fish?'

'No,' they answered.

He said, 'Throw your nets on the right side of the boat and you will find some.' When they did they were unable to haul in the net because of the large number of fish.

Then the disciple whom Jesus loved said to Peter, 'It is the Lord!' as soon as Simon Peter heard him say, 'It is the Lord,' he wrapped his outer garment around him (for he had taken it off) and jumped into the water. The other disciples followed in the boat, towing the net full of fish, for they were not far from shore, about a hundred yards. When they landed they saw a fire of burning coals there with fish on it, and some bread.

Jesus said to them, 'Bring some of the fish you have just caught.'

Simon Peter climbed aboard and dragged the net ashore.

It was full of large fish, 153, but even with so many the net was not torn. Jesus said to them, 'Come and have breakfast.'

None of the disciples dared ask Him, 'Who are you?'

They knew it was the Lord." John 21:4-12

Most people who read that story never really notice the number 153. After the last few pages, though, the 153 probably caught your eye. Very good. *"To search out a matter is the glory of kings."*

Let's think for a minute, why in the world would God have thought it important enough for us to know that there were 153 fish? He could just as easily have used the phrase, "a lot", or "many", or "a bunch", or even "over a hundred". Obviously the number 153 must have been important. Scholars spent countless hours on that for centuries. Men like Newton, Augustine and DiVinci, plus scores of others dating back to the very first century, knew that there must be a hidden meaning, but it alluded them. Finally, about a hundred years ago an army officer named Lt. Col. R. Roberts had an idea.

Roberts counted the number of people referred to in the four gospels that were in some manner blessed by Jesus. The number incredibly totaled 153. In retrospect, it probably should not have been so difficult to figure out. In Mark 1:17, when Jesus was first calling to Andrew and his brother, Simon, He said, *"Come follow me, and I will make you fishers of men."*

I can not for the life of me imagine that anyone could still be around who has read this far in this book who could still want to throw up a flimsy debate, so for the sake of fairness I will put forth one myself. Isn't it possible that John counted up the number of people in the Gospels that Jesus touched in some way and were blessed? Knowing what you already know, having read so much of the undeniable genius of God in the Bible, I can see you shaking your head at such a ridiculous thought, but let's address this question anyway.

Yes, it is possible that John could have counted the people and come up with the 153 number, but could he have arranged for Matthew, Mark, Luke and himself to write stories about exactly 153 people? You see, that is what he would have had to have accomplished because the Greek letters that make up the number

153 also spell out "Sons of God." Only the God of all creation could have arranged all of that to happen in the life of Jesus and the writings of the four gospels. Hopefully you, like me, are totally flabbergasted. Like the shadow of the gigantic human cross moving across the desert for 40 years, with an ox, a lion, a face of a man, and an eagle on the four edges, only an all powerful God could arrange for the net to bring 153 fish ashore.

So that you will have a record in case you ever need it, below is the list of the 153 people blessed by Jesus in the Bible:

Description	Scripture (# of people)
1. The leper	Matthew 8:2-4 (1)
2. Centurion and servant	Matthew 8:5-13 (2)
3. Peter's mother in law	Matthew 8:14-15 (1)
4. Two devil possessed	Matthew 8:18 (2)
5. Palsied man and bearers	Matthew 9:2 (5)
6. Jairus and his daughter	Matthew 9:18-25 (2)
7. Woman with issue of blood	Matthew 9:21-22 (1)
8. Two blind men	Matthew 9:27-31 (2)
9. Man who was dumb	Matthew 9:32-33 (1)
10. Eleven Apostles	Matthew 10:1-4 (11)
11. Man with withered hand	Matthew 12:10-13 (1)
12. Blind, dumb, devil possessed	Matthew 12:22 (1)
13. Brothers of Jesus	Matthew 13:55 (4)
14. Syro-Ph woman and daughter	Matthew 15:22-28 (2)
15. Father and son with seizures	Matthew 17:14-18 (2)
16. Blind men at Jericho	Matthew 20:30-34 (2)
17. Simon the leper	Matthew 26:6 (1)
18. Mary, sister of Lazarus	Matthew 26:7 (1)
19. Centurion	Matthew 27:54 (1)
20. Salome	Matthew 27:56 (1)
21. Mary, wife of Cleopas	Matthew 27:56 (1)
22. Mary Magdalene	Matthew 27:56 (1)
23. Joseph of Arimathea	Matthew 27:57-60 (1)
24. Man with unclean spirit	Mark 1:23-26 (1)
25. Deaf and dumb man	Mark 7:32-35 (1)
26. Blind man	Mark 8:22-26 (1)

27. Son of the widow of Nain	Luke 7:12-15 (1)
28. A woman, a sinner	Luke 7:37-38 (1)
29. Joanna and Susanna	Luke 8:3 (2)
30. Another man (follow me)	Luke 9:59-62 (1)
31. The seventy disciples	Luke 10:1-9 (70)
32. Martha	Luke 10:38-42 (1)
33. Crippled woman	Luke 13:11-13 (1)
34. Man with dropsy	Luke 14:2-4 (1)
35. Ten lepers	Luke 17:12-14 (10)
36. Blind man	Luke 18:35-43 (1)
37. Zacchaeus	Luke 19:2-6 (1)
38. Malchus	Luke 22:50-51 (1)
39. Thief on the cross	Luke 23:42-43 (1)
40. Two disciples at Emmaus	Luke 24:13-32 (2)
41. Nicodemus	John 3:1-21 (1)
42. Samaritan woman	John 4:7-26 (1)
43. Nobleman and sick son	John 4:46-50 (2)
44. Invalid man at pool	John 5:1-9 (1)
45. Man blind since birth	John 9:1-41 (1)
46. Lazarus	John 11:1-44 (1)
47. Mary, mother of Jesus	John 19:25 (1)

Total: 153 people touched by Jesus
In Greek, the number 153 spells "Sons of God"

CHAPTER FOURTEEN

One of the most important statements given to us by God is found in Hosea 4:6. We all need to memorize it, think about it vary carefully, and actually do something about it. The verse is, *"My people are destroyed from lack of knowledge."*

Obviously God was not saying that we would be destroyed from lack of knowledge of the literary classics, or lack of knowledge of algebra, or lack of knowledge about how to sell more computers or fast food, or for that matter, lack of any kind of knowledge that we humans might think is so important in our own personal or business lives.

When God said, *"My people are destroyed from lack of knowledge."* He meant only one thing; the knowledge of His existence, His Son's existence, and how we can become a part of His eternal kingdom. Every other kind of knowledge is meaningless in comparison to that. In truth, nothing at all even matters without that imperative knowledge as the base.

King Solomon was the wisest man who ever lived. During his forty year reign he accomplished more, accumulated more, and maybe learned more than any other person who ever lived. Other kings and queens, like the Queen of Sheba, traveled to his court just to be awed by all that he possessed, and how fabulous his kingdom was. In Ecclesiastes 2:10-11, he tells us about his phenomenal life, *"I denied myself nothing my eyes desired; I refused my heart no pleasure. My heart took delight in all my work, and this was the reward for all my labor. Yet when I surveyed all that my hands had done and what I had toiled to achieve, everything was meaningless, a chasing after the wind; nothing was gained under the sun."*

Solomon had started out on the perfect track. He obviously was the chosen son of King David, the person in the Bible of whom is said, *"The Lord has sought out a man after His own heart and appointed him leader of His people."* 1 Samuel 13:14

Can we imagine anything better than starting out life as the son of the only man in the Bible described as being a man after God's own heart?

At first Solomon did not disappoint. The first part of his life was lived totally according to the very first commandment, *"You shall have no other gods besides me."* Exodus 20:3

When he was made Israel's king, he had a dream in which he humbly asked God for only one thing, *"So give your servant a discerning heart to govern your people and to distinguish between right and wrong."*

The Lord was pleased that Solomon had asked for this. So God said to him, 'Since you have asked for this and not for long life or wealth for yourself, nor have you asked for the death of your enemies but for discernment in administering justice, I will do what you have asked. I will give you a wise and discerning heart, so that there will never have been anyone like you, nor will there ever be. Moreover, I will give you what you have not asked for - both riches and honor -so that in your lifetime you will have no equal among kings." 1 Kings 3:9-13

Solomon's primary accomplishment during his forty year reign was to build the first temple to God, which was built exactly to God's specifications; including the outer court, where the sacrifices took place, the Holy place, and the Holy of Holies, which housed the famous Ark of the Covenant.

God kept His word with Solomon and we find, *"King Solomon was greater in riches and wisdom than all the other kings of the earth. All the kings of the earth sought audience with Solomon to hear the wisdom that God had put in his heart."* 2 Chronicles 9:22-23

One of those who came to visit King Solomon was the Queen of Sheba, which we now know as Ethiopia. After being given the grand tour of Jerusalem and asking Solomon quite a few very hard questions, she said, *"The report that I heard in my own country about your achievements and your wisdom is true. But I did not believe these things until I came and saw them with my own eyes. Indeed, not even half was told me; in wisdom and wealth you have far exceeded the report I heard. How happy your men must be! How happy your officials, who continually stand before you and hear your wisdom! Praise be to the Lord your God, who has delighted in you and placed you on the throne of Israel. Because of the Lord's eternal love for Israel, He has made you king, to maintain justice and righteousness.*

And she gave the king 120 talents of gold." 1 Kings 10:6-10

We need to stop right here. Did you catch the number 120? The Holy Spirit must be involved in here somehow in an important way. And He certainly is. Jesus even mentions this momentous visit in Luke 11:31, *"The Queen of the south will rise at the judgement with the men of this generation and condemn them; for she came from the ends of the earth to listen to Solomon's wisdom, and now One greater than Solomon is here."*

We need to digress for a moment, for obviously every important historic event is not chronicled in the Bible, at least not in the surface text. It could be that, underlying the surface Biblical text, that may very well be the case, and although a fairly solid set of hidden coding is currently being frantically researched by numerous reputable scholarly groups with the use of high speed computers, the debate is still ongoing, so we will not address it in these pages. Having seen just a few examples, though, of the intricate interweaving of such things as the meanings of names, numbers, and types and shadows throughout the 66 books of the Bible by the true Author, further hidden coding should not be all that surprising. Again though, although intriguing, such is not in the scope of this book.

I do think it important, though, and extremely fascinating, for us to go for a moment to another historical source. In "searching out a matter" we must dig into many reputable sources to uncover actual events not discussed in the Bible. Obviously we need to consult other reference materials in order to study such things, for example, as what resulted in history after Daniel eleven was written. And now we will look at a fascinating reference called the Kebra Nagast.

To quote from the introduction of the first English translation made in 1922 of this reference, also known as the Ethiopian Royal Chronicles, "The Kebra Nagast, or The Book of Glory of the Kings, has been held in the highest esteem and honor throughout the length and breadth of Abyssinia for a thousand years at least, and even today it is believed by every educated man in that country to contain the true history of the Solomonic line of kings in Ethiopia, and is regarded as the final authority on the history of the conversion of the Ethiopians from the worship of the sun, moon, and stars to that of the Lord God of Israel."

The Kebra Nagast relates many of the events found in the Word of God; from of the creation story and the Garden of Eden, through Noah and Abraham; all the way up to Jesus and beyond, to the evangelistic work of Mark. It is a remarkable work in that it gives a look at events from a different perspective than what is normally found in the Bible. One of the pivotal parts of the Kebra Nagast relates to The Queen of Sheba's visit with Solomon and what happened later that we don't read about in Kings or Chronicles in our Bible.

According to that text, Solomon and the Queen of Sheba were married and had a son, Menyelek. This may be alluded to in 2 Chronicles 9:12 with the statement, *"King Solomon gave the Queen of Sheba all she desired and asked for."* We learn in the Kebra Nagast that when the Queen left to go back to Ethiopia she left Menyelek behind to grow up in Solomon's palace and be schooled by the priests in the things of the God of Israel. By the time the boy was nineteen and his mother died, he was very much a young man of God, in the order of the young Daniel at the same age. Before he left to take the twenty five hundred mile trip back to Ethiopia to assume the throne, his father, Solomon, had an exact replica of the Ark of the Covenant made to take with him.

Menyelek and some of the more devout priests were so distraught over the idolatry taking place in Israel at that time, which we will discuss later, that they secretly swapped the replica for the true Ark of the Covenant and took it with them to Ethiopia. Interestingly, the Bible in a way confirms that this quite possibly could have indeed happened, because the last time the true Ark is mentioned is in 2 Chronicles 8:11, when referring to his first wife, who was Egyptian, Solomon said,

"My wife must not live in the palace of King David of Israel, because the places the Ark of the Lord has entered are holy."

Up until then, if anyone other than a priest from the tribe of Levi tried to touch the Ark he would die, such as Uzzah. After Solomon died, though, an enemy king supposedly stole it. Later, in 2 Chronicles 35:3, King Josiah has the stolen ark returned. In all previous scriptures the Ark is always referred to in its formal name, the Ark of the Covenant. That is not so in the King Josiah story, and after that the Ark is mysteriously missing from biblical accounts.

Did Menyelek really take the true Ark of the Covenant back to Ethiopia with him? Very reliable sources have surfaced in the last twenty five years that not only concur that the Ethiopian Royal Chronicles are correct, but that until very recently the Ark remained in Ethiopia. Robert Thompson, a member of the Canadian Parliament and Canada's ambassador to NATO confirmed that the story about the Ark of the Covenant having been constantly guarded in underground chambers for three thousand years was fact. Incidently, in the closing days of the brutal Ethiopian civil war, Mr Thompson flew to Ethiopia and rescued the last princes and princesses of the Ethiopian royal family. That family, the descendants of Menyelek, is the longest lived monarchy in history, although the current Emperor is currently living in exile in England.

As an aside, the most famous Emperor from the Solomonic dynasty in modern times was Haile Selassie, who reigned from 1930 to 1974. His baptismal name means "Power of the Holy Trinity," and Selassie called himself "The Lion of the Tribe of Judah." Sound familiar? Time Magazine made him their Man of the Year in 1936 and later in life, as the longest serving head of state in the world, Selassie was given precedence at world functions such as the state funerals for John F. Kennedy and Charles de Gaulle.

In 1988 the great grandson of Emperor Selassie, Prince Stephen Mengesha, who now is in exile in Canada, appeared in a televised interview and confirmed that the Ark of the Covenant was still being secretly guarded in Aksum, Ethiopia. In the interview Mengesha even showed official government photographs of Queen Elizabeth II and Prince Phillip of England being escorted by Emperor Selassie to the secretly guarded resting place of the ancient Ark.

Three years later, during that hectic time of the civil war, the Israelis flew tens of thousands of Ethiopian Jews out of battle scarred Ethiopia to their new homeland in Israel. These Jews were the descendants of the priests who accompanied Menyelek on his trek from Jerusalem, with the Ark of the Covenant, to take over the throne at the age of 19. As we saw in Part One, this return of those Jews fulfilled God's prophecy concerning that event.

Several extremely credible sources have now told us that at the same time as these flights were occurring, the Israelis sent a plane into Ethiopia with soldiers who were all from the priestly tribe of Levi. These uniformed priests carried the Ark in the prescribed manner onto the plane and back to its home in Jerusalem, where it is now hidden safely away, awaiting the rebuilding of the temple, which God tells us in the minutest of detail in chapters 40 through 44 of Ezekiel will actually occur.

As an aside, those four chapters are preceded by the two chapters, Ezekiel 38 and 39, in which God also tells us about the coming battle He calls the battle of "Gog and Magog." In that prophecy God foretells that Russia and Iran, aided by Syria, Lebanon, Sudan, and Turkey will invade Israel. Incidently, in the 2,500 years since God prophesied about the battle of Gog and Magog, Russia and Iran (Persia) have never been military allies, until today. Now that is something to ponder.

Before we leave Ethiopia and get back to the story of Solomon we should look at a related story in the New Testament that happened with Philip, one of the Apostles, after Jesus had arisen and returned to His Father. In the accounting, Philip was traveling on the road from Jerusalem to Gaza when, *"he met an Ethiopian eunuch, an important official in charge of all the treasury of Candace, queen of the Ethiopians."* Acts 8:27

"This man had gone to Jerusalem to worship, and on his way home was sitting in his chariot reading the book of Isaiah the prophet. The Spirit told Philip, 'Go to that chariot and stay with it.'

Then Philip ran up to the chariot and heard the man reading Isaiah the prophet. 'Do you understand what you are reading?' Philip asked.

'How can I,' he said, 'unless someone explains it to me?'

So he invited Philip to come up and sit with him.

The eunuch was reading this passage of scripture: 'He was led like sheep to the slaughter, and as a lamb before the shearer is silent, so He did not open His mouth. In His humiliation He was deprived of justice. Who can speak of His descendants? For His life was taken from this earth.' (Isaiah 53:7-8)

The eunuch asked Philip, 'Tell me please, who is the prophet talking about, himself or someone else?' Then Philip began with that very passage of Scripture and told him the good news about Jesus.

As they traveled along the road, they came to some water and the eunuch said, 'Look, here is water. Why shouldn't I be baptized?' And he gave orders to stop the chariot. Then both Philip and the eunuch went down in the water and Philip baptized him. When they came up out of the water, the Spirit of the Lord suddenly took Philip away, and the eunuch did not see him again, but went on his way rejoicing." Acts 8:27-39

Can you imagine being baptized by a minister and as soon as you come out of the water the minister literally disappears.

That's what happened to this high ranking official of Ethiopia. He was sitting in his chariot, reading God's Word, but not understanding it. Out of the blue this fellow runs up and offers to help him. The guy then goes through some of the three hundred prophecies in the Old Testament (Greek Septuagint), probably explaining some of the types and shadows that we looked at, and then explains to him that the Messiah has just recently come in the flesh and has been crucified and arose from the dead. The eunuch is convinced and gets baptized. Then this mysterious scripture teacher vanishes into thin air right before his eyes. If that eunuch had any smattering of doubts before God beamed Philip out of there, those doubts obviously vanished when Philip vanished.

That is what we know of the event from the Bible. We now can put more pieces together. The Ethiopian Christian Church was started immediately after that supernatural happening, and every Gospel and letter written by an Apostle went to Ethiopia and was painstakingly translated from the Koine Greek into the extremely complex Ethiopic language. The Greek language is one of the most precise languages ever invented, but the Ethiopic, with its 210 characters, is even more highly regarded for capturing the minutest detail an author wants to include. Compare it to the 26 letters in the English language or the 24 letters in the

Greek language and you can imagine how precise Ethiopic really is. The reason I mention this is that the very oldest complete manuscripts we have today of the New Testament are the Ethiopic manuscripts. Do you suppose the needed complexity of Ethiopic is coincidence? Not for a minute.

We took that lengthy detour from Solomon to the Ethiopian connection for a reason. When we debarked we had seen that the Queen of Sheba had brought Solomon 120 talents of gold, and the number 120 gave us a clue that the Holy Spirit was about to do something major. We certainly can use the word major in describing the creation of a continual God fearing lineage from the union of Solomon and the Queen that would most probably safeguard until the appointed time the Ark of the Covenant, the true representation of Jesus (as we will see later), as well as the preservation in the most detailed form possible of the New Testament, the good news of the worldly appearance and redeeming work of the Anointed One, Jesus the Messiah.

The Queen of Sheba did not travel 2,500 miles to Jerusalem with 120 talents of gold for King Solomon by accident. Yes, God gave mankind free will to chose eternal destruction, but when it comes to history (His Story) things are not left to random chance. God sees to it that His story moves along toward the final result He desired when He first spoke, *"Let there be light,"* with the light that Albert Einstein learned was the first light; the primal light, the Shekinah glory of God.

But now, let's return to our story of Solomon. In the very next verse after the Queen of Sheba leaves to return to Ethiopia, we learn, *"The weight of the gold that Solomon received yearly was 666 talents."* 1 Kings 10:14.

Oh boy! Did you catch that? The number 666 just broadsided us before we got past the first sentence. What a gigantic clue. Satan, evil, has made its appearance big time.

And he certainly did. We know that he came on the scene to tempt God's first children in the garden of Eden. The one and only commandment God had given to them is found in Genesis 2:16, *"And the Lord God commanded the man, 'You are free to eat from any tree in the garden; but you must not eat from the tree of the knowl-*

edge of good and evil, for when you eat of it you will surely die." Only one thing forbidden, and mankind can't stand to feel like he is not in charge of every single thing in his life, so he eats it. Can anything be more stupid than that?

So the number 666 shows up in the story of Solomon. To this point we know from what we already read that *"King Solomon was greater in riches and wisdom than all the other kings of the earth."* 2 Chronicles 9:22. He had it made. His father, David, had been the only man ever recorded to have been a man after God's own heart. Solomon had intelligence and wealth beyond compare, plus the complete respect and honor of everyone on the world. What could 666 possibly foretell?

There was one thing that God had commanded. Just like in the garden, God gave Solomon everything he could possibly have desired, with the exception of one forbidden fruit. That fruit and the eating of it is written about in 1 Kings 11:1-6,

"King Solomon, however, loved many foreign women besides Pharaoh's daughter - Moabites, Ammonites, Edomites, Sidonians and Hittites. They were from nations about which the Lord had told the Israelites, 'You must not intermarry with them, because they will surely turn your hearts after their gods.'

Nevertheless, Solomon held fast to them in love. He had seven hundred wives of royal birth and three hundred concubines, and his wives led him astray. As Solomon grew old, his wives turned his heart after other gods, and his heart was not fully devoted to the Lord his God, as the heart of David his father had been. He followed Ashtoreth the goddess of the Sidonians, and Molech the detestable god of the Ammonites. So Solomon did evil in the eyes of the Lord; he did not follow the Lord completely, as David his father had done."

The result, of course, was that the entire Hebrew nation turned from the true God of creation and started worshiping idols made of wood and stone, gods that could neither hear, speak, or act. And the result of the foolishness of Solomon was the destruction of Israel and bondage in Babylon, and the scattering to the winds that lasted until May 15, 1948, the exact date foretold by God that He would rebirth their nation and give them one more chance.

We started this chapter with the first phrase of Hosea 4:6, let's now look at the King James Version of that phrase, as well as what God tells us in the next one, *"My people are destroyed for lack of knowledge: because thou hast rejected knowledge, I will also reject thee."*

So where do we begin to get that knowledge that obviously is the most crucial to have. The answer is stated plainly in Proverbs 1:7, *"The fear of the Lord is the beginning of knowledge."*

Dumitru Duduman said it better than I could ever say it,

"On judgement day, neither you nor I will be asked what we read or how many degrees we hold. All that we will be asked is whether or not we lived the will of God. If we did not, there will be no explanation and no excuse. The only thing that will help us then is to live our lives for God now."

There will be no debate that day.

CHAPTER FIFTEEN

There is a misconception that we need to quickly clear up which has to do with the word "fear." When we read in Proverbs that *"The fear of the Lord is the beginning of knowledge"*, we are not to think that we are to be "afraid" of God. Jesus told us in Matthew 22:37 that the greatest commandment is to, *"Love the Lord your God with all your heart and with all your soul and with all your mind."* Obviously we don't really love people we are afraid of. The Biblical word fear is translated in The New Collegiate Edition of The American Heritage Dictionary as "Extreme reverence or awe."

With what we have seen so far in these pages, it is not difficult at all to have extreme reverence and awe for God. His knowledge and intellect are so far superior to ours that our brain is like an ant's brain compared to His. He knows absolutely everything. If that isn't awesome, nothing is.

Once we can resolve in our minds not only that God exists, which was obviously done in this book through His fulfilled prophecies, but that He did indeed communicate to us through His Bible, we do for a fact have a starting point for gaining knowledge. The verse in proverbs could actually be read as,

"Extreme reverence and awe of God is the beginning of knowledge."

God has told mankind so much in His Word that was totally overlooked. Man has a history of not wanting to take God's word in a matter. Consequently, mankind has lived under false beliefs about very important things until he finally stumbles along and finds out that God had plainly stated the truth all along. One example that probably caused God to shake His head in disbelief for centuries was man's notion that the world was flat.

In Isaiah 40:22 of God's Word it is stated very simply,

"He sits enthroned above the circle of the earth." How much more plainly could God have said it? The earth is round, not flat.

"He sits enthroned above the circle of the earth." is as easy to understand and straightforward a statement as ever was made,

kind of like, *"In the beginning God created the heavens and the earth."* Genesis 1:1

On March 15,1493, however, when Christopher Columbus returned to Spain after his heralded voyage of "discovery", something never before seen occurred. As Columbus approached the throne of King Ferdinand and Queen Isabella, they rose to meet him. When he knelt to kiss their hands, they raised him up and ordered a chair brought for him to sit in as he told them his unbelievable story. Neither one of those two actions by the royal couple had ever been witnessed. Columbus was a true visionary, a man in Europe without peer. From that day forward, whenever the King went out in his carriage, Columbus sat beside him, an unknown privilege to anyone not of royal blood. But why not? Columbus had discovered a brand new truth beyond compare; the earth was a circle. Had people only taken a clue from the meaning of his name, Christopher, which means Christ bearer, they might have paid more attention to what was right under their collective noses all along, *"He sits enthroned above the circle of the earth."*

It isn't exactly like God had hidden the fact of the earth being round in some obscure place like a genealogy or a listing of tribes of Israelites. In fact, let's see what God says about Himself in the full context of that statement in Isaiah:

"Do you not know? Have you not heard? Has it not been told to you from the beginning? Have you not understood since the earth was founded?

He sits enthroned above the circle of the earth, and its people are like grasshoppers. He stretches out the heavens like a canopy, and spreads them out like a tent to live in.

He brings princes to naught and reduces the rulers of this world to nothing. No sooner are they planted, no sooner are they sown, no sooner do they take root in the ground, then He blows on them and they wither, and a whirlwind sweeps them away like chaff.

'To whom will you compare me? Or who is my equal?' says the Holy One. Lift your eyes and look to the heavens. Who created all these? He who brings out the starry host one by one, and calls them each by name. Because of his great power and mighty strength, not one of them is missing."

Why do you say, O Jacob, and complain, O Israel, 'My way is hidden from the Lord; my cause is disregarded by my God'?

Do you not know? Have you not heard? The Lord is the everlasting God, the creator of the ends of the earth. He will not grow tired or weary, and his understanding no one can fathom." Isaiah 40: 21-28

It also was not hidden in those statements by God, that He told us for the umpteenth time in His Bible, that He created everything. Yet the debaters of our day are now theorizing that it all happened by random chance. Random chance, now there is a notion for us to swallow. Of course, with a straight face they matter of factly drag out that proof of all proofs, that if you give a monkey a typewriter, and assume that the monkey lives forever and the typewriter never wears out, the cute little ape will eventually type the complete works of Shakespeare. That little ace in the hole of theirs is suppose to end all argument. Who in the world could challenge such logic as that?

In 2002, C.N. Miller, did the unthinkable. He actually put his unique mathematical mind to the task of delving into the "undebatable" monkey story. I had the privilege of interviewing Mr. Miller in 2007 for this book and found that he is still in awe of the absurdity that his findings proved.

Without going through all of the lengthy mathematical procedures Mr. Miller used, allow me to briefly summarize his results. We can say that he bent over backwards in trying to be lenient on the side of the debaters. Most striking is the fact that instead of making the monkey type everything Shakespear ever wrote, he only had the primate type the actual words, "The Complete Works of Shakespeare." In Miller's calculations he didn't even make the monkey use spaces or capitalize the letters. He only asked that the little ape type the 29 characters in sequence. Obviously that seems reasonable. He even went further and removed every key from the typewriter except the 26 actual letters in the English language.

His first findings came out so outlandish that he gave the poor single monkey another big break by giving him some companions to help in the project. He first enlisted 999 others for the task, but then got really generous and brought in another 999,900 of the typing wizards. His next assumption was that these hairy typists could each type a hundred words, or five hundred characters per minute, non stop forever.

Wanting to give the apes and their kin folk debaters an even bigger chance to type that one little 29 character phrase in a reasonable amount of time, Miller thought up the incredible; he pretended that each of those little guys were as lucky as lottery winners who win lotteries with the odds of one in twelve million.

So these were Miller's overly generous assumptions; a million monkeys, typing five hundred letters per minute non stop, each with the luck of a twelve million to one lottery winner, having to type only 29 letters in a row, with typewriters that had only 26 keys. Imagine if these poor little animals had to type the phrase in Ethiopic with its 210 characters.

The results of all of the mathematical calculations was that the year the first monkey would type the phrase correctly and win the gold ribbon would be in year: 99,430,800,000,000,000,000,000,000

If we assume the earth to have been around ten billion years for these million weary monkeys to type, the number of years before the first one reaches the 29th letter will be another 994.3 trillion years. This random chance thing is a tough row to hoe.

As an aside, C.N. Miller's name is Christopher, like Columbus's, meaning Christ bearer. The world should not have needed Christopher Columbus to prove that the world was not flat. God had already stated that fact. And you and I should not need Christopher N. Miller to point out to us the absurdity of random chance playing any roll in God's story. God does not leave anything to chance. Through His infinite wisdom and knowledge, He not only knows, *"the end from the beginning, from ancient times, what is still to come"*, His guiding hand has been involved in every aspect.

The sad truth is that almost every one of us has nodded our head in agreement with the logic of this little innocent sounding, logical monkey story. Why? Because almost every one of us today was indoctrinated at a very early age by the educational system to believe that evolution is not a theory but a fact. The smartest person in the last 150 years was probably Charles Darwin because he knew from the outset that his theory was full of holes.

At the beginning of his book, <u>The Origin of the Species,</u> that changed the course of human thinking, Darwin wrote a sentence that most people paid no attention to. Darwin himself wrote, "To suppose that the eye with all its inimitable contrivances for adjusting the focus to different distances, for admitting different amounts of light, and for the correction of spherical and chromatic aberrations, could have been formed by natural selection, seems, I freely confess, absurd in the highest degree."

"Absurd in the highest degree", yet mankind, not inherently wanting to be accountable to anyone, not even a truly just and perfect God, jumped at this "absurdity to the highest degree", and a new science that would eventually evolve into its own religion was born. This pseudo science was to have such impact on modern mankind's thinking that we need to at least take a cursory examination of it here; because although it is rapidly fading from the scientific community, as we shall see, it still lingers on in the educational system, as outmoded "science" always does, and its profound effect of leading the masses away from an eternal life with God is unfortunately becoming a sad reality, as we will also discover.

Even though Solomon let his lust for foreign women cloud his thinking, God told him, and us, in 1 Kings 3:12 that he would be the wisest man ever, *"I will give you a wise and discerning heart, so that there will never have been anyone like you, nor will there ever be."* With this in mind, we should ponder what God directed Solomon to write in Ecclesiastes 7:9, *"This only have I found: God made man upright, but men have gone in search of many schemes."* The theory of evolution is one of the most insane, and dangerous, *"schemes"* man has ever uncovered.

We saw that mathematically it would take a million extremely lucky monkeys almost a zillion years before one would actually type a 29 letter sequence without mistake. One can not even remotely fathom the zillion times zillions of years it would take for random chance to stumble upon the correct manufacture of a living cell with its phenomenal complexity.

Scientists think that they know what comprises a one cell organism, but even with their brainpower and high speed computers they can't come close to creating life. How could man have been so gullible as to fall for such a notion? And the even greater insanity is that we are still allowing it to be taught to our children.

A cute but profound little story goes like this. In the year 9436 scientists proudly tell God they finally know how to create life just like He did. God says, "That's great, show me." So the scientists pick up some mud to start, whereby God stops them and says, "Oh, I thought you meant from scratch."

I feel silly to even waste our time looking into this, but since the young minds of our world are being fed this absurdity, let's at least see why Darwin knew his theory was faulty from the beginning. Actually he didn't even know just how faulty it was because in the mid 1800's when he was speculating about these matters mankind did not have a fraction of the knowledge it now has about such things as the complexity of an eye.

Forgetting about the completely insane notion that life could start on its own by random chance, in its simplest form the theory of evolution rests on the notion that once life has been established, mutations occur that are beneficial to the organism. These good mutations are kept and any useless mutations that might occur are done away with. These good mutations keep improving the organism until eventually you have a complete animal that can see and hear and touch and think. That is about it in a nutshell. Pretty simple, and it may even sound logical.

Now, let's be overly generous to the evolutionists and pretend that through billions of years of good mutations being kept we have a creature that has developed a body and a brain. We'll even simplify things outlandishly by supposing that an eye would function somewhat with only one optic nerve. To even be more extremely naive let's say that somehow a useless eyeball formed on the outside of the creature's body through a series of useless mutations that the body did not reject, as the theory states that it would.

OK, so now we have a brain inside a body and an eyeball somehow attached to the outside. We know that the way eyesight is developed an optic nerve starts growing outward from the optic center of the brain. We won't even discuss how this optic center formed when sight had thus far never been accomplished. At the same time the optic nerve is growing outward from the optic center of the brain, another optic nerve must be growing from the eyeball and moving toward the brain so that the two can connect.

Imagine now if you will that first optic nerve dangling out of the brain with nothing to connect to. According to the theory that first little mutant nerve would be completely useless, and thus would not be kept in succeeding generations. The same would be true of the mutant optic nerve growing out of the eyeball. Any thinking person will obviously see the complete fallacy of the entire theory at this simplest level. In reality, there are over a million such nerves growing towards each other with the innate ability to each match up exactly to its counterpart.

None of this makes one iota of sense, and Darwin himself knew it. The above little ridiculous example doesn't begin to describe what would have to occur for the complexity of sight to be achieved, and all of this in an organism that wouldn't have a clue what sight was or that it could be useful. Each of the needed millions and millions of mutations that would be necessary to create sight would have been discarded as useless mutations long before the end result would have been realized. And we haven't even begun to look at hearing, touch, taste, smell, etc.

But you and I went to school and saw drawings in a book that showed evolutionary changes that brought a single cell from primal soup all the way up to man. And we believed it. Of course we not only had those drawings in our text books, but we also had paragraphs in there describing the findings of the links from one step to the next. These were even named for us. Unfortunately, the Nebraska Man, which was so all important to the outcome of the ground breaking Scopes monkey trial in 1925 turned out to be nothing but the tooth of an extinct pig. Of course, what you and I saw was a drawing of a somewhat slouched over, hairy man. Talk about literary license. From an old pig's tooth an artist drew a cave man and we were fed it as gospel.

The hoax continued. The Southwest Colorado Man found his way into our text books, too, and it turned out to have been based solely on a dug up tooth as well. This time, though, the tooth was finally admitted to have been one from a horse.

The big name draws, however, were Cro-Magnon Man, Neanderthal Man, and Peking Man. Do you remember having to study the differences of those for our school tests. In the end they all turned out to be modern humans. Then there is Lucy.

Lucy is my all time favorite. In 1974, paleontologist Dr. Donald Johanson found a partial fossil skeleton in Hadar, Ethiopia. It is about the size of a chimpanzee and appears to be female. The find included a jaw, a part of a hip, and some other bones. The age was estimated to be 3.2 million years. This latest find has been unanimously heralded by evolutionists as the true transitional form, the sought after missing link. Scientists lovingly named her Lucy, and she became the toast of the town.

Lucy's jaw was obviously an ape jaw, but because the femur and pelvis were more robust than most chimps, and the knee seemed at a little different angle than most chimps, it was felt that she could have walked upright. But then a wee little problem arose. Unfortunately, and very reluctantly, it was learned that the knee bones had been found a year earlier than the "rest" of Lucy, and they were actually two hundred feet deeper in the earth, and at an entirely different location of only slightly more than a mile and a half away. Talk about a stretch, but look at your child's school book and you will still find Lucy as the top proof for evolution. Totally amazing. Lucy is the latest in the list of complete and dramatic disappointments, however, the theory lives on, seemingly healthy as ever, in the educational system that just won't let go. In fact, Lucy came to the United States for viewing in August, 2007, but no signs were posted showing that the bones were found in different years, miles apart, and at different depths. This wild hoax lives on.

Dr. G. Jeffrey wrote, "There never has been one scientific discovery that supported the theory of evolution, not one, despite a constant search during the last 150 years. The museums and universities have more than 100 million fossils collected from every area of the earth, and the truth is this: there is no fossil evidence that supports the evolutionary theory of the gradual development of life from simple to complex."

Science Digest Special reported that, "Scientists who utterly reject evolution may be one of our fastest growing minorities....

Many of the scientists supporting this position hold impressive credentials." The truth is that since that report they may actually have become the majority.

Professor Soren Lovtrup, an embryologist, wrote in his book, Darwinism: The Refutation of a Myth, "I believe that one day the Darwinism myth will be ranked the greatest deceit in the history of science."

British knighted astronomer, Dr. Fred Hoyle, wrote,

"The common sense interpretation of the facts suggest that a superintellect has monkeyed with physics, as well as with chemistry and biology, and that there are no blind forces worth speaking about in nature. The numbers one calculates from the facts seem to me so overwhelming as to put this conclusion almost beyond reasonable question."

A fellow astronomer George Greenstein added, "As we survey all the evidence, the thought insistently arises that some supernatural agency must be involved. Is it possible that suddenly, without intending to, we have stumbled upon scientific proof of the existence of a Supreme Being?"

MIT physicist, Dr. Vera Kistiakowsky has recorded her conclusion by saying, "The exquisite order displayed by our scientific understanding of the physical world calls for the divine."

A formerly outspoken evolutionist who has made a total about face is Dr. Henry Morris. He asserts, "Many believe in evolution for the simple reason that they think science has proven it to be a "fact" and, therefore, it must be accepted...In recent years a great many people... having finally been persuaded to make a real examination of the problem of evolution, have become convinced of its fallacy and are now convinced anti-evolutionists."

We could fill the rest of the book with quotes from scientists who have totally deserted evolution, but I think it is even more fascinating and eye opening to read what those who are still somehow professing to be evolutionists are actually saying. For example, evolutionary scientist, Arthur Keith, interestingly stated, "Evolution is unproved and unprovable. We believe it only because the only alternative is unthinkable."

Professor G.A. Kerkut said it quite plainly, "It is therefore a matter of faith on the part of the biologist that biogenesis (evolution) did occur and he can choose whatever method of biogenesis happens to suit him personally; the evidence for what did happen is not available."

Evolutionist Solly Zuckerman admitted, "The record of reckless speculation of human origins is so astonishing that it is legitimate to ask whether much science is yet to be found in this field at all."

A die hard supporter of evolution, T.L. Moor, actually wrote, "The more one studies paleontology, the more certain one becomes that evolution is based on faith alone." It sounds like his science has totally flown out the window. And Moor's fellow paleontologist, Dr. Niles Eldridge went even further by writing, "We paleontologists have said that history of life supports the story of gradual adaptive change, all the while really knowing that it does not." Even a politician could be thrown in jail for admitting such as that.

Let's end with the look at those who are unimaginably still backing the theory of evolution by citing a Nobel prize winner in chemistry, Dr. Harold Urey, who wrote, "All of us who study the origin of life find that the more we look into it, the more we feel it is too complex to have evolved anywhere."

He even astoundingly added, "We believe as an article of faith that life evolved from dead matter on this planet."

But let's leave these totally confused souls who know, and often admit, that evolution is a hoax, and end these quotes with a very distinguished 1981 Nobel winner of physics who brings up a good point that we will endeavor to clarify a little later. Stanford University Professor, Dr. Arthur L. Schawlow, another of the long list of very credible scientists who have recently completely abandoned any belief at all in evolution, wrote,

"It seems to me that when confronted with the marvels of life and the universe, one must ask why and not just how. The only possible answers are religious...I find a need for God in the universe and in my own life."

The Theory of Evolution and the notion that the world and everything in it somehow created itself was preposterous from the beginning, and the author of the idea, Charles Darwin, knew that it had as many holes as a spaghetti strainer, and even admitted it. However, as insane as it was, it had one big thing going for it. For the first time in the history of mankind there was now a kind of plausible possibility that mankind might not have to be accountable to a higher power than himself. This had always been a dream of man since creation.

Until Darwin's ideas came along, man *knew* that God existed. He may not have chosen to obey Him or worship Him, but he *knew* without doubt that He was there. When we study history we find people running from God, or ignoring Him altogether, but they never had the desirable option of thinking that God did not exist. That option never crossed their minds.

Psalm 19:1-4 said it plainly, *"The heavens declare the glory of God; the skies proclaim the work of His hands. Day after day they pour forth speech; night after night they display knowledge. There is no speech or language where their voice is not heard. Their voice goes into all the earth, their words to the end of the world."*

After Darwin came up with his ideas, that statement in Psalm 19 was just as true, but for the first time man could ignore it and feel relief from the pressure of accountability. Now man could be the creator of his own destiny. What an intoxicating thought that was. And now that the truth of evolution as a bogus theory is really coming to light, people the world over are very reluctant to give up that alluring thought. They don't want God.

We have seen that the scientific community that is still attempting to hold on to such an unprovable theory has admitted that at this point they are doing it as a "matter of faith." They would rather toss out all that science has previously been grounded in, such as provability, and hang their hat on the nail of faith, than give up their accountability to no one but self and turn to faith in God. Unfortunately, these men and women do not know what you and I have already learned in these pages, that God's existence is not a matter of faith. God proved his existence by fulfilled prophecy, exactly as he said he would.

" I am God, and there is none like me. I make known the end from the beginning, from ancient times, what is still to come." Isaiah 46:10

We might surmise that one of the big reasons God set up fulfilled prophecies as proof of his existence was for our generations. Until evolution, mankind did not need such proof. Unfortunately, modern man does. Isn't it phenomenal that He cared enough for us to put this failsafe plan in motion? But once again, God does not leave things to chance. God is in control.

We will examine more prophecies, types and shadows, names, and numbers. We will even look at one of the most startling fulfillments you could ever imagine, one that took an extremely dramatic turn within the past few years. It is an Indiana Jones type adventure that you will never forget. Additionally, we will examine my very favorite prophecy of all time. But evolution needed to be addressed before we could continue, and you will understand why more completely in the next chapter.

CHAPTER SIXTEEN

Since we can know for a certainty, by the thousands of fulfilled prophetic scriptures, not only that God exists, and that He communicates to us through His Word, we can also be sure that Satan and his evil forces also exist. The name Satan is used 59 times in the Bible, devil is talked about 38 times, and the word demon is used 66 times. On top of that Satan is referred to many other times in such ways as the dragon, or a snake.

God tells us quite a lot about him, even going back to when he was named Lucifer and was one of the three top archangels. God actually talks to him in Ezekiel, *"This is what the Sovereign Lord says: 'You were the model of perfection, full of wisdom and perfect in beauty. You were in Eden, the garden of God, every precious stone adorned you: ruby, topaz, and emerald, chrysolite, onyx, and jasper, sapphire, turquoise and beryl. Your settings and mountings were made of gold; on the day you were created they were prepared .*

You were anointed as a guardian cherub, for so I ordained you. You were on the holy mount of God; you walked among the fiery stones. You were blameless in your ways from the day you were created till wickedness was found in you.

Through your widespread trade you were filled with violence, and you sinned. So I drove you in disgrace from the mount of God, and I expelled you, O guardian cherub, from among the fiery stones.

Your heart became proud on account of your beauty, and you corrupted your wisdom because of your splendor. So I threw you to the earth. I made a spectacle of you before kings.   By your many sins and dishonest trade you have desecrated your sanctuaries. So I made fire come out from you, and it consumed you, and I reduced you to ashes on the ground in the sight of all who were watching. All the nations who knew you are appalled at you; you have come to a horrible end and will be no more." Ezekiel 28:12-19

These are obviously not just brief mentionings of Satan. He obviously exists, and God tells us all about him, in quite a lot of detail. In Isaiah God tells a similar story, including, *"How you have fallen from heaven, O morning star, son of the dawn! You have been cast down to earth, you who once laid low the nations!*

You said in your heart, 'I will ascend to heaven; I will raise my throne above the stars of God; I will sit enthroned on the mount of assembly, on the utmost heights of the sacred mountain.

I will ascend above the tops of the clouds; I will make myself like the Most High.'But you are brought down to the grave, in the depths of the pit." Isaiah 14:12-15

Obviously this marvelous archangel, on the order of Michael and Gabriel, was not satisfied with his position. Although he was only a created being, as we are, Satan wanted more. He wanted to be God. Does that sound vaguely familiar? But we learn in Revelation that God sent Michael to put Satan in his place and end this heavenly revolt.

"And there was war in heaven. Michael and his angels fought against the dragon, and the dragon and his angels fought back. But he was not strong enough, and they lost their place in heaven. The great dragon was hurled down - that ancient serpent called the devil, or Satan, who leads the whole world astray. He was hurled to the earth, and his angels with him." Revelation 12:7-9

We know also that there were a third of the total angel population involved in the revolt because God's Word sometimes refers to angels as stars, such as in Revelation 12:4 where we read that, *"His tail swept a third of the stars out of the sky and flung them to earth."*

Additionally we know what happened to them by reading Jude, one of the half brothers of Jesus, *"And the angels who did not keep their positions of authority but abandoned their own home - these he (God) has kept in darkness, bound with everlasting chains for judgement on that great Day,"* Jude 6

Did this actually take place or was it somehow symbolic? Jesus Himself mentions that He saw Satan cast out. In Luke 10:18 Jesus says, *"I saw Satan fall like lightning from heaven."*

Think of all of the fulfilled prophecies we have looked at. The fulfillment has never been symbolic. The fulfillment is always literal. Always. Satan is on our earth. He exists.

There is an interesting encounter in Daniel. If you recall, Gabriel was the angel who gave Daniel the amazing prophecies we read about earlier; all about the future life of Alexander the Great, and the very detailed foretellings of the heirs to his kingdom, phenomenal details that read like a newspaper report.

Daniel had prayed for understanding of dreams that he knew were from God. In response to that prayer, God sent Gabriel, and this is how Daniel reported the first words Gabriel spoke, *"He said, 'Daniel, you who are highly esteemed, consider carefully the words I am about to speak to you, and stand up, for I have now been sent to you.' And when he said this to me I stood up trembling.*

Then he continued, 'Do not be afraid, Daniel. Since the first day you set your mind to gain understanding and to humble yourself before your God, your words were heard, and I have come in response to them. But the prince of the Persian kingdom resisted me twenty - one days. Then Michael, one of the chief princes, came to help me, because I was detained there with the king of Persia. Now I have come to explain to you what will happen to your people in the future, for the vision concerns a time yet to come." Daniel 10:11-14

There obviously are things going on in the unseen world that we know nothing about. Mankind is often so smug in its assumed knowledge of how the world around us works, and we can't even see the most important part, the other dimension.

In the above accounting, Daniel had prayed, Gabriel had been sent immediately, but Satan and his forces delayed him twenty one days (notice 7 X 3) until the angel with the real might, Michael, showed up. Michael is someone we definitely want on our side in a pinch.

The main thing I wanted to point out here, though, is that Satan was on the earth then, trying to thwart God's plans.

Does that mean that Satan is actually a threat to God? Not in the least. Remember, Satan is just a created being. He is not all knowing, or all seeing, or all powerful. God created him. And God is God. He is in total control. It is all His Story. In fact, as we will see, Satan was created for the purpose of doing exactly what he has done so far and will continue to do. And his antics are all for our eventual good. God is the Most High. He alone is sovereign. All history is His Story.

That being said, Satan is not dumb. He can read God's Word. In fact, immediately after Jesus was baptized by John the Baptist, He went into the wilderness and was tempted by Satan.

In the process, Satan quoted scripture, for we read in Matthew 4:5-6, *"The devil took Him to the holy city and had Him stand on the highest point of the temple. 'If you are the Son of God,' he said, throw yourself down. For it is written: "'He will command his angels concerning you, and they will lift you up in their hands, so that you will not strike your foot against a stone.'"* Notice that Satan quoted Psalm 91:11-12

Satan therefore knew what some people refer to as the first prophecy in Scripture, the verses in Genesis 3:14-15 in which God says to Satan after the temptation of Eve, *"I will put enmity between you and the woman, and between your offspring and hers, He will crush your head, and you will strike His heel."*

As an aside, we will show that there actually is another prophecy that precedes this one, possibly the most monumental prophecy of all of them. But that is for later.

Notice in that scripture that God made known to us that Satan was going to have his own offspring. That is important.

So Satan knew from the outset that God would send an offspring of Eve to destroy him. Many of the stories of the Old Testament have to do with Satan trying to stop that offspring from arriving. In fact, we read in Revelation 12:4, *"The dragon stood in front of the woman who was about to give birth, so that he might devour her child the moment it was born."* And he stayed in front of that "woman" throughout the Old Testament history of Israel, continually trying to do exactly that.

It wasn't difficult for Satan to surmise that the offspring that was to crush him would be of the lineage of Abram. We saw in Genesis 14:19 that Melchizedek blessed Abram, even before God changed his name to Abraham. In the very next chapter Abram laments to God, *"You have given me no children; so a servant in my household will be my heir."*

Then the word of the Lord came to him: 'This man will not be your heir, but a son coming from your own body will be your heir." Genesis 15:3-4

Then to cap it off as far as Satan was concerned, a few verses later God promises Abram that his descendants would get the promised land, the former Garden of Eden, *"To your descendants I give this land, from the river of Egypt to the great river Euphrates."* Genesis 15:18 (In Genesis 2:11-14 we are told the four rivers that were the boundaries of the Garden of Eden, and the two rivers mentioned above were two of those four rivers. Israel now sits where the Garden of Eden once was.)

From then on Satan tried unsuccessfully to stop the births of the line from Abram, in hopes of killing the one who would later crush him.

In talking about Satan, Jesus Himself said in John 8:44,

"He was a murderer from the beginning, not holding to the truth, for there is no truth in him. When he lies, he speaks his native language, for he is a liar and the father of lies."

So Satan, lying like he did to Eve in the Garden, when we read in Genesis 3:4, *"You will surely not die.' the serpent said to the woman."*, whispered little lies to Sarai telling her to suggest that Abram have their child with Hagar, her Egyptian maidservant. Abram agreed, of course, and Hagar gave birth to a son, the father of the people who today primarily make up the Islamic world. Of him, God said, *"You shall name him Ishmael, for the Lord has heard of your misery. He will be a wild donkey of a man; his hand will be against everyone and everyone's hand against him, and he will live in hostility toward all his brothers."* Genesis 16:11-12 (This sounds very much like another fulfilled prophecy.)

God, though, as always, had everything under control. In Genesis 17:19 God tells the patriarch when he is 99 years old, *"Yes, but your wife Sarah will bear you a son, and you will call him Isaac. I will establish my covenant with him as an everlasting covenant."* Isaac by the way means "he laughs" and I somehow think that God was laughing at Satan's shenanigans. He does have a sense of humor.

Satan wasn't through, though, because when Isaac's wife, Rebekah, gave birth, *"there were twin boys in her womb. The first to come out was red, and his whole body was like a hairy garment, so they named him Esau. After this, his brother came out with his hand grasp-*

ing Esau's heel, So he was named Jacob." Genesis 25:25-26 (Esau was also called Edom, 'red')

The name, Jacob, means "he grasps the heel." Does that evoke a picture that Esau could have been trying to crush the head of Jacob while the twin brothers were still in the womb?

It looks like Satan had tried to go past lying and into murder, as Jesus said he had been doing from the beginning. But again, God was in control. He had talked to Rebekah before the birth, *"The Lord said to her, 'Two nations are in your womb, and two people from within you will be separated; one people will be stronger than the other, and the older will serve the younger."*

Genesis 25:23 (Once again, if we look at the descendants of Esau we can see that we have another fulfilled prophecy.)

Interestingly, a thousand years later God says of these twins, *"Was not Esau Jacob's brother?' the Lord says, 'but Esau I have hated, and I have turned his mountains into a wasteland and left his inheritance to the desert jackals. Edom may say, "Though we have been crushed, we will rebuild the ruins."*

But this is what the Lord almighty says, "They may rebuild, but I will demolish. They will be called the wicked land, a people always under the wrath of the Lord. You will see it with your own eyes and say, 'Great is the Lord - even beyond the borders of Israel." Malachi 1:2-5

Today, the land that the Edomites inhabited is now the Negev Desert in Southern Israel, adjacent to Jordan. More fulfilled prophecy to put on the stack of the thousands of others.

With all of Satan's continual efforts in the Old Testament to kill the lineage of the baby that would one day crush his head, he failed miserably. We read what happened when we read the full account that we started a few pages back, *"The dragon stood in front of the woman who was about to give birth, so that he might devour her child the moment it was born. She gave birth to a male child, who will rule over all the nations with an iron scepter. And her child was snatched up to God and to His throne."* Revelation 12:4-5

We did see when we looked at some of the fulfilled prophecies of Jesus that Satan tried murder again when Christ was born, by whispering to King Herod and talking him into trying to kill all the male children under two who were born in Bethlehem, but obviously God thwarted that plot as well.

Since all of those attempts to get rid of the anointed one failed, Satan has had to change his tactics. Following the completed work of Christ, when He ascended back to the Father, Satan's modus operandi has been to do everything in his power to get mankind to believe his lies that God does not even exist, that the Bible is not his Word, and that Jesus is not divine.

Satan still is delusional in his hopes that he can somehow stop the inevitable and usurp God. He understands the big picture. It is almost comical when someone says, "Satan tried to stop me from getting to the 'women's ministry bake sale' today by giving me a flat tire, but I made it anyway." In the first place, Satan is not at all intimidated by church bake sales. In the second place, she probably drove over a nail. Satan is one being. He is not everywhere at once, and his efforts are larger in scope.

Yes, Satan is still around. In fact, in 1 Peter 5:8 we are told,

"Be self controlled and alert. Your enemy the devil prowls around like a roaring lion looking for someone to devour."

In speaking of Satan, Jesus said In John 10:10, *"The thief comes only to steal and kill and destroy."* And he does have his demons to do the work of trying to keep individuals in the dark.

Modern man thinks that the struggles that he goes through in this life are part of the natural order of things. That really is not the case at all. There truly is an unseen world, and some of it is dark and evil. God tells us through Paul, *"our struggle is not against flesh and blood, but against the rulers, against the authorities, against the powers of this dark world and against the spiritual forces of evil in the heavenly realms."* Eph. 6:12

There is a spiritual realm that modern man has no notion exists. In that other dimension entities are fighting for their very eternal existence. Satan, his princes, and his demons, know that unless they can somehow defeat God's plan, they have no eternal hope at all. And they are doing everything in their limited power to turn mankind away from the only Sovereign God that has ever been, the Creator of everything. Their ways are evil and they hate us, God's love child, more than you could ever imagine.

In the final analysis, of course, Satan is doomed to destruction. Jesus emphatically told us in John 16;11, *"The prince of this world now stands condemned."* And also in John 12:31, Jesus said, *"The prince of this world will be driven out."* The die has been cast.

In the meantime, though, Satan has recently made one of his slickest moves ever. The name of this ploy is the Theory of Evolution. The *"father of lies"* knows enough to include a grain of truth in a lie to make it believable. In the history of the world there is evidence of some gradual changes within a species. Human athletes today are obviously stronger and faster than they were in the past. Roger Bannister's four minute mile, which was once thought to be the unthinkable, is a common occurrence today. Little advances like that led the original observers of the Darwinian idea to take the gigantic leap of faith into thinking that all of evolutional theory must be true. Satan is a cunning liar. Mankind grabbed hold hook, line, and sinker.

And now, after several generations of teaching everyone Satan's most successful lie, even die hard believers think that maybe evolution was the way God created things. To be honest, Darwin's false science theory, invented by Satan, wouldn't normally be a very big thing. Eventually it will fade away like the scientific "fact" that the earth is flat. No real harm done.

In the meantime, though, this lie of all lies has caused the masses of humanity either to outright believe that there is no Creator at all, or to at least doubt little portions of God's true Word. The latter alternative, Satan knew, would be the most devastating. He was probably smart enough to know that eventually man would figure out that the Theory of Evolution was ridiculous, which is beginning to happen right now. But he also knew that if those little doubts took root, apostasy would grow. But, as we will see, God is still smiling on His throne.

CHAPTER SEVENTEEN

"My people are destroyed from lack of knowledge." Hosea 4:5

The little doubts created by the belief in Satan's masterpiece lie, the Theory of Evolution, are causing drastic changes not only among non believers and their every day lives and beliefs, but inside the church as well. The privilege many suffered and died for only five hundred years ago is rapidly being discarded as unnecessary. The consequences are more than tragic.

In the second and third chapters of Revelation, Jesus wrote seven letters to seven churches. These seven churches actually existed in the year Jesus dictated His letters to His beloved disciple, John. However, as is the case with much of God's Word, there also were secondary meanings, as we have seen with such things as the Cross of Christ with His four major defining characteristics on the ends moving across the wilderness toward Jerusalem for forty years. Yes, the banners of the four outside Hebrew tribes actually existed, and were delineated by the ox, the lion, the eagle, and the face of a man.

As we have learned, though, those drawings represented Jesus as a servant, the king of kings, fully God, and yet fully human.

Likewise, not only were those seven letters written to seven real churches, but they were also written to the seven definitively separate church ages, as we shall see.

Church in letter	Church Age	Dates
Ephesus	Apostolic Age	Before 100 AD
Smyrna	Age of Persecution	100 AD to 313 AD
Pergamum	Imperial Church Age	313 AD to 590 AD
Thyatira	Age of Papacy	590 AD to 1517 AD
Sardis	Age of Reformation	1517 AD to 1730 AD
Philadelphia	Age of Missions	1730 AD to 1900 AD
Laodicea	Age of Apostasy	1900 AD to ?

In all seven letters to these church ages Jesus starts out by saying something about himself, which corresponds to that age. He then gives a commendation, a complaint, a correction, and a promise. One exception is that with Smyrna and Philadelphia he has no complaint at all. Obviously, during the Age of Persecution, when His followers were being thrown to the lions and still refused to denounce Him, Jesus was pleased. He refers to Himself in the opening of the letter to Smyrna (The Age of Persecution) by saying, *"These are the words of Him who is the first and the last, who died and came to life again,"* Revelation 2:8

And this is what happened to the martyred souls who stood fast. They also *"came to life"* again. The promise to them was,

"He who overcomes will not be hurt at all by the second death." Revelation 2:11

The other church to receive no complaint at all was the church at Philadelphia, the Age of Missions (1730 to 1900). Jesus begins in Revelation 3:7 with, *"These are the words of Him who is holy and true, who holds the key of David. What He opens no one can shut, and what He shuts no one can open."*

Along with the saints who endured the Age of Persecution, the believers during the Age of Missions were definitely the most holy. And they were the most true to God's Word. They also held the key to His Kingdom and took it to the ends of the world, in all the areas the Holy Spirit opened up for them to go. In the promise section of the letter they were told, *"Him who overcomes I will make a pillar in the temple of my God. Never again will he leave it."* Revelation 3:12

In addition to the two exceptions of the churches that received no complaints, in two of the church letters there were no commendations at all. Those churches that Jesus had nothing at all good to comment about were Sardis and Laodicea, our church age. We will mention later what is said to our age, represented by the church at Laodicea, but first let's look at Pergamum, the Imperial Church Age, that took away the Bible.

The Imperial Church Age began with a good event for believers, the conversion of Constantine which resulted in the end of the age of persecution. Constantine even made Christianity the official religion of the Roman Empire. This eventually, of course, led to the Age of Papacy. In the letter to Pergamum Jesus starts out by saying. *"These are the words of Him who has the sharp, double-edged sword."* Rev. 2:12

From what we saw in the opening description of Jesus to the churches at Smyrna and Philadelphia, His comments about Himself deal with something pertinent to the individual church age. Smyrna was dealing with the death of the Age of Persecution, and the Philadelphia saints of the Age of Missions were holy and true and evangelizing the world.

Now, with Pergamum, the Imperial Church Age of 313 AD to 590 AD, Jesus immediately mentions that He has the *"sharp, double-edged sword."* The double-edged sword in the Bible always refers to God's Word, for instance, we are told to take up the full armor of God, including, *"the sword of the Spirit, which is the Word of God,"* Ephesians 6:17

A problem which endured for over a thousand years was that the Word of God was completely taken away from the people. On orders from Pope Damasus I, in 382 AD, Jerome translated the Word of God into Latin. This translation was refined somewhat into what is known as the Vulgate, and from then on God's Word was no longer read by the common man. Instead it was held that only the "Church" could interpret for the people what God had said. Of course, as the church became more and more corrupt during the Age of Papacy, the religious leaders really did not want the true Word of God to be known. The religious leaders were too busy trying to find ways to increase their coffers by such means as the selling of indulgences and fake relics to their flock. By the time a thousand years had passed, no one knew what God had truly said about anything. These truly were the "Dark Ages."

God's statement, *"My people are destroyed from lack of knowledge."* was a complete reality during this terrible time in human history.

Then, in the early 1380's, a man by the name of John Wycliff decided that enough was enough. There was no printing press at that time but he translated God's Word back into the language of the people and painstakingly copied his translations by hand. Wycliff then sent out pairs of poor preachers, called Lollards, or mumblers, to try to get the real Word of God out to the masses. The church retaliated by persecuting and killing many of these Lollards, but although the translation was totally banned from being read, copies of this common language English translation continued to circulate, under threat of death. Wycliff himself died only two years after his translation was completed.

Common people being able to read for themselves God's Word was a gigantic threat to the church, and torturous burning at the stake became common for people accused of the "sin' of reading the Bible in English. The numbers of those martyred in that manner continued to increase for a few hundred more years. Unknown thousands were killed in that horrifying manner, but still people persisted in hiding away even a single page, and reading it over and over until it literally fell apart. Neighbors would meet secretly with anyone who had such a copy, knowing that if they were caught they would burn. Literacy even increased in England and Europe because people wanted to learn how to read the precious pages. No one took the privilege of being able to read God's own Words lightly.

There are even documented cases of parents being burned at the stake because they had the audacity to teach their children the Lord's Prayer or the Ten Commandments. Children were even forced to light the fires that would burn up their daddies in the hope that they, too, would learn just how serious an offense it was to be able to read or recite God's Holy Word.

If people from that time had been able to time travel to today and could see the dusty, completely unread Bibles on our current shelves, we can only surmise that they would weep uncontrollably. Entire villages were actually condemned to the stake during that period for reading just a few pages to each other. And although we freely can read it, we don't.

Finally another Bible hero came along by the name of William Tyndale. About fifty years before Tyndale's birth, believed to be in 1494, Gutenberg had invented the printing press. As a young man Tyndale became quite a proficient Greek Scholar. After reading old Greek texts he became so enthralled with what he learned that he knew his calling was to share it with his fellow man.

In a meeting with other students he heard one say very positively, "The Bible is not necessary. It is all foolishness to talk about translating it into English for the people to read. All they need is the word of the pope. We had better be without God's laws than the pope's laws."

Tyndale jumped up, and striking a clenched fist on a table, shouted, "I defy the pope and all his laws; and, if God spares me, I will one day make the boy that drives the plow in England to know more of the scriptures than the pope does!"

Obviously Tyndale very quickly became enemy number one of the pope, and to save his own skin he was forced to hide out in Hamburg, Germany. The story from then on is one of intrigue that is exciting reading, but the short of it is that Tyndale succeeded. In 1525 The Tyndale Bible went to press.

The next ten years were spent by Tyndale in trying to smuggle Bibles into his beloved England. He was finally caught in 1536 and he, too, was put to the flames of the stake. His last words were, "Lord, open the king of England's eyes."

Seventy years after that, another king, James I, did indeed open his eyes and authorize that a new Bible translation be undertaken. Seven years later, in 1611, the King James Version of God's Word was printed for literally everyone to read.

The western world had heard the shrieks and cries of thousands and thousands who had been burned alive for the privilege of reading just one page of God's Love Letter, now people like you and I could learn about God and His plan for His children whenever they wanted. Satan had kept mankind in the dark for over twelve hundred years. He obviously now needed a new plan.

Following the 1611 printing of the first King James version Bible, the church made a very quick about face. From being in the dark itself, it lightened up the world with the truth of God. Jesus, therefore, was able to allude to the new Age of Missions' church as being, *holy and true.*

These new members of a church with the Word of God as their guide learned from the scriptures that they could actually talk to God, and moreover, that He would listen and act on those prayers. Men like George Mueller came to the front. If you are not acquainted with Mr. Mueller, he lived in the 1800's and felt strongly that he should show his fellow man that God answers prayer. To do this he decided to start an orphanage and tell no man his needs. His idea was that he would only tell God his specific needs in starting the orphanage, and in its continued maintenance. He later published his daily journal which is still in print today. The results are startling. They speak of how specifically needed funds or supplies would show up time and time again, although no one but God knew about the need.

Mueller's is one of the most fascinating and awesome stories you will ever read. In the end, when he died at the age of 92, George Mueller had seen over ten thousand orphans go through his orphanage and school that he also founded. Every single need had always been mysteriously met, often to the penny, and at the last possible moment. Additionally, he had received extra monies amounting to more that seven million dollars which he was able to pass along to other missions, often hearing back that the sum he had been led to send was the exact amount that they needed on that exact day. Mueller's final tally was that he had seen more than 50,000 specific answers to his prayers.

Mueller's being able to pray in the first place only came about because he and others like him were now able to read the Bible for themselves. This costly privilege, bought by the burnings at the stake of untold others before him, allowed him to learn that God was a personal God, a God that longed for communion with His children. Mueller learned that God was a God of mercy, compassion and grace; and above all, love. Mueller, and the rest of his *"holy and true"* church learned quickly that God is loving, faithful, and unchanging. Mueller's church learned that God's Word is always trustworthy and true.

Then came Satan's lie of all lies, Evolution. Man now had an option. No longer did man need to be responsible to anyone. Man could now doubt that God even existed, and it rapidly became politically correct to do so. With the fact of God's existence out of the way, the Bible became totally useless. And if Jesus was needed it was only as a good, moral teacher, on a par with others like Gandhi, Confucius, Mohamed, or Buddha.

Of course, you and I have already seen through the countless fulfilled prophecies that we have studied that God does exist. There can be no question once we know the facts. The debate is over on that count. God knew it would be. He told us to search in that direction when He said, *"I am God, and there is none like me. I make known the end from the beginning, from ancient times, what is still to come."* Isaiah 46:10

Likewise, since God used the Bible to communicate those prophecies to us in over eight thousand scriptures, it is just as obvious that the Bible is His Word. No other book contains His fulfilled prophesies.

We also know that from His Word that Jesus fulfilled the 332 prophecies, plus all the numerous types and shadows generously laid out within the Old Testament, so we can be just as sure that Jesus was the Anointed One God said He would send.

Finally, as we will see, Jesus Himself completely took away the option of looking at Him as only a good, moral teacher. The only options Jesus gave us for Himself were that He was either God in the flesh, or He was a lunatic or a liar.

CHAPTER EIGHTEEN

You and I may not know each other at all. If we do have a passing acquaintance, we probably don't know each other very well. That is natural. Even people who have been around each other for some time don't truly know each other's real goals, desires, likes and dislikes, challenges and fears. Once we start developing a relationship, be it friendship or love, the way we open up is by sharing our memories.

In addition to the ox, the lion, and the eagle, Jesus is always depicted by the image of the face of a man. Jesus was human. Even the staunchest debater doesn't question that. We know for certain that He lived, so He was human. Even Flavius Josephus, the well respected Jewish historian mentioned Jesus twice in his historic works, and Josephus was definitely not a believer that Jesus was the Messiah.

Josephus was born in 37 AD, a few years after Jesus was crucified, lived until 100 AD, and probably knew some of the same people Jesus knew. But Josephus was a Jew. He had even been a priest before he became commander of the Jewish forces in Galilee until 70 AD when Rome destroyed Jerusalem. He spent his latter years in Rome under the patronage of Roman Emperors who commissioned him to write the History of the Hebrew people. He remained a staunch believer in Judaism.

The Greek translations of the works of Josephus probably have been tampered with by followers of Jesus because they do read as if he, too, may have been a follower, but we can be certain that, in truth, he never abandoned his Jewish heritage.

We can, however, look at the ancient Arabic version of what Josephus wrote of the period, and be confident that it is accurate. In that version we read, "Similarly Josephus the Hebrew (sic). For he says in the treatises that he has written on the governance of the Jews: 'At this time there was a wise man who was called Jesus. And his conduct was good, and he was known to be virtuous. And many people from among the Jews and the other nations became his disciples. Pilate condemned him to be crucified and to die."

Later in the written history of Josephus, the Greek and Arabic translations agree exactly that his original writings included the following paragraph concerning the martyrdom of the half brother and leader of the first Christian church in Jerusalem, "Since Ananus was that kind of person, and because he perceived an opportunity with Festus having died and Albinus not yet arrived, he called a meeting of the Sanhedrin and brought James, the brother of Jesus (who is called 'Messiah') along with some others. He accused them of transgressing the law, and handed them over for stoning."

It is interesting to historians that James was referred to as the "brother of Jesus" when it was always common in the writings of Josephus to refer to someone as "the son of" someone. Nowhere else does Josephus, in all of his voluminous work, delineate someone as someone else's brother. Evidently Josephus did at least recognize that Jesus was someone very special. At any rate, there is not any question that Jesus lived, or for that matter, that He was crucified.

So, we have this man, a regular human, who has gathered some other regular guys around Him and they are starting to become friends. They obviously liked each other or they would not have stayed together beyond the first few days. And in the evenings after supper they naturally sat around the fire for a while in the evenings and talked. There is nothing at all strange about that. Had we lived back then, you and I could imagine fitting in, kind of like being at camp, or college, or some other situation in which we are getting to know the people we are fairly newly associated with.

The natural progression of opening up to each other would have occurred, and gradually the people would have shared memories; memories of their home lives, memories of the towns they grew up in, memories of events from their past. This is how we let people know about us. This give and take of memories inevitably became more personal. It always does. Then Jesus shared this memory, *"I saw Satan fall like lightning from heaven."* Luke 10:18

Can you imagine the quietness that ensued? "What did He just say?" Thoughts have got to be running all over the place,

"I've never known Jesus to lie to us, but He now is saying that He was in heaven when Satan fell, and he saw the whole thing." The Bible doesn't give us the reaction of those present that evening, but we can surely imagine at least the diversity of thoughts at that moment in that little band of "regular guys."

And that was not the only very odd thing that he shared with them as they became closer to each other. He often matter of factly made references to actually having been in heaven, and having seen things that "regular guys" just don't see. At one point He said, *"Your father Abraham rejoiced at the thought of seeing my day, he saw it and was glad.*

'You are not yet fifty years old', the Jews said to Him, 'and you have seen Abraham!'

'I tell you the truth,' Jesus answered, 'before Abraham was born, I am." John 8:56-58

Not only did He tell them that He witnessed it, but He said the unthinkable by calling Himself, "I am"; the same name that God told Moses to tell the Israelites when asked who had sent him, *"God said to Moses, 'I AM WHO I AM. This is what you are to say to the Israelites: I AM has sent me to you."* Ex. 3:14

This obviously is pretty crazy stuff from an ordinary, moral teacher. As we noted, Jesus was either a liar, a lunatic, or both; or else He was God in the flesh.

In Luke 15:7 Jesus said, *"I tell you that in the same way there will be more rejoicing in heaven over one sinner who repents than over ninety-nine righteous persons who do not need to repent."* Now let's be serious, how was He suppose to know stuff like that unless He had been there?

And not only did He constantly talk about having seen things in heaven first hand, but He continually made statements that sounded like He thought the world revolved around Him and that He was somehow perfect. For instance, Jesus blatantly said in Matthew 28:16, *"All authority in heaven and on earth has been given to me."*

This crazy talk of His was constant. He said, *"Do not think that I have come to abolish the law and the prophets; I have not come to abolish them but to fulfill them."* Matthew 5:17

He even dared to say, *"I am the way and the truth and the life. No one comes to the Father except through me."* John 14:6

Nobody continually says stuff like that without having everyone around him get fed up with such ludicrous remarks and walking away. Wouldn't you if someone you knew kept on making such grandiose statements about himself? Confucius, Mohamed, Gandhi, and Buddha never talked like that. They were smarter than that. They knew that everyone would be so totally turned off that they would end up telling their stories to a wall.

So why did this band of friends stay around Jesus? The answer is simple: at the same time Jesus was talking crazy, he was also performing miracle after miracle after miracle. And these were not little magic tricks. These were things like turning water into wine, healing crippled people, giving sight to the blind, hearing to the deaf, and even raising the dead. Obviously these things were not myths, because the disciples stayed. There is no other logical answer.

Let's face it, Jesus even claimed to be God. That's right, He did. Although debaters have said that Jesus made no claim, their comments come from lack of knowledge. And interestingly, Jesus made the claim over and over, and in different ways.

In the story of the Samaritan woman at the well, we read,

"The woman said, 'I know that Messiah' (called Christ) 'is coming. When he comes he will explain everything to us.' Then Jesus declared, 'I who speak to you am He." John 4:25-26

Then in Matthew 16:15-17, *"But what about you?' He asked, 'Who do you say I am?' Simon Peter answered, 'You are the Christ, the Son of the living God.' Jesus replied, 'Blessed are you, Simon son of Jonah, for this was not revealed to you by man, but by my Father in heaven."*

In John 12:45, *"When he looks at Me, he sees the one who sent Me."*

Also, *"If you really knew Me you would know My Father as well. From now on, you do know him and have seen him."* John 14:7

In Matthew 26:63, *"The high priest said to Him, 'I charge you under oath by the living God: Tell us if you are the Christ, the Son of God.'*

"Yes it is as you say,' Jesus replied."

Those around Him listened to all these outlandish claims, and we can be sure that initially at least, they wondered. But the miracles kept happening, and as may be the case with you or me, the doubts eventually vanished. They knew. They believed.

Then, they saw Jesus die on that cross. It was obvious that He felt pain like any man. He bled like any man. He died like any one of them would have, had they, too, been crucified.

Nothing that He said had really been provable. Not really. The miracles were phenomenal. But in the end, Jesus bled, and Jesus died. Their dream world came crashing down. Jesus was, in the end, human.

This was a confused, scared, embarrassed group of eleven. Judas, one of their own, was dead. Jesus, their leader, their hope for high government appointments when Jesus established his kingdom, was in the tomb. All they wanted to do was hide. How could they have been so dumb as to have wasted three years of their lives following a lunatic. Obviously that was what He had been. He couldn't have even been just a liar, because a liar would not have lied his way to a Roman flogging and a heinous death on a cross. A liar would have stopped short of that. No, He had to have been a complete lunatic. And they had all been duped.

But what about the miracles? They obviously weren't fake. Maybe God had just answered the prayers of a lunatic. Surely they had seen God answer prayers before. You and I just read that George Mueller saw over 50,000 miraculous answers to specific prayers in his lifetime. That must have been the only logical answer the eleven could think of. A lunatic that somehow got His prayers answered. God, in his mercy, probably answered the prayers for those blind and deaf folks.

You and I hear people today say that Jesus was just a good, moral, wise teacher. We can be sure that the disciples didn't for a minute entertain that option. No, if Jesus was not God, he was just a lunatic, crazy as a bat, and they were the dumbest eleven men on the planet. We can be sure that John, Andrew, Peter, and James couldn't wait to get back to the solitude of their lives as fisherman on that big Lake of Galilee. They probably didn't ever even want to hear the name, Jesus again. What a nightmare!

Those eleven had the advantage of living with Jesus for over three years, but you and I have an advantage that they did not have. You and I have seen the precision of God's Word. We have seen how Einstein came up with E=MC2. We have seen how God told man about such things as germs, long before people knew things existed that were smaller than the eye could see. We have seen that Pleiades really is the gravitational center of the Milky Way.

You and I know that God mentioned Arcturus, and it is indeed the "Runaway Star." Those eleven couldn't have imagined that there was anything like String Theory that would prove that God was right when he alluded to rolling up the flat universe like a ball. There are scores of things that we now know, that they didn't have a clue about.

On top of all those things, they didn't have all of the fulfilled prophecy that we have today. They couldn't see that the deserts around Jerusalem would one day become true garden spots that would be responsible for most of the fruit consumed in Europe, or that the Dead Sea would actually separate, exactly as God had said that it would.

They obviously had no idea that their Hebrew language would disappear, only to be miraculously revived, as God predicted. And they most certainly could not even guess that their nation would be disbanded, but come back together in one incredible day, just as predicted, and that miracle upon miracle, Israel would become a nation on the very date, May 15, 1948, that the Sovereign God said would be the date.

Those eleven had lived with Jesus, but you and I have God's very own Word that has proven over and over and over to be completely supernatural. It was seemingly lost for centuries, but was brought back into existence exactly when it was needed most. Without it, we too, might be deceived and destroyed.

As I was writing these words I decided to stop for a bite of food. While taking a break I opened my Bible at random and "by coincidence" read the following scripture. Notice that the Psalmist, in

Psalm 19:89-96, when using words like law, precepts, statutes, and commands is describing God's Word, the love letter we have with the thousands of fulfilled prophecies.

"Your word, o Lord, is eternal; it stands firm in the heavens. Your faithfulness continues through all generations; you establish the earth and it endures. Your law endures to this day, for all things serve you.

If your law had not been my delight, I would have perished in my infliction. I will never forget your precepts, for by them you have preserved my life.

Save me, for I have sought out your precepts. The wicked are waiting to destroy me, but I will ponder your statutes. To all perfection I see a limit; but your commands are boundless."

(A coincidence is when God decides to remain anonymous.)

No, the disciples did not know for a certainty, like we now do, that God's Word is so utterly infallible. And they could not see the big picture, like we can. If God had given them the knowledge He has given us, they might have been more open to expect what came next. They might have expected a risen Jesus.

CHAPTER NINETEEN

It is completely incredible to realize that you and I can know more about Jesus than the disciples did the day after Christ was crucified. But it is true. Ponder it for a moment and you will be totally amazed. Yes, they had been with the Master for three years, and they had seen first hand not only His love, gentleness, and wisdom, but also His supernatural power.

On the other hand, not only do we have so many more fulfilled prophecies that obviously strengthen our "knowing", but we also have the entire New testament, which teaches us so much that they could not know about the big picture of why Jesus came, and His plans for the future. Granted, books of the New Testament are titled with names of some of those original eleven, like Matthew, John, and Peter, but we must remember that although their names are on those books, it was the Holy Spirit of God who was truly the author. The second book of Timothy, verse 3:16, tells us emphatically, *"All scripture is God breathed."*

People of today too readily forget that fact; *"All scripture is God breathed."* It wasn't men who could see into the future the phenomenal fulfillment of the prophecies we have studied.

It was God. We are told, *"For prophecy never had its origin in the will of man, but men spoke from God as they were carried along by the Holy Spirit."* 2 Peter 1:21

The same is true of every other word in the sixty six books of the Bible. Every single letter was *"God breathed."* Jesus told us in Matthew 5:18, *"I tell you the truth, until heaven and earth disappear, not the smallest letter, not the least stroke of the pen, will by any means disappear from the Law until everything is accomplished."* Actually, this is one scripture that I prefer the King James version which says, *"For verily I say unto you, Till heaven and earth pass, one jot or one tittle shall in no wise pass from the law, till all be fulfilled."*

There is just something about the archaic words *"one jot or one tittle"* that creates more of a mental picture for me than *"stroke of the pen."* In either case, though, the meaning is clear; every single letter in the Bible was authored by God. Everything is there for a reason. Every single phrase has a meaning. And remember, *"It is the glory of God to conceal a matter; to search out a matter is the glory of kings."* Proverbs 25:2

The eleven disciples did have the thirty nine books of the Old Testament, but not one of the twenty seven books of the New Testament had been dictated by the Father until some years after Jesus was crucified, and there are things revealed in each of those books that probably were unknown by the disciples the day He died. Obviously they new nothing about the resurrection and its meaning for mankind, because it had not even occurred, but also they knew nothing about the future events of the world, like we can know by studying the books of the New Testament. As we said, it is a truly awesome thought that we can know more about God and His plan just by sitting in our living room and reading our Bible than the men knew who actually walked with Jesus every day of his three year ministry. To not take advantage of such a privilege may be the most absurd act of modern man.

It's not that our society doesn't read. Every single day virtually everyone in every nation reads something. We read novels. We read magazines. We read business and trade materials. We read meaningless gossip columns. We read inane forwarded e-mail jokes. We read advertisements. We even read comic strips. For goodness sake, we even read cereal boxes as we eat our breakfasts. But we do not as a whole ever read the most important words ever written; words that came directly from the mind of the Creator and Author of everything.

God was loving enough to give us His thoughts and plans; everything we need to know for our lives on this earth and beyond into eternity; yet sadly, less than 50% of the people in North America can even name the first book in God's Word. Just to be clear, it is Genesis.

It isn't that we are living five hundred years ago and don't have access to a God's Word. The average American household owns three Bibles, and 92% of the individuals own at least one copy. The Bible is the world's all time best seller, with twenty million copies sold each year. Gideans International even gives away forty five million copies a year.

Polls tell us, though, that 80% say the Bible is too confusing to read. How many of those do you think ever even opened one up and tried. 64% say they are just too busy to read it. As a result one third of Americans think Billy Graham delivered the Sermon on the Mount. One fourth don't even know why Easter is celebrated. Even a remarkable 80% of people who claim to be "born again Christians" think that the Bible says "God helps those that help themselves.", which was really said by Ben Franklin.

God gave us the commandment in several places to read his Word daily. For instance, Joshua 1:8 commands us, *"Do not let this Book of the Law depart from your mouth; meditate on it day and night."*

In fact, listen to how detailed God was in telling us to keep His Word in front of us at all times, *"These commandments that I give you today are to be upon your hearts. Impress them on your children. Talk about them when you sit at home and when you walk along the road, when you lie down and when you get up. Tie them as symbols on your hands and bind them on your foreheads. Write them on the doorframes of your houses and on your gates."* Deuteronomy 6:6-9

Instead, though, man reads his cereal box. Is it any wonder that the debaters on both sides could give no proofs for their stands. God hit it on the head when He said in Hosea 4:6,

"My people are destroyed from lack of knowledge."

There is a cute but profound little statement, "Bible means **Ba**sic **I**nstruction **B**efore **L**eaving **E**arth." We won't get that on a Wheaties box. Enough said.

Getting back to our point of departure, the eleven disciples on that fateful day did not have the knowledge we can have. They knew enough, though, to know that Jesus could not have been a good, wise, moral teacher. The statements He had made over and over precluded that option, unless He also was God.

Those today who label Jesus in such a manner don't realize that they, too, do not really have the option to call Him that. As we now know, He was either God or He was a lunatic. The proof of which one he actually was lies in one place, the empty tomb.

Everything having to do with Jesus revolves around that one place. Nothing else matters in discussing Jesus unless we can resolve the question about the resurrection. Anything else is irrelevant until that is proved or disproved. The Bible even makes that fact totally clear.

In God's Word we read, *"And if Christ has not been raised, our preaching is useless and so is your faith. More than that, we are then found to be false witnesses about God, for we have testified about God that he raised Christ from the dead. But he did not raise Him if in fact the dead are not raised. For if the dead are not raised, then Christ has not been raised either. And if Christ has not been raised, your faith is futile; you are still in your sins. Then those also who have fallen asleep in Christ are lost. If only for this life we have hope in Christ, we are to be pitied more than all men."* 1 Corinthians 15:14-19

You and I who have seen some of the thousands of dramatically fulfilled prophecies and types and shadows, know not only that God exists; we also know that the Bible is God's communication with us. And we can *know* totally from God's Word that Christ arose from the dead. We can concur with the scores of statements such as that of the Psalmist, *"All your words are true."* Psalms 119:160

For a debater, though, who has not come to that solid knowledge, is there any way to prove that not only was there an empty tomb, but that Jesus Christ really and truly arose from the dead after three days, exactly as He said He would? Although God's *"words are true"*, is there any outside historical proof?

Quite frankly, as we have seen from man's former "knowledge" that the world was flat, to his current "knowledge" that everything was created by random chance, it should now be obvious to us that the Bible is the surest way to find the truth in a matter. For the sake of the debater, though, let's see what light history can shed on the topic of Christ's resurrection.

The best place to start is to go back to the most trusted and unbiased historian of that day, Flavius Josephus. We initially looked at the first part of his entry about Jesus, but let's now look at his entire report, again according to the extremely reliable Arabic translation that we know were the historian's own words: "At this time there was a wise man who was called Jesus. And His conduct was good, and He was known to be virtuous. And many people from among the Jews and the other nations became His disciples. Pilate condemned Him to be crucified and to die. And those who became his disciples did not abandon His discipleship. They reported that He had appeared to them after His crucifiction and that he was alive; accordingly, He was perhaps the Messiah concerning whom the prophets have recounted wonders."

We need to be crystal clear about one very important fact in reading the above report from Josephus in this account that he knew was going to be part of the official history of the Jewish people; Josephus was a Jew's Jew. He did not have a Christian bone in his body. If there had been any way at all to squelch the idea that Jesus rose from the dead, Josephus would have surely included it. Like all religious Jews of his time, he would have mentioned anything he could have to stop Christianity.

It was the Jewish religious community that pushed for the crucifiction of Jesus in the first place. They hated Him and wanted him dead because they considered Him a threat to their way of life and their standing in the community. Josephus knew all of that, and if he could have been some assistance to the Jewish cause, he would gladly have done it. Fortunately, though, Josephus was above all a historian. He wanted his masterpiece Jewish history to be completely true and accurate. Therefore, there is not even a hint in it that there was any proof that the resurrection did not occur. That glaring omission speaks volumes.

Let's be realistic, if there had been a way to stop any talk about a risen Jesus, not only the Jewish leaders, but the Romans as well, would have done it. If they could have produced a body, there is no question but that they would have quickly done it. Obviously, no body could be produced.

It's not as if Jesus was buried in a secret tomb. Everyone knew where it was to begin with, but in fairness to any debaters we won't even go into any of the Biblical accounts here. We will look totally at outside facts. The only viable option to the resurrection really happening was that the disciples stole the body and perpetrated a hoax.

Roman soldiers were very skilled at their work of crucifying criminals. Jesus did not come off that cross alive. Pilate himself was involved in this crucifiction. The captain in charge would have been very, very sure that the accused man, Jesus, was dead. We don't even have to read the Biblical accounts of the soldiers sticking a spear in him to be sure of that. We can know from common sense that Jesus died. Not only the Romans, but the Jewish leaders would have made very sure that Jesus, their nemesis, was very, very dead.

So, as we said, since it is irrefutable that everyone but the disciples of Jesus would have wanted it known that Jesus not only died, but that He stayed dead, there are only two plausible options; either He arose, or the disciples stole his body and from then on lied.

Not too many years after the crucifiction, the first letter to the Corinthians was sent by Paul. In it, he made the following statement about Jesus after He supposedly arose, *"He appeared to Peter, and then to the Twelve* (By this time Judas had been replaced with Matthias). *After that he appeared to more than five hundred of the brothers at the same time, most of whom are still living, though some have fallen asleep. Then He appeared to James, then to all the apostles."* 1 Corinthians 5:5-6

We don't offer this scripture as proof of anything. We only quote it because we know that this letter by Paul was widely circulated. Don't you imagine that if there had been any way to disprove the claim that five hundred people saw a risen Jesus at the same time, the Jewish leaders would have done it. Surely they could have gotten one of that crowd to confess that it was a lie if it was. We have to realize that the Jewish leaders had a lot at stake, and they obviously had a whole lot of power. But again, they could bring no one forward to admit that Paul had lied. We can be sure that Josephus would have put at least one paragraph in his report had they found only one talkative soul.

Let's not lose sight of the fact that, knowing how easy it is to prove God's existence by his fulfilled prophecies, and knowing also how easy it is to prove that he communicated to us through the Bible by not only his prophecies but the other amazing examples we have looked at, and knowing that the life and death of

Jesus fulfilled all three hundred of the prophecies of the coming Anointed One, it is ludicrous for us not to just take God's Word for the fact that Jesus arose. However, in case anyone could possibly think they need more, we'll continue to explore the option of what would be the biggest hoax in history.

We can know a little more by looking at the disciples themselves. These were not educated men. They were ordinary laborers. From what they even wrote about themselves we can grasp that they probably were not the sharpest tools in the shed. None of them were public speakers, which even back then, as today, was one of the scariest things for anyone not accustomed to it to do. And they obviously were not the bravest bunch around because we know they all scattered and went into hiding when Jesus was arrested. Sure, Peter was a hot head, but as far as we know only John was even brave enough to witness the crucifiction.

So what did they have to gain by fabricating a story about Jesus raising from the dead. Without that story they could return to their peaceful lives as fisherman and the like. By concocting such a ridiculous story they knew that they would be hunted down, tortured, and probably killed. Obviously a lie like that wasn't going to bring them riches. The truth is that they had nothing at all to gain by such a hoax.

But let's suppose they did in fact make up the whole thing, fearful as they were of the authorities, and even of having to persuade large groups of people by preaching it. The only possible reason could have been to somehow save face for having been so gullible as to have followed a lunatic. Remember, that was their only real choice at the time of describing Jesus. Without a true resurrection these disciples had to believe that Jesus was crazy. They were smart enough to know that no sane man would lie about something that he knew would get him tortured and killed.

Modern man, of course, should be just as smart as those disciples were. No sane man would make up a lie that would gain him nothing, knowing that that lie would bring about his own torture and death. And here lies the biggest proof of all.

These timid disciples set out in different directions, mostly on their own, to tell people this incredible story which would bring them no gain whatsoever, knowing the consequences.

Most had little or no contact with each other. Let's see what happened to them.

Simon Peter started out preaching this remarkable tale in Jerusalem before he eventually reached Rome. He was executed by Nero by crucifiction either in 64 or 67 AD, however unlike Jesus, he was head down.

Andrew, Peter's brother, went to Achaia (Southern Greece) and Scythia (Ukrane and Southern Russia). Like his brother and Jesus, Andrew was also crucified, however his crucifiction was spread eagle style, and his death took three excruciating days.

James stayed and preached in what is now modern Israel. He might have traveled farther except he was beheaded by King Herod Agrippa I in 44 AD.

Philip, who we saw was responsible for the story going to Ethiopia after he told the Eunuch about it, went to Phygia in central Turkey, where he was tied to a pillar and stoned to death.

Bartholomew really got around. He preached in what is now Iraq, Iran, Turkey, India, Egypt, Arabia, and Ethiopia. His end was reached in Baku on the Caspian sea where he was actually very painfully skinned alive. He was then beheaded.

Thomas, who we know as Doubting Thomas, did his preaching in Iraq, Iran, and India. His death came by being burned first, then speared with a javelin in Madras, India.

The lesser known James, known as James the Less probably because he was smaller than John's brother, James, was killed for his preaching in Egypt.

Jude, also known as Thaddaeus, preached in Iraq before joining Simon the Zealot in Persia (Iran) where both were beaten to death with sticks and clubs.

Simon the Zealot first preached in Egypt before he met his cruel end with Jude in Persia.

John, the brother of James, was the only one of the original eleven who died of natural causes. He preached in Turkey and Asia Minor. Of course, although he was not martyred for what he preached, he was lowered in boiling oil head first, and when he survived was banished to the Isle of Patmos in the Aegean Sea, which was like being sent to do hard labor in a prison rock quarry. It was not a resort and he was a very old man at the time.

Matthais, the one who replaced Judas, preached in Turkey before being killed in Ethiopia for his preaching by being nailed to the ground with spikes and then beheaded.

Paul, who originally persecuted the Christians himself, was often beaten, stoned, flogged, and in other ways unmercifully tortured before he eventually was beheaded in Rome.

Finally, James, the half brother of Jesus, who thought his brother was insane when He was alive, started telling the resurrection story and was stoned to death for it, as we saw in the account by Josephus.

All fourteen were tortured for telling the story, and only one did not die at the hand of his captors because of it.

Now, let's be just the least bit realistic. Is there any way in our wildest imaginations that we could believe that these fourteen men, all but two totally alone at their deaths, undergoing the most heinous forms of torture, including being skinned alive, hundreds and thousands of miles apart from their nearest conspirator, knowing that all they had to do was recant the story to stop the torture and their own painful death, would have kept up a lie that could do no one any good at all, about a man that they knew to be a lunatic?

To believe that not a single one of them, in unheard of agony, knowing that the others would probably never find out anyway, would not have given in to the excruciating pain and said the simple words that their torturers wanted to hear, stands alone as the craziest belief possible. We could scour the planet and never find fourteen men who would go through what these men went through, totally isolated, for a meaningless hoax.

Only a real encounter with the true risen Christ could explain the reality of what happened in the lives of these men. There is no other explanation. Jesus actually arose from the grave, exactly like He said He would. There is no other possibility.

Peter stated it plainly for us when he said, *"We did not follow cleverly invented stories when we told you about the power and coming of our Lord Jesus Christ, but we were eyewitnesses to His majesty."* 2 Peter 1:16

We have all heard that truth is more incredible than fiction. This truth, that Jesus rose from the grave, is more than that, not just because it is so astonishing a fact, but because of what it means for you and me.

If you recall, a few chapters back we quoted one of the smarter men alive today, Nobel winner in physics, Dr. Arthur L. Schawlow, who said, "When confronted with the marvels of life and the universe, one must ask why and not just how. The only possible answers are religious...I find a need for God in the universe and in my own life."

God exists. The Bible is how He communicated with us. Every word of it is true. Jesus is the Son of God and He rose from the dead. These, we have seen, are easy. They are provable.

But what about the "why's" of it all? These, Dr. Schawlow says, are what we must ask, and there are many. Why did God create this whole thing to begin with? Why did he write the Bible? Why does man exist? Why did Jesus have to die?

And then there are the "what's." What's the next big event that will happen on earth? What is the future of the world? For that matter, what is our future? What is our role in this whole thing? In fact, what exactly is the meaning of life?

Ahead we will look at more prophecies, types and shadows, and other similar things that are always fun because they make us say "Wow", and we will read a true life "Indiana Jones" type story that is going on as this page is being typed. It is phenomenal. But additionally, we will also answer the truly deep questions. And just as we have already read things in prior pages that we had never heard of before, in pages to come we will learn answers to things that we never had answers to before.

In fact, we may never have even had the questions. We are going to learn the "why" and the "what" of it all.

PART FOUR

PART FOUR

CHAPTER TWENTY

We have learned three undebatable truths, through proofs that are completely unquestionable: that God exists and is the creator of everything, that He communicated with us through His infallible Word, and that Jesus is the Messiah sent by God and that He arose from the dead and is Himself divine.

But what does it all really mean? How do those three facts explain all the why's and what's we long to understand? Is there really any purpose to everything? Unfortunately, just believing that God exists and that Jesus is the Son of God does us no good whatsoever. God told us, *"You believe that there is one God. Good! Even the demons believe that - and shudder."* James 2:19

To get past the shuddering stage we need to understand that everything we look at as history is really His Story, not our story. Rick Warren probably said it best in the first line of his powerful book, <u>The Purpose Driven Life</u>, when he said to all of us, "It's not about you."

What a sobering thought that is for any of us. Let's read again, very slowly, that opening line, "It's not about you."

Let those words truly sink in, because they tell it all.

Of course, in this self centered world we live in, that truth is nowhere to be observed. The famous soliloquy by the melancholy Jaques in William Shakespear's <u>As You Like It</u> starts out with the famous line, "All the world's a stage, and all the men and women merely players; they have their exits and their entrances." The fact is, though, that deep down we all believe that we have the starring roles. Our little universes revolve around us. Probe the innermost recesses of even the most religious appearing people we know and the same feeling is even prominent with them. We are a self centered people.

The fact is, though, that it is <u>not</u> all about us. If we are to search for the meaning of life within our own lives, the search will come up empty. Sure, in our lives we could do some good for ourselves, or for our families, or even for our fellow man, but in the end it is all, as Solomon told us, *"a chasing after the wind."* Ecclesiastes 2:11

If any of us really think that this life we live, in itself, could have meaning, try to think of anything that any human could do today that would be meaningful four million years from now. Or what about seventeen million years from now. Solomon's full quote is, *"everything was meaningless, a chasing after the wind. Nothing was gained under the sun."* Ecclesiastes 2:11

Unfortunately for Solomon, the wisest man ever, he did not have what we have to search out and learn from. He did not have the majority of God's Word. Solomon only had about a third of the Old Testament, and not a single word of the New Testament. We are told in the Bible that even the prophets of Solomon's day, *"searched intently and with the greatest care"* trying to learn the knowledge we now have access to. That Biblical passage surprisingly ended with this startling statement, *"Even angels long to look into these things."* 1Peter 1:12

Rick Warren said in his second paragraph, "If you want to know why you were placed on this planet, you must begin with God. You were born *by* His purpose and *for* His purpose."

So let's do as Warren suggests and begin with God. We must realize, however, as Paul Tillis said, "It is as blasphemous to define God as to deny Him." God is too big, too powerful, too everything, to actually be able to define. He obviously is larger than all the universe, since He created it. And He is powerful enough to have created it just by speaking it into existence. He is beyond time, beyond any spacial dimension, beyond anything we could possible imagine.

He exists, and He is God, Creator of what exists, and Supreme over all. Everything about us is indescribably minuscule compared to God. To forget that fact is a mistake of the most gigantic order. The thought that mere mortals would be so ludicrous as to think that debating His very existence would in any manner be meaningful to the truth, is totally laughable. *"For in Him we live and move and have our being."* Acts 17:28

God has, however, told us volumes about His attributes and His characteristics. The most meaningful to us, and the most important for us to search into, is the fact that *"God is love."* 1 John 4:8

Don't pass over this statement in God's own Word too hastily. In this statement is the reason you and I even exist. In these words is the meaning for everything. The fact that you and I are living, breathing, thinking creatures is all summed up in those three phenomenal words, *"God is love."* If this had not been the case, God would have never spoken in the first place. Every single event is directly linked to that one simple phrase. And nothing else impacts our future as does *"God is love,"*

One of the most incredible books of our time is Gene Edwards' beautiful work, <u>The Divine Romance</u>. The first exquisite paragraphs tell us where to really begin to answer all the why's and what's that Nobel prize winning scientist, Dr. Arthur Schawlow, encouraged us to answer. Read them carefully and comprehend the unearthly scene:

> *"He was alone.*
>
> The first tick of time had never sounded, nor had the unending circle of eternity yet commenced. There were neither things created nor things uncreated to share space with Him.
>
> He dwelt in an age before the eternals, where all there was ... was God. Nor was there space for anything else. He was the uncreated. He was the ALL.
>
> In this non-time of so long ago, there was but one life form ... the highest life.
>
> *He was also love.*
>
> Passionate, emotional, expressive ... love.
>
> In this God, dwelling so all alone, there was a paradox: though He was alone, He was also love. Yet there was no *counterpart* for Him to love. A love so vast, so powerful, yet, there was no "other than."
>
> Then life pulsated, light blazed in newfound glory as revelation ascended in Him, as He cried from within the council of the Godhead.
>
> *There can be two.*
>
> 'I ... the living God ... shall have a counterpart!'
>
> Exalting in revelation, He consecrated His whole being to this one task: to have ... *a bride.* For one brief moment the infinite solitude retreated." By Gene Edwards

It is all so easy to understand, with the magnificent imagery of Gene Edwards. In the Creator's own words,*"God is love"*, but He had no one to love. We have the truth of the mystery of the trinity, God the Father, the Son, and the Holy Spirit, which although truly exists, is unfathomable to the finite human mind. But the trinity, although three separate persons, is still one. That trinity, the Godhead, being totally love of the highest order had nothing to love. There were the three persons who made up the Godhead, the One God, but there was no "other" on which to bestow His uncomparable love. We can only vaguely imagine the need such an all loving being must have had for someone to love, the need for ... *a bride.*

That is our starting point. In fact, that is "the" starting point of everything. Without *"God is love,"* nothing at all makes sense. Without *"God is love,"* there would be nothing.

Chapter Twenty-One

God created mankind because *"God is love,"* and a love that indescribable must be manifested in a love relationship with an "other." That love should not, dare we say "could not," exist for all of eternity with no "other" to love and be loved in return. Mankind is the necessary "other." God made man as His "other."

In order to have an "other" to love, and to be loved by, any being would want the other to be of like nature. A robin seeks a robin, a dolphin seeks a dolphin, and a giraffe seeks a giraffe.

In the very same manner, we read, *"Then God said, 'Let us make man in our own image, in our likeness. ... So God created man in His own image, in the image of God He created him; male and female He created them."* Genesis 3:26-27

The problem is that love that is manipulated or coerced in any way is not true love. God obviously knew that. In the sixty six books of the Bible we find the word love used 808 separate times. God is the expert on love. He knew that He could not create an "other" that expressed only a robotic kind of love, and be satisfied with that kind of love. You and I are made *"in His image"* and we can fully understand that fact.

In order for love to be real and meaningful, it must be returned to us by choice. Anything else is not truly love. Therefore, God had to create us with free will. We had to have the ability to return His love or reject it. In the end, it had to be our choice to love Him or not. The idea of predestination dies with that one simple fact. Mankind was not created as robots. You and I have free will, just like God does. That is the <u>only</u> way God would have it. It is the only way to have honest love.

The necessity of free will, of choice, brings with it the necessity of two things to choose from. Mankind could have been given free will, but it would have been completely meaningless without something other than God to choose. We could tell a child that he could have any puppy in the pet store to bring home and love, but if there is only one puppy in the store, the child's free will in the matter is actually non existent.

With that as a fundamental fact, God had to also create an alternative for His longed for love recipient. He was forced to give mankind someone else to choose to love. The created angel, Lucifer, was the needed possible "other suitor" for you and me; a being so opposite from God that a real choice could be made.

Everything about God is crystal clear. There are no gray areas. Let's examine just a few of God's attributes:

"The Lord is righteous in all His ways." Psalm 145:17

"God is light; in Him there is no darkness." 1 John 1:5

"There is no one holy like the Lord." 1 Samuel 2:2

"All His ways are just. Upright and just is He." Deut. 32:4

"All Your words are true." Psalm 119:160

We could go on and on for page after page, but the bottom line is that everything about God is good, pure, holy, righteous, honest, faithful, etc., etc., etc. It is easier to just say that God is perfect, and He can not be in the presence of darkness (sin).

Satan, on the other hand is the total opposite. In John 10:10 Jesus said that he *"comes only to steal and kill and destroy."*

He went on to tell us, *"He was a murderer from the beginning, not holding to the truth."* John 8:44

Everything that God is, Satan is not, and vice versa.

The other problem lies in the fact that if mankind had been created perfect like God, not being able to even be in the presence of sin, we would have been forced to choose Him. We would once again be devoid of free will. If you and I had been created exactly like God, our choice between returning God's love or choosing Satan and sin would have been moot. Once again, we would have had no true free will, and our love would have been robotic in nature. Remember, God wants us to be able to choose to love Him. He wants honest love.

The truth is obvious, though. Mankind was not made perfect. And it was by God's choice that we weren't. The Psalmist states clearly, *"Surely I was sinful at birth, sinful from the time my mother conceived me."* Psalm 51:5

We were not just born with a sin nature, but we were also conceived that way. Ponder that. It had to be so. This is the only way that you and I and the rest of mankind could have a choice. It was a risk on God's part to design His plan that way, but it had to be. Every single person could reject him, but He had to give mankind an honest to goodness choice in the matter. Eternity would be a long time to spend with a love that He *knew* was not truly and freely given. Remaining alone would actually be preferable. And lest we forget, the end result of this entire creation was to determine how God would spend eternity. It is His Story.

The story, then, unfolds in the Garden of Eden. God created mankind with the ability to choose. He created also the alternative to his love, the lure of sin and Satan. And He inserted inside mankind the needed element, a predisposition to sin, in order to allow for an honest choice. He then let the story play out. He did not, though, just walk away and wait.

The desired end result of a *bride* was way too important for God to just leave things to random chance. From this point forward His Story is chronicled in His Word, the ultimate love letter. It is a story of the most perfect Being that ever was, courting the object of His love, us.

God *knew* what would happen. Remember, it was God that created both man and Satan. The rebellion in the heavens by Satan and his band of angelic cronies was planned to happen by God for our sake. It was the only way for him to give us the needed choice. And Satan played his part to the fullest.

Once the stage had been set, the world created, and mankind placed on the stage, Satan answered his call on cue.

Of course, first, God gave the most important of all his prophecies. God told His creation of love, *"And the Lord commanded the man, 'You are free to eat from any tree in the garden; but you must not eat from the tree of the knowledge of good and evil, for when you eat of it you will surely die."* Genesis 2:16-17

Satan walked on the stage of history, His Story, and uttered his first big lie by starting with a question, *"Did God really say,"You must not eat from any tree in the garden?"*

The woman said to the serpent, 'We may eat fruit from the trees in the garden, but God did say, "You must not eat from the tree that is in the middle of the garden, and you must not touch it, or you will die."

Then came the big lie.

'You will not surely die,' the serpent said to the woman, 'For God knows that when you eat of it your eyes will be opened, and you will be like God, knowing good and evil." Genesis 3:1-5

Satan played his part exactly as God knew he would, and of course, woman and man did exactly as God knew they would as well. They had to. They had been conceived with a sin nature. Give man a forbidden fruit, and he will go for it. Even Solomon, the wisest man to ever live, chased after the one thing he had been commanded not to go near, foreign women. Give any of us forbidden fruit, with the thought that we can pick it without any repercussions, and leave us to our own inbuilt sin nature, and we can lay odds that we will jump at it every time. A baby doesn't have to be taught to lie. Ask the child the very first time he is caught marking on the wall with a crayon if he was the one who did it, and he will cutely and innocently say, "no, it wasn't me."

God knew what would happen. He also knew that He had said, *"You will surely die."* But, He also had a plan in place to redeem the ones who in the future would decide to choose His pure and righteous love. The failsafe plan, as we will show through more types and shadows and prophecy, was Jesus.

"He was chosen before the creation of the world." 1 Peter 1:20

The entire Bible, from beginning to end, explains this incredible, perfect plan, which allows for the needed sin in God's beloved to be cancelled the minute we make the decision to choose to love Him. *"As far as the east is from the west, so far has he removed our transgressions from us."* Psalm 103:12

Once we have our eyes opened to the different parts of God's plan we can see the super intelligent genius of it all.

The plan is so utterly simple, yet through the centuries virtually no one has understood it. It all starts with *"God is love,"* and having no "other" to love.

Being God, and all powerful, He creates a beloved for Himself. He knows, though, that the true love He wants in return from His beloved must involve her free will to be able to make the choice to love Him or to reject Him and choose another.

He also knows that in order to make that choice a real choice, He must also create that other possible suitor that His beloved could choose, one totally opposite from Himself, such as Satan, who incidently also was the most beautiful angel God ever created. Creating Satan so beautiful was done so as not to stack the deck in His own favor. God did not want the choice to be an obvious one. He made Satan and sin desirable.

God also knew that He must instill in His beloved the ability to actually choose Satan. To choose Satan took the ability to be able to tolerate sin, the very thing that Satan would use to court her with.

Finally, God knew that if His beloved did do what He longed for, and actually chose Him, something would have to be done to get rid of His beloved's no longer needed inbuilt sin nature; since sin is so totally abhorrent to Him that it is a completely impossibility for Him to be in the presence of it.

The fact is that God's intolerance of sin is such that looking at his beloved still in sin would be like you or I looking at our little baby girl in a crib all covered with hideous venomous snakes crawling all over her precious little body. The snakes would obviously have to be instantly thrown out of the crib before we could pick up our baby girl and caress her. The same is true of the sin attached to God's beloved. It must be removed.

"Before the creation of the world" God established a way to get rid of the snakes in the crib. The Way, as we said, is Jesus. God's Word, spoken by Jesus himself said, *"I am the way and the truth and the life. No one comes to the Father except by me. If you really knew me, you would know my Father as well. From now on you do know Him and have seen Him,"* John 14:6-7

Every book of the Bible tells us in different and fascinating ways the ingenious plan that God cleverly devised to get rid of His beloved's sin, once she had truly committed to be His betrothed. In the process they also tell us what the future holds, both on earth, as well as in the other dimension we call heaven.

Our searching out of these things in pages to come will be exciting, and very often extremely surprising. *"To search out a matter is the glory of kings."* Proverbs 25:2

CHAPTER TWENTY-TWO

John 4:24 states it very simply, *"God is spirit."*

You and I find it completely impossible to understand that word, "spirit." We are material beings and understand fully only what our five senses can interpret. This has always been the case. Everyone knows the old King James version of John 3:16, *"For God so loved the world that He gave His only begotten Son, that whosoever believeth in Him should not perish, but have everlasting life."*

What most people don't know is that the entire third chapter in which that verse is found is a conversation with one of the religious leaders of the day, Nicodemus, who had come secretly at night to learn from Jesus. He knew Jesus had the answers to life but was afraid of being seen by the other Pharisees.

Let's look at the verses leading up to that famous verse.

"Now there was a man of the Pharisees named Nicodemus, a member of the Jewish ruling council. He came to Jesus at night and said, 'Rabbi, we know you are a teacher who has come from God. For no one could perform the miraculous signs you are doing if God were not with Him.'

In reply Jesus declared, 'I tell you the truth, no one can see the kingdom of God unless he is born again.'

'How can a man be born when he is old?' Nicodemus asked. 'Surely he cannot enter a second time into his mother's womb to be born!'

Jesus answered, 'I tell you the truth, no one can enter the kingdom of God unless he is born of water and spirit. Flesh gives birth to the flesh, but the Spirit gives birth to spirit. You should not be surprised at my saying, "You must be born again." The wind blows wherever it pleases. You hear its sound, but you can not tell where it comes from or where it is going. So it is with everyone born of the Spirit.'

'How can this be?' Nicodemus asked.

'You are Israel's teacher,' said Jesus, 'and do you not understand these things? I tell you the truth, we speak of what we know, and we testify to what we have seen, but still you people do not accept our testimony. I have spoken to you of earthly things and you do not believe; how then will you

believe if I speak of heavenly things? No one has ever gone into heaven except the one who came from heaven - the Son of Man. Just as Moses lifted up the snake in the desert, so the Son of Man must be lifted up, that everyone who believes in Him may have eternal life." John 3:1-15

Obviously Nicodemus did not understand spiritual things. Neither does modern man. Obviously a non believer never will understand spiritual things, but unfortunately it seems that most Christians have even given up trying, and have changed Christianity into something that is a far cry from what God intended it to be. It is hard to fathom but there are now 440 different denominations within Christianity, and although each one of them points to individual scriptures as their basis, most have ended up far afield. The big picture seems to be hidden.

Let's just quickly look at some of the different forms of modern churches that label themselves Christian:

1- There are a myriad of churches that teach that in order to get into heaven we must never sin while we are here on earth, even though no man in history has been able to keep all of the Old Testament commandments other than Jesus.

2- There are the other churches who feel their main duty is to get behind "Christian" causes. Social reform seems to be the requirement to be a good Christian in these churches.

3- There are many that totally concentrate on teaching good, moral values.

4- We have some that stress the fact that no one can be a real Christian unless he possesses "gifts of the Spirit," primarily the speaking of tongues. Otherwise a person is not "Spirit filled" so certainly could not be a complete Christian. Interestingly, although God tells us that some will receive the "gift of tongues," He very plainly shows us that not all will receive each gift when God asks, *"Are all apostles? Are all prophets? Are all teachers? Do all work miracles? Do all have gifts of healing? Do all speak in tongues?"* 1 Corinthians 12:29

5- Some churches stress living in a type of humility.

6- Others stress living in poverty is the needed ingredient.

7- The fastest growing today, and the one that really packs in the crowds, purposefully concentrates on God as a kind of spiritual Santa Claus. Everything in those churches stresses having faith in God for the good life here on earth. The best of the "prosperity" preachers can point to their own Rolls Royces as the proof that they are truly preaching the Gospel. They never even see the fact that not a single one of the Apostles of Jesus ever got "the good life". All lived basically penniless. These prosperity churches obviously overlook what you and I read about how desperately the Apostles lived and how tragically they died. If they do see the fourteen lives and deaths we examined, those church members must think the Apostles lacked the faith needed to have the "good life" here on earth. What an aberration of the true Gospel of Christ.

8- We also have the big worship churches. True Christianity to them only revolves around the "spiritual worship experience." These churches make us believe we can summon the Holy Spirit at exactly 11:15 every Sunday morning by singing with tears on our cheeks. It is uncanny how He always does seem to show up on time. Of course, He leaves as we head to our cars at 12:30. I guess the Holy Spirit has a game to watch.

Worship is wonderful, but not at the expense of *"searching out the matter."*

9- Then we have some who don't believe in the Holy Spirit at all.

10- There are those who talk about missions, like the one in a small Georgia town that we watched spend $600,000 on an organ while millions of their "brothers and sisters" in other countries don't even have a Bible to read.

11- Now we even have churches headed up by gays, because they are "good, loving" people, even when God's Word clearly commands in Leviticus 18:22, *"Do not lie with a man as one does with a woman; that is detestable."* The king James version uses the word "abomination" in place of "detestable."

God even destroyed Sodom and Gomorrah for the homosexual "lifestyle." These modern thinking churches, though, respond that verses like that are Old Testament. They conveniently overlook the fact that God even mentions it over and over in the New Testament as well, with terms like "perversion" such as, *"Men committed indecent acts with other men, and received in themselves the due penalty for their perversion."* Romans 1:27

God goes on to tell us in 1 Corinthians 6:9, years after Jesus was crucified for our sins, *"Do not be deceived: neither the sexually immoral nor idolaters nor adulterers nor male prostitutes nor homosexual offenders ... will inherit the kingdom of God."* The truth is that Jesus even mentions it in a similar list in verse 15 of the very last chapter of the Bible as being one of the things that will keep people out of the kingdom of God. Yet our modern churches embrace homosexual ministers. Unreal!

(Obviously, this is not a politically correct book. That's OK, though, as Jesus Himself was never politically correct. And as to the Father, well, we won't go into the very real "wrath of God.")

12- Unbelievably, we even have had a gigantic number of known child abusers allowed to continue to lead congregations. These sick humans even still demand the respect of the term "Father." Of course, Jesus forbade the term "Father" anyway, when He said in Matthew 23:9. *"And do not call any one on earth 'father,' for you have one Father, and He is in heaven."*

When we consider these pedophile preachers, the old humorous statement, "A few were called, and a lot of others just went," has become extremely serious.

13- We have already mentioned the growing number of churches that teach that Jesus was only a good, moral teacher, when we now know that Jesus never left that option open.

14- And of course, we have the thousands of churches that now pick and choose which scriptures they want to believe.

We could fill many more pages with the different churches that are based on teaching family life, and the ones that revolve totally around healing, and the perfect choir music churches. Of course, we can't forget the churches based on icons, or saints, or traditions, or individual prophetic revelations. And then there are the ones based on self sacrifice, and the political reform churches, and the ones based on being just a friendly gathering place (Those, of course, have super food). We even have churches that base their religion on secular education of their children, and as an off shoot we also have some fabulous sports complex churches.

The list could go on and on. As we said, there are 440 denominations, including 600,000 clergy, and the differences can stretch beyond our imagination. Almost all of them even quote a few scriptures each week to back up the points they want their congregations to focus on that week. Some even are able to "study' an entire chapter of the Bible in the service, again with the hidden agenda of driving home a personal point the "teacher" wants to make. And surprisingly, out of it all, a few people are actually "born again" (In the words of Jesus), and become a part of the "bride" that His Story is all about.

In 1966 Billy Graham made the famous statement, "The harvest is ripest within the church." We can be sure he had no idea just how true that was going to become. Taken as a whole, the modern church has sadly become the church of Laodicia, the last church Jesus wrote a letter to in the book of Revelation.

As you recall, the church of Laodicia represents our church age, The Church of Apostasy. The American heritage Dictionary defines apostasy as "an abandonment of one's religious faith." As we have seen, the Christian church as a whole has obviously slipped into that. It is now the Church of Laodicia, which was one of only two churches of the seven that got no commendation from Jesus at all. The other one that received no commendation was Sardis. Jesus had nothing good to say about either church.

In fact, difficult as it may be to swallow, let's read what Jesus Himself said about our church age. You will recall that Jesus always starts his letters to the seven churches by describing Himself in a manner that points to something about that church that is the root problem in that age. With our church He mentions "Amen," which is the highest form of faith and belief, "faithful and true witness," which we obviously are not, and "God's creation", which we threw out the window when Satan gave us evolution. So brace yourself for His letter to us.

"To the angel of the church in Laodicea write: These are the words of the Amen, the faithful and true witness, the ruler of God's creation. I know your deeds, that you are neither cold nor hot. I wish you were either one or the other! So, because you are lukewarm - neither hot nor cold - I am about to spit you out of my mouth. You say, 'I am rich; I have acquired wealth and do not need a thing.' But you do not realize that you are wretched, pitiful, poor, blind, and naked. I council you to

buy from me gold refined in the fire, so you can become rich; and white clothes to wear, so you can cover your shameful nakedness, and salve to put on your eyes, so you can see.

Those whom I love I rebuke and discipline. So be earnest and repent. Here I am! I stand at the door and knock. If anyone hears my voice and opens the door, I will come in and eat with him, and he with me.

To him who overcomes I will give the right to sit with me on my throne, just as I overcame and sat down with my Father on His throne. He who has an ear, let him hear what the Spirit says to the churches." Revelation 3:14-22

Now, that is a heavy, heavy letter. And it is even more sobering when we realize that it was written directly to you and to me. Jesus dictated that letter to His beloved disciple John while he was on the Isle of Patmos, after He had saved him from death, when John had been lowered head first into the vat of boiling oil. Jesus obviously saw our church age as absolutely pathetic.

Because we do not have the needed total faith and belief, and because we are not faithful and true witnesses of who He really is and what His visit to earth was all about, and because many have even given up belief in God altogether because of the lie of evolution and its lure of non responsibility to God by its outright denial of Him, Jesus said very plainly that He was going to spit our church out of his mouth. Can you imagine Him saying anything worse to us? He obviously loathes what our church has become. And when we look at the prophecies that are soon to be fulfilled, which we will, we will find that He will indeed spit most of us out of His mouth.

On the other hand, He does give us as individuals hope beyond compare. He is still standing at the door, knocking. He still loves us as individuals. He mercifully still wants us as his "other". If we are earnest and repent, which means a complete reversal of mind, and unfalteringly choose Him over Satan and sin, He will still take us as His bride and we will actually sit with Him on His throne. What a phenomenal thought that is. What an incredible opportunity we still have. The choice is pretty simple. We either will be spit out of His mouth, or we will sit with Him on His throne in heaven.

But are there no churches within the church as a whole today that are still true to the Gospel of Christ? Of course there are. There are thousands of individual lay people and church leaders in most denominations who could proudly be named Theophilus, the person to whom Luke addressed both his Gospel and the book of Acts, which means, "one who loves God." These are saints who search out the truly spiritual things of God with no agenda but to find what God wants them to know, and then they apply these things in their own earthly lives. Many of these true Children of God are in constant communications with Him through prayer.

Unfortunately, the average Christian prays less than two minutes a day and the average minister prays only slightly more, at five minutes per day. When we take out the large amounts of time that the true saints pray, it is obvious that a lot of people who call themselves Christians, as well as thousands of church leaders, must not communicate with God at all during a normal day. Spiritual things become very hard to discern for a person who never communicates with the God who is spirit.

As a result our churches are moving more and more away from what God intended. In actuality, the big buzz phrase today in church circles is "people friendly churches." These churches cross all denominational lines. They started in the more traditional church denominations that saw church attendance drastically decline in the 1980's and 1990's. These declines devastated revenue, which unfortunately has become one of the biggest parts of a church's life. As a result, the people friendly church was born; a type of church that would try to offend no one, thereby bringing more people into the pews, along with their donations.

One of the big changes instituted by people friendliness has been the elimination of any talk about the ugly word, sin. Obviously, bringing up a person's sin might make him feel uncomfortable, thus driving him and his billfold away. The second thing that had to be tossed out of the church was the use of the offensive word, blood. Hymn books have actually been rewritten in order to eliminate that terribly offensive word. Now that you and I know what we do, you will understand and find it interesting when we notice that those were the hymns written in the eighteenth and nineteenth centuries by the people of the Mission Church Age, the age that Jesus had not one single complaint about in His letter to the Church at Philadelphia.

In the next chapter we are going to find out that these are two of the main things God wants us to search out in order to fully understand spiritual things. We are going to do this by examining what probably is the most intriguing and important examples of types and shadows in the entire Bible. It will be an utterly fascinating study.

And coming up shortly will be the answer to the question that has haunted mankind since the beginning. For possibly the very first time in print we will be given the true meaning of life. It is amazing that it has thus far been totally overlooked.

By "searching out these matters" the way we are, you and I are combating the problem God described in His statement, *"My people are destroyed from lack of knowledge."* Hosea 4:6

CHAPTER TWENTY-THREE

The Bible, when taken as a whole, is so simple in explaining God's plan, His Story; and yet it is so intricate and complex as to completely deny any human authorship.

We are certainly going to find that to be true as we examine the information in these next chapters. Only God could have laid out what we are now going to delve into.

We ended the last chapter by bringing up the fact that the modern "people friendly" church is trying to completely eliminate any discussion or reference to anything having to do with sin or blood. The truth is that these are the very two things God would want His church to concentrate on. These are the things we must truly understand in order to become the bride that He so longingly desires. These are "spiritual things."

Let's first crystalize our thinking on two facts. First, that "God is spirit." And second, His bride, therefore, must be spirit as well. According to 1 Thessalonians 5:23 you and I are made up of three parts, *"spirit, soul and body."* There is some argument among "deep thinkers" as to whether the soul and spirit are the same. This verse plainly tells us that they are not. However, they obviously are intertwined. The soul consists of those things that are not physical that make us individuals; our thoughts, memories, traits, etc. One of the wonderful truths God explains to us in His Word is that these things will live on. We are told that the real us, *"live in the tent of this body."* 1Pet 1:13

Yes, this body we live in is best described as a tent, and not a house, because it is so very temporary. The real us will live on.

We read in the very first book of the Bible a story about Rachel giving birth to Jacob's youngest son, Benjamin, who would complete the twelve sons that make up the twelve tribes of Israel. *"And it came to pass, as her soul was departing, (for she died) that she called his name Ben-o-ni: but his father called him Benjamin."* Genesis 35:18 (KJV)

The importance of that verse to us in this study is that it is the first place in the Bible that shows that the soul, the individuality of you and I, lives on. That theme is carried out throughout God's Word in such places as in the words of Jesus Himself, *"Do not be afraid of those who kill the body but cannot kill the soul. Rather, be afraid of the One who can destroy both soul and body in hell."* Matthew 10:28

Now, please read slowly the following truths. We need to fully comprehend this information in order to understand much of what the whole of God's Word talks about. It is critical that we get a firm grasp of the "spiritual thing" that God is teaching us. Very few people really understand the entire idea of blood sacrifice and the absolute need for it, but what we are going to cover now will begin to clarify everything. God did not set in motion things in a haphazard manner. He is a God of reason.

Ask anyone what the name Adam means, and we will get the response, "man." In actuality, the Hebrew word for man is "ish." The truth is that Adam is spelled in Hebrew with three letters: The first letter, Aleph, pronounced "ah", actually means "the first." The second letter, Dalet, is pronounced like a "d". The third letter, Mem, sounds like "m". Those last two letters spell "dam", the Hebrew word for "blood." Adam, therefore, really means, "the first blood."

Leviticus 17:11 (KJV) tells us, *"The life of the flesh is in the blood."* That word "life" in Hebrew is "nefesh", which additionally means "soul." A more literal translation actually could be, *"The soul of the flesh is in the blood."* This will become extremely important as we *"search out the matter."*

Now, let's put some pieces together. We must remember that God has staked the proof of his very existence on the fact that every single one of His prophecies comes to pass. God's very first prophecy, and maybe the most important foretelling of all, was *"You are free to eat from any tree in the garden; but you must not eat from the tree of the knowledge of good and evil, for when you eat of it you will surely die."* Genesis 2:16-17

This prophecy stated clearly that if His creation, His "other," experienced sin, he would surely die. Let's remember those prophetic words.

The story of Adam and Eve is not a children's Sunday School story. The story of Adam and Eve sets the stage for His Story. In fact, immediately following this very first prophecy in the Bible, *"You will surely die,"* God began to make known His innermost motives as He inserts in His Word the first of hundreds and hundreds of scriptures dealing with marriage, the "shadow" of things to come between Himself and His "other."

We read just six verses later, in Genesis 2:24, *"For this reason a man will leave his father and mother and be united* to *his wife, and they will become one flesh."* The story goes on in the next verse to say, *"The man and his wife were both naked, and they felt no shame."* Sin had not yet been manifested.

You and I now understand, though, that it was imperative for sin to exist in order for God's love creation to have another possible suitor besides God. For God to eventually receive true love from the "other" there had to be the real possibility that the "other" could choose someone else. The response to the love call could not be coerced. If Satan was to be a viable alternative to God as a suitor, man had to possess a nature that was not totally repulsed by sin, the very being of Satan.

The story continues, of course, by mankind eating the forbidden fruit and manifesting the first sin. The verse after they both ate it tells us, *"Then the eyes of both of them were opened, and they realized they were naked; so they sewed fig leaves together and made coverings for themselves."* Isn't it interesting that God showed us in this very first story that mankind would somehow hope that he could cover up sin all by himself, thus negating the *"You will surely die"* prophecy? Much of the Bible is devoted to God mercifully teaching man that this is impossible. Man can not cover the sin nature by himself. The entire Law and commandments in the Old Testament were put into place partially for that reason, to teach us that on our own we can not succeed in covering the sin that is in us. It requires divine assistance. Only God can do it for us.

Adam and Eve tried to hide from God, as many of us do, but of course this was impossible, too. After the Lord confronted them and discussed with them what they had done, and the results that would befall both them and Satan, an often minimized verse is inserted that understates the love that God has for His object of affection, *"The Lord God made garments of skin for Adam and his wife and clothed them."* Genesis 3:21

That compassionate act was in itself a shadow, a foretelling that God Himself would make the covering for the sin that He had been forced to allow into mankind. Moreover, in that act God described that the ultimate covering would be done through a death. By using the skin of an animal, God instituted the sacrificial substitution necessary for mankind. An animal was slain in order to give of its skin for the covering of man's sin.

It was the first death mankind had witnessed. It was the first shedding of blood. We are not told the details, but the odds are that it was a lamb. The other missing detail in the Biblical account of that first sacrificial act was that God probably wept.

God knew that this was the picture of what was to come, that part of Himself, the Son part, would one day be that innocent lamb, *"The lamb slain from the creation of the world."* Revelation 13:8

God knew that the time would painfully come when, *"For God so loved the world, that He gave His one and only Son, that whoever believes in Him shall not perish, but have eternal life."* John 3:16

CHAPTER TWENTY-FOUR

God, being a totally just God, and knowing that since He was the One who put the sin nature in mankind in the first place, in order to allow man to have honest to goodness free will, knew that in order to be just, He must be the One to eventually pay the price necessary to remove it, once man had exercised his free will and made the choice to return God's love.

Being a perfect God, He also knew that He must give Satan intelligence, in order for the alternative suitor to be given any chance to be chosen. Once again, God did not want the ultimate choice we make to be a manipulated one. He gave us free will.

With this intelligence, Satan knew that the only chance he ultimately would have for survival would be to stop the offspring of the woman who was foretold to come and crush his head. We have already seen a few cases of how he tried to do that, such as with the attempted murder in the womb of Jacob by his twin brother Esau, and the attempted killing of Jesus Himself by means of the slaughter of the baby boys by King Herod.

Satan also knew, from witnessing the act of the covering of mankind's evidence of sin by the initial sacrifice in the garden, that it would be prudent of him to try to stop the "shadow" of the act of sacrifices that were being made by mankind throughout Old Testament history. One such attempt can be seen in the account of Moses trying to talk Pharaoh into letting the Israelites go. Just as we have already looked at a few "types" of Jesus in the Old testament, in Pharaoh we see a Biblical "type" of Satan.

Much of the Moses's and Pharaoh's back and forth arguing between each plague had to do with whether or not the Pharaoh would allow the people to take animals with them that could be used for sacrifices, and in what manner he might allow it. In one place in the story the Pharaoh seems to relent with the sacrifice part, but says they must perform the sacrifices there in Egypt.

It is very interesting to note that Moses' response was, *"We must make a three day journey into the desert to offer sacrifices to the Lord our God, as He commands us."* Exodus 8:27

There is another shadow of the crucifiction of Jesus that had occurred earlier when Abraham was told to take his son, Isaac, and offer him for a sacrifice. In that story, which we will look at later, Genesis 22:4 says of Abraham as he and the boy were traveling to do the Lord's will, *"On the third day Abraham looked up and saw the place in the distance."* We mention this only to show how detailed the pictures are of the future events they depict. Obviously, Jesus was three days in the grave, as Jonah was three days in the belly of the fish. The intricacy of the similar types and shadows depicted in the thirty nine Old Testament books, written over a thousand year period, foretelling an event the men God used to write down His words could not even guess at, once again denies human authorship. Here for example, with Moses, Abraham, and Jonah, we see the very same shadow of the three days Jesus would spend traveling into hell itself.

Getting back to Pharaoh, finally, before the last plague, which is itself the plague of the death of the firstborn, we read, *"Then Pharaoh summoned Moses and said, 'Go, worship the Lord. Even your women and children may go with you; only leave your flocks and herds behind."* Exodus 10:24

Satan's very last defiance was to try to stop the needed sacrificial animals from going with the people. He must have felt that if he could stop the shadows, maybe he could somehow stop the prophesied coming event that would secure his demise.

"But Moses said, 'You must allow us to have sacrifices and burnt offerings to present to the Lord our God. Our livestock too must go with us; not a hoof is to be left behind." Ex. 10:25

Satan knew the importance of the blood sacrifices in spiritual things, but our modern "people friendly" churches don't want them discussed at all. Could it be that Satan is still trying to make a last ditch effort for his survival? Remember, his only semblance of victory could only be accomplished by our destruction, and God said, *"My people are destroyed from lack of knowledge."* Hosea 4:6

As we know, the Israelites left Egypt, which typifies the world, when Pharaoh could not stand up against the plague of the death of the firstborn. This too, obviously, was a shadow showing that Satan would not be able to withstand the result of the death of The Firstborn. The types and shadows abound throughout the Old Testament as forms of fulfilled prophecy. They are to be found in virtually every historical event, every chapter in His Story, and every chapter of God's Word.

As the Hebrew people entered their forty year trek through the wilderness, spread out by tribe, in the manner God directed, a multimillion person human cross, they were also given instructions by God for what may well be the most important plan of types and shadows He had ever laid out. We will be truly amazed at what we will examine in these instructions.

Before we do, though, we need to briefly study one other type and shadow story that had occurred earlier in order to make a few points. Please remember that when we say "type and shadow story", the events always actually happened. These are not just stories that God dictated to people. We lose the incredible truth that God actively participated in historical events if we somehow just look at these as stories. Yes, they do illustrate what was to come, but God supernaturally influenced actual historical events to give us these pictures of future events that were to happen. He did not create us and then walk away.

We alluded to this incident earlier when we mentioned Abraham being told to sacrifice his son. Let's now read the actual, fascinating story, keeping our eyes open for the shadows of the main event that was to come.

"Some time later God tested Abraham. He said to him, 'Abraham!'

'Here I am,' he responded.

Then God said, 'Take your son, your only son, Isaac, whom you love, and go to the region of Moriah. Sacrifice him there as a burnt offering on one of the mountains I will tell you about.'

Early the next morning Abraham got up and saddled his donkey. He took with him two of his servants and his son Isaac.

When he had cut enough wood for the burnt offering, he set out for the place God had told him about. On the third day Abraham looked up and saw the place in a distance. He said to his servants, 'Stay here with the donkey while I and the boy go over there. We will worship and then we will come back to you.'

Abraham took the wood for the burnt offering and placed it on his son Isaac, and he himself carried the fire and the knife. As the two of them went on together, Isaac spoke up and said to his father Abraham, 'Father?'

'Yes, my son?' Abraham replied.

'The fire and wood are here,' Isaac said, 'but where is the lamb for the burnt offering?'

Abraham answered, 'God himself will provide the lamb for the burnt offering, my son.' And the two of them went on together.

When they reached the place God had told him about, Abraham built an altar there and arranged the wood on it. He bound his son Isaac and laid him on the altar, on top of the wood. Then he reached out his hand and took the knife to slay his son. But the angel of the Lord called out to him from heaven, 'Abraham, Abraham!'

'Here I am,' he replied.

Do not lay a hand on the boy,' he said. 'Do not do anything to him. Now I know that you fear God, because you have not withheld from me your son, your only son.'

Abraham looked up and there in a thicket he saw a ram, caught by its horns. He went over and took the ram and sacrificed it as a burnt offering instead of his son. So Abraham called the place The Lord Will Provide. And to this day it is said, 'On the mountain of the Lord it will be provided.'

The angel of the Lord called to Abraham from heaven a second time and said,'I swear by myself, declares the Lord, that because you have done this and have not withheld your son, your only son, I will surely bless you and make your descendants as numerous as the stars in the sky and as the sand on the seashore. Your descendants will take possession of the cities of their enemies, and through your offspring all nations on earth will be blessed, because you have obeyed me." Genesis 22:1-18

There obviously are numerous similarities between this story and the crucifiction of Jesus. Since our purpose in relating this episode was not to do a verse by verse comparison, we will just list ten of the similarities along with the verse numbers. Hopefully you will take your own Bible and study them in depth for yourself. Remember, *"to search out a matter is the glory of kings."* Proverbs 25:2

Similarity	Isaac	Jesus
1 - Only begotten Son	Genesis 22:2	John 3:16
2 - Offered on a mountain, hill	Genesis 22:2	Matt 27:33
3 - Took donkey to sacrifice	Genesis 22:3	Mark 15:27
4 - Two men went with him	Genesis 22:3	Luke 23:33
5 - Three day journey	Genesis 22:4	1 Cor 15:4
6 - Son carried wood up hill	Genesis 22:6	John 19:17
7 - God provide the lamb	Genesis 22:8	John 1:29
8 - Son was offered on wood	Genesis 22:9	Luke 23:33
9 - Ram in thicket of thorns	Genesis 22:13	John 19:2
10- The seed would multiply	Genesis 22:17	Isaiah 53:10

Neither Abraham nor Isaac as they experienced this event, nor Moses as he later chronicled it, could possibly have understood the real significance of these ten details. They could not see into the future and see the ultimate sacrifice, Jesus Christ, the Son of God. To those three, and to all the readers of the account during Old Testament times, the episode was surely of utmost importance, but only in so far as the faith of Abraham resulted in the promise given by God to bless his offspring.

The point we need to understand is that God's going to the trouble to orchestrate all of those details, and then to have them written down, was solely for our benefit. Prior to the actual death and resurrection of Jesus, no human could have benefitted by such an elaborate shadow of things to come. Additionally, the early church did not need it because they were already absolutely convinced that God existed, the Bible was his communication to us and that Jesus was the true Son of God, come down from heaven as their Savior.

No, these prophecies in the form of types and shadows were primarily for you, for me, and for the debaters. We are the ones who can benefit from their existence. We are the ones who needed convincing that God is real, His Word is exactly that, and Jesus is the only way to eternal life. These types are for us.

Chapter Twenty-Five

The Biblical picture that may well be the most important of the many types and shadows God gave us to explain spiritual things is the tabernacle. God obviously feels that it is so important that He actually discussed it in fifty chapters of His Word.

The very first mention of the tabernacle was given by God to Moses on Mt. Sinai in Exodus 25:8 after the Israelites had walked away from their 400 year bondage to the Pharaohs.

God told Moses, *"Then have them make a sanctuary for Me, and I will dwell among them. Make this tabernacle and all its furnishings exactly like the pattern I will show you."* The word "pattern" in that scripture is the Hebrew word, "tupos", from which we get our word, "type."

God then proceeded to take an inordinate amount of space, 225 verses, to describe in the minutest of detail exactly how the tabernacle was to be constructed and laid out. We are not exaggerating at all. God even gave instructions as to the color of thread to be used in weaving the different parts, the type of wood to be used in the furniture, the position of everything, even the ingredients in the incense to be burned.

As you can imagine from our study so far, every single material is a type or shadow. It would take a book larger than this one to cover every minute part, so we won't even attempt it here. For example, though, the wood that had to be used was acacia, which is a very thorny tree that derives its name from the Hebrew root word for "to pierce." Obviously that is a shadow of the crown of thorns Jesus would later have pushed into his skull.

For now, though, we will just examine an overview of the tabernacle. It was a rectangle of 150 feet by 75 feet. The first thing one would encounter when he entered was the altar for the sacrifices (Crucifixion). Next came the laver, a brass basin for washing (Repentance). Next came the entrance into a big tent, the first half of which was the Holy Place, which consisted of a lampstand with seven candles (The seven churches in Revelation we studied), a table of shewbread (Jesus, the bread of life), and an altar of incense (the prayers of the saints).

In the back part of the tent, walled off with a very thick *"curtain of blue, purple and scarlet yarn and finely twisted linen, with cherubim worked into it by a skilled craftsman."* Exodus 26:31, was the Most Holy Place, or Holy of Holies, which contained the Ark of the Covenant. Inside the Ark were the two unbroken tablets of the Ten Commandments (Jesus, the only One who did not sin), a jar of manna (Jesus, the bread of life), and the rod that budded after it was dead (The resurrection of Jesus) that had been used by Aaron, the brother of Moses and the first high priest. On top of the ark was the golden "atonement" covering with two cherubim facing each other.

This area, or covering, is called the Mercy Seat.

"There, above the cover between the two cherubim that are over the ark of the testimony, I will meet with you and give you all my commands for the Israelites." Exodus 25:22. It was in the Holy of Holies that God would actually dwell. It was only there that He would commune with man, and at that, only with the ceremonially clean High Priest once a year.

You and I can now understand that because God had put a sin nature in mankind, in order for us to have free will, God could no longer have direct contact with His children that He loved. We must understand that God is totally Holy. He can not have sin in His presence any more than light and darkness can coexist. By giving mankind the sin that was necessitated by free will, God effectively walled Himself away from us. This sad reality had to happen in order to achieve the desired eternal end, a bride who had truly chosen to love God.

Fortunately that necessary separation of God from man that began when mankind first manifested sin in the garden, ended the moment Jesus died on the cross, for we read, *"With a loud cry, Jesus breathed His last. The curtain of the temple was torn in two from top to bottom."* Mark 15:37-38

In the Old Testament days, however, God had to remain separated from man. As we said, the only person who could communicate with God was the ceremonially clean High Priest, and then only on the Day of Atonement, best understood by breaking the word down into "at one ment." That day would later become known as Yom Kippur, the Jewish day of repentance, and the holiest and most solemn day of the year.

Two chapters back we learned that God told us that the life, or soul, of the flesh is in the blood. God went on to tell us in that same scripture, *"and I have given it to you to make atonement for yourselves on the altar; it is the blood that makes atonement for one's life."* Leviticus 17:11

Once the tabernacle had been constructed exactly as He told them, God laid out instructions as to how the Israelites were to substitute an animal's blood for their own blood on the Day of Atonement. There were actually to be three animals involved, a bull and two goats.

"Aaron is to offer the bull for his own sin offering to make atonement for himself and his household. Then he is to take the two goats and present them before the Lord at the entrance to the Tent of Meeting. He is to cast lots for the two goats - one lot for the Lord and the other for the scapegoat. Aaron is to bring the goat whose lot falls to the Lord and sacrifice it for a sin offering. But the goat chosen by lot as the scapegoat shall be presented alive before the Lord to be used for making atonement by sending it into the desert as a scapegoat." Leviticus 16:6-10

The word "scapegoat", by the way, was first coined by William Tyndale when he combined "escape goat" into "scapegoat" in 1530 AD, when he translated the first English Bible from the Latin Vulgate. At any rate, all three animals mentioned above were types of Jesus. There has been some erroneous teaching that the scapegoat represents Satan; however, Satan can obviously never take away the sin nature from man. The confusion occurred because the original Hebrew describing the scapegoat says "the other goat for Azazel." "Azazel" literally means, "the one to be sent away"; however, someone noticed Satan referred to as Azazel in The Book of Enoch, which is not even in God's Word. The Book of Enoch was actually referring to Satan also as "one to be sent away."

God goes on with his instructions by saying that after the bull is killed for the sins of the High Priest, *"He is to take some of the bull's blood and with his finger sprinkle it on the front of the atonement cover; then he shall sprinkle some of it with his finger seven times before the atonement cover.*

He shall then slaughter the goat for the sin offering for the people and take its blood behind the curtain and do with it as he did with the bull's blood: He shall sprinkle it on the atonement cover and in front of it." Leviticus 16:14-15

Lest we start wondering why all this killing and bloodshed was necessary, let's remember that God's first prophecy was that once man's sin nature was manifested, *"You shall surely die."*

And since the life and the soul *"is in the blood,"* man's own blood, or adequate substitutionary blood, must be shed. This entire shadow showed that God had already devised the plan *"from the foundation of the world"* to fulfill the prophecy and still allow us to live. We need also to realize that the death referred to in the prophecy was our spiritual death. The death we experience on earth is itself a shadow of the more important and devastating spiritual death. Earthly death is only a transition from our fleshly selves to our spiritual selves, our real selves.

God's instruction continued, after the sacrifice of the bull and the goat, and after the blood of both had been presented to God at the Mercy Seat and found acceptable to substitute for the needed death of both the priest and the people, *"He shall take some of the bull's blood and some of the goats blood and put it on all the horns of the altar. He shall sprinkle some of the blood on it with his finger seven times to cleanse it and to consecrate it from the uncleanness of the Israelites."* Leviticus 16:18-19

The above act finalized the acceptance of the substitutions for dying, which allowed for the forgiveness of any prior sins and the sending of them away. Therefore, God then said, *"He shall bring forward the live goat. He is to lay both hands on the head of the live goat and confess over it all the wickedness and rebellion of the Israelites - all their sins - and put them on the goat's head. He shall send the goat away into the desert. ... The goat will carry on itself all their sins to a solitary place."* Leviticus 16:20-22

As we said, all three of these animals represented Jesus and what was accomplished on the cross. His death was first of all for himself, because, since He was fully human, He had to have the sin nature inside Him. Some "scholars" argue that point, referring to His divinity, but Hebrews 4:15 says very clearly about Jesus, *"we have one who has been tempted in every way, just as we are, yet was without sin."* Had there been no sin nature in Him, He could not have been tempted. In fact, to put an end to that debate God tells us in James 1:13, *"God cannot be tempted by evil."* Therefore, since Jesus was tempted, the humanity of Jesus, with its necessary sin nature, had to die. The shadow of the bull's death represented that necessary death.

The second animal, the sacrificed goat which was God's lot, was a shadow of the death of Jesus that was a completely acceptable substitution for us.

The sin in mankind could in no way be brought into the presence of God, just as darkness could not come into the presence of light. God, being Holy could not allow sin to be brought to the Mercy Seat. Jesus, however, took all of mankind's sin, for we read in 2 Corinthians 5:21, *"God made Him who had no sin to be sin for us."* His crucifiction, therefore, like the scapegoat, took our sins, *"as far as the east is from the west, so far has He removed our transgressions from us."* Psalm 103:12

The sacrificial system during Old Testament times was only temporarily in place until God knew that the timing was right for Him to become the needed substitution Himself, in the form of Jesus. As we have seen, Jesus said in John 14:9, *"Anyone who has seen me has seen the Father."* God prophesied the punishment with, *"You shall surely die,"* but He also told us in Romans 6:23, *"For the wages of sin is death, but the gift of God is eternal life in Christ Jesus our Lord."* God put sin in man, but He Himself paid the price to remove it.

The commandments were put into place to prove that no man could keep them. No man but Jesus could live without sin. Once that proof was established over a fifteen hundred year period, God could provide the only answer. Until the abysmal failure of man to redeem himself was made obvious, God provided the temporary covering in the form of animal sacrifice. What some people have looked at as meaningless was in reality God's long-suffering mercy. These are the spiritual things God wants us to search out and understand.

Romans 3:21-26 has been agreed on by many as the one section in God's Word that best describes all of the Bible.

Those verses tell us, *"But now, a righteousness from God, apart from the law, has been made known, to which the Law and the prophets testify. This righteousness from God comes through faith in Jesus Christ to all who believe. There is no difference, for all have sinned and fall short of the glory of God, and are justified freely by His grace through the redemption that came by Christ Jesus. God presented him as a sacrifice of atonement, through faith in His blood. He did this to demonstrate His justice, because in His forbearance He had left the sins committed beforehand unpunished - He did it to demonstrate His justice at the present time, so as to be just and the One who justifies those who have faith in Jesus."*

In the middle of those verses we see Jesus described as a *"sacrifice of atonement."* Obviously He was. The Greek word that is translated there, though, is Hilasterion. That word is only used one other place in the entire New Testament. We find it in Hebrews 9:5, describing the tabernacle, *"Above the ark were the cherubim of the Glory, overshadowing the atonement cover."*

The Greek word used for atonement cover, the Mercy Seat, is the same word, "Hilasterion." Yes, Jesus was the sacrifice of atonement, but He is now the Mercy Seat in the true heavenly tabernacle. You and I do not have to offer blood at this new Mercy seat. We only need offer the fact that we have made our choice, and that our choice is Him. We want to be His bride.

We'll close this mini study of the tabernacle by reading a little more from the New testament. *"The law requires that nearly everything be cleansed with blood, and without the shedding of blood there is no forgiveness.*

It was necessary, then, for the copies of the heavenly things to be purified with these sacrifices, but the heavenly things themselves with better sacrifices than these. For Christ did not enter a man made sanctuary that was only a copy of the true one; He entered heaven itself, now to appear for us in God's presence. Nor did He enter heaven to offer himself again and again, the way the high priest enters the Most Holy Place every year with blood that is not his own. Then Christ would have had to suffer many times since the creation of the world. But now He has appeared once for all at the end of the ages to do away with sin by the sacrifice of Himself. Just as man is destined to die once, and after that to face judgement, so Christ was sacrificed once to take away the sins of many people; and He will appear a second time, not to bear sin, but to bring salvation to those who are waiting for Him." Hebrews 9:22-28

CHAPTER TWENTY-SIX

When we were in school we learned very quickly that the things our teachers mentioned over and over were probably the things that were the most important. They were the things that we would probably find on the test. The same is true with God.

We saw that there are an unbelievable fifty chapters devoted in God's Word to the topic of the tabernacle, so quite obviously He feels that to be extremely important for us to understand completely. By the same token, there are at least 272 places in the Bible that mention the word, blood. Think about that, a whopping 272 times God wanted our attention directed to an understanding of the importance of blood in spiritual matters.

It might be prudent for us to take one more look at this spiritually important subject. Maybe we should find out why Satan, through his new "people friendly" church program, is trying to keep us from ever even mentioning it. Why is it so important a subject that Satan has gone to the trouble of even having the word, blood, removed from old, traditional hymns.

In chapters back we looked at some astronomical odds against random chance having ever occurred. With blood, we can far surpass any figure we have thus far talked about. On July 12, 1997, Dr. David Humphreys, of McMaster University, gave a speech at the University of Waterloo in Canada. The title of the speech was "Evidence for a Creator." In the speech, Dr. Humphreys brought up the fact that the hemoglobin molecule in our blood is made up of twenty amino acids. These acids are found elsewhere in nature and can be isolated.

Using simple mathematical probability, Dr. Humphrey showed that these twenty amino acids can be arranged by chance into combinations totaling ten to the 650th power. With all of these possible combinations, however, there is only one correct combination for the complex hemoglobin molecule that is essential for the blood system, and thus for life. The odds, then, for one hemoglobin mol-

ecule to ever form by random chance is One in 10000000000000000
00000000000000000000000000000000000000000000000000000000000
00000000000000000000000000000000000000000000000000000000000
00000000000000000000000000000000000000000000000000000000000
00000000000000000000000000000000000000000000000000000000000
00000000000000000000000000000000000000000000000000000000000
00000000000000000000000000000000000000000000000000000000000
00000000000000000000000000000000000000000000000000000000000
00000000000000000000000000000000000000000000000000000000000
00000000000000000000000000000000000000000000000000000000000
00000000000000000000000000000000000000000000000000000000000
00000000000000000000000000000000000000000000000000000000.

We did not even bother to put commas where they should be because there obviously is not a name for such a figure. Dr. Humphreys went even further and showed that if we allow for a thousand combinations to be made every second, there could only be ten to the 67 power of sequences in five billion years, his estimate of the age of our earth. Obviously we would need about fifty billion years to go through all of the sequences possible. Granted, random chance says that the first molecule could have been formed by chance early on, but what about the second, and the third, etc., etc. Dr. Humphreys once again very convincingly ended that ridiculous evolution debate that you and I discussed earlier.

The silliness of the theory of evolution, however, is not the reason we brought up Dr. Humphreys' speech. We have here a pretty good clue of the importance of blood to God. Remember what we learned in Leviticus 17:11, *"The life of the flesh is in the blood,"* and that Hebrew word for life, nefesh, also means soul. Our entire spiritual being is mysteriously linked to our blood. That critical verse went on to say that *"it is the blood that makes atonement for the soul."*

Since seven is God's favorite number, let's look at six more things in addition to <u>atonement</u> that the blood does. Acts 20:28 tells us, *"Be shepherds of the church of God, which He bought with His own blood,"* so obviously the blood <u>purchased</u> us.

Colossians 1:19-20 says of Jesus, *"For God was pleased to have all his fullness dwell in him, and through Him to reconcile to himself all things, whether things on earth or things in heaven, by making peace through His blood, shed on the cross."* The blood of Jesus, therefore, made <u>peace</u> between God and us.

The blood <u>purifies</u> us, for we read, *"the blood of Jesus purifies us from all sin."* 1 John 1:7

Additionally, in Revelation 5:9 we are able to see Jesus *"redeemed us to God by the blood,"* so the blood was able to <u>redeem</u>.

The word <u>justified</u> means that God now can look at us as if we are "just" like Jesus. The blood of Jesus is what had the ability to do that for us, as we read *"we have now been justified by His blood."* Romans 5:9

And the number seven thing can be found in Hebrews 13:12. The King James Version of that verse says, *"Wherefore Jesus also, that He might sanctify the people with His own blood, suffered without the gate."* So number seven is that wonderfully religious word, <u>sanctify</u>. The Greek word originally used in that verse is "hagios", which was actually better translated in the NIV version of the Bible with, *"And so Jesus also suffered outside the city gate to make the people holy through his own blood."* The blood, therefore, had the power to make you and me <u>holy</u> in the sight of God. Incredible!

In the beginning of this book we said that the existence of God did not need to be taken on faith, because He proved His very existence through His fulfilled prophecies. We did, though, make the statement that there was one important thing that we did need to take on faith. That one important thing is whether the blood of Jesus was actually sufficient as far as the Father was concerned.

Since we now know that the Bible is God's Word, the way He communicated with us, the above seven scriptures and many, many more like them, assure us fully that we can not only have-faith that when Jesus presented His own blood at the real Mercy Seat (the hilasterion) in heaven, the Father accepted it as the for-ever acceptable substitution for our own sin tainted blood, but we can go beyond faith to the level of absolute knowledge. In other words, we not only can have faith, but we can now know without a shadow of a doubt that the shed blood of Jesus at Calvary was more than enough to take away the sin in us, so that if we choose Him, we will be an acceptable bride.

As we saw, the Age of Missions of the church (1730 to 1900), was written to without any complaint whatsoever by Jesus Himself in the very last book of the Bible, in His letter to the Church of Philadelphia. What the saints who were a part of that church age believed, and how they acted, should be a model for us today. One of those Godly people was a man named Lewis E. Jones, who was inspired to write a song during a camp meeting in Mountain Lake park, Maryland.

The words of that song have been sung millions of times since that memorable night. Satan wants them gone. We might be well served to read the third stanza and the refrain:

Would you be whiter, much whiter than snow?
There's power in the blood, power in the blood.
Sin stains are lost in its life giving flow.
There's wonderful power in the blood.

There is power, power, wonder working power
In the blood of the lamb.
There is power, power, wonder working power
In the precious blood of the lamb.

Does that song mean that there were some magical qualities in the blood of Jesus that gave it special power over any one else's blood? No, the quality that made it so powerful was that it belonged to the only person who ever lived a totally sinless life.

As we recall from reading Hebrews 4:15, *"We have one* (Jesus) *who has been tempted in every way, just as we are - yet was without sin."*

It was the sinless life that Jesus lived that gave his shed blood the power to do the two things that were necessary for us to become the "other" for God. Only the blood of the sinless Lamb of God could be acceptable as a substitute for mankind's punishment that was made necessary by the very first prophecy, *"You shall surely die."* And only the shed blood of the only sinless person ever, could send our past sins and future repented sins *"as far away as the east is from the west,"* as was pictured in the scapegoat being sent into the wilderness.

With those two necessities accomplished the remaining piece to the puzzle was put on each of us individually in the choice we made. As the Old Testament is chock full of types and shadows about the coming person and life of the Messiah, the New Testament is also full of types and shadows of our future.

Two of the most obvious, however, that to our knowledge have never been never taught about or put in print, are the "type" and "shadow"seen at the crucifiction. We all know the story, *"Two other men, both criminals, were also led out with Him to be executed. When they came to the place called the Skull, there they crucified Him, along with the criminals - one on His right, the other on His left."* Luke 23:32-33

Those two criminals were a "type" of you and me. And the "shadow" of our future is made even clearer as the story unfolds.

"One of the criminals who hung there hurled insults at Him: 'Aren't you the Christ? Save yourself and us!'

But the other criminal rebuked him. 'Don't you fear God,' he said, 'since you are under the same sentence? We are punished justly, for we are getting what our deeds deserve. But this man has done nothing wrong.'

Then he said, 'Jesus, remember me when you come into your kingdom.'

Jesus answered him, 'I tell you the truth, today you will be with me in paradise." Luke 23:36-43

Do you see clearly the shadow of the future? Some people will obviously reject Jesus and their death will be complete like the first thief's was. Some, however, will acknowledge their sins and repent, and then put their faith in Jesus for their eternal lives like the second thief did. The last group will hear, *"today you will be with me in paradise."*

I have refrained thus far from inserting anything personal in this book because this did not seem like the place for any personal testimony. My wife has even very wisely reminded me of that fact. I will say, however, that I could fill another entire book with the supernatural occurrences that have happened with the writing of virtually every chapter.

There was one thing that happened that I feel you should be aware of. One verse that I had wanted to include in the book seemed to mysteriously elude me for weeks on end. I knew it was in the Bible, but try as I might, I could not find it. For weeks I used everything at my disposal to try to find the verse, but to no avail. Finally I gave up, thinking that maybe I was somehow mistaken and it didn't really exist at all.

That night I went to bed dog tired. I woke up about an hour later and felt that I was *supposed* to get up and turn on the TV. This was the very last thing in the world I wanted to do and I even grumbled about it as I stumbled blurry eyed into our den to obey this *nudge*. I turned on the TV just as an old black and white war movie ended. I didn't even sit down. I just stood there in front of the TV set as the credits of the actors rolled on and on. All I could think of was my cozy bed. Finally, the credits quit rolling and plain as day on the TV screen were the words I had searched in vain for, and had given up ever finding,

"My people are destroyed from lack of knowledge." Hosea 4:6

I tell that story because I believe it to be so important for you to know how important I believe God thinks that statement really is. His bride is being *"destroyed from lack of knowledge."*

You and I have seen enough types and shadows in our study so far to know without any doubt that they always come true. And just as the shadow of the cross moving across the desert toward Jerusalem culminated in the real wooden cross, and just as the type of the brazen serpent on the pole that God told Moses to erect eventually became fact when God made Jesus *"who had no sin to be sin for us."* 2 Corinthians 5:21, we can know for a certainty that the future for each of us will take the form of one of the shadows of the two thieves that were crucified along with Jesus.

For any person who now possesses that knowledge to still choose the complete destruction of the first thief, instead of choosing to be in paradise with both the second thief and Jesus, would be utterly ludicrous. Of course, we still do have free will. You and I can choose to be whichever thief we want; however, there is no third choice. We have only two options. And, there is no guarantee of a tomorrow. This minute is decision time. Putting off a choice is making a choice, and it is the wrong one.

Assuming we both made the correct choice, we will now be looking at what God tells us is coming next, both on the earth, and in heaven. In the next chapter we will actually put in words the meaning of life. After that we will examine in some detail our personal futures, as well as the future of mankind as a whole. Along the way we will meet the real life "Indiana Jones" in his quest for the Ark of the Covenant, and discover what he has found that could have real implications for our immediate futures here on earth. Exciting reading is right ahead.

PART FIVE

PART FIVE

CHAPTER TWENTY-SEVEN

There is a book in the Old Testament that seldom is talked about the way it should be. It is a small book that most ministers only bring out of the closet on Mothers' Day. The book we are referring to is the lovely, four chapter book of Ruth. It is a simple little heartwarming story of a man from Bethlehem in Judah, named Elimelech, and his wife Naomi. A famine came to the land so the couple took their two sons and moved to Moab, a land in which food was still available,

The family lived there even after Elimelech died and the two sons married Moabite women, Orpah and Ruth. Then both sons died and all three women find themselves as widows. Later, when they learned that the famine in Judah was over, *"Naomi and her two daughters-in-law prepared to return home from there."* Ruth 1:6

As they start the journey, *"Naomi said to her two daughters-in-law, 'Go back, each of you, to your mother's home. May the Lord show kindness to you, as you have shown to your dead and to me. May the Lord grant that each of you will find rest in the home of another husband."* Ruth 1:8-9

This is when the story really gets all warm and fuzzy. Naomi gives them more reasons for staying in Moab. *"At this they wept again. Then Orpah kissed her mother-in-law good-by, but Ruth clung to her."* Ruth 1:14

This brings the words by Ruth that are used in churches in every town on Mothers' Day, *"Where you go I will go, and where you stay I will stay. Your people will be my people and your God my God. Where you die I will die, and there I will be buried. May the Lord deal with me ever so severely, if anything but death separates you and me."* Ruth 1 16-17

It is a touching scene, and certainly makes for a nice, loving Mothers's Day message, but that is not at all why God put the Book of Ruth in His Word. It is a fabulous message, though, for our "people friendly" church environment. However, God wants us to *"search out the matter"* much deeper, for when we do we find a message that is even more heartwarming and wonderfully eternal.

The story goes on as Naomi and Ruth begin living in Bethlehem as the destitute widows that they truly are. With no means for support, Ruth says to Naomi, *"Let me go to the fields and pick up the leftover grain behind anyone in whose eyes I find favor."*

"Naomi said to her, 'Go ahead my daughter.' So she went out and began to glean in the fields behind the harvesters. As it turned out, she found herself working in a field belonging to Boaz, who was from the clan of Elimelech." Ruth 2:2-3

Boaz takes kindly to her and at one point even tells her, *"Come over here. Have some bread and dip it in wine vinegar."*

Things progress to the point that Naomi instructs Ruth to, *"Wash and perfume yourself and put on your best clothes. ... When he lies down, note the place where he is lying. Then go and uncover his feet and lie down. He will tell you what to do."* Ruth 3:3-4

While Boaz was asleep, *"Ruth approached quietly, uncovered his feet and lay down. In the middle of the night something startled the man, and he turned and discovered a woman lying at his feet.*

'Who are you?' he asked.

'I am your servant Ruth,' she said. 'Spread the corner of your garment over me, since you are a kinsman-redeemer." Ruth 3:7-9

It was the custom at that time for a relative of a deceased kinsman to be able to redeem the deceased man's property from his widow and marry the widow, assuming he is willing and can pay the price, *"in order to maintain the name of the dead with the property."* Ruth 4:5

Boaz was willing, but there was a nearer kinsman redeemer than Boaz. The story ends, however, with the first kinsman redeemer being unable to be the redeemer, so Boaz pays the price and is also willing to marry Ruth. The story has a happy ending as Boaz becomes the kinsman redeemer and Ruth's husband. Their grandson turns out to be King David.

Virtually every verse in the Book of Ruth is a type or shadow of someone or something to come. Since we saw several chapters ago that Biblical names have meanings, let's start to search out the matter there. Elimelech means "My God is King," and Naomi means "my joy." Obviously Israel's God was King, and we read about Israel in Zephaniah 3:17, *"The Lord thy God in the midst of thee is mighty; He will save, He will rejoice over thee with joy, he will rest in his love, He will joy over thee with singing."* (KJV). Naomi represents Israel.

Orpah means hard of neck. We can find the term, stiff necked, throughout God's Word and it always means someone who won't turn to God. We find it first in Exodus 34:9 when Moses describes the Israelites to God after he finds them worshiping the golden calf by saying, *"this is a stiff necked people."* And Jeremiah in chapter 7:26 says, *"They were stiff necked and did more evil than their forefathers."* Even Stephen, in one of the very best sermons ever recorded says to the people, *"You stiff necked people, with uncircumcised hearts and ears! You are just like your fathers: You always resist the holy spirit."* This sermon resulted in Stephen becoming the first martyr for Christ as he was stoned to death for his remarks. The end of the matter is that Orpah is a type of the people who resist God's love call.

Ruth means companion, obviously the type of follower who is destined to become God's bride.

And Boaz means strength, such as is found throughout God's Word in places such as Exodus 15:2 and Psalm 28:7 which say, *"The Lord is my strength."* Boaz represents Jesus.

Naomi represents Israel, Orpah is the group of unbelievers, Boaz is Jesus Christ, and Ruth is the true church. And the shadows in the story are numerous. For instance, did you notice that Boaz (Jesus) offered bread and wine to Ruth (The Church)? This is the same thing we saw Melchizedek do when he met Abraham, and we already know that Melchizedek was certainly a type of Jesus. The bread and wine, of course, represents the last supper, the holy communion still partaken of by the church today.

The kinsman who was first in line but was unable to be the redeemer represents the Law. God gave the Israelites the law, consisting of the commandments, but history proved that no one could go through life and keep all of them. If people had to rely on the Law to get to heaven, no one would ever make it in. Remember, God is totally holy and no one who is not holy can be in his presence. It is only when we are covered by the holy blood of Jesus that we are able to enter heaven and stand in His presence. We cannot earn our way in.

One of the most important shadows in the story is when Ruth asks Boaz to *"Spread the corner of your garment over me."* Let's think back to our quote from Romans 3:25, which says in speaking of Jesus, *"Whom God has set forth to be a propitiation through faith in His blood."* (KJV)

We've learned that word, propitiation, was the Greek word, hilasterion, which meant mercy seat. Its other translation is covering. In the Old Testament, which was written in Hebrew, the word used to describe the mercy seat above the ark was kapporeth, which also means covering. Therefore, when Ruth pulled Boaz's cover over herself she was demonstrating in dramatic fashion what Christ did for us on the cross. He covered our sins.

And please don't forget the incredible fact that the book of Ruth was written over a thousand years before Jesus even walked this earth. That would be an important point if there were still any debaters left to talk to.

Overshadowing all the many types and shadows in the book of Ruth is the fact that God is painting a picture of the future for the believer as His bride, His "other." The Bible is filled with example after example of God trying to point out our aimed-for marriage to him for eternity. In fact, God is so intent on telling us about marriage in His Word that he uses the words marriage, bride, husband, etc., 773 times. Think about that, there are a gigantic amount of 773 times that God wants our attention to be focused on an upcoming marriage to Him. There are even many, many other verses that allude to it but don't actually use one of those words. Our union to God is utmost on His mind.

Marriage is obviously one of the very most important spiritual themes of the Bible. We saw that Nicodemus did not understand spiritual things when he met Jesus at night in secret and he could not understand what Jesus was telling him. Modern man does not understand spiritual things either. One of the biggest problems is that mankind does not see the big picture that we have been going over and over. Once we understand that since"*God is love*," and He wanted someone to love and be loved by in return, the reason for all of creation becomes clear.

Secondly, once we realize that in order for us to be able to truly accept God's love and also to love Him back, we had to be given free will. And by understanding that, we can understand the need for the creation of Satan, as well as the need for our inbuilt sinful nature. Once we can grasp these basic realities we can begin to understand other spiritual things.

These basics also give us the meaning of life, so here it is. The meaning of this life of ours is summed up in three things:

1 - The courting period by our two suitors

2 - Our decision as to which one we will choose, and

3 - An engagement period with the one we choose.

That is the meaning of life. People have searched for several millenniums for the meaning of life and all the while it was very simple. Anything other than those three things are, as Solomon said, "*a chasing after the wind.*" Nothing else has eternal meaning. Wealth, happiness, good deeds for mankind; none of these last forever. How we handle those three things is the only thing in this life with lasting, eternal significance.

To bring it down to our level, let's sum up the meaning of life in a way that we can easily understand. Let's pretend that you and I are a young lady who has two young men, Jack and Sam, vying for our hand in marriage. Jack is perfect husband material, while Sam, although charming and exciting in spurts, would obviously be a terrible husband. After a little fling with Sam we finally decide on Jack to be our husband for life. The next step is as plain as day, we must put Sam totally out of our life. We cannot be engaged to Jack and still keep seeing Sam on the sly. That just will not work.

The above situation sums up the three parts of the meaning of life. It is crystal clear. With the last thought, however, what we will discuss next will be extremely controversial in modern church circles.

It should be obvious that if we can't keep seeing Sam on the sly and hope for our engagement to end with a walk down the isle in the above pretend situation, it is just as imperative that we can't keeping cavorting with Satan and expect to be able to sit down at the marriage feast of the Lamb.

Interestingly, though, much of the modern church, the Church of Laodicia, advertises very enticingly that we can. The idea goes back to the mid sixteenth century when John Calvin proposed two thoughts that are still staunchly defended by many today. Calvin called these two ideas "God's Election" and "Perseverance of the Saints." The first means "predestination" and the second means "once saved always saved." Both stemmed from Calvin's basic belief that man did not have free will. Calvin obviously did not see the big picture as we have.

Predestination simply means that God chose who would be saved and who would be destroyed before anyone was even born. The thought is that your course and mine are completely predetermined, no matter what, and there is no way to change it. The Presbyterian Church, of course, still believes the same thing today. There are a some scriptures which taken by themselves seem to back that thought, and very Godly and learned people understandably defend it avidly. But the Bible needs to be taken as a whole, and the entirety of God's Word does not back up the concept of predestination.

A simple example is the lives of the Apostles. Why in the world did they need to waste their whole lives, and die horrible deaths, trying to preach to people whose destinies were already predetermined. Many books have been written pro and con on the subject, so we will not elaborate further by going through hundreds of scriptures on both sides of the debate. We will just say that it is clear, but only if we look at the big picture, that God wanted a bride who would choose to love him, not a robot. This being the case, any debate over predestination is moot because predestination supposes the creation of people who have no choice but to love God. They have no free will.

As we said, we admit that there are some very Godly people who staunchly defend the concept, but we do find it interesting, though, that these people even bother to try to evangelize anyone, when the people they are preaching to have supposedly been predetermined either to end up in heaven or hell, no matter whether anyone explains God and the Bible to them or not. For that matter, why do they even feel the need for any churches or pastors at all, especially since these same people also believe that "once saved always saved." Remember, both concepts rest on the notion that mankind has no free will.

The idea of predestination does not seem to be keeping people from heaven, though, because the group who believe in it do, in fact, do an admirable job of trying to spread the good news of the gospel. The second concept of "once saved always saved", however, does need to be somewhat addressed. That doctrine could and, probably does, create eternal problems for some.

Taken at its extreme, Calvin's idea that once a person makes his decision to choose Jesus, there is nothing at all that person can do to break the engagement. In other words, once a person has that shining religious moment and repents of his sins and takes Jesus into his heart, he can then go on a rampage of raping and beating little old ladies, murdering elementary school children weekly, and tearing the do not remove tags off mattresses every morning before breakfast. You can even hear some with that belief say that since Hitler was a Christian as a young lad, he will definitely be in heaven. The millions of screaming humans that were killed will not even be considered as a problem. They can even point to some scriptures that seem to irrefutably back them up. Don't be concerned, though, neither Hitler nor the serial killer who raped and slaughtered over twenty young college girls, even though he was once an altar boy, will be sitting next to you at the marriage feast of the Lamb. By the same token, the once on fire Christian who changes his mind and turns to Buddha later in life won't have a seat at the feast either.

Of course, the "once saved always saved" believer, which include the largest protestant denominations, will just sluff those examples off by saying that those folks were never really believers in the first place. It seems that even if they don't believe in predestination, they believe that God does take away a persons free will the minute he becomes a true follower. They have to believe that or the entire "once saved always saved" house of cards falls apart.

Yes, God is more than able if He so desires to keep people from changing their mind during the engagement period, but that is not God's nature. He does not make us love Him, and he does not make us stay faithful to Him. God will still allow people to have free will on the very last day of the Millennial reign of Christ talked about in Revelation 20:7-8,

"When the thousand years are over, Satan will be released from his prison and will go out to deceive the nations ... to gather them for battle. In number they are like the sand on the seashore." Remember, these people as numerous as the sand have lived with Jesus as Lord of lords for a thousand years, and they still have free will to choose Satan, and do.

God wants a bride who has made the decision to love Him without any coercion, and sticks to that love. The engagement part of the meaning of life is extremely important. Even Calvinists would have to agree that just as the engagement ring that Jack gives us is not a license to have a continual affair with Sam, so a one time decision to choose God does not give us free reign to partner with Satan whenever and as often as we want.

To be fair to the "once saved always saved" believers, it is very plain that Satan cannot snatch a believer away from God.

Jesus stated that in John 10:28 in a very clear manner in speaking of his sheep, which are the true Christians, *"no one can snatch them out of my hand."* It is very true that a believing Christian can in no way ever be snatched away from Jesus.

On the other hand, there are scores of verses that talk about how believers can fall away of their own accord, because of their free will. Jesus himself makes too many statements to quote, like the following one from Matthew 10:22, *"He who stands firm to the end will be saved."* God's Word even talks about believers *"if they fall away."* in Hebrews 6:6 and many other places.

The problem may actually go back to the verses like, *"Believe in the Lord Jesus and you will be saved."* Acts 16:31. We have already seen that just believing in one God doesn't help us at all, for we read, *"You believe that there is one God. Good! Even the demons believe that - and shudder."* Acts 2:19

Part of the problem though goes deeper, into our translation of the original Greek word, pistevo, into our simple word believe.

Pistevo is an active verb that has its root in the noun, pistis, which is usually translated as faith. Pistevo occurs 550 times in the New Testament, most frequently as a command or instruction, and being an "active verb" means that it is something we are to continue to do. As Dr. Gene Scott so wonderfully coined a new verb, to faithe, we are to continue to "faithe" in Jesus every day. But there is more that is almost never mentioned.

Strong's Greek dictionary gives the meaning of the word, pistevo,

> to have faith in a person or thing,
> to trust,
> to commit to,
> to have credence or moral conviction of the truthfulness of
> God, and to have reliance upon Christ for salvation.

All of those, remember, are to be done on a continual basis. To make a one time "testimony of faith," as the modern church calls it, and then to sit back and wait for our heavenly life, doesn't quite seem to be enough when we actually discover what the word that God used really means. Let's not forget,

"My people are destroyed from lack of knowledge." Hosea 4:6

Choosing God means all of the above. To examine the Biblical "believe" word, pistevo, even further, let's look at Bauer's Greek Lexicon (BDAG revised 2,000 AD). Bauer's says, pistevo means:

> To entrust oneself to an entity in complete confidence
> To believe in
> To trust, <u>with implications of total commitment</u> to the
> One who is trusted.

Yes, Jesus did everything that needs to be done for our salvation and entrance into the wedding feast. We can't earn our own salvation by being a perfect person. In fact, we can't earn our salvation in any way at all. *"For it is by grace you have been saved, through faith - and this not from yourself, it is the gift of God - not by works, so that no one can boast."* Eph. 2:22

That being said, the engagement part of the meaning of life is more than a one time prayer, or statement, or the filling out of a decision card. The engagement period, including every day for the rest of our lives, should be filled with faith, trust, and total commitment to Jesus. It should be a time of constantly trying to develop a deeper relationship and love for our future husband. Love entails trust and faithfulness and spending time together.

Our engagement period and subsequent marriage to God, to Jesus, is the reason for all of creation. It is the very utmost important thing to God. He does not want it taken lightly, like our modern day Christianity does. The end result of modern day Christianity, the Church of Laodicia, is written in red in God's Word, where Jesus says, *"because you are lukewarm - neither hot nor cold- I am about to spit you out of my mouth."*Rev.3:16 Did you notice that Jesus is writing to His church, not to a bunch of unbelievers, and He is going to spit them out of his mouth? That should put the lid on the "once saved always saved" idea. The engagement time doesn't always end in "I do."

The entire Bible is full of shadows of what our engagement and marriage to Him should be. The book of Esther is an example. You probably know the story. Esther, a young Jewish girl, is given the chance to vie for the king's affection in competition with scores of other beautiful young virgins. Marriage and the crown of the Queen awaited her if she became chosen. *"She had to complete twelve months of beauty treatments prescribed for the women, six months with oil of myrrh and six with perfumes and cosmetics."* Esther 2:12

At the end of that time, on the day she was to present herself to the king, she could choose to wear anything in the elaborate storehouse of garments that she wanted. And she could pick any of the jewels that she wanted to wear. The fact is that if she were not chosen, she could keep whatever she wore that night. That could be quite an incentive to pick the costliest gems by worldly standards, because if she didn't get to become queen just one bauble could feed her family for years. Strangely, though, the book of Esther 2:15 tells us, *"When the turn came for Esther ... to go to the king, she asked for nothing other than what Hegia, the king's eunuch, suggested. And Esther won the favor of everyone who saw her."* Not surprisingly, the end result was that Esther became queen. She listened to the servant, who represents the Holy Spirit, as to what God would want her to wear, and she ended up on the throne beside him.

Clothes play a very important part in many of the shadows in God's Word. Remember Ruth 3:3, where Naomi told Ruth,

"Wash and perfume yourself and put on your best clothes." Even in the letter to the Church of Sardis, which got no commendation from Jesus, we find, *"Yet you have a few people in Sardis who have not soiled their clothes. They will walk with me, dressed in white, for they are worthy."* Revelation 3:4

All the references in the Bible to cleaning up and to fine clothes or white clothes or the clothes that God prefers, are shadows of the person's righteousness. God wants us to "clean up" and stop courting Satan.

One example of wearing clean clothes that probably also deals with the timing of Christ's second coming is found In Exodus 19:10, *"And the Lord said to Moses, 'Go to the people and consecrate them today and tomorrow, have them wash their clothes and be ready by the third day, because on that day the Lord will come down on Mount Sinai in the sight of all the people."* Although this verse obviously deals with clean clothes and the righteousness we are discussing, we might make note that 2 Peter 3:8 says, *"With the Lord a day is as a thousand years."* Could this verse mean that Jesus is coming back after two thousand years? That question is for a later chapter.

The point we are trying to make is that if we listen to the teaching of the modern day Laodician church we might be totally and frighteningly surprised in the end. Pay very close attention to the following words of Jesus In Matthew 7:21-23,

"Not everyone who says to me, 'Lord, Lord,' will enter the kingdom of heaven, but only he who does the will of my father who is in heaven. Many will say to me on that day, 'Lord, Lord, did not we prophesy in your name, and in your name drive out demons and perform many miracles?' Then I will tell them plainly, 'I never knew you. Away from me, you evil doers."

We have not been promised a rose garden in this earthly Christian life. That is not a part of the meaning of life. Those who teach that all we need do is show God that we have faith that He will keep us healthy because we can "stand on" a few scriptures of promise, or prove our faith by "believing for" a new Cadillac, or even prove our Christian faith by believing God will forgive us no matter how often we continue to commit the same old sin over and over and over and over, even if we read that what we are doing every day is a total abomination to the Lord; those and their eager followers of the "easy" Christian life could be in for a very rude and eternal shock.

The very first sermon Jesus preached, after being tempted in the wilderness, was *"Repent, for the kingdom of heaven is near."* Matthew 4:17. In the same verse we read that *"From that time on"* Jesus preached the very same thing, repent. To repent means to turn away from something. It means to stop doing those things. It doesn't mean to say I'm sorry and then keep right on doing them, knowing that God hates it.

God didn't stop putting prophecy and types and shadows in His Word to us at the end of the Old Testament. The New Testament is full of the same things, unfortunately we do not have the luxury of looking back at everything like we do the Old Testament. One of the shadows in the New Testament that deals with marriage is found in Ephesians 5:22, *"Wives, submit to your husbands as to the Lord. For the husband is the head of the wife as Christ is the head of the church, his body, of which he is the savior."*

It would be comical if it weren't so sad when we see churches and pastors actually have heated arguments about such verses, and congregations and denominations actually split up over their differences, when the root problem lies in their inability to see the big picture and discern that God's Word is primarily spiritual in focus.

Sure, God wants us to make our earthly marriages resemble as closely as possible our future marriage to Jesus in heaven, but the primary reason for verses like the above is to teach us that we should submit to our future, all wise, loving, divine husband. God is not telling wives that they are to be submissive to some earthly jerk of a husband who beats them and their children. God is much more realistic, and way more understanding than that. These verses are shadows that are meant to teach us to listen to and fully commit to the perfect wisdom of God.

Bauer's translates further the Greek word, pisteusantes, which is seen in our bibles as "believed", in verses such as Ephesians 1:13, *"Having believed you were marked in Him* (Jesus) *with a seal, the promised Holy Spirit,"* as: (those) who made their commitment. So, to believe in Jesus means to be committed to Him.

This fifth part of our book is devoted to what the future holds. Since the first part of our future entails the engagement period to Christ, we need to know the full implications of what that includes. The editor of Bauer's (BDAG), William Danker, sums up what the original Greek word for "believe" really means in the following statement: "When one has faith he enters into a state of trust. Additionally, while one can commit his eternal destiny to Christ (ie, trust him for eternal life), commitment means committing ones life (ie, deciding to follow Christ in obedience)."

A gigantic problem lies in the fact that since very few people who call themselves Christians today have actually read God's Word, virtually no one knows what Jesus even said. How, then are they able to "follow Christ in obedience." And again, since most of our Church of Laodicia teaches the "once saved always saved" doctrine, even the few who have read their Bible seem to think that Jesus gave us instructions just because He enjoyed hearing His own voice. They admit that the instructions were good, but just like the Ten Commandments, they were only suggestions. And it matters not if we heed the "suggestions."

The modern Christians are for the most part convinced that whether they make the called for attitude adjustment or not, doesn't really matter. They are certain that no matter what they do, say, or think, Jesus will feel so overwhelmingly privileged that they even acknowledged His earthly existence and realized that He died on the cross for them, that He will open His loving arms in a warm greeting whenever they depart this earth, and everything will be fine and dandy.

The spiritual truth is in Jesus' own words, *"Enter through the narrow gate. For wide is the gate and broad is the road that leads to destruction, and many enter through it. But small is the gate and narrow the road that leads to life, and only a few find it."* Matthew 713

"Therefore everyone who hears these words of mine and puts them into practice is like a wise man who built his house on a rock. ... But everyone who hears these words of mine and does not put them into practice is like a foolish man who built his house on the sand. The rain

came down, the streams rose, and the winds blew and beat against the house, and it fell with a great crash." Matthew 7:24-27

"For many are invited, but few are chosen." Matt. 22:14

"Anyone who does not carry his cross and follow me cannot be my disciple." Luke 14:27

"If anyone would come after me, he must deny himself and take up his cross and follow me. For whoever wants to save his life will lose it, but whoever loses his life for Me and for the gospel will save it. What good is it for a man to gain the whole world, yet forfeit his soul." Mark 8:34-37

It all sounds very much like the Christian life is pretty bad. It sounds like it is made up of days and nights of walking on egg shells, wondering if we are doing all the "do's" and not doing the "don't's". With all that we have said, though, the truth is that the engagement period with Christ is nothing like that at all. Being engaged to someone is suppose to be a time of unbridled joy, and the fact is that once we are committed to love Jesus and completely trust Him with every aspect of our lives, peace and joy are two words that describe our new lives. There is no other experience like it known to man.

Jesus promised us, *"Come to me, all you who are weary and burdened, and I will give you rest. Take my yoke upon you and learn from me, for I am gentle and humble in heart, and you will find rest in your souls. For my yoke is easy and my burden is light."* Matthew 11:28-30

In the next chapters we will find out how exciting our future here on earth and in heaven will be, and we will learn about specifics God has foretold are coming. Life will be fantastic.

CHAPTER TWENTY-EIGHT

An engagement period is a time for two people to really get to know each other intimately, to understand the other person's desires, needs, background, thoughts, idiosyncracies, beliefs, and ways of doing things. God, of course, already knows every single thing there is to know about us. In speaking about God, King David said,

"O Lord, you have searched me and You know me. You know when I sit down and when I rise; You perceive my thoughts from afar. You discern my going out and my lying down; You are familiar with all my ways. Before a word is on my tongue you know it completely, O Lord.

You hem me in - behind and before; You have laid your hand upon me. Such knowledge is too wonderful for me, too lofty for me to attain." Psalm 139:1-6

"For You created my inmost being; You knit me together in my mother's womb." Psalm 139:13

God even says in Jeremiah 1:4, *"Before I formed you in the womb I knew you."* And Jesus tells us, *"And even the very hairs of your head are all numbered."* Matthew 10:30

There is nothing about us that God doesn't know, and yet He loves us anyway. That may be the most remarkable revelation of the entire Bible. God loves you and me with a love that we could never ever understand. He tells us plainly, *"I have loved you with an everlasting love."* Jeremiah 31:3. And lest we need reminding, *"For God so loved the world that He gave His only begotten Son."* John 3:16

The engagement period, then, is for us to get to know God, and more importantly to actually develop a deep, personal relationship with Him. Let's start with trying to get to know who He really is. That sentence is ludicrous at best, because God is "too everything" for us to really know who He is. Our finite minds could never fully comprehend the infinite, and God is infinitely everything that is good. He is infinitely wise, infinitely just, infinitely loving, etc. God is infinitely "everything" that is good. God is truly wonderful to the extreme. No words could even come close to describing all the awesome qualities of God.

In addition to the fact that *"God is spirit,"* a gigantic problem arises in the understanding of God in the truth that God, although one being, is also three separate and distinct beings. Not only can we not fully comprehend the spirit world, our minds are at a total loss to absolutely grasp the concept of the Trinity. Our inability to understand, however, has nothing to do with the fact that God really is made up of three individuals; three beings who each have their own personalities. God the Father, the Son, and the Holy Spirit are independent and at the same time "one." As the hymn writer, Reginald Heber, from the time of the non condemned Church of Philadelphia, wrote in 1826, "God in three persons, blessed Trinity."

Before we reach heaven and attend the wedding feast which we will discuss later, while we are maturing into the "bride," we are God's children. He is our Father. It is another concept of God's love for us that is carried throughout His Word as a main theme. In fact, and this is really startling, of the 31,174 verses in God's Word, the words child, daughter, son, father, etc., are used 7,008 times. It would be difficult to find a more prominent theme in the Bible than that of our relationship as children of God.

Actually, when we realize that there are many, many more verses that allude to this parent/child relationship without one of those words, we can see that almost every other verse in the Bible gives us insight into the fact that while we are in this fleshly tent of an earthly body, God wants us to look to Him as our Father. Interestingly, even though the phrase "our Father" is used throughout the Bible, the religious leaders of Christ's day were probably appalled when He taught us to pray in Matthew 6:9 (KJV), *"Our Father which art in heaven, Hallowed be thy name."* Obviously Jesus was teaching us that God wants us to talk with him in that Father/child manner. He wants us to relate to him as the loving Father He really is.

The definition of the Hebrew word, Abba, is "Daddy," "Dear Father," or "Papa." It is a term of endearment that is a much more intimate expression than the Hebrew word for father, "av," which means, "one who gives strength to the family." (Remember Boaz, whose name means strength and represented Jesus in the story of

Ruth.) We mention the term, Abba, because there is a wonderful verse that says, *"You received the spirit of sonship. And by Him we cry, 'Abba, Father.' The Spirit Himself testifies with our spirit that we are God's children. Now if we are God's children, then we are heirs - heirs of God and co-heirs with Christ."* Romans 8:15-17. Chapter 8, incidently, is said to be the jewel in the crowning book of the Bible, Romans.

"How great is the love the Father has lavished on us, that we should be called the children of God." 1 John 3:1

God truly is, *"The father of compassion and the God of all comfort, who comforts us in all our troubles."* 2 Corinthians 1:3

We have often mentioned in this book that it would be wise for us to learn from the saints who lived during the Church Age of Missions between 1730 AD and 1900 AD since they were, along with the believers of the Persecuted Church Age between 100 AD and 313 AD, the only two churches in the letters in Revelation that Jesus had nothing bad to write about. One of those Age of Missions Christians was a wonderful Quaker lady by the name of Hannah Whitall Smith, who was born in 1832. She wrote two books that should be mandatory reading for any follower of Jesus today.

The two books written by this down to earth, Godly lady that we cannot recommend highly enough for anyone who chooses to spend this life and the next with God instead of Satan, are The Christian's Secret of a Happy Life and The God of All Comfort. The inspiration for the title of the second book, of course, was taken from the above scripture in 2 Corinthians.

We can all benefit beyond words from reading and understanding the practical truths in the following excerpts from the last chapter, "God Is Enough," of The God of All Comfort.

"The all-sufficiency of God ought to be as complete to the child of God as the all-sufficiency of a good mother is to the child of that mother. We all know the utter rest of the little child in the mother's presence and the mother's love. That its mother is there is enough to make all fears and all troubles disappear.

It does not need the mother to make any promises; she herself, just as she is, without promises and without explanation, is all that the child needs.

My own experience as a child taught me this, beyond any possibility of question. My mother was the remedy for all my own ills, and, I fully believed, for the ills of the whole world, if only they could be brought to her. And when anyone expressed doubts as to her capacity to remedy everything, I remembered with what fine scorn I used to annihilate them, by saying,

'Ah! but you don't know my mother.'

And now, when any tempest tossed soul fails to see that God is enough, I feel like saying, not with scorn, but with infinite pity. 'Ah, dear friend, you do not know God! Did you know Him, you could not help seeing that He is the remedy for every need of your soul, and that He is an all-sufficient remedy. God is enough, even though no promise may seem to fit your case, nor any inward assurance give you confidence. The Promiser is more than His promises; and His existence is a surer ground of confidence than the most fervent inward feelings.'

His simple existence is all the warrant your need requires for its certain relieving. Nothing can separate you from His love, absolutely nothing, neither death nor life, nor angels, nor principalities, nor powers, nor things present, nor things to come, nor height, nor depth, nor any other creature. Every possible contingency is provided for here; and not one of them can separate you from the love of God which is in Christ Jesus.

After such a declaration as this, how can any of us dare to question or doubt God's love? And since He loves us, He cannot exist and fail to help us. Do we not know by our own experience what an imperative necessity it is for love to pour itself out in blessing on the ones it loves; and can we not understand that God, who is love, who is, if I may say so, made out of love, simply cannot help blessing us. We do not need to beg Him to bless us, He simply cannot help it.

Therefore God is enough! God is enough for time, God is enough for eternity. God is enough!" By Hannah Whitall Smith

What a wonderful way for all of us to look at our true Abba, Father. In the next chapter we will find out how Hannah Smith from the Age of Missions got such assurance about God, her heavenly Father, and how we can have it, too. Before we do, however, let us look at one of Hannah's contemporaries, another phenomenal lady named Fanny Crosby.

Miss Crosby was born twelve years before Hannah Smith, in

1820 in Putnam County, New York. As a baby she seemed to have some eye problems and a man claiming to be a doctor put something on her eyes that burned them severely, resulting in total and permanent blindness. Her mother was a Godly woman who read the bible to Fanny as a child, which led to Fanny virtually memorizing the entire Word of God.

Throughout her life Fanny had a love real affair with God, and incredibly she wrote over 9,000 hymns, many of which are still being sung in churches today. Her engagement period with God is a testament to just how deep the relationship can become.

Not being able to see may have opened her spiritual eyes to see God better than most of us. At one point she was asked if she would want to regain her sight if she could. Fanny's answer was, "Oh no, I want the first face I ever see to be the face of Jesus."

Before we find out how we, too, can have the assurance about our Abba and future husband the same way Hannah Whitall Smith and Fanny Crosby did, let's listen to the words of Fanny's most beloved, 1873 hymn, "Blessed Assurance."

> Blessed assurance, Jesus is mine!
> O what a foretaste of glory divine!
> Heir of salvation, purchase of God,
> Born of His Spirit, washed in his blood.
>
> Perfect submission, perfect delight,
> Visions of rapture now burst on my sight;
> Angels descending bring from above
> Echos of mercy, whispers of love.
>
> Perfect submission, all is at rest
> I in my Savior am happy and blest,
> Watching and waiting, looking above,
> Filled with His goodness, lost in His love.
>
> This is my story, this is my song,
> Praising my Savior, all the day long;
> This is my story, this is my song,
> Praising my Savior, all the day long.

Chapter Twenty-Nine

As to the second person of the trinity, the Son, we can learn a lot about the love and compassion of the human side of Jesus by reading the four separate accounts of His life in Matthew, Mark, Luke, and John. Even a cursory reading of those gospels will give us insight into His thoughts, emotions, desires and goals. To understand more about Jesus from a spiritual point of view, however, the remaining books of the New Testament may be even more helpful. For example, let's see what God wrote in the first chapter of Hebrews about the his Son, Jesus:

In the past God spoke to our forefathers through the prophets at many times and in various ways, but in these last days he has spoken to us by his Son, whom he appointed heir of all things, and through whom he made the universe. The Son is the radiance of God's glory and the exact representation of his being, sustaining all things by His powerful word. After He had provided purification for sins, He sat down at the right hand of the Majesty in heaven. So He became as much superior to the angels as the name He has inherited is superior to theirs.

For to which of the angels did God ever say, 'You are my Son; today I have become your Father?'

Or again, 'I will be His Father and He will be my Son?'

And again, when God brings his firstborn into the world, he says, 'Let all God's angels worship Him.'

In speaking of the angels he says, 'He makes his angels winds, his servants flames of fire.'

But about the Son he says, 'Your throne, O God, will last forever and ever, and righteousness will be the scepter of your kingdom. You have loved righteousness and hated wickedness; therefore God, your God, has set you above your companions by anointing you with the oil of joy.'

He also says, 'In the beginning, O Lord, you laid the foundations of the earth, and the heavens are the work of your hands. They will perish, but you remain; they will all wear out like a garment. You will roll them up like a robe; like a garment they will be changed. But You remain the same, and your years will never end."

To which of the angels did God ever say, 'Sit at my right hand until I make your enemies a footstool for your feet." Hebrews 1:1-13

Did you notice that according to the Father, it was through Jesus that He made the universe, and it was Jesus who laid the foundations of the earth and the heavens? Obviously, it was not His human side that did that. It is also worth noting that the Father says that the throne of Jesus will last forever and ever. Jesus is not just a teacher on the order of Mohammed, Buddha, or Gandhi. Jesus is God. Jesus, the Son, created everything. He created you, and He created me. Jesus is God.

Probably the very best description of Jesus is found in God's Word in the letter God had Paul write to the Colossians. We should read it very slowly and very carefully, and we should read it over and over. It should change our attitudes.

"He is the image of the invisible God, the firstborn over all creation. For by Him all things were created; things in heaven and on earth, visible and invisible, whether thrones or powers or rulers or authorities; all things were created by Him and for Him. He is before all things, and in Him all things hold together. And He is the head of the body, the church; He is the beginning and the firstborn among the dead, so that in everything He might have the supremacy. For God was pleased to have all his fullness dwell in Him, and through Him to reconcile to himself all things, whether things on earth or things in heaven, by making peace through His blood, shed on the cross." Colossians1:15-20

We need to get a firm grasp on the reality that Jesus is the *image of the invisible God,"* and *"all things were created by Him and for Him."* As Rick Warren said, "It is not all about us." Everything was created by Jesus and for Jesus. Without Him arrogant man would not even exist. There is not a point to debate. Without Jesus our lives are not just a *"chasing after the wind;"* our lives would not even exist. What could be more plain? Modern man thinks he can take Jesus or leave Him and it doesn't really matter. The truth is that Jesus is God. This world was made by Him and for Him. We are only players. The only thing that gives us humans any semblance of importance at all is the fact that He loves us. With all our faults, He still loves us.

Let's continue reading the next paragraph in Colossians because in it there is something that is of utmost importance that
we need to fully comprehend.

*"Once you were alienated from God and were enemies in your minds
because of your evil behavior. But now he has reconciled you by Christ's
physical body through death to present you holy in his sight, without
blemish and free from accusation - if you continue in your faith, established and firm, not moved from the hope held out in the gospel. This is
the gospel that you heard and that has been proclaimed to every creature
under heaven."* Colossians 1:21-23

The thing we need to focus on in the above paragraph is the
gigantic word, if. We have been reconciled to God, *"if you continue
in your faith."* Through the death of Christ we are presented to the
Father as holy, *"if ...."* God looks at us as if we had no blemishes, *"if
... ."* No one, including Satan, can accuse us of anything, *"if ... ."*

The *"if"* is our part in our own salvation. The *"if"* is the only
way we enter eternal life as the bride of Christ. The *"if"* is the
only thing that keeps us from an eternal life with Satan. And the
"if" is not a one time statement or prayer. It is not filling out a
decision card or walking down a church aisle one time. It is not
doing more "rights" than "wrongs" as most religions teach.

The *"if"* is one thing only, and it is a continual thing. The only
requirement, the only thing that makes a difference, is to *"continue in your faith, established and firm."* And remember, that word,
faith, in the original Greek means "to trust with implications of
total commitment to the one who is trusted."

It isn't a one time thought; it is a continual lifetime <u>commitment</u>.

Stop doing that *"if"* and we may have just as well have never
started. In fact, stopping may be worse than not starting.

*"It is impossible for those who have once been enlightened, who have
tasted the heavenly gift, who have shared in the Holy Spirit, who have
tasted the goodness of the word of God and the powers of the coming age,
if they fall away, to be brought back to repentance, because to their loss
they are crucifying the Son of God all over again and subjecting Him to
public disgrace."* Hebrews 6:4-6

Are we harping on this subject? Yes, and we know that what
we are saying is going to make many of the modern church lead-

ers irate, because most teach the "once saved always saved" doctrine. Thousands of times ministers have stood in front of congregations and with a "knowing" smile on their face said, "Jesus said on the cross, *'It is finished.'* He didn't say, 'to be continued.'" Then the entire congregation laughs. Then the minister goes on to tell us that there is nothing at all that we can do to ever loose our salvation once we believe that Jesus died on the cross to save our sins and arose three days later." Remember, though, it is the modern church, the Church of Laodicia, about which Jesus Himself said, *"Because you are lukewarm - neither hot nor cold - I am about to spit you out of my mouth."* Revelation 3:16

Yes, Jesus said in John 19:30, *"It is finished."* And His part definitely was. Jesus had done what He needed to do. But we have a part, too. We need to fully trust that His blood was sufficient to erase our sins and satisfy the necessary death part of the prophecy, *"You shall surely die."* We <u>additionally</u> need to be "committed" to Him as the Lord of our lives, as defined in "pistevo," and we need to do the *"if you continue"* part.

Lets examine our first part first, how do we get the faith that is talked about in that Greek word, pistis, that obviously encompasses not just head knowledge, but a heart felt commitment to allow Jesus to be Lord of our lives? The answer is once again not going to be what this Church of Laodicia teaches. Ask any Christian who has any modern Bible teaching at all and he will immediately quote the King James Version of Romans 10:17, *"So then faith cometh by hearing, and hearing by the word of God."* The NIV translates that verse as, *"Consequently, faith comes from hearing the message, and the message is heard through the word of Christ."* Both versions tell us that faith comes from the "word." Today's teaching in most churches, therefore, tells us that we get faith solely by reading the Bible, God's Word.

The error in that is that the original Greek word for "word" in that particular verse was "rhema," not "logos," which can be somewhat different. Logos normally refers to the written Word of God, but not always. Rhema refers to an oral revelation or insight from God through his Holy Spirit, but again, not always. A rhema word can also be a written word.

Pentecostal or Charismatic churches will forget the "but not always" part of what we just said and dogmatically say that faith only comes from hearing an utterance from the Holy Spirit, primarily through prayer.

The truth of the matter is that faith normally comes by a combination of both things. We must study God's Word to even understand what the "Good News" is, and we must be in prayer so the Holy Spirit can really teach us and draw us close to Jesus.

Although reading and studying God's Word is not only exciting but is also a faith builder, there must additionally be personal communication with Him as well. Thousands of people through the ages have studied God's Word and not become true followers of Christ. Oral Roberts once recalled being taken on a tour of a leading seminary by the Dean. After meeting the head of the Bible Studies Department, Dr. Roberts commented in shock to the Dean that the man was not even a Christian. The Dean responded, "We know, but he knows the Bible better than anyone else here."

Yes, we need to study the Bible. God even wants us to *"search out the matter."* However, we also need direct communications with the person of God. We need to pray. Educators tell us that the thing that separates man from all other living creatures is the opposable thumb. That is a difference, but the main separating distinction is that man is the only one of God's creations that prays.

Since rhema is the Greek word used for "word" in the verse, *"So faith cometh by hearing and hearing by the word of God,"* and since rhema includes hearing from God in ways outside the written word, it stands to reason that prayer is an integral part in gaining faith. Prayer is also a main ingredient to *"continue in your faith, established and firm."*

As far as the obtaining of faith, many a person who now is totally in love with God started their very first prayer with something ridiculous like, "If you are really there, God, ..."

I count myself in that group. What we find is that if that stumbling prayer is sincere, God will almost invariably take that opening to somehow show that He really and truly is there. Remember, God is a very personal God who really wants to make himself known to us so that we will desire to develop the relationship further. And being God, He knows how to go about doing it in any situation we might give Him.

Often the first prayer a person makes is in response to a need. Many times the first time someone hits their knees is in desperation. And normally we see that God somehow responds. In fact, brand new believers often experience more miracles in the first few months of their lives than more seasoned believers do in years. This may be God's way of making sure that someone who begins to draw close to Him will continue to come to Him. We saw Jesus perform miracle after miracle as He walked this earth, and God's Word tells us, *"Jesus Christ is the same yesterday and today and forever,"* Hebrews 13:8

The key is to continue to pray, and to continue to study His Word. Unfortunately, most do not, and they loose out on everything. One of the most famous parables given by Jesus is the parable of the Sower:

"A farmer went out to sow his seed. As he was scattering his seed, some fell along the path, and the birds came and ate it up. Some fell on rocky places, where it did not have much soil. It sprang up quickly, because the soil was shallow. But when the sun came up the plants were scorched, and they withered because they had no root. Other seed fell among thorns, which grew up and choked the plants. Still other seed fell on good soil, where it produced a crop - a hundred, sixty or thirty times what was sown. He who has ears let him hear." Matthew 13:3-9

Jesus explained very few parables, but this one was so important that He went on to explain it to His disciples. It is so important to us also, that we need to truly concentrate on

His explanation. Jesus goes on to say:

"Listen to what the parable of the sower means: When anyone hears the message about the kingdom and does not understand it, the evil one comes and snatches away what was sown in his heart. This is the seed sown along the path. The one who received the seed that fell on rocky places is the man who hears the word and at once receives it with joy. But since he has no root, he lasts only a short time. When trouble or persecution comes because of the word, he quickly falls away. The one who received the seed that fell among the thorns is the man who hears the word, but the worries of this life and the deceitfulness of wealth

choke it, making it unfruitful. But the one who received the seed that fell on good soil is the man who hears the word and understands it. He produces a crop, yielding a hundred, sixty or thirty times what was sown." Matthew 13:18-23

For those who believe that faith only comes through the uttered word because of the use of the Greek word "rhema" for "word" in Romans 10:17," we need to point out that in this parable the Greek word, "logos," was used for each "word," which refers to God's written word. As we said, both prayer and Bible study are integral in producing faith.

Another point we will make is that although the "once saved always saved" thinkers will say that only the last group in the parable became believers, in reality even Jesus Himself points out that the second group received the word with joy, so they obviously were believers for at least a short time. Likewise, the third group believed, but fell away because of troubles or persecution caused by the word, and the third group believed but fell away because of the normal everyday worries of the world and making money.

As we mentioned, the key to "continuing" is in both daily Bible study and prayer. The Bible study obviously is exciting, as we have seen with just the examples of the prophecies and types and shadows we have looked at thus far in this book. For some people that is easier than the prayer part. That being the case, we will look a little more closely at prayer and see if we can touch on a point or two that might be helpful in that realm.

In this final part of this book we are looking at the future of this world, and more importantly at our own individual futures. In Chapter 27 we learned that the meaning of life included three things:

1 - The courting period by our two suitors,

2 - Our decision as to which one we will choose, and

3 - Our engagement period with the one we choose.

We are briefly touching on the three persons of the Trinity.

In the last chapter we looked at God the Father, being exactly that, our Father. And in this chapter we have looked at descriptions in God's Word of Jesus, the Son, being truly God, the Creator of everything.

At the same time we are endeavoring to explore the third part of the meaning of life, the engagement period, which is our immediate future here on earth. In the next chapter we will be briefly discussing the third member of the Trinity, the precious Holy Spirit, thereby introducing all three individuals who make up the One to whom we are betrothed. Additionally, in the next chapter we will be looking at some exciting parts of what may be the main ingredient of our engagement period, prayer.

We will even touch on another mysterious spiritual being that plays a part in this story, angels.

Obviously we could spend volumes talking about this phenomenal engagement period between man and Spirit, and the wonderful possibilities it presents, but we have so much more of the exciting and little known that needs to be explored that we will move on after the next chapter to other extraordinary topics.

In later chapters we will be looking at the most wonderful of all prophecies. We will read about the real life Indiana Jones and his search for the Ark of the Covenant, which has already yielded possibly the most startling find ever made. We will discuss briefly what God tells us is going to happen in the end times, and how those things relate to our current events. And we will actually take you into heaven to see what it will really be like. Additionally we will find out the mystery of why God said in Proverbs 25:2. *"It is the glory of God to conceal a matter; to search out a matter is the glory of kings;"* and how that pertains directly to you and to me. We have encountered some wonderful things so far, but they may pale in comparison to what is ahead.

CHAPTER THIRTY

Are not all angels ministering spirits sent to serve those who will inherit salvation?" Hebrews 1:14

Angels do exist. The Bible mentions angels 110 times, in addition to scores of other times that they are talked about in other terms. Jesus mentioned them matter of factly in places such as when He told Peter to put his sword away the night He was arrested and said, *"Do you think I cannot call on my Father, and he will at once put at my disposal more than twelve legions of angels?"* Matthew 26:53

They are here on this earth, and each believer has his own guardian angel. We can know that for certain, because in talking about children Jesus said, *"See that you do not look down on one of these little ones. For I tell you that their angels in heaven always see the face of my Father in heaven."* Matthew 18:10

It may even be that your guardian angel looks just like you. For a clue to that astonishing possibility let's retell a story from the New Testament. Peter was in prison, *"sleeping between two soldiers, bound with two chains, and sentries stood guard at the entrance. Suddenly an angel of the Lord appeared and a light shown in the cell. He struck Peter on the side and woke him up. 'Quick, get up!' he said, and the chains fell off Peter's wrists."* Acts 12:6-7

The angel then led Peter out of the prison. *"They passed the first and second guards and came to the iron gate leading to the city. It opened for them by itself, and they went through it. When they had walked the length of one street, suddenly the angel left him."* Acts 12:10

After the angel left, Peter went to some friends' house who had been praying for him. *"Peter knocked at the outer entrance, and a servant girl named Rhoda came to answer the door. When she recognized Peter's voice, she was so overjoyed she ran back without opening it and exclaimed, 'Peter is at the door!'*

'You are out of your mind,' they told her. When she kept insisting that it was so, they said, 'It must be his angel." Acts 12:15

Obviously we don't know if our guardian angel really does look like us, but isn't it interesting that God found it important to include that incident in His Word. There must be something that He wants us to learn from that response. Obviously Peter's friends thought that his angel would be like him. It is fun to ponder, especially knowing that God did not put words in the Bible for no reason. Every single word is there for a purpose.

The main reason we included that story was to point out the obvious, angels are mighty and powerful spiritual beings. They are not floating on clouds and playing harps. Someone once painted a phenomenal word picture. In it were two very powerful looking, intense angels, standing side by side, looking down at their earthly charge, a person just like you and me. They were obviously extremely attentive, ready to answer the man's call for assistance at a moments notice. It was noticeable that they were more than capable of handling any situation that might be presented. These were experienced and mighty beings, eagerly anticipating the need to jump into action instantly. Their faces were determined and their strong bodies taught.

Suddenly one of the angels tensed. "He is about to pray," he said to his ready comrade. Both sets of wings fluttered slightly and a massive amount of air was displaced. Swoosh, swoosh. The slow beating of the phenomenal wings gave proof of the readiness of the mighty angels to obey the forthcoming command. Nothing could stand in their way to perform their upcoming duty. These spiritual warriors anticipated action.

The man's head bowed. The angels leaned closer. Swoosh, swoosh, swoosh, swoosh. The man's words were slowly uttered, "Dear God, please bless this bountiful meal." The angels' heads plaintively dropped in disappointment. Then, sadly but obediently they straighten back up, to wait for another day.

In the meantime they could only hope upon hope that they would one day be placed into action, any action. They had been created to do, not to wait.

How sad is that story, but how true to real life. Miracles still happen, and mighty angels are standing at the ready. But mankind seldom asks more than to bless our evening meals. What a waste.

As we said, though, new believers normally come to God in response to a specific need. And God usually seems to turn His angels loose to do what only they can do, the supernatural. It's not that our asking for things should be the main part of our prayer life; it shouldn't. But it is normally a first step, and as any other engaged man, God wants to let His bride-to-be know that He is trustworthy and able and caring. This is only reasonable.

The early days of any engagement are about encouraging the development of the relationship. From there, conversations become deeper, more meaningful, and more satisfying. Or at least, they should. Relating our needs eventually becomes a very small part of our prayer life. If not, it should. The engagement period is not just a time to get to know about Jesus through Bible study. It is a time to really get to know Him, in a very personal way. That is what our prayer life should become.

As time goes on, many things are added in addition to asking for things. We personally had the privilege as a hospice volunteer to spend quite a bit of time with the saintly Dr. Alfred Smith in his final months before going home to be with his Lord. Dr. Smith, often called the "Dean of Gospel Music," was a composer of hymns, a soloist, song leader, and authority on church music and its history. He was a fascinating man who had started his career as Billy Graham's first song leader. Among the many hymns he wrote was the well known and loved, "Surely Goodness and Mercy."

Having traveled extensively, and knowing intimately many of the most famous people in the religious world, his numerous stories were literally unparalleled treasures. One of the most profound was about a time when he was allowed to personally examine the original journals of George Mueller, who as we recounted earlier, built and maintained orphanages and schools in England by only praying for the needs instead of telling people about them. Dr. Smith said that in studying the journals he was impressed by one haunting statement that was written in the margins of many, many of the pages. The simple but very incitefull statement was, "The fruit of prayer is found in the garden of praise." We would all do well to memorize it, and actually learn from it. George Mueller left us a nugget with that statement, scribbled often in the margins: answers for needs come when we praise God in our prayers. They don't come by begging. They don't come because of whining. They don't come because we do a great job of explaining the need; God already knows all about that. Answers come because we turn the need over to Him completely, and then spend our prayer time praising Him. "The fruit of prayer is found in the garden of praise."

Yes, praise is one of the things that enters into our prayer life as it grows deeper. So, too, is thanksgiving, adoration, repentance, searching, and virtually anything else imaginable.

A mature prayer life is unrushed, and it is an honest and open communication between two people who love each other very much.

Mother Teresa of Calcutta quite obviously was one of the truly Godly people of the last century. A reporter once asked her what she said when she prayed to God. Mother Teresa simply answered, "I listen."

With a "cute" air about him, the reporter pushed the subject further by asking, "Well, what does God say?"

Mother Teresa's response was, "He listens."

What this saintly woman described was the true end result of a mature prayer life. Just as two lovers don't need to use words to convey their love for each other as they sit together under the stars, a wonderfully intimate prayer is often silent.

The person who was reputed to be quite possibly the closest to God of any person in the past thousand years was an extremely simple monk who lived in the 1600's by the name of Brother Lawrence. A collection of conversations with him and letters by him were first published after his death in 1691 in a book called, The Practice of the Presence of God. Although it was published several times after the first publishing, it was finally published again and widely distributed in 1895 with an introduction by the wonderful Quaker lady we read about earlier, Hannah Whitall Smith. The book has since then been published often, and is still widely circulated. You would have no trouble at all buying a copy on-line or in many book stores.

We recommend highly that you do.

For now, though, let's learn a few things from the 1895 copy of this exceptional work. We need to first know that Brother Lawrence (1610-1691) was a humble cook in a monastery in Lorraine, France. What was exceptional about him was the fact that he was so close to God. In the words of M. Beaufort, Grand Vicar to Cardinal de Noailles, with whom the conversations that appear in the book transpired,

"As Brother Lawrence had found such an advantage in walking in the presence of God, it was natural for him to recommend it earnestly to others; but his example was stronger inducement than any arguments he could propose. His very countenance was edifying, such a sweet and calm devotion appearing in it as could not but affect the beholders."

What was Brother Lawrence's secret? Very simply, the title of the book says it all, he constantly practiced being in the presence of God seven days a week. He was in nonstop communion and communication with his Father and his Lord. Here are the words of Brother Lawrence himself in the tenth letter he wrote to M. Beaufort:

"Pray remember what I have recommended to you, which is, to think often of God, by day, by night, in your business, and even in your diversions. He is always near you and with you; leave Him not alone. You would think it rude to leave a friend alone who came to visit you; why, then, must God be neglected? Do not, then, forget Him, but think on Him often, adore Him continually, live and die with Him; this is the glorious employment of a Christian. In a word, this is our profession; if we do not know it, we must learn it."

This should be every Christian's "words to live by."

In that paragraph was a question that should be drummed into our minds, "You would think it rude to leave a friend alone who came to visit you; why, then, must God be neglected?"

We need to imagine asking a friend over to our house and immediately ushering him into a seat in the living room, and then walking out, not to return until the next day, or the next.

It would be completely unthinkable for anyone to do such a thing, and yet, many, if not most, people who claim to be Christian invite Jesus into their hearts and lives, and then totally neglect Him, day after day after day. Rude is too nice a word.

We already mentioned that the average Christian spends less than two minutes per day talking to the Lord. Many only say "Dear Father" when they have some need that they can't resolve by themselves. Weeks or even months may go by between prayers. Or if they pray daily it may be nothing more that to ask the blessing at dinnertime. Or some might go so far as to pray every night at bedtime, asking protection for their kids.

Is it any wonder that Jesus made the statement He did in Matthew 7:23 about the last day, *"Then I will tell them plainly, I never knew you. Away from me."*

Of course, in the weak defense of those described above, they will probably be able to say that their minister gave the impression that their prayer life wasn't really all that important because, "once saved always saved." Are you beginning to see the real eternal life problems with that doctrine; a doctrine that almost prohibits debate because the thought is that to dispute it shows an unbelief, or at best a disrespect, for the love and power of God?

Yes, Jesus is all loving, and if He so desired He could save those who make a one time emotional walk down a church or crusade aisle, but then rudely leave Him sitting in a living room seat of their heart from then on; but over and over and over God's Word makes it clear that Jesus wants, and even demands more from a future bride than that. Even spending a precious hour of our time every Sunday morning doesn't guarantee a relationship with Jesus. It takes time truly spent with him in prayer that waters the bud of admiration into true love for Him.

True love can not develop in a relationship based on an occasional couple of brief minutes spent with a person. We spend more than that with the person who cuts our hair. In order to really fall deeply in love with anyone takes time. To fall in love with Jesus is no different. It takes time. Lots of time. But it is so worth it. Nothing at all compares to it.

When we train ourselves as Brother Lawrence did to practice the presence of God, we invariably find that prayer is a two way communication. God really does talk with us. It is hard to describe, as even Jesus told Nicodemus that spiritual things are hard to describe, but that doesn't make them any less real. Yes, it may not be with words, but God does communicate with everyone who genuinely makes an all out effort to get to know and love Him. God is very clear in His Word. He gives us a promise we can always rely on, *"Come near to God and He will come near to you."* James 4:8

God listens to us when we pray. Isaiah 38:5 says, *"This is what the Lord says, 'I have heard your prayer and seen your tears."* And God responds. In fact, He promises us, *"Call on me and I will answer you and tell you great and unsearchable things you do not know."* Jeremiah 33:3

Until we have truly made the effort to spend quality time in prayer we will not understand how He communicates with us, and lovingly communes with us. Describing the results to someone who hasn't genuinely done it is like trying to describe to someone who has never soared the emotions one feels flying in a glider for the very first time. We must do it to experience it, but it is very, very real, and it is incomparably wonderful.

Is it easy to practice the presence of God to the point that we achieve the results Brother Lawrence did? No, it takes effort, but fortunately he told us what to do. In the second conversation with M. Beaufort, Brother Lawrence said:

"That in order to form a habit of conversing with God continually, and referring all we do to Him, we must at first apply to Him with some diligence; but that after a little care we should find His love inwardly excite us to it without any difficulty."

The key is to do it, and do it until we form a habit of it. Brother Lawrence says that "we must at first apply to him with some diligence." Obviously that means there will be some effort at first. It doesn't come naturally. We are too accustomed to thinking about ourselves all the time, or the work we need to do, or the diet we are currently on, or any one of a million other things, than thinking of God. To form the habit of thinking about and talking with God we need to make the effort to do it. It may not be easy, although to some it may, but the end result surpasses anything words could ever convey. Staying in the presence of God results in a constant state of contentment, no matter what troubles may surround us. Additionally, beyond that, it is a New Testament instruction; a commandment if you will.

Christians are constantly searching for God's will. If they would only search in God's Word they would find that the only place "God's will for you" is mentioned, instructs us to remain in constant communications with God in prayer. The virtually never followed commandment is, *"Be joyful always; pray continually; give thanks in all circumstances, for this is God's will for you in Christ Jesus."* 1 Thessalonians 5: 16-18

There are only three things in that "commandment." We are to be joyful always. We are to pray continually. And we are to be thankful in all circumstances. That is God's will for our lives. The *"pray continually"* part is by all means the most important, because if we are in constant communications with Jesus we cannot help but fall so in love with him that everything else will fall into place. We will, without question, even fall so much in love with Him that the seemingly impossible commandments He gave us in the Sermon on the Mount, such as in Matthew 5:44 and 48, *"Love your enemies and pray for those who persecute you,"* and, *"Be perfect therefore, as your heavenly Father is perfect,"* will become much easier, because we will so want to please Him.

Brother Lawrence has given us very practical advice concerning how to do it; we must just diligently do it, no matter what, until it becomes a habit.

Additionally, though, God has given us another answer that will help tremendously. That answer lies with the third person of the mysterious trinity, the precious Holy Spirit.

Jesus told His disciples the night before He was crucified,

"If you love me, you will obey what I command. And I will ask the Father, and he will give you another Counselor to be with you forever - the Spirit of truth. The world cannot accept him, because it neither sees him nor knows him. But you know him, for he lives with you and will be in you." John 14:15-18

Please notice that there was another big "if" in that statement by Christ. It is an "if" that is normally overlooked by today's

Christian who is so often spoon fed only good news, never with any contingent requirements. Ask virtually anyone who has been trained in our Church of Laodicia and they will tell you that the Holy Spirit comes immediately when a person is gracious enough to "accept" Jesus. They sincerely believe that Jesus almost owes us the Holy Spirit's help, and that it is an automatic gift.

Let's read those first words from the lips of Jesus again,

"If you love me, you will obey what I command." It is then that Jesus sends us the Holy Spirit to help us in so many remarkable ways. Yes, loving Him and obeying Him are the *"if"* that must occur before we can hope to receive the Holy Spirit. God's Word reiterates that fact by saying, *"the Holy Spirit, whom God has given to those who obey him,"* Acts 5:32

Unfortunately so many ministers of the no responsibility, easy religion of today's Christianity tell the congregation when eight year old Billy comes up from the water of baptism that Billy now has the Holy Spirit in him who will guide him throughout his life. If that were true, why is it that forty years later Billy hasn't spent any time at all developing his relationship to the Jesus he supposedly calls Lord?

No, the acts of joining a church and even being baptized do not of themselves guarantee the precious gift of the Holy Spirit. Remember, "believing" in Jesus is the word "pistevo" which includes committing to, trusting, loving and obeying. But you and I are already well aware of that.

Jesus goes on to explain, *"All this I have spoken while still with you. But the Counselor, the Holy Spirit, whom the Father will send in my name, will teach you all things and will remind you of everything I said to you,"* John 14:25-26

In the King James version, the name, Holy Spirit, appears 89 times, and the name, Holy Ghost, appears 111 times. Additionally, the Holy Spirit is referred to often by other names, such as the Spirit of God, the Spirit of Christ, the Comforter, the Counselor, the Teacher, the Eternal Spirit, etc., but He is still the same person. And the Holy Spirit is a person. He is the third member of the Godhead, and He will come and live within us and help us in too many ways to count.

Just imagine, we can have God inside us. It is an incredible thought, but true. Allow these words of Romans 8:11 to sink in, *"And if the Spirit of him who raised Jesus from the dead is living in you, he who raised Christ from the dead will also give life to your mortal bodies through his Spirit who lives in you."* What a remarkable verse. We can have the same powerful God living inside us in the person of the Holy Spirit.

He will assist us in so many ways, even in our prayer life, as we are told in Romans 8:26-27, *"The Spirit helps us in our weakness. We do not know what we ought to pray for, but the Spirit himself intercedes for us with groans that words cannot express. And he who searches our hearts knows the mind of the Spirit, because the Spirit intercedes for the saints in accordance with God's will."* This is the assistance we mentioned that will help us "practice the presence of God" like Brother Lawrence.

The Holy Spirit will also convict us about sin, for Jesus said about the Holy Spirit, *"When he comes, he will convict the world of guilt in regard to sin and righteousness and judgment: in regard to sin, because men do not believe in me; in regard to righteousness, because I am going to the Father, where you can see me no longer; and in regard to judgement because the prince of the world now stands condemned."* John 16:8-11

The second part pertains to the help the Holy Spirit will give us during our engagement period with Christ. He will help us by pointing us to righteousness, and convicting us of sins that we commit, or contemplate committing. By so doing we may make the necessary adjustment to either repent if we did it already, or avoid it if we haven't.

However, just because we have the help and guidance of the Holy Spirit doesn't mean that we lose our free will. We can still resist him. Remember when we read from Stephen's sermon, *"You stiff-necked people with uncircumcised hearts and ears! You are just like your fathers; you always resist the Holy Spirit."* Acts 7:51

Yes, it is possible for us to resist the leading of the Holy Spirit, and Satan's demons do all they can to entice us to do exactly that. Unfortunately some people do fall for their sweet talk, but it is a simple task not to, because the Bible tells us in James 4:7, *"Resist the devil and he will flee from you."* Just as we are to avoid any other suitor when we are engaged to be married in our worldly lives, the same is true in our more important spiritual lives.

Let's read that piece of advice in God's Word in its entirety, *"Submit yourselves, then, to God. Resist the devil and he will flee from you. Come near to God and he will come near to you. Wash your hands, you sinners, and purify your hearts, you double minded."* James 4: 7-8

We are double minded so long as we try to keep Satan as a suitor after we have been betrothed to Jesus, and that simply will not end up with the result we hope for. We need to keep our minds focused on the actual heavenly marriage. The first century Christians were said to be "so heavenly minded that they were no earthly good." Quite frankly, that should be us. We should forget about the role models in our current religious society that are "so earthly minded that they are no heavenly good," thinking that they can still win the heavenly prize while at the same time cavorting with the deceiver. Our minds, hearts, and entire life need to be devoted to God.

When asked what the most important commandment was, Jesus answered, *"Love the Lord your God with all your heart and with all your soul and with all your mind. This is the first and greatest commandment."* Matthew 22:37-38

We do that when we "practice the presence of God." We do that as long as we *"pray continually."* Jesus expounded on this necessity very succinctly, so let's pay very close attention to His words:

"I am the true vine and my father is the gardener. He cuts off every branch in me that bears no fruit, while every branch that does bear fruit he prunes so that it will be even more fruitful. You are already clean because of the word I have spoken to you. Remain in me, and I will remain in you. No branch can bear fruit by itself; it must remain in the vine. Neither can you bear fruit unless you remain in me.

I am the vine; you are the branches. If a man remains in me and I in him, he will bear much fruit; apart from me you can do nothing. If anyone does not remain in me, he is like a branch that is thrown away and withers; such branches are picked up, thrown into the fire and burned. If you remain in me and my words remain in you, ask whatever you wish, and it will be given to you. This is to my Father's glory, that you bear much fruit, showing yourselves to be my disciples.

As the Father has loved me, so have I loved you. Now remain in my love. If you obey my commands, you will remain in my love, just as I have obeyed my Fathers commands and remain in his love. I have told you this so that my joy may be in you and that your joy may be complete." John 15:1-11

In those few verses Jesus used the word "remain" eleven times. We remain in him by following the instructions of Brother Lawrence and thinking about Him, praying with Him, and communicating with Him all the time; during our business time, in our recreational time, in all of our time. The end result is in that last statement, our joy in this life will be complete, plus our joy in our eternal life will be indescribable.

As important as this discussion of our Christian life in this temporary tent of flesh is, the time we have referred to as our engagement period, which is our extremely brief immediate future until you and I return to our true spiritual home, we will now move to an examination of God's foretelling of events to come on this earth and in eternity. We will next talk about the most important and exciting prophecy that is found in the Bible.

Before we close this chapter and move on, however, let us emphasize as strongly as possible that the most important, as well as most rewarding, necessity in our lives is for us to do everything in our power to really develop our relationship with God and the person of His son, Jesus Christ. For our Christian walk to mature we must move into the area of complete love and trust in our Savior. That can only happen through much time spent with Him in prayer. That being said, there is nothing at all that is as important as our daily prayer life. Not only should we talk to Him constantly as we go through our daily lives, and keep Him continually foremost in our minds, but we should also form the habit of setting aside uninterrupted time each and every day in which we can truly get into quality prayer time. This is the time that the Bible talks about in Psalm 42:7 in which, *"Deep calls to deep."*

Set aside enough time that you won't feel rushed. If it requires getting up earlier, do it. If you must give up a TV show, do it. Whatever it takes, do it. There is nothing as important in our lives as that time spent with the Creator of the universe, the Creator of everything that ever was or ever will be. It is a privilege beyond compare, and it normally results in such unbelievable love being poured out from both parties that neither one will want to break away. It is in those minutes that God will truly fulfill the promise he gave us when He said, *"Call on me and I will answer you and tell you great and unsearchable things you do not know."* Jeremiah 33:3

PART SIX

CHAPTER THIRTY-ONE

When we look at what is to come on earth in the near future there are two chapters in God's Word that spring to mind, Ezekiel 38 and 39. Those two chapters describe in quite a bit of detail the war of Gog and Magog. There is some debate among Biblical prophecy scholars as to whether or not this war is actually describing the same war that we refer to as the very last battle on earth, the one we know of as Armageddon. Most scholars lean toward the thinking that they are two very separate and distinct wars, and we do too; however, we probably will not know for sure until the war actually takes place, and quite frankly, it really and truly doesn't matter which camp is right.

The one thing that is becoming more and more clear is the fact that current events seem to be leading anyone in either camp to believe that it is right around the corner.

We will read a little bit from those chapters, but first let's explain the list of participants in alphabetical order:

Beth Togarmah is now Turkey

Cush is now Sudan

Gog and Magog are Uzbekistan, Kazakstan, Kurdistan, Tajikistan, Turkmenistan, and others.

Gomer is now north central Asia Minor

Meshech is now the Russian Federation

Persia is now Iran

Put is modern Lybia

Rosh, meaning "head," is Russia

Tubal is now eastern Russia

Almost all of these are Islamic states, with many being the home of Islamic terrorists. Interesting in this list that we will find in Ezekiel 38 is the absence of Egypt, Jordan, Yemen and Saudi Arabia, the four nations that broke allegiance with the Arab League of Nations over Hezbollah's attack on Israel, and four countries who are currently distancing themselves from Iran due to the nuclear weapon concern. And isn't it interesting that for the first time ever we are seeing Russia align itself with Iran?

Now let's read what God told Ezekiel to write, the very same Ezekiel that we saw in Part One of this book who was told to lie on his sides for a certain number of days as a part of the prophecy that gave the exact day in which Israel would become a nation in May of 1948. And as a point to ponder, remember that the prophecy we are going to look at could not have even possibly occurred for twenty five hundred years after it was given to Ezekiel to write, because Israel was not even a nation from Ezekiel's time until 1948.

"The word of the Lord came to me: 'Son of man, set your face against Gog, of the land of Magog, the chief prince of Meshech and Tubal; prophesy against him and say: This is what the Sovereign Lord says: I am against you, O Gog, chief prince of Meshech and Tubal. I will turn you around, put hooks in your jaws and bring you out with your whole army ... Persia, Cush and Put will be with them ..., also Gomer with all its troops, and Beth Togarmah from the far north with all its troops - the many nations with you.

Get ready, be prepared, you and all the hordes gathered about you, and take command of them. After many days you will be called to arms. In future years you will invade a land that has recovered from war, whose people were gathered from many nations to the mountains of Israel, which had long been desolate. They had been brought out from the nations, and now all of them live in safety. You and all your troops and the many nations with you will go up, advancing like a storm; you will be like a cloud covering the land.

This is what the sovereign lord says: On that day thoughts will come into your mind and you will devise an evil scheme. You will say, 'I will invade a land of unwalled villages; I will attack a peaceful and unsuspecting people - all of them living without walls and without gates and bars. I will plunder and loot and turn my hand against the resettled ruins and the people gathered from the nations, rich in livestock and goods, living at the center of the land." Ezekiel 38:1-12

So where is America in all of this? Can we imagine Russia and her Islamic allies mounting an attack like this against Israel if America is still the super power of the world? It seems pretty unlikely to say the least. So, where is America? Strangely, America is never mentioned in Biblical prophecy, although a minority of Biblical Prophecy scholars point to the next verse as a remote possibility. The verse reads, *"Sheba and Dedan and the merchants of Tarshish and all her villages will say to you, 'Have you come to plunder? Have you gathered your hordes to loot, to carry off silver and gold, to take away livestock and goods and to seize much plunder?"* Ezekiel 38:13

Sheba and Dedan refer to Saudi Arabia, Yemen, and Kuwait, who will evidently be nervously on the sidelines. Tarsish is probably eastern Europe. The thought by the few who see the USA at all in scripture is that since the word for "villages" could also have been translated as "young lions," that could refer to the young lions of England, namely Canada, Australia, and the United States. We personally feel that to be a pretty big stretch by those who hope upon hope that the United States is still around and a world power.

In the very unlikely chance that "villages" did refer to America, she obviously is only talking at this point, without any military strength at all, or at least any will to engage. The more likely reality is that America will have either passed her glory by normal time erosion, as all empires do, or she will have been quickly knocked back into the nineteenth century by an Electro Magnetic Pulse bomb or the like, which Iran may soon be able to launch, in the manner North Korea and China are already capable of doing. Another possibility, of course, is that the ridiculous political correctness that is so prevalent in America today allowed the war on terror to be lost in any of several possible scenarios. At any rate, America will not be a factor in this upcoming war, which is probably quickly approaching.

This should not really come as any surprise to any of us who have seen God's many prophetic proofs of his existence. We know that He is here, and that He has a vested interest in how nations obey His commands and repay Him for His blessings. On March 30, 1863, Abraham Lincoln told his fellow American citizens the following:

"We have been the recipients of the choicest bounties of heaven. We have been preserved, these many years, in peace and prosperity. We have grown in numbers, wealth and power, as no other nation has ever grown. But we have forgotten God. We have forgotten the gracious hand which preserved us in peace, and multiplied and enriched and strengthened us; and we have vainly imagined, in the deceitfulness of our hearts, that all the blessings were produced by some superior wisdom and virtue of our own. Intoxicated with unbroken success, we have become too self-sufficient to feel the necessity of redeeming and preserving grace, too proud to pray to the God that made us!

It behooves us, then, to humble ourselves before the offended Power, to confess our national sins, and to pray for clemency and forgiveness."   Abraham Lincoln, 1863.

Obviously the American people did not pay attention to the truth of what Abe Lincoln had to say. They didn't then, and they haven't since. In fact, since then America has done just about all it could do to throw God out of the country, by banning prayer in school, slaughtering millions of babies, inviting Hindus and Moslems to pray in its Senate, and effectively doing all in its power to tell God that He is not wanted or needed. Every action, though, whether it is national or individual, brings about results, either positive or negative. No, America will not be a power anymore when the war of Gog and Magog occurs, but we should not be at all surprised.

Forgetting what could have or should have been, though, let's continue on with finding out how God tells us this quickly approaching, important and exciting battle will play out:

"Therefore, son of man, prophesy and say to Gog: 'This is what the Sovereign Lord says: In that day, when my people Israel are living in safety, will you not take notice of it? You will come from your place in the far north, you and many nations with you ... a great horde, a mighty army. You will advance against my people Israel like a cloud that covers the land. In days to come, O Gog, I will bring you against my land, so that the nations may know me when I show myself holy through you before their eyes." Ezekiel 39:14-16

Now we are beginning to see something really important; this war will be orchestrated by God Himself in order to stop the debate about Him. This invasion has been planned by God for the reason, as He explains, *"so that the nations may know me."*

Obviously this book you are reading will not have reached the masses of the world. They will still need more proof that God is among us.

The prophecy continues;

"This is what will happen in that day: when Gog attacks the land of Israel my hot anger will be aroused, declares the Sovereign Lord. In my zeal and fiery wrath I declare that at that time there shall be a great earthquake in the land of Israel." Ezekiel 38:18-19

We stopped just momentarily to make note of that word "wrath." It could become very important in our future study.

God's prophecy goes on to describe the "earthquake,"

"The fish of the sea, the birds of the air, the beasts of the field, every creature that moves along the ground , and all the people on the face of the earth will tremble at my presence. The mountains will be over-turned, the cliffs will crumble and every wall will fall to the ground. .... I will pour down torrents of rain, hailstones and burning sulfur on him and on his troops and on the many nations with him. And so I will show my greatness and my holiness, and I will make myself known in the sight of many nations. Then they will know that I am the Lord." Ezekiel 38:22

God goes on to describe the battle and how He will destroy the Russian/Iranian led coalition army. After it is over God says,

"Then those who live in the towns of Israel will go out and use the weapons for fuel. ... For seven years they will use them for fuel. They will not need to gather wood from the forest, because they will use the weapons for fuel." Ezekiel 39:9-10

This leads many to think that there will be usable nuclear weaponry left over that could be converted to civil use.

"On that day I will give Gog a burial place in Israel, in the valley of those who travel east toward the sea. It will block the way of travelers, because Gog and all his hordes will be buried there.

For seven months the house of Israel will be burying them in order to cleanse the land. ... Men will be regularly employed to cleanse the land. Some will go throughout the land and, in addition to them, others will bury those that remain on the ground. At the end of seven months they will begin their search.

As they go through the land and one of them sees a human bone, he

will set up a marker beside it until the gravediggers have buried it. ... And so they will cleanse the land." Ezekiel 39:11-16

Once again, this sounds very much like the clean up operation after a nuclear explosion. We obviously cannot know for sure until this shortened battle really takes place, but it could be that the earthquake God described is a nuclear bomb, or it could be that there will actually be an earthquake and then a nuclear explosion. Whatever the case, it will be very obvious that God's hand will have been involved with the protection of His people, Israel, so that both they and other nations will know for a certainty that He exists, and He is present.

One of the several reasons that we lean toward thinking that this battle is the next big event prophesied in God's Word and not the very last battle at Armageddon is the fact that Israel will spend so much time on the clean up operation after it is over, and that they will be using the left over weaponry for fuel for seven years following it. That does not sound at all like what would happen in the time that has been described in the Bible that will follow Armageddon. We will look at that a little bit later.

Whether this upcoming battle that God foretells will occur is the last battle on earth described in Revelation, or is, as we believe, just a precursor to the seven year tribulation that we will discuss later, two things should be extremely apparent to us.

The first obvious thing is that if we are keeping up with current events at all we should see that for the first time in history the nations described in this prophecy are definitely aligning themselves to make such a move. The second thing we should now know for a certainty is that God's prophecies always come to pass, and always in a very literal way. All of His prophecies that should have occurred by now have in fact happened, and all of them happened just as God said they would. Lest we forget. God told us, *"I am God, and there is none like me. I make known the end from the beginning, from ancient times, what is still to come."* Isaiah 46:10

The most exciting prophecy God ever made, though, makes not only the above prophecy about the war of Gog and Magog, but all the fulfilled prophecies we have previously examined, pale in comparison. Additionally, it may not only be the most fantastic prophecy for us, but it may well be for God as well. We say that because He did not just give it once, but He foretold it about 2,400 times in His Word. There is no other event, passed or future, that He predicted nearly that often.

This monumentally important prophecy is none other than the truth that Jesus is coming back to earth. This is not just a doctrine that is talked about in churches. This is not just a metaphysical topic of discussion by spiritualists. Jesus is actually going to walk back on this earth in a body that men and women will be able to see and touch. And it may be quite soon. Jesus will come back once again to be with His creation. You and I will witness it. There can be no statement more profound.

Over and over Jesus spoke very plainly about His return:

"Do not let your hearts be troubled. Trust in God; trust also in me. In my father's house are many rooms; if it were not so, I would have told you. I am going to prepare a place for you. And if I go and prepare a place for you, I will come back and take you to be with me that you also may be where I am." John 14:1-3

We saw that the first coming of Jesus was foretold three hundred times, and Jesus literally fulfilled each one of them. God told us eight times that often that Jesus would come again. As we said, Jesus Himself talked about it constantly, but the Bible is full of other ways it is foretold as well, such as what happened when the disciples watched Him ascend into heaven after His forty days on earth that followed His resurrection.

Of that ascension we read:

"They were looking intently up into the sky as He was going, when suddenly two men dressed in white stood beside them. 'Men of Galilee,' they said, 'why do you stand here looking into the sky? This same Jesus, who has been taken from you into heaven, will come back in the same way you have seen Him go into heaven." Acts 1:10-11

Two thousand, four hundred times we are told by God in His Word, His infallible communication to us, that Jesus is coming back. We can take it to the bank. Jesus is coming back. Once we have a clear understanding of what that entails, there can be no more exciting knowledge than that. In the next chapters we will attempt to clarify as much as is known about how that will take place, when it probably will happen, and what is in store for His true bride, those who continue to pistevo.

CHAPTER THIRTY-TWO

We said some chapters back that we can ascertain what is really important to God, and therefore to us, the exact same way we can find the thoughts of a good teacher, by looking at what is repeated over and over and over. There is nothing mentioned as often throughout God's Word as the second coming of Jesus. Two thousand four hundred times it is discussed in the Bible.

In fact, out of the 216 chapters in the New Testament, we can find references to the return of Jesus in 212 of them. Think about that, God wanted us to be so aware that Jesus was going to come back to earth again that He foretold it in 212 chapters out of 216. That should be eye opening.

With all of that repetition, however, there is some confusion within the church as to whether or not Jesus will actually return twice. The answer is a very definite yes, and no. The scripture that is at the root of the debate is the following:

"Brothers, we don't want you to be ignorant about those who fall asleep, or to grieve like the rest of men who have no hope. We believe that Jesus died and rose again and so we believe that God will bring with Jesus those who have fallen asleep in him. According to the Lord's own word, we tell you that we who are still alive, who are left till the coming of the Lord, will certainly not precede those who have fallen asleep. For the Lord Himself will come down from heaven, with a loud command, with the voice of the archangel and with the trumpet call of God, and the dead in Christ will rise first. After that, we who are still alive and are left will be caught up together with them in the clouds to meet the Lord in the air. And so we will be with the Lord forever." 1 Thessalonians 4;13-17

The original Koine Greek word that was later translated as "caught up" in that verse was "harpazo." About 400 AD the word, Harpazo, was translated into the Vulgate as the Latin word, "raeptius," from which we get our exciting and somewhat controversial English word, "rapture." We say the rapture is somewhat controversial because a minority of Christians are not convinced that it is going to happen. That is OK, though, as they will just be pleasantly surprised when it happens to them, if they happen to be alive on the day it occurs.

The truth is that if we look at the Bible as a whole, as well as the individual scriptures that discuss it, the rapture has to happen. Exactly how it will happen, we don't know. But it will happen just as surely as the war of Gog and Magog will come to pass, and it could very well take place before that battle is over.

God has established His modus operandi. He always takes his children out of harms way before His wrath is let loose on disbelieving and disobeying mankind. Shadows can be seen in God's Word of that method of doing things, prophesying the rapture. In the well known story of the flood, God takes those who "pistevo" Him out of the path of His wrath when He lifts Noah and his family above it in Noah's ark. The ark is in fact a shadow of the rapture.

In the same manner, prior to God's wrath destroying Sodom and Gamorrah because of their homosexual practices, God removes the only righteous man in the cities, Lot, and his family. In fact, let's look at a very revealing verse in the description of that story.

Lot, when told to flee the city with his family before the disaster occurs, asks to be allowed to flee to a small town that was near enough to run to. The scripture then says:

"He said to him, 'Very well, I will grant this request, too;

I will not overthrow the town you speak of. But flee there quickly because I cannot do anything until you reach it." Genesis 19:21-22

Isn't it revealing that God is telling us that He <u>cannot</u> let forth His wrath until His people are safely out of harms way. What a comfort that should be to all of us. This is why we feel the rapture will occur before the battle of Gog and Magog. Remember when we examined that upcoming battle in the last chapter, we read in Ezekiel 38:19, *"In my zeal and fiery wrath I declare that there shall be a great earthquake."* If God's wrath is going to be experienced on earth, His children will be taken out beforehand. God won't change His modus operandi.

How will the rapture take place? We are not told exactly, but we do know some things. For instance, God's Word tells us, *"Lis-*

ten, I tell you a mystery: We will not all sleep, but we will all be changed - in a flash, in the twinkling of an eye, at the last trumpet. For the trumpet will sound, the dead will be raised imperishable, and we will be changed. For the perishable must clothe itself with the imperishable, and the mortal with immortality." 1 Corinthians 15:52-53

Tim LaHaye and Jerry Jenkins wrote a fabulously successful and entertaining series of books that were then made into movies, called <u>The Left Behind Series</u>. They told a story of those who would be left behind when the rapture occurred. The series read like science fiction, but it may be very close to fact.

This rapture will occur, but it is not the time referred to as the Second Coming of Christ. Yes, Jesus will call His saints to heaven, both those who are dead and those who are still alive, but He Himself will not actually descend to earth again at that time. That is why we answered the question about Christ coming twice with a yes and a no. In reality it is more of a no than a yes. He may get close, but His feet will not walk the earth until at least seven years later.

Yes, the rapture must occur, and it must take place before the last seven year tribulation period for many reasons. We mentioned that God must take His children out of harms way before He displays His wrath; but also, we shall see that the marriage supper of the Lamb will occur in heaven at the same time the tribulation is happening on earth. Additionally, those who are raptured have a real and distinct role to play in the later Millennial Kingdom, so they must have been changed into their future spirit form. These things we are about to discuss should cause those who now "pistevo" Jesus to tingle all over.

We saw earlier that all of the disciples of Jesus except John died horrible deaths because of their preaching of the Gospel. As we learned, they even tried to kill John in Rome by dipping him head first into a vat of boiling oil in 95 AD. God miraculously saved him, though; and the Emperor Domitian, knowing that it had to have been a miracle, did not try any other methods of killing him. Instead Domitian had John exiled to the Ilse of Patmos in the Aegean Sea to do hard labor.

God saved John because He had one more extremely important task for him. While on Patmos, Jesus came to John and actually dictated many of the words in the last book of the Bible, Revelation. Additionally He allowed John to supernaturally view and record what was going to happen in the last seven years, both the events on earth as well as the events that would occur during the same time period in heaven. It is a phenomenal book that incidentally is the only book in the Bible of which we are told, *"Blessed is the one who reads the words of this prophecy."* Revelation 1:3

The first words of Jesus to John in Revelation 1:8 were,

"I am the Alpha and Omega,' says the Lord God, 'who is, and was, and who is to come, the Almighty." (As an aside, and remembering our study of numbers, we can see 1, being the Creator, and 8 being Jesus. We will see that combination later on in an astounding verse.)

Jesus goes on to dictate chapters two and three verbatim, which comprise the letters to the seven churches that we studied earlier, with the last letter to the church of Laodicia, our church, the lukewarm church of which He says, *"So, because you are lukewarm - neither hot nor cold - I am about to spit you out of my mouth."* Revelation 3:16

John then goes on to write in amazing detail the future seven year period he is allowed to see that makes up the last seven years immediately preceding the day Jesus returns. Additionally, John writes about what will happen after Christ's return. Enough books to fill several libraries have been written about the events John foresaw and recorded.

We, however, are just going to briefly cover in a few paragraphs the events that will take place on earth. Quite frankly, for those who truly make Jesus the Lord of their lives and develop a loving relationship with Him now, what happens on earth during those seven years are completely unimportant. Those true followers of Jesus will not be here to see any of it anyway. Surprisingly, the relatively few churches that spend any time studying prophecy at all, seem to concentrate on that section, which is totally irrelevant to a true believer. I suppose some people might get scared enough of the tribulation years to run to Christ; though, it makes more sense that the thought of an eternity in hell would cause that response a lot quicker than the comparatively short seven years of the tribulation.

At any rate, in a nutshell, the following is what those who are left behind can look forward to according to God's always accurate prophecies in the books of Daniel, Revelation, Joel, Zephaniah, and elsewhere. It would take another complete book to even partially go over all of the scriptures and their explanations of the tribulation period here on earth. Since enough books on that subject have already been written to fill a couple of libraries, we will just give a quick overview here; for as we said, current Christians will have already been raptured anyway. The following will be our own personal interpretation of those seven year events, laid out in as abbreviated and simplistic a fashion as possible.

First let's go back to our old friend Daniel. Probably the most well known of the prophecies in the book of Daniel come from an interpretation he gave to King Nebuchadnezzar about a dream the king had. The king made the task a little harder than normal by insisting that Daniel even tell him what the dream was. With God as his advisor, though, Daniel didn't even have any trouble with that part of it, for we read;

"You looked, O king, and there before you stood a large statue - an enormous, dazzling statue, awesome in appearance. The head of the statue was made of pure gold, its chest and arms of pure silver, its belly and thighs of bronze, its legs of iron, its feet partly of iron and partly of baked clay. While you were watching, a rock was cut out , but not by human hands. It struck the statue on its feet of iron and clay and smashed them. Then the iron and clay, the bronze, the silver, and the gold were broken to pieces at the same time and became the chaff on the threshing floor of the summer. The wind swept them away without leaving a trace. But the rock that swept the statue became a huge mountain and filled the whole earth." Daniel 2:31-35

Daniel goes on to interpret the dream for the king with the same intricate accuracy that we saw earlier was the mark of God's prophecies in that book. He describes the head of gold as the kingdom of Babylon, the chest of silver as the Medo-Persian Empire, the belly and thighs of bronze as the Greek Empire under Alexander that we studied early on, and the legs of iron as the Roman Empire.

There were two legs, of course, which foretold that the Roman Empire would be divided, which obviously it was. Rome was the first capital; but under Emperor Constantine an eastern capital was established in Constantanople, which is now Istanbul, Turkey. In reality, the eastern leg of the Roman Empire outlasted the western leg by about a thousand years. The dream, and others that Nebuchadnezzar had, and the interpretations by Daniel of them, foretold very accurately those four main empires. The toes and the rock that smashes the toes and becomes a huge mountain covering the future earth foretell an empire and event that is still to come. Scholars know that the rock is a type of Jesus. His second coming and establishment of a worldwide earthly kingdom are not at all in question. What is somewhat in question is the make up of the end time empire that is represented by the toes, the empire that Christ will smash.

For years Biblical scholars evidently forgot the eastern leg of the Roman Empire, the leg that in reality was the most successful and long lasting. Since common western thought for years about the Roman Empire has focused on Rome, western Biblical scholars have concentrated their interpretation of coming events on a resurgence of power in Rome, or at least Europe. With the foundation of the European Union coming at a time when a plethora of end time prophecies were so obviously being fulfilled, starting with the rebirth of the Jewish nation of Israel, all the scholars immediately said "Aha, the EU is going to be the prophesied end time empire." They were all so sure about it that a mountain of books were written and speculation began as to which ten European nations would make up the ten toes, and which European nation the antichrist would come from who would lead this end time European empire into the tribulation. Even today, with the EU far over the anticipated number of ten nations, almost all the scholars are still holding strong to those views. Of course, they have to. They sold millions of books and lectured so emphatically that it would be too embarrassing to admit that they were wrong.

What they all failed to pay attention to was the original Roman Empire. The fact is that the scope of that empire covered the following countries in addition to Italy and Greece: Turkey, Iraq,

Syria, Lebanon, Libya, Jordan, Egypt, Ethiopia, and Morocco. Isn't it striking that all of the nations that made up the ancient Roman Empire are now very Islamic, with the exception of Italy and Greece? That being said, it probably is not surprising to you that we personally feel strongly that the upcoming, end time, ten nation empire from which the antichrist will arise will be an Islamic federation of some sort.

We will, however, state that Syria may not be a big part of it. At least not Damascus. For God told us in Isaiah 17:1, *"See, Damascus will no longer be a city but will become a heap of ruins."* This has not happened yet; but since God said it, it will. Syria is not even mentioned in Ezekiel with the list of countries in the war of Gog and Magog, so the possibility is that Israel may get fed up with Syria's terrorist influence and one day retaliate. Or it could be the United States. What we can say is that Syria is definitely not the place to invest in property.

Our feeling, then, is that sometime in the future the Islamic nations mentioned above, minus Syria, but plus a few others, will form a union of some kind which will be the predicted end time ten nation empire. A man, who we feel strongly will also be Islamic, will arise on the international scene who will be extremely charismatic, and he will lead the world to believe that he can bring order back into the world, following the disaster of the war of Gog and Magog and the upheaval caused by it. This is the person we know as the antichrist.

This man will sign a seven year peace agreement with Israel. This agreement, however, will be broken in the middle of the seven years. The signing of this agreement will usher in the seven years of tribulation. Please remember, we are just going to be mentioning the rough highlights of those seven years' events here on earth, since those of you who "pistevo" Christ now will be gone when it happens, due to either death or the rapture.

Up until this time in history, God will have been very patient with mankind, trying to lovingly court His creation. With the beginning of the tribulation, though, things change. God will show his awesome power in ways man has never before experienced, but with His same goal in mind, to cause man to choose Him over Satan and evil. Revelation describes in detail terrible things that will occur on earth in hopes of causing mankind to wake up and turn to God. These things are described one at a time as seven seals are broken and seven trumpets sound. They include such things as war, famine, pestilence, death, earthquakes, hail, fire, the sun diminishing, and plagues. It will be a terrible time to be on earth. Fortunately we won't be.

Although the true Christians will have been taken to heaven before this ordeal commences, God will raise up 144,000 believers during this time to spread the word of how people can still be saved and live with God for eternity. God still will be wooing people with these 144,000 ministers. In Revelation 7:4 we read, *"144,000 from all the tribes of Israel."* Verses 5 through 8 then describe that there will be 12,000 from each of the twelve tribes of Israel.

This obviously is very unlike what Jehovah's Witnesses teach, which is that they will be the 144,000. It is almost comical when studying that cult to see that they originally believed that when they reached 144,000 members, that would be it. Of course, now they have about six million members so they have been forced to change their doctrine to say that the best 144,000 Jehovah's Witnesses will go to heaven and the rest will join Jesus in His millennial reign. That doctrinal change isn't surprising when we find that they changed doctrines 148 times between 1917 and 1928 alone. Of course, since they don't believe in the Trinity, they do not believe that Jesus is God either. In fact, they somehow amazingly came up with the thought that the archangel, Michael, was the first being created and is therefore the only begotten son of God. This means, of course, that they miss out on the celebration of Christmas. Obviously, though, not even believing that Jesus is God will cause them even bigger problems than that.

As we shall see when we look in more detail at what is going on in heaven at this same time, these 144,000 Messianic Jewish ministers do quite a phenomenal evangelical job, because a giant world wide revival takes place.

God also foretells that He will send two Old Testament witnesses to explain the Gospel of Jesus to the world, with obviously even more people turning to God because of their preaching.

Some feel that those two witness will be Enoch and Elijah, since both of them went to heaven without dying. Some scholars, however, believe that they may be Moses and Elijah. There is no way to be sure, of course, but we personally feel that the two witness will in some way be reminders of the Old Testament Law and the New Testament Gospel of Jesus. Those are the two "witnesses" God sent in the past.

In Revelation 11:3, God foretells, *"And I will give power to my two witnesses and they will prophesy for 1,260 days, clothed in sackcloth."* And He goes on to tell us, *"These men have power to shut up the sky so that it will not rain during the time that they are prophesying; and they have the powers to turn the waters into blood and to strike the earth with every kind of plague as often as they want."* Revelation 11:6

Lest we think any of this is fantasy, let's remember that it would have seemed fantastic to have thought that the three hundred prophecies of the first coming of Jesus would have been fulfilled literally as well. For that matter, it was a fantasy to believe that Israel would again become a nation, or that most of the fulfilled prophecies we have studied would have come to pass. But they all did, exactly as God foretold that they would.

During the first three and a half years of the tribulation the antichrist will gain more and more power. He will defeat some who don't agree with him, and he will literally become a world dictator such as the world has never seen.

One of the big things the antichrist will do will be to try to establish a one world religion, with his sidekick, the "false prophet" as its head. This false prophet is described in Revelation 13:11, *"Then I saw another beast coming out of the earth. He had two horns like a lamb, but he spoke like a dragon."* We believe very strongly that the two horns are a reference to a melding of two religions, the Apostate Christian church, which will not believe that Jesus is God, and Islam, which also does not believe Jesus is God. As we know, Islam recognizes Jesus as a prophet and believes that he was not crucified but will return with the Mahdi and will then slaughter all Christians and Jews. Can you imagine such a thing? As to the false prophet himself, we believe that he will be an Apostate Pope. We need to realize that a Moslem today reveres

Mary and will even kiss the ring of a Pope so long as he is not wearing a cross. An Apostate Pope would be perfect casting for the false prophet.

In the very middle of the seven year tribulation on earth the antichrist will enter the then rebuilt temple in Jerusalem and be declared as God. This is the *"abomination that causes desolation,"* that Daniel 11:31 foretells. In speaking of the false prophet, Revelation 13:12 says that he *"made the earth and its inhabitants worship the first beast,"* the antichrist.

We then read in God's prophecy of the false prophet, *"he deceived the inhabitants of the earth. He ordered them to set up an image in honor of the beast* (Antichrist) ... *all who refused to worship the image to be killed. He also forced everyone, small and great, rich and poor, free and slave, to receive a mark on his right hand or on his forehead, so that no one could buy or sell unless he had the mark, which is the name of the beast or the number of his name.*

This calls for wisdom. If anyone has insight, let him calculate the number of the beast, for it is man's number. His number is 666." Revelation 13:14-18

Some people today are concerned about accepting the number 666, but they need not be worried at all. Remember, so long as we make the decision to become "engaged" to Jesus now, and *"remain in Him"* by staying faithful to Him with the help of the precious Holy Spirit, we will either die or we will be raptured before the tribulation even begins. Either way, the big decision, which is the big part of the meaning of life, will have already have been made and we will escape all the events leading up to and including the mark of the beast. By fully giving our lives to Jesus today, the number 666 has no meaning in our lives. We won't be here to witness that abomination.

For those who are alive during the tribulation, though, the decision to take that mark will be the most horrendous decision of their lives. Although it will seem like a wise thing to do for the moment, because rejecting it will bring about terrible hardships and possible death from the antichrist, those who accept it will be doomed, for we read:

"If anyone worships the beast and his image and receives his mark on the forehead or on the hand, he, too, will drink of the wine of God's fury, which has been poured full strength into the cup of His wrath. He will be tormented with burning sulfur in the presence of the holy angels and of the Lamb. And the smoke of their torment rises forever and ever. There is no rest day or night for those who worship the beast and his image, or for anyone who receives the mark of his name. This calls for patient endurance on the part of the saints who obey God's commandments and remain faithful to Jesus." Rev. 14:9-12

Please notice once again that those who choose Jesus during the tribulation will also be required to *"obey God's commandments and remain faithful to Jesus."* It won't be a one time decision without any further requirements. We need to really grasp hold of this reality in light of the teaching of today's church of Laodicia and its dangerous "once saved always saved" doctrine.

About this time on earth an angel will be sent to give mankind one last chance, for John tells us, *"Then I saw another angel flying in midair, and he had the eternal Gospel to proclaim to those who live on the earth - to every nation, tribe, language and people. He said in a loud voice, 'Fear God and give Him glory, because the hour of His judgement has come. Worship him who made the heavens, the earth, the sea and the springs of water."* Revelation 14:6-7

With all of the last efforts of God to save as many people as will listen to His wooings, through His 144,000 Messianic Jewish ministers, the two witnesses, and the angel telling everyone about Jesus, there will then be a lot of new believers, ones who "pistevo" Jesus. This results in either a second rapture of sorts or a mass martyrdom like has never occurred. We can't be sure, but either way, the new saints are taken to heaven.

At this point God's wrath is sent forth with full force. Seven bowls of his wrath now pour down on the remaining mankind, which results in terrible boils on humans, the seas and rivers turn to blood, there is great unbearable heat and darkness, and gigantic hail. These last years are the Great Tribulation.

Finally, several nations become so fed up with the state of affairs the antichrist has led them into, that they start to rev(gigantic battle is set to take place in the valley of Jezreel tha rounds Mount Migeddo. The battle is referred to as Armaged-don, but it never really occurs, for as it begins, Jesus, who has had enough, returns to earth, this time not as a meek Servant and Lamb to be slaughtered, but as the King of kings and Lord of lords. *"On that day His feet will stand on the Mount of Olives, east of Jerusalem, and the Mount of Olives will be split in two from east to west."* Zechariah 14:4

God says of that day, *"Look, He is coming with the clouds, and every eye will see him, even those who pierced him; and all the peoples of the earth will mourn because of him. So shall it be! Amen."* Revelation 1:7

This will be the day that twenty four hundred prophecies will be fulfilled. It may well be the most monumental day in the history of mankind, or in His Story. Jesus Himself told us of this day often, with statements like, *"For the Son of Man is going to come in his Father's glory with His angels, and then He will reward each person according to what he has done."* Matthew 16:27

Romans 14:11 says, *"As surely as I live' says the Lord, 'every knee will bow before me."* This will be that day. It is going to happen. For those who are in Him, what a wonderful day that will be.

Our prayer is that everyone who has read this book to this point will never have to face the horrors of the seven year tribulation period immediately preceding the return of Christ, but we know that is unrealistic. If, however, you happen to be one who still does have the possibility of being on earth during those terrible years, and even having a worse future beyond that, God is courting you this very moment. A coincidence is when God decides to remain anonymous, so it is a loving God that put this book in your hand and made the effort to nudge you to read it. He truly desires you for His bride.

You can accept his engagement ring this very minute. You don't need any special instructions or words. The veil has been torn from top to bottom so that you can talk to God all by yourself. Commit yourself to him and "pistevo" him from now on. You will then understand the scripture in Romans 15:12 about Jesus, *"One who will arise to rule over the nations; the Gentiles will hope in Him."* Christ will become your hope, too.

We actually barely skimmed over the tribulation time on earth because we feel it to be immaterial to you who "pistevo." Now, though, we will look at things that <u>will</u> matter to you, and they will be exciting. There is still a lot to cover.

We still will *"search out"* matters that you may have never even heard of before, things that will send chills up your spine. In the process we will explore the time frame of when the end times will happen, and we will meet the modern day Indiana Jones and see what he has found that will play a part in that time table. Additionally we will learn about what was going on in heaven, where we will be during those seven years on earth that we just looked at. And we will find out what our lives will be like immediately after Jesus touches down once again on planet earth. And finally we will learn what our long term eternal future in heaven will be like. The anticipation mounts.

CHAPTER THIRTY-THREE

There are several areas of debate concerning end time prophecy among Bible scholars as well as different Christian denominations. As we have mentioned, such things as whether or not the war of Gog and Magog is the same thing as the battle of Armageddon can spur heated discussions. Likewise, the role of the European Union or the probable birthplace of the antichrist can unfortunately be the catalysts for even breaking Christian families and churches apart. Although there can be verses quoted to support either sides of these debates, and the many others that cause tension among believers, what Christians tend to forget is that who is right and who is wrong doesn't matter a twit. Those who truly "pistevo" Jesus won't be a part of those days.

We must admit, though, that it can be fun speculating on future events. God's prophecies, however, are not meant so much to allow humans to see exact details of the future as they are to first of all prove to us that God is there, the Bible is His Word, and He is in control; and secondly, to give us a solid hope and firm faith that His promise of taking care of His bride in the future will come to pass literally, just as the fulfilled prophecies we studied earlier came about the way He said they would.

Quite frankly, even the timing of these end time events is not of major importance to us in contrast to the importance of the assurance that they will indeed occur; and that those who "pistevo" Him now will in fact get to spend eternity with Him in heaven. Additionally, the timing is not that important because even if the Biblical end times are not really all that close, our personal "end times" are. Our lives on earth are very, very short. They are but a comma in the gigantic tome that is His Story.

Let's examine what may be a very revealing prophecy;

"Just as man is destined to die once, and after that to face judgment, so Christ was sacrificed once to take away the sins of many people; and He will appear a second time, not to bear sin, but to bring salvation to those who are waiting for him." Hebrews 9:27-28

We don't want to stir up a brand new controversy and debate, but it may be interesting to look at that first phrase again, *"man is destined to die once."* The King James version states it even more emphatically by saying, *"it is appointed unto man to die."* With that thought, could the rapture actually be kind of a mass death of the saints? We saw earlier that we are told that we will be changed *"in the twinkling of an eye."* Doesn't that automatically happen at death anyway? When we die we don't lie in the grave or some type of limbo for some specified time. We instantly, upon death, become our true spiritual beings.

The change occurs *"in the twinkling of an eye."* We are not dogmatic at all about this, because we do strongly believe the prophecy of the Rapture will definitely occur, and it will take God's children away from the earth before His wrath hits; however, it may not be in any supernatural fashion as most rapture buffs have pictured. It may actually happen in such a way that those who are left behind will not suspect that anything spiritual has taken place. This is just a point to ponder.

No matter how it will all come about, we are commanded to keep *"Looking for that blessed hope, and the glorious appearing of the great God and our Savior Jesus Christ."* Titus 2:13 (KJV)

Jesus gave us the following words, *"Be careful, or your hearts will be weighed down ... with the anxieties of life, and that day will come upon you like a trap. For it will come upon all those who live upon the face of the earth. Be always on the watch, and pray that you may be able to escape all that is about to happen, and that you may be able to stand before the Son of Man."* Luke 21:34-36

Just as we learned that we must "remain" in Him during our engagement period, God gave us the following instruction through the beloved disciple John, *"And now, dear children, continue in Him, so that when He appears we may be confident and unashamed before Him at His coming."* 1 John 2:28

Jesus also told us, *"Remember, therefore, what you have received and heard; obey it, and repent. But if you do not wake up, I will come like a thief, and you will not know at what time I will come to you."* Revelation 3:3

So, when will all of this take place? We can't know for sure the exact time, for Jesus told us, *"No one knows about that day or hour, not even the angels in heaven, nor the Son, but only the Father. Be on guard! Be alert!"* Mark 13:32

Unlike the prophecy we looked at earlier in Daniel that told mankind the exact day Jesus would come the first time, we have not been given the exact time of His second coming. This was done so that man throughout the past two thousand years would be constantly on their toes in fear of Jesus coming when they were not *"abiding"* in Him. God did not want men to lose focus on Him by telling them that it would be a long number of years before He came back. He wanted them to "remain" in Him so that when their natural death occurred, their personal "end times," they would be ready. The lack of prophesying the exact date was an act of mercy on God's part. He did, however, tell us the following, *"Now learn this lesson from the fig tree: as soon as its twigs get tender and its leaves come out, you know that summer is near. Even so, when you see these things happening, you know that it is near, right at the door."* Mark 13:28-29

Since the fig tree often symbolizes Israel in God's Word, many prophecy scholars have thought that this reference was about the nation of Israel being reborn in 1948 or Jerusalem being recaptured in 1967, and since the next verse, Mark 13:30, says, *"this generation will certainly not pass away until these things have happened,"* there have been entire books written on whether a generation meant forty years, seventy years or one hundred years.

The fact is that the Greek word that has been translated as generation is "genea," which also means age, nation, time, or race. It is very possible that Jesus was just telling us that just as we can tell what is happening by a tree budding, we should also be able to tell the end times are upon us by the things we see happening around us, such as the things He described in the verses immediately preceding that verse, such as wars, rumors of wars, earthquakes, famines, persecution against Christians, and people claiming to be Him. Jesus did end that discourse, though, with the following words of advice, *"What I say to you, I say to everyone: 'Watch!'"* Mark 13:37

In speaking about interpreting the times, Jesus also said,

"When you see a cloud rising in the west, immediately you say, 'It's going to rain,' and it does. And when the south wind blows, you say, 'It's going to be hot,' and it is. ... You know how to interpret the appearance of the earth and the sky. How is it that you don't know how to interpret the present time?" Luke 12:54-56

We are going over these verses just to make the point that although the scripture referring to the fig tree may or may not have to do with the rebirth of Israel or the capture of Jerusalem, there really is no way to be dogmatic about it. We need to be careful, therefore, not to get too caught up in end time prophecy teaching that emphatically states that the rapture or the tribulation is going to happen at a specific date or year. God's prophecy is easy to interpret in hindsight, but quite a bit harder for future events, unless God wants the timing to be clear to us like He did with the timing of the first appearance of Jesus. As to end time prophecy, God seems to have purposefully kept things a little bit hazy to make sure we all "remain" in him at all times.

We probably also need to reiterate one more time that it really shouldn't matter to us how close the end times are, do to the fact that any of us could face our personal "end times" as soon as five minutes from now. In fact, God tells us:

"Now listen, you who say, 'Today or tomorrow we will go to this or that city, spend a year there, carry on business and make money' Why, you do not even know what will happen tomorrow. What is your life? You are a mist that appears for a little while and then vanishes." James 4:13-14

The truth is, though, that due to human nature, we are all curious about such things as the timing of the final days; and since God gave us scores of clues about it, let's examine some of them and see just how close this current world is to seeing the ultimate change, the return of Christ as the King of kings.

One of the reasons God gave such detailed genealogies in His Word was so mankind could get an accurate feel for His timetable. The Jewish calender, although flawed as we shall see, was set up to do just that. As this sentence is being typed in 2007, it is currently 5768 AM, or Anno Mundi, on the Jewish calender. Anno Mundi is Latin for "from the creation of the world."

One of the errors with that date was made deliberately. The primary author of the modern Jewish calender was a man named Yose ben Halafia, who died in 160 AD. Halafia was a student of Rabbi Akiva ben Joseph. As a 90 year old living legend, Rabbi Akiva ben Joseph gave his blessing to the leader of an unsuccessful revolt against the Romans in 132 AD by declaring its leader, Bar Kokhbah, as the "star out of Jacob," Israel's long awaited Messiah. Later, when Yose ben Halafia was designing the Jewish calender he decided to point the Daniel prophecy that accurately foretold the exact day Jesus rode into Jerusalem away from Jesus and to Bar Kokhbah.

Since part of the dating relied on the time period of the Medo-Persian Empire, Yose ben Halafia just conveniently left out the reigns of eight of the Persian emperors. He started with Darius, Cyrus' father-in-law, then included Cyrus, Artaxerxes, Ahasuerus, and ended up with the other Darius who Alexander the Great defeated. These five added up to 53 years.

We now know for a certainty that there were really thirteen Persian emperors who reigned a total of 207 years, but the calender Yose ben Halafia came up with to keep the Jews from believing in Jesus still exists, with those missing 154 years. If we add those missing years in, we would now be at 5922. But that is not the end of the Jewish calendar problem.

Without getting bogged down in all of the other details of mistakes that quite frankly were just honest miscalculations in things such as the age of Abraham's father, which cost the calender 60 years, and mistakes in the year the Abrahamic covenant was given as well as the length of the second temple, which together caused a shortfall of 22 years, the Jewish calender should actually have already passed the year 6000 AM.

Why are these Jewish calender discrepancies so important? As we have seen, all of God's prophecies that involve time are always based on the Jewish year which has 360 days.

And lest we forget, the Jewish people are still God's chosen people. Even the New Testament which is strictly a Christian part of the Bible states that fact very emphatically:

"I do not want you to be ignorant of this mystery, brothers, so that you may not be conceited: Israel has experienced a hardening in part

until the full number of the gentiles has come in. And so all Israel will be saved ... As far as the gospel is concerned, they are enemies on your account; but as far as election is concerned, they are loved on account of the patriarchs, for God's gifts and His call are irrevocable. Just as you who were at one time disobedient to God have now received mercy as a result of their disobedience, so they too have now become disobedient in order that they too may now receive mercy as a result of God's mercy to you. For God has bound all men over to disobedience so that He may have mercy on them all." Romans 11;25-32

Had Israel as a whole been aware of Daniel's prophecy that foretold the day their Messiah would appear, and had they worshipped Him as their Savior, which He was, we Gentiles would have been left in the cold. As it was, only the Jews' main religious leaders knew about that prophecy, and since Jesus wasn't a worldly king at that time like they expected Him to be, and since accepting Him would have threatened their cushy positions, they led the people to reject Him. As we saw earlier, because of this rejection, Jesus said to them; *"If you, even you, had only known on this day what would bring you peace - but now it is hidden from your eyes."* Luke 19:42

This hardening on the part of the Jews, however, will end. Remember what we just read, *"Israel has experienced a hardening in part until the full number of Gentiles has come in."* The second coming of Christ for the Christians will be an acceptance of their Messiah for the Jews. They missed His first coming; but because of God's love for and promise to the patriarchs, Abraham, Isaac and Jacob, the Spiritual eyes of Israel will be wide open at His second appearing. Both Jewish and Gentile believers will pistevo Jesus and live with Him eternally.

We went through all of this so that you will understand that the timing of the prophecies for the Jews for their coming Messiah is the same as the timing for the Christian's longed for second coming of Christ. Both religions now see it as happening as soon as the year 6000 is reached. If you recall, 2 Peter 3:8 told us, *"With the lord a day is like a thousand years,"* and there are numerous scriptures in the Jewish religion, both in the Old Testament as well as their other holy writings, that point to that glorious occurrence happening between the sixth and seventh day. Of course, the first shadow was when God created the world in six days and rested on the seventh.

The same is true for the Christians who can point to many similar shadows. Our favorite is probably in the story of the transfiguration of Jesus. In that account Jesus is on a mountain with Peter, James and John. The description of the magnificent event reads as follows:

"There He was transfigured before them. His face shown like the sun, and His clothes became as white as light. Just then there appeared before them Moses and Elijah, talking with Jesus.

Peter said to Jesus, 'Lord, it is good for us to be here. If you wish, I will put up three shelters - one for you, one for Moses and one for Elijah.' While he was still speaking a cloud enveloped them, and a voice from the cloud said, 'This is my Son, whom I love; with Him I am well pleased. Listen to Him.'

When the disciples heard this, they fell facedown to the ground, terrified. But Jesus came and touched them. 'Get up,' He said, 'Don't be afraid.' When they looked up they saw no one except Jesus." Matthew 17:2-8

The reason we started at verse two is that the first verse is the important one for us at this moment. It reads, *"**After six days** Jesus took with him Peter, James and John, the brother of James, and led them up a high mountain by themselves."* Matthew 17:1

We have made the point over and over that God did not put words in His Bible just to take up space. Each word has a meaning. There is nothing in this story or what precedes it to show any reason for God to start this story with the phrase, *"**After six days.**"* The transfiguration that occurred obviously is a shadow of the Christ that was to come, Jesus at His second appearing. The six days can only allude to the scheduled timing, the six thousandth year since the beginning of recorded time.

Another very interesting part of this story has to do with Peter wanting to put up the three shelters. Very few Bible teachers seem to put two and two together, but Peter's offer to do this is intricately woven into the framework of one of the seven Jewish feasts. We do not have the space to cover all of the feasts in this book, but we suggest strongly that you *"search out the matter"* for yourself. There may be more of prophetic interest in the feasts of Israel than in any other area.

God's Word says, *"Therefore do not let anyone judge you ... with regard to a religious festival. ... These are a shadow of the things that were to come; the reality, however, is found in Christ."* Colossians 2:16-17

There are seven feasts. The first three clearly were shadows of Christ's first coming, and the fourth one, Pentecost was a shadow of the coming of the Holy Spirit. Those four have all been fulfilled. The final three are shadows of the second coming of Jesus. The very final one is called Tabernacles, or booths.

*"Live in booths for **seven days**: All native-born Israelites are to live in booths so your descendants will know that I had the Israelites live in booths when I brought them out of Egypt.*

I am the Lord your God." Leviticus 23:42-43

Even today, Israelites leave their homes and move into temporary "booths" made out of branches. They normally leave gaps in the branches to be able to see the stars at night. At the end of the seven days they move back to their permanent homes. In our discussion thus far we haven't come to the fact that Jesus will reign on earth for one thousand years. That makes seven thousand years from the beginning until the return of God's children to their permanent home in heaven. I'm sure it is now easy to see the shadow of that homecoming event in the seven day festival of "booths." Paul even talks about *"the earthly tent we live in."* 2 Corinthians 5:1

When Peter suggested that he build shelters for Jesus, Moses and Elijah on the Mountain of Transfiguration we can be sure it was a shadow of this very thing.

There is another description of the same transfiguration event found in Luke. The only difference is that the second account begins with the phrase, *"about **eight days** after Jesus said this,"* because Jesus is talking about something different immediately preceding the event. We can see in this, however, that God is showing us a like shadow of two different future events, the second coming of Jesus, and the return to His heavenly glory after the millennial reign is over.

In case it might seem that we are straying from a possible timetable, what we are showing is that the Jewish prediction of their

Messiah and the Christian prophetic timetable for the second coming of Christ are one and the same, and are both linked to the Jewish calender, which in reality should be giving today's date at somewhere around 6000 AM.

As Christian's, of course, if the date of our Lord's return corresponds to the Jewish six day or six thousand year projection, we would expect to find prophetic verses also showing a two day span between His ascension and His return, and we aren't disappointed. If you recall, several chapters back when we were discussing clean clothes being a shadow of righteousness, we looked at Exodus 19:10, which says,

*"And the Lord said to Moses, 'Go to the people and consecrate them today and tomorrow. Have them wash their clothes and be ready by the **third day**, because on that day the Lord will come down on Mount Sinai in the sight of all the people."*

We can obviously see that God is telling us to become righteous in the two days (two thousand years) that Jesus is gone, because on the third day Jesus is coming back. That thought is reiterated in Hosea:

*"Come, let us return to the Lord. ... After **two days** He will revive us; on the **third day** He will restore us, that we may live in His presence. Let us acknowledge the Lord; let us press on to acknowledge Him. As surely as the sun rises He will appear; He will come to us like the winter rains, like the spring rains that water the earth."* Hosea 6:1-3

There is no doubt that the Bible is telling us over and over that Christ will return after a two day, or two thousand year, absence. We can even see shadows foretelling it in places such as the miracles of Jesus. For instance, Jesus was once told that His good friend Lazarus was sick unto death. But God's Word then says, *"Yet when He heard that Lazarus was sick, He stayed where He was **two more days**."* John 11:6

The general time frame for Christ's second coming, therefore, is 6,000 years after the creation, and two thousand years after His ascension, which incidently occurred about 2003 Jewish years ago. Looking at those parameters, we can say that the second coming may be right at the door.

To get away from Biblical prophetic verses for a moment, though, let's do something that Jesus mentioned we could do, which is, *"interpret the appearance of the earth."* Luke 12:56

In 500 BC there were about a hundred million people on the earth. Population kept gradually increasing until the world population finally topped a billion people sometime between 1800 and 1850. By 1960 the figure had exploded to three billion people. A short forty years later it had doubled again when the world population hit an astounding six billion people. Obviously we are now in an exponential curve of gigantic proportions.

If we were to forget about the roughly 240 years that are actually missing on the Jewish calender, and if we were to be extremely generous and say that the United Nations or some other entity could somehow stabilize the population growth to just a mere doubling every forty years, as was the case with the last doubling, instead of a continuation in the exponential curve we are actually in, planet earth would still have approximately 400 billion people 240 years from now.

Let that figure sink in; four hundred billion people. There is no way at all that the earth could sustain that many people. There would not be enough food. There would not be enough water. There would not even be enough oxygen to breath. Jesus alluded to the fact that we could use our sense of reason and *"interpret the appearance of the earth and sky."* Do we need to be hit on the head with a hammer to get our attention?

Jesus is coming again, this time as the King of kings and Lord of lords. Cock your head and listen closely. The next sound you hear may be the sound of a trumpet.

CHAPTER THIRTY-FOUR

The rapture could occur today. There is not a single prophecy that must be fulfilled before that glorious event can happen that hasn't already come to pass. Additionally, every end time prophecy has already been fulfilled that needs to occur before the beginning of the seven year tribulation, with the possible exception of the war of Gog and Magog, and that event could be very close.

August 16, 2007, the Shanghai Cooperative Organization met in Bishkek, Kyrgyzstan. Russian, Iranian, Chinese, Kazakh, Turkmenistan, Krygyz, Tajik, Uzbek, Mongolian, and Afghan presidents were all in attendance. That surely sounds like an excellent start to the roll call for the war of Gog and Magog alliance. And as we have mentioned, although we believe that war will precede the tribulation, some scholars believe that war to be the same as the final war, Armageddon, and they, of course, could be correct.

The only thing that we know for a certainty that still needs to happen is the rebuilding of the Jewish Temple in Jerusalem, along with the necessary priests and items to reimplement sacrifices, etc.; and those things do not actually have to be in place until the midpoint of the tribulation when Daniel 11:31 tells us of the antichrist, *"His armed forces will rise up to desecrate the temple fortress and will abolish the daily sacrifices. Then they will set up the abomination that causes desolation."*

It seems, though, that everything is already in motion for the Temple to be rebuilt and everything else that would be needed to be in place. Things are happening today in Jerusalem.

One of the necessities that seemed to be lost for all time was the definite certainty of the priestly line. The Temple priests had to be from the line of Aaron, the brother of Moses, of the tribe of Levi. In Exodus 29:9 God gave instruction concerning Aaron and his sons, *"The priesthood is theirs by a lasting ordinance."* The same *"ordinance"* was repeated about Aaron by God in several other passages, such as, *"He and his descendants will have a covenant of a lasting priesthood."* Numbers 25:13

The Hebrew word for such a priest is Cohen, and many have asserted their direct lineage going back 3300 years. Therefore, around the world, Cohens or Kohanims have served in the priestly positions for centuries. But who could be sure if the line was pure? There were quite obvious differences between such priests in different parts of the globe; differences in stature, skin coloration, hair and eye color.

Finally, Dr. Karl Skorecki, whose family had a tradition of being Cohen, entered the picture. Being a nephrologist and top level researcher at the University of Toronto and Rambam-Technion Medical Center in Haifa, Israel, he had been involved with breakthroughs in molecular genetics. To cut to the chase, Dr. Skorecki and his team have isolated a DNA marker, now known as the Cohen Modal Haplotype, which is being used to identify direct priestly descendants of Aaron who can rightfully administer in a yet to be built new Temple.

The Temple Institute in the Old City of Jerusalem has already made the linen priestly garments that the Kohanim priests would be required to wear in the new Temple.

Additionally, well over 500 Kohanim priests have to date been fully trained to fulfill the Temple worship duties in this rebuilt Temple, including the administering of animal sacrifices and the playing of the harp and lyre. On top of that, about one hundred of the required Temple implements have been made and are ready for use right now, including the commanded menorah made in strict accordance to the instructions God gave in Exodus. This menorah, which is a six and a half foot candelabra with seven branches, was cast with ninety two pounds of pure gold at a cost of over $400,000. Remember, the Bible tells us that this new Temple will be up and operational by the 3 ½ year mark of the tribulation. That doesn't seem to be an insurmountable problem at all.

Another prophetic necessity is a red heifer for the cleansing sacrifice for the priests and the Temple and Temple objects. Numbers 19:2 commands the use of *"A red heifer without defect or blemish and that has never been under a yoke."* The Temple Institute is currently raising just such a breed of cattle at a ranch near Mount Carmel in northern Israel. In fact, a few years back Rabbi Reichman of the Temple Institute did certify a perfect red heifer, however it was later bruised and a few white hairs grew at the spot of the bruise and was therefore disqualified. We can be certain, though, that at the appropriate time God will be sure that the perfect animal will be available for the cleansing ritual.

The only two remaining needs to complete the requirements necessary to fulfill end time prophecy are the Temple itself and the oil needed to anoint Jesus upon His return.

The money for the rebuilt Temple is already available, and from what we can ascertain the probable location will be on the Temple Mount over the East Gate, some distance from the current Islamic Dome of the Rock, and there is plenty of room for both structures.

As to the needed oil for the anointing of Jesus, it was lost in 70 AD. One of the five designated ingredients for anointing oil given in Exodus 30 came from a very rare *afars'mon* plant. At the time the Romans destroyed Jerusalem and the Temple in 70 AD there were only two groves of the plant, one in Jericho and the other in Ein Gedi. Jewish rebels burned both of those groves as they were escaping. Some Jewish religious leaders have said through the years that Temple services could not be reinstituted without this special oil, but something could change even that. As we know, experts said that Israel would never be a nation again, but it is. *"Nothing is impossible with God."* Luke 1:37

In discussing the Temple objects and the coming of the Messiah there are two of the Dead Sea Scrolls that we will find interesting to quickly examine. As you probably know, the Dead Sea Scrolls were discovered between 1947 and 1956 in eleven caves on the shore of the Dead Sea, about thirteen miles from Jerusalem. These caves were very close to the ancient ruins of Qumran.

The Scrolls were evidently a library of a Jewish sect called Essenes who were strict, Torah observant, followers of Jesus. The find included 900 documents, representing over 350 separate works in multiple copies, written between 200 BC and 68 AD in Hebrew, Aramaic and Greek. Most of the Scrolls were copies of the books of the Old Testament, including nineteen copies of Isaiah, twenty five copies of Deuteronomy, and thirty copies of Psalms. They are the oldest group of Old Testament manuscripts ever found. In fact, the Isaiah Scroll, found relatively intact, is a thousand years older than any previously known copy.

Included in the Scrolls are never before seen Psalms attributed to King David and Joshua. There are even prophecies by Ezekiel, Jeremiah and Daniel that are not found in our Bible. Also of interest are the last words of Joseph, Judah, Levi Naphtali, and Amram, the father of Moses. Obviously it was the archeological find of the century.

The Temple scroll found in cave eleven is the longest scroll, measuring almost 28 feet long. Most scrolls were made of animal skin, although there are a few of papyrus, and one of copper. Many contained a number of surprises, such as unknown stories about people such as Enoch, Abraham, and Noah. Also of surprise to many was the fact that all of the books of the current Old testament were included except for Esther, and almost every word was identical to what we already had, showing how thoroughly God preserved His Word through the centuries.

One of the big advantages to the finding of the Dead Sea Scrolls was to silence much debate that had gone on for years. For instance, the intricately prophesied accounts of the heirs to Alexander's kingdom that we looked at early on from Daniel eleven, had been steadfastly claimed by many sceptics through the ages to have been written after the events actually occurred. It was thought that they were way too close to the reality of the actual events to have been written as prophecy. Many thought that they were too accurate even for God Himself to have foretold. The Dead Sea Scroll of Daniel, however, squashed that debate because it was obvious, even by carbon dating, that the newly found copy predated most of the real events. As Gomer Pyle would say "Surprise, surprise!"

One of the works found in the Dead Sea Scrolls that is not included in our Bible was numbered 11Q13 in case you ever want to read it in its entirety. The title of this fascinating work is "The Coming Of Melchizedek", the priestly character in God's Word that we learned earlier was a "type" of Jesus. We will now quote from this exciting work, indicating Biblical references that were included in the scroll in italics, and putting in parenthesis and bold type the actual Book, chapter and verse, plus our comments:

"And concerning what scripture says, *'In this year of Jubilee you shall return, every one of you, to your property'* (Lev.25:13) ... *'because God's remission has been proclaimed.'* (Deut. 15:2) The interpretation is that it applies to the Last Days and concerns the captives, just as Isaiah said; *'To proclaim the jubilee to the captives'* (Isa. 61:1 As an aside, this is the verse Jesus first read in the Temple and proclaimed that He had come to fulfill.) from the inheritance of Melchizedek, who will return them to what is rightfully theirs. He will proclaim to them the jubilee, thereby releasing them from their debt of all sins.

Then the Day of Atonement shall follow after the tenth Jubilee period, when he shall atone for all the Sons of Light. ... For this is the time decreed for the Year of Melchizedek's Favor, and by his might he will judge God's holy ones and so establish a righteous kingdom, as it is written about him in the Songs of David; *'A Godlike being has taken his place in the council of God; in the midst of divine beings he holds judgement.'* (Ps.82:1)

Scripture also says about him; *'Over it take your seat in the highest heaven; a divine being will judge the peoples.'* (Ps. 82:2) Concerning what scripture says; *'How long will you judge unjustly, and show partiality to the wicked? Selah'* (Ps.82:2), the interpretation applies to Belial (Satan) and the spirits predestined to him, because all of them have rebelled, turning from God's precepts and so becoming utterly wicked. Therefore Melchizedek will thoroughly prosecute the vengeance required by God's statutes. Also, he will deliver all the captives from the power of Belial, and from the power of all the spirits destined to him. (Note that it is the spirits, or fallen angels, that are predestined to Satan, not humans.)

Just as it is written concerning him; *'who says to Zion "Your divine being reigns"* (Isa. 52:7) *"Zion"* is the congregation of all the sons of righteousness, who uphold the covenant and turn from walking in the way of the people. *"Your divine being"* is Melchizedek, who will deliver them from the power of Belial.

Concerning what the scripture says, *'Then you shall have the trumpet sounded loud." Lev. 25:9)*

This previously unknown work is interesting in several aspects, among which is not only the stating of things we already knew about Jesus and what will happen the day He returns, but also the insistence of our turning from walking "in the way of the people." Once again we see that "pistevo" requires much more that just a belief in Jesus.

Additionally, although a few television Bible teachers have lately been teaching that Melchizedek could be a son or grandson of Noah, even though Hebrews 7:3 says he was *"Without father or mother, without genealogy,"* this ancient Dead Sea Scroll writing gives even more credence to our view that not only was Melchizedek a type of Jesus who gave wine and bread to Abram, exactly like the last supper, and accepted the first tithe from him, but this mysterious person named Melchizedek was in fact Jesus, the same Jesus who later came as the Lamb of God.

The scroll that physically stands apart from all the others is the Copper Scroll, labeled 3Q15 and discovered in cave three in 1952 by an expedition sponsored by the Jordan Department of Antiquities. In almost every way it was different from its companion scrolls. It was found all by itself, tucked away in the very back of the cave, and was written in a different form of Hebrew than all the rest. And, of course, it was the only scroll made of copper. It was also found in two parts because evidently when it was rolled up two thousand years ago the thin copper sheet snapped into two separate sections. When found, it was so badly oxidized that it would crumble if anyone touched it.

After almost five years of debate as to how to open it, the scroll was sent to Manchester College of Technology in England, where it was decided to open it by using a very fine saw to cut it into segments. Can you imagine the pressure the first person must have felt who was given the task of cutting into such a delicate and immensely valuable treasure? The technique worked, however, and after the scroll had been cut very painstakingly into 23 sections, the experts were able to piece it together into a decipherable form. What they found when they translated it was such a startling discovery that everyone present was completely awestruck. On it was an inventory of holy treasures and where they were hidden.

Included on the scroll were paragraphs such as the following:

"In the desolation of the Valley of Achor, under the hill that must be climbed, hidden under the east side, forty stones deep, is a silver chest, and with it, the vestments of the High Priest, all the gold and silver with the Great Tabernacle and all its treasures."

A total of 64 such instructions were listed on the Copper Scroll. However, the instructions weren't as easy to follow as one might suspect, and although hundreds of would be treasure hunters went out scouring the countryside, nothing turned up.

Enter on the scene Indiana Jones; although he might better be nicknamed Texas Jones or South Carolina Jones. His real name is Vendyl Jones, though he prefers to drop the "V" and "L" from his first name and call himself "Endy" Jones.

Born in 1930 in Sudan, Texas, to a Christian family, Jones was totally fascinated as a boy with the stories in the Old Testament. Although he never did actually "pistevo" Jesus, he decided to become a Baptist preacher. As we learned earlier, "some are called and a lot of others just went." Vendyl Jones "just went." He attended Southwestern Theological Seminary for a short time, got a degree from Bible Baptist Seminary, and then attended Bob Jones University in Greenville, S.C. While still in his early twenties he got a job pastoring the Dungan Baptist Church on the border of North Carolina and Virginia in 1955. Not really being a Christian, but enamored by the Old testament stories, Jones then decided to become a Jew.

He headed back to Greenville, S.C., and at age 25 began learning Hebrew in the Talmud Torah alongside elementary school children under Rabbi Henry Barneis. About ten years later, he established an organization called the Institute for Judaic-Christian Research. Wanting to become even more "Jewish", in 1967 he left South Carolina and headed to Israel to study in the Department of Judaica at Hebrew University. Two days after he arrived, however, the Six Day War erupted and he volunteered to become a spotter for the Israeli army.

As soon as the war was over, Texas or South Carolina Jones's real mission came to fruition. It seems that in 1960 he had read about the Dead Sea Copper Scroll and couldn't get the treasures off his mind. He got a job with an excavation team in Qumran. Since then, that has been his life. With very little financial backing, or the blessings of Israel, Jones was a driven man. Year after year he laid out the copies of the Copper Scroll that he had, and planned and dug, and then he dug and planned. Finally, his efforts payed off, but probably not as he expected. His little team, following clues from the Copper Scroll, found a small, very old juglet with something in it.

Jones took his find to Hebrew University where the contents were tested by the Pharmaceutical Department and found to be some kind of oil. The department started to buzz a little. Then a lot. Experts were called in. Could it be?

Chinese experts who specialize exclusively in chemical compositions of ancient oils confirmed by carbon 14 dating that the contents of the flask was 2,000 year old oil. Then the unthinkable began to be thinkable. As the testing went on, the contents of the oil were irrefutably determined to be the exact ingredients God had commanded in Exodus 30 that the original holy anointing oil be made from, including the long lost and never to be revived *afars'mon* plant.

"Nothing is impossible with God." Luke 1:37

Cock your head and listen closely. A trumpet sound, you say?

CHAPTER THIRTY-FIVE

Vendyl Jones, is still calling himself Endy Jones, and is now a self proclaimed Pharasee on the order of those Christ encountered while on earth the first time. Endy currently spews anti Jesus statements on a daily basis and looks forward, as a very strict Jew, to the first coming of the Jewish Messiah. That is who he believes the anointing oil he found will anoint. A highly thought of Rabbi in Jerusalem recently made the statement, "Wouldn't it be ironic if the hoped for Jewish Messiah and Jesus turn out to be one and the same." As we have seen, He will.

Who knows for sure what will be the final outcome for Endy Jones. He may live to be a part of the coming tribulation.

If so, based on the testimony of the 144,000 Jewish witnesses or the two witnesses that will come from heaven, Endy may still make the decision to "pistevo" Jesus. Of course, he also might not. He has free will. If that is his future, he may still live through the entire seven tribulation years and get to see his oil used; however, he will witness it from a different perspective than we will, assuming we remain committed to Jesus now. If Endy's rejection of Jesus remains strong, he will witness the anointing with a natural body, while our bodies at that time will be very different. But let's back up and see how we will arrive at that event, the anointing of Jesus as King of kings.

Obviously, if we make Jesus the lord of our lives, God's Word foretells that we will either die, or we will be raptured prior to the seven year tribulation. Either way, we will be in heaven while the tribulation occurs on earth. Thank heaven.

Most people have no idea about what heaven is like, or if in fact it even exists. The AARP magazine for September/October 2007 had an article entitled "Life After Death," for which they conducted an exclusive survey of Americans over age 50 and their thoughts concerning an afterlife. 73% of the respondents said they believed in an afterlife of some kind. When asked what it takes to get there, the largest group, 29%, said to "believe in Jesus," although most of them probably just think that knowledge of His existence and what He did would suffice. We have seen that it takes more than just a mental acknowledgment of His having existed in order to "pistevo" Him. We must also remember that this survey was taken of seniors. Obviously a similar survey of younger Americans would probably have a much smaller percentage that would give any thought to even believing in Jesus as being of any help at all in getting to heaven.

The next largest group of afterlife believers, 25%, said that those who "are good" will get in. Many of those, if asked, would probably have called themselves Christians. If pressed they would be forced to admit that they think the suffering Jesus did during his crucifiction was for nothing, since in their opinion those who were "good" were going to be saved anyway.

The rest were split in half between those who believe that everyone will make it no matter what, and those who think that believing in "one God" is enough. Obviously that group never read what we have read, *"You believe that there is one God. Good! Even the demons believe that - and shudder."* Acts 2:19

Almost a fourth of all those surveyed believed in reincarnation, and interestingly, the percentage was even higher, at 31%, for those believing in reincarnation who lived in the northeast. Of course, reincarnation is a big theme of eastern religions such as Hinduism, which is on the upswing in America. As an aside, the U.S. Government allows religious visas on a regular basis. Due to that, untold numbers of Hindu chefs are brought into the United States each year for the sole purpose of preparing foods for the myriad of Hindu gods, which obviously are just idols made of stone, wood or plastic. What a country!

Mike Evans, in his book, <u>The Final Move Beyond Iraq</u>, talks about wanting to weep as he watched Hindus bowing down and worshiping a black ball about the size of a bowling ball. And today there are almost a billion Hindus in the world worshiping that stone ball, or thousands of other similar things made of stone, wood or plastic that they call their gods. We need to recall that God said, *"My people are destroyed from lack of knowledge."* Hosea 4:6

Islamic terrorists, of course, believe that they can get an automatic trip to heaven by blowing to pieces themselves and any infidels, even if those infidels are innocent little babies. They, however, believe that their holy book, the Koran, is the true word of God and that the Bible is false. They have never been presented with the fact that the Bible contains thousands of God's prophecies that have already come true, whereas the Koran contains a total of none. God's lament is true with them as well, *"My people are destroyed from lack of knowledge."* Hosea 4:6

Marilyn vos Savant is listed in the <u>Guinness Book of World Records</u> as the most intelligent person in the world, having been recorded at age 10 with an IQ of 228, the highest level possible for a 23 year old. Millions look for her column first each Sunday in the Parade newspaper Sunday supplement. Her books are best sellers. We have enjoyed many of her answers to questions from readers, and we have learned a lot, such as her quotes about what we should be able to do; for example, "Be able to tell whether garments that look good on a hanger actually look good on you," or "Be able to blow out a dinner candle without sending wax across a table," or "Be able to hiccup silently, or at least without alerting neighbors to your situation. The first hiccup is the exception."

We aren't being critical; Marilyn vos Savant also says some things that are more profound. But isn't it interesting that we humans can't wait to read what the smartest person among us has to say, when even Marilyn vos Savant's phenomenal IQ would be like the IQ of a piece of dust compared to the IQ of the God who created everything? Even with that as a fact, we turn to her for answers to questions instead of looking at what the Genius behind all of creation has to tell us. Just as God's fulfilled prophecies prove His existence, we reiterate that they also prove the Bible to be the way He communicated with us. His Word is where we will find the answers to any questions about heaven.

For years, unfortunately many Biblical scholars believed that end time prophecy and descriptions of heaven were probably allegorical and not literal. Much of this belief can be traced back to Augustine, the Bishop of Hippo from 396 AD to 430 AD. Augustine was one of the most prolific Christian writers of all time, and many of his works, such as his <u>Confessions</u>, are still widely read today and are wonderful classics of excellent Christian thought.

Quotes from the writings of Augustine are profound and worth taking the time to seriously ponder, such as, "God loves each of us as if there were only one of us," or "He who created us without our help will not save us without our consent," or "If you believe what you like in the gospels, and reject what you don't like, it is not the gospel you believe, but yourself."

Unfortunately, Augustine did not have the plethora of fulfilled end time prophecies that we have to look at. He obviously was not able to see Israel become a nation again and her Hebrew language come alive. He was not able to see the Holy Land blossom again and Israel become a major producer of citrus and flowers for the rest of the world as was foretold. And in his day he obviously could not witness the aligning of the exact nations described in Ezekiel 38 against an Israel that didn't even exist. Because of this lack of the knowledge that we are privileged to have, Augustine did not believe in a literal fulfillment of end time and heavenly prophecies.

Those who were present and wrote about Augustine's death experienced final words that bear repeating. Several friends were at his bedside when Augustine died. They sat there with tears in their eyes and discussed his lifelong contributions to the church for several minutes afterward. Then miraculously, Augustine opened his eyes one more time and spoke. The words were astonishing, "I have seen Jesus. All that I have written is as straw." He then left his earthly tent forever.

Augustine had witnessed the phenomenal majesty of the Lord of lords. He had seen heaven. Everything he had written was worthless compared to the reality of it. He had been in the presence of Jesus and had seen what you and I will someday see. Words could never do it justice, but with the aid of God's Word, we will humbly try.

Most people never try to imagine heavenly things because it is difficult for humans to visually paint a picture of what a spiritual place could be like. We need to clear up the basics first. Heaven really is a place. It is not a state of mind. We are told throughout

God's Word that different things here on earth are only shadows of the real things in heaven. For instance, in speaking of the earthly tabernacle and its furniture, God tells us that they are *"the copies of the heavenly things."* Hebrews 9:23 We will be looking in detail of what heaven will be like as we go further, but for now let's just realize that it is a real place with real *"things;"* not a misty, ethereal, intangible environment. Jesus told us when He was leaving:

"Do not let your hearts be troubled. Trust in God; trust also in me. In my father's house are many rooms; if it were not so, I would have told you. I am going there to prepare a place for you. And if I go and prepare a place for you, I will come back and take you to be with me that you also may be where I am" John 14:1-3

One of the questions people ask is, "Where is heaven?" Could it be someplace beyond our universe? The answer is probably yes, but not as we might imagine. As you recall, modern string theorists are convinced that there are parallel universes. They liken them to slices of bread in a loaf. As we saw from the statement God made about the heavens in Hebrews 1:11, one day He *"will roll them up like a robe."* This is consistent with string theory of the universes being parallel. String theory also suggests that the parallel universes are very close to each other.

Our personal opinion is that heaven is where we are, except consisting of faster moving energy. To explain what we mean, let's look at the basis of everything material as being the atom. As we know, the atom is made up of electrons, protons and neutrons. Each one of those composing parts is nothing but energy. The slower the energy moves the more solid it is. The energy making up the table in front of you is not moving nearly as fast as the energy that makes up the air around you, but it is all the same energy. The only difference is its speed.

The heavenly realm is a spiritual realm. We know from what Jesus told us in John 4:24, *"God is spirit."* We also know from 1 John 1:5 that *"God is light."* That is not just a figure of speech. Throughout the Bible the same point is made and those who saw His glory saw a radiant, brilliant light.

Although we have not delved into the Hebrew codes in this book because they have not been proven definitively as yet, there is one code in the first chapter of Genesis that is fascinating in regard to this train of thought.

In case you are not aware of the Hebrew Code phenomena, very simply stated, there is ongoing research with high speed computers that is discovering possible hidden codes beneath the surface of the Biblical text. Going back to people like Isaac Newton, many people have believed that God concealed a hidden communication from mankind temporarily with what is called "equal letter spacing." For us laymen that just means that there are things hidden in the text of the Bible that can be read by reading every fourth or fifth or sixth letter, etc. So far, entire paragraphs lying underneath the original Hebrew and Greek text have been found by high speed computers, and the relevance to the common text where they are found is uncanny. Obviously a long sentence or paragraph goes way beyond the possibility of random chance that early skeptics applied to the phenomenon.

For our discussion, however, let's just look at one very short ELS discovered a few years ago by the late Jewish genius, Yacov Rambsel. Underneath Genesis 1:17, which discusses the creation of light, Rambsel found three very interesting adjacent sequences. The first sequence in six letter intervals spelled the Hebrew *bait a'or*, which means "lighthouse." Adjacent to it was a sequence that spelled in Hebrew *mohar harah*, which means "speed conceived." At another letter interval was the name *Jehovah Adonai aleph*. *Jehovah Adonai*, of course, is one of the names of God, and *aleph* means thousand.

As we discussed previously, Hebrew letters, like in Latin, also have numeric values. By taking the four letters that spell Jehovah to the second power as indicated by *Adonai*, we have a *yod* equaling 100, a *heh* equaling 25, a *vav* equaling 36, and the final *heh* another 25. Adding those together we have 186, and of course, when we add the three zeros for the *aleph*, we have a grand total of 186,000 for the name of God, which we now know is the speed of light in miles per second. From the things we have already seen in this book, it is not too far fetched to believe that God did indeed encode the fact that He was the speed of light for our generation, with the knowledge of what the speed of light is, to find when we *"search out the matter."*

All of this information was just to make the point that we believe heaven to be right here with us, with the difference being the speed of the energy of the earthly things versus heavenly things. God is spirit. He is 186,000 miles per second. We and our surroundings are physical, and our energy makeup moves much, much slower. This possibility is made more interesting when we consider the fact that up to now nothing in our world moves faster than the speed of light. This is naturally only our own personal theory, but it is interesting to ponder in light of the thousands of recorded instances in which the two parallel universes seem to have been perceived at the same time.

As we said, there have been thousands of such recorded occurrences, but one that may be of exceptional interest to us for this discussion was reported by *Guidepost Magazine* in 1970. We are using this *Guidepost* referenced happening because they have an excellent historical reputation for doing everything possible to verify anything that appears in their publication. This incredible story met all of their hard to meet criteria for accuracy.

The main characters in this true story were Dr. S. Ralph Harlow and his wife, Marion. Both are very credible witnesses. Dr. Harlow has an A.B. from Harvard, an M.A. from Columbia, and a PhD from Hartford Theological Seminary. Let's relive the actual events in Dr. Harlow's own words:

"The little path on which Marion and I walked that May morning was spongy to our steps, and we held hands with the sheer delight of life as we strolled near a lovely brook. It was May, and because it was examination reading period at Smith College where I was a professor, we were able to get away for a few days to visit Marion's parents.

We frequently took walks in the country, and we especially loved the spring after a hard New England winter, for it is then that the fields and woods are radiant and calm yet showing new life bursting from the earth. This day we were especially happy and peaceful; we chatted sporadically, with great gaps of satisfying silence between our sentences.

Then from behind us we heard the murmur of muted voices in the distance, and I said to Marion, 'We must have company in the woods this morning.'

Marion nodded, and turned to look. We saw nothing, but the voices were coming nearer - at a faster pace than we were walking - and we knew that the strangers would soon overtake us. Then we perceived that the sounds were not only behind us but above us, and we looked up.

How can I describe what we felt? Is it possible to tell of the surge of exaltation that ran through us? Is it possible to record the phenomenon in objective accuracy and yet be credible?

For about ten feet above us and slightly to our left was a floating group of glorious beautiful creatures that glowed with spiritual beauty. We stopped and stared as they passed above us.

There were six of them, young beautiful women dressed in flowing garments and engaged in earnest conversation. If they were aware of our existence they gave no indication of it. Their faces were perfectly clear to us, and one woman, slightly older than the rest, was especially beautiful. Her dark hair was pulled back in what today we would call a ponytail and although I cannot say it was bound at the back of her head, it appeared to be. She was talking intently to a younger spirit whose back was toward us and who looked up into the face of the woman who was talking.

Neither Marion nor I could understand their words although their voices were clearly heard. The sound was something like hearing but being unable to understand a group of people talking outside a house with all the windows and doors shut.

They seemed to float past us and their graceful motion seemed natural - as gentle and peaceful as the morning itself. As they passed, their conversation grew fainter and fainter until it faded out entirely, and we stood transfixed on the spot, still holding hands and still with the vision before our eyes. It would be an understatement to say we were astounded. Then we looked at each other, each wondering if the other had seen.

There was a fallen birch tree just there beside the path. We sat down on it and I said, 'Marion, what did you see? Tell me exactly, in precise detail. And tell me what you heard.'

She knew my intent - to test my own eyes and ears to see if I had been the victim of hallucination or imagination. And her reply was identical in every way to what my own senses had reported to me."

As we mentioned, there have been thousands of recorded meetings with spiritual beings, made by very credible witnesses. As a hospice volunteer we heard and read of many interesting encounters. One that was not uncommon was that of an older gentleman who, in the days before he passed over, told his volunteer very rationally that his deceased brother had come to visit him on two separate occasions. Each time he said that his brother had told him that he would come to get him at exactly noon the following Sunday. When Sunday came the gentleman did take his very last earthly breath, at exactly noon.

One of our favorite examples was of a little girl of about four who had a terminal illness. She started telling her mother about a nice man who kept visiting her and describing a beautiful place that he was going to take her, where she would be sick no more. The description of the lovely land with colorful flowers was in amazing detail. The mother, of course, humored her precious daughter about her new imaginary friend. One day she asked the little girl if her friend had a name. "Yes," the girl matter of factly stated, "his name is Malachi." There was no earthly way that this innocent little child could know that Malachi in Hebrew means "my angel."

Did Dr. and Mrs. Harlow see angels on that wooded path that unforgettable day? With nothing concrete to base it on, our own inclination is to think that they saw fellow earthlings who had already passed over into the spirit world that we know as heaven. Could one of those beautiful ladies have been one of your own departed relatives? We believe it to be quite possible. How Dr. Harlow described the women is perfectly in line Biblically with what we have been told our new bodies will be like on the other side. In fact, let's examine that right now.

God tells us what to expect regarding our resurrection bodies:

"But someone may ask, 'How are the dead raised? With what kind of body will they come?' ...

"What you sow does not come to life unless it dies. When you sow you do not plant the body that will be, but just a seed, perhaps of wheat or

of something else. But God gives it a body as He has determined, and to each kind of seed He gives its own body."

"All flesh is not the same: Men have one kind of flesh. ... There are also heavenly bodies and earthly bodies; but the splendor of the heavenly bodies is one kind, and the splendor of the earthly bodies is another."

"So will it be with the resurrection of the dead. The body that is sown is perishable, it is raised imperishable; it is sown in dishonor, it is raised in glory; it is sown in weakness, it is raised in power; it is sown a natural body, it is raised a spiritual body.

If there is a natural body, there is also a spiritual body. So it is written; 'The first man Adam became a living being'; the last Adam (Jesus), a life giving spirit. The spiritual did not come first, but the natural, and after that the spiritual. The first man was of the dust of the earth, the second man from heaven. As was the earthly man, so are those who are of the earth; and as is the man from heaven, so also are those who are of heaven. And just as we have borne the likeness of the earthly man, so shall we bear the likeness of the man from heaven." 1 Corinthians 35-49

The key here for us in *"searching out the matter"* is that our resurrection bodies will be like the resurrection body that we know Jesus had for the forty days he spent here on earth after he arose; the body that over five hundred people saw and talked with, and which was described to us in the infallible Word of God. *"And just as we have borne the likeness of the earthly man, so shall we bear the likeness of the man from heaven."*

The chapter continues:

"I declare to you, brothers, that flesh and blood cannot inherit the kingdom of God, nor does the perishable inherit the imperishable. Listen, I tell you a mystery: We will not all sleep, but we will all be changed - in a flash, in the twinkling of an eye, at the last trumpet. For the trumpet will sound, the dead will be raised imperishable, and we will be changed. For the perishable must clothe itself with the imperishable, and the mortal with immortality. When the perishable has been clothed with the imperishable, and the mortal with immortality, then the saying that is written will come true: 'Death has been swallowed up in victory.'

"Where, O Death, is your victory?

Where, O Death, is your sting?"

The sting of death is sin, and the power of sin is the law. But thanks be to God! He gave us the victory through our Lord Jesus Christ.

Therefore, my dear brothers, stand firm. Let nothing move you. Always give yourselves fully to the work of the Lord, because you know that your labor in the Lord is not in vain." 1 Corinthians 15:50-58

Like a good teacher, God tells us over and over that our bodies will be like the one Jesus had when He left the grave.

"But our citizenship is in heaven. And we eagerly await a savior from there, the Lord Jesus Christ, who, by the power that enables Him to bring everything under his control, will transform our lowly bodies so that they will be like his glorious body." Philippians 3:20-21

"Dear friends, now we are children of God, ... we know that when He appears, we shall be like Him." 1 John 3:2

So what can we expect our bodies to be like? What was the resurrection body of Jesus like? We know from God's Word that Jesus walked: *"Jesus himself came up and walked along with them."* Luke 23:15

We know from many verses that Jesus ate and talked. For instance, *"On one occasion while He was eating with them, He gave them this command: 'Do not leave Jerusalem, but wait for the gift my Father promised, which you have heard me speak about. For John baptized with water, but in a few days you will be baptized with the Holy Spirit."* Acts 1:4-5

Of course, Jesus could be touched like an earthly person: *"Then He said to Thomas,'Put your finger here, see my hands. Reach out your hand and put in into my side. Stop doubting and believe."* John 20:27

It was then that *"Thomas said to Him, 'My Lord and my God."* John 20:28

Following that worshipful statement, Jesus spoke of us by saying, *"Because you have seen me, you have believed; blessed are those who have not seen and yet have believed."* John 20:29

You, dear believing reader, are blessed.

Although Jesus walked like we do, he also could pass through doors and walls. For instance, *"When the disciples were together, with the doors locked for fear of the Jews, Jesus came and stood among them, and said, 'Peace be with you!' After He said this he showed them His hands and side. The disciples were overjoyed when they saw the Lord."* John 20:19-20

298   Unlocking God's Secrets: Past, Present, and Future

Think about it, one day you will have a body that is free enough to walk through solid objects like walls. And in many places Jesus just appeared instantly. In fact, there were shadows of this ability to translate Himself and others even before he was crucified. A simple example is found when Jesus got into the boat following the episode we are all familiar with, when He walked on water. God's Word tells the story:

"They saw Jesus approaching the boat, walking on the water; and they were terrified. But He said to them, 'It is I; don't be afraid.' Then they were willing to take Him into the boat, and immediately the boat reached the shore where they were heading." John 6:19-21

Most people read that scripture and miss that phenomenal word, *"immediately."* Imagine what happened. Jesus got into the boat and "instantly" it was at their destination. This was long before Scotty was beaming up people on Star Trek. And this was real. This wasn't science fiction; this was supernatural reality. And you and I will have a body that will allow us the same luxury. We will be able to translate ourselves from one place to another instantly, just by thought. What an exciting life we have in store for us!

Speaking of this fantastic ability to translate ourselves as Jesus did, it is interesting that it was foretold about the very end times that *"knowledge shall be increased."* Daniel 12:4 KJV, and that is happening at an astronomical rate right now. For example, an Associated Press report dated August 28, 2007, says:

"Two German physicists claim to have done the impossible ...Dr. Gunter Nimtz and Dr. Alfons Stahlhofen, from the University of Koblenz, ... have conducted an experiment in which microwave photons - energy packets of light - traveled "instantaneously" between a pair of prisms that had been moved from a few millimeters to up to one meter apart. Although these photons had traveled farther, they arrived at their detector at exactly the same time.

Nimtz told *New Science* Magazine: 'This is the only violation of special relativity that I know of.'"

The duo say being able to travel faster than the speed of light would lead to a wide variety of bizarre consequences. For instance, an astronaut moving faster than it would theoretically arrive at a destination before leaving, they said.

What these scientists have discovered is very probably not the ability to move faster than the speed of light, God's speed, but the phenomenon of translation that was foretold by God in His Word. Wonderfully, it will be a real part of our lives in heaven, as well as for us when we return to earth for the time we will spend here during the coming Millennial Kingdom.

The next part, unplanned but fittingly numbered with God's number for perfection, seven, will be exciting. Now that we have an idea of the kind of bodies we will have, we will learn about the things we will see, the events that will occur, and what our lives will actually be like both in heaven and during the earthly Millennial Reign of Christ. By simply making Jesus the Lord of our entire lives now, we will be rewarded beyond what we could comprehend in the future, a future that will be eternal, a future that will be unbelievably exciting. In a word, it will be heavenly.

PART SEVEN

Chapter Thirty-Six

The little girl's "Malachi" and the older gentleman's brother both came at the appointed time. You and I will be ushered into heaven by an angel or loved one as well, unless as the signs seem to indicate, the rapture occurs rather soon, in which case Jesus Himself will come down and take us to the place of our true citizenship. No matter who escorts us it is possible that the first sight we will see could be the same as that of John the Revelator:

"When I turned I saw ... someone 'like a Son of Man,' dressed in a robe reaching down to His feet and with a golden sash around his chest. His head and hair were white like wool, as white as snow, and His eyes were like blazing fire. His feet were like Bronze glowing in a furnace, and His voice was like the sound of rushing waters. ... His face was like the sun shining in all its brilliance.

When I saw Him, I fell at His feet though dead. Then He placed his right hand on me and said, 'Do not be afraid. I am the First and the Last. I am the Living One. I was dead, and behold I am alive forever and ever. And I hold the keys of death and Hades.'" Revelation 1:12-18

Can you imagine what that moment will be like? Every emotion we have ever felt will be rushing through us all at once. In 1999 Bart Millard was looking through some old school notebooks of his from eight years earlier, the year his father had died of cancer. In the margins of several pages Bart had written the phrase, "I can only imagine," He wrote it as he was thinking of the glory his father must be experiencing in the presence of Jesus. With that as a title, Bart penned the lines of a song.

"Surrounded by your Glory, what will my heart feel?
Will I dance for you, Jesus? Or in awe of you be still?
Will I stand in your presence, or to my knees will I fall?
Will I sing 'Hallelujah!'? Will I be able to speak at all?
I can only imagine! I can only imagine!

Probably, our initial reaction will be the same as John's; *"When I saw Him, I fell at His feet as though dead."* Rev 1:17. Nothing we have ever remotely experienced could prepare us for His majesty, His Glory, His complete awesomeness. I am fully convinced that the most arrogant or unfeeling among us will be able to do nothing but fall at His feet, trembling, or as though dead. St. Augustine said on his deathbed, after that experience,

"I have seen Jesus, all that I have written is as straw."

When we are finally able to speak, the only conceivable words that could come from our lips will have to be those words of Doubting Thomas, *"My Lord and my God."* John 20:28.

"I can only imagine," but I hunger for that day.

How much time it will take, we can not say, but eventually our senses will begin to be able to process the lesser awesome sights of our new surroundings. Lesser we say, because nothing will ever rival our first encounter with the creator of everything, *"The Word of life."* 1 John 1:1.

Eventually we will look around and be awestruck in every direction. The first thing that may take our breath away may be the same thing that John saw next:

"And there before me was a throne in heaven with someone sitting on it. And the one who sat there had the appearance of jasper and carnelian. A rainbow, resembling an emerald, encircled the throne. Surrounding the throne were twenty-four other thrones, and seated on them were twenty-four elders. They were dressed in white and had crowns of gold on their heads. From the throne came flashes of lightning, rumblings and peals of thunder. Before the throne seven lamps were blazing. These are the seven spirits of God. Also before the throne was what looked like a sea of glass, clear as crystal.

In the center, around the throne, were four living creatures, and they were covered with eyes, in front and in back. The first living creature was like a lion, the second was like an ox, the third had a face like a man, the fourth was like a flying eagle. Each of the four living creatures had six wings and was covered with eyes all around, even under his wings. Day and night they never stopped saying:

'Holy, holy, holy is the Lord God Almighty,
who was, and is, and is to come.'

Whenever the living creatures give glory, honor, and thanks to him

who sits on the throne and lives forever, the twenty-four elders fall down
before him who sits on the throne, and worship him who lives forever
and ever. They lay their crowns before the throne and say:
  'You are worthy, our Lord and God, to receive
  glory and honor and power, for you created all
  things, and by your will they were created and
  have their being."   Revelation 4:2-11.

Wow! All of the combined resources and talent of all the movie studios in the world could never come close to duplicating what this scene must be like in real life. There is no word to describe it. And lest we forget, God's prophecies come true, literally. What we are reading, we will someday witness for ourselves. Talk about chills going up your spine. We will see the throne of God in person. "Wow!" is the only word.

And lest we forget also, at the exact same time you and I are standing awestruck by what we are witnessing in heaven, those who do not "pistevo" Jesus today will be just beginning to realize a world being run by a mad man, the antichrist, who by then will have come on the scene on planet earth.

To clarify further our fellow participants, none of those who have died rejecting Christ throughout history will be involved at this time either. God's Word tells us very plainly, as we will later see, that they will be raised at a later resurrection. The only people who will be witnessing what is being described here will be those who died "in Christ" or were raptured, plus the permanent heavenly residents. Additionally, we will mention now that what we are looking at in this chapter will end at the end of the earthly tribulation. At that time, as we shall see, those of us who are in heaven during this time will return to earth, but still in our Christlike heavenly bodies.

But let's continue. Obviously the tribulation on earth will be orchestrated from heaven, so we will be witnessing the activity that precipitates those terrible seven years. God's Word foretells what we will watch transpire:

Then I saw in the right hand of him who sat on the throne a scroll
with writing on both sides and sealed with seven seals. And I saw a
mighty angel proclaiming in a loud voice, 'Who is worthy to break the

seals and open the scroll?' But no one in heaven or on earth or under the earth could open the scroll or even look inside of it. I wept and wept because no one was found who was worthy to open the scroll or look inside. Then one of the elders said to me, 'Do not weep! See, the Lion of the tribe of Judah, the Root of David, has triumphed. He is able to open the scroll and its seven seals.

Then I saw a Lamb, looking as if it had been slain, standing in the center of the throne, encircled by the four living creatures and the elders. ... He came and took the scroll from the right hand of him who sat on the throne. And when He had taken it, the four living creatures and the twenty-four elders fell down before the Lamb. Each one had a harp and they were holding golden bowls full of incense, which are the prayers of the saints. And they sang a new song;

'You are worthy to take the scroll and to open its seals because you were slain, and with your blood you purchased men for God from every tribe and language and people and nation. You have made them to be a kingdom and priests to serve our God, and they will reign on the earth."
Revelation 5:1-10

Let's stop here and discuss something very important about your personal future. Did you catch what was said in that last line? *"And they will reign on the earth?"* Revelation 5:10.

That *"they"* is you. You personally. This is not just a little song that was being sung for musical entertainment. This was a very important prophetic uttering in God's Word, and it will just as surely come to pass as the foretelling of Jesus being born in Bethlehem, or Israel becoming a nation on May 15, 1948, or a person named Cyrus being born and growing up to free God's people from Babylonian bondage, or that Alexander the Great would unite the Greek tribes into a mighty nation that would conquer the world.

"And they will reign on the earth" literally means that you personally will have a very specific job of authority as a ruler in Christ's kingdom government on earth during His millennial reign. You can laterally exchange the *"they"* with your name. That is a very deep, profound statement, that carries with it responsibility. As we will see, there will be cities, etc., on earth exactly as there are today. They will be in the same locations, and they will probably

have the same names. And there will be nations. The difference is that they will have kings, because the earth will be under a kingdom government, with Jesus as the King of kings.

With that as a truth, does it now make more sense why we have been trying to drive home the prophetic verse, *"It is the glory of God to conceal a matter; to search out a matter is the glory of kings."* Proverbs 25:2.

The above prophetic verse in revelation did not say that "some of them will reign on earth". It said, *"They will reign on earth,"* so obviously, if you pistevo Jesus now, you <u>will</u> be placed in a position of authority in the millennial kingdom. The thought we think worth pondering is whether or not part of the criteria for choosing those of higher authority, such as the millennial kings, will be the time and effort spent *"to search out a matter."* And could the *"matter"* be the Word of God? Let's not forget, Jesus said the exact same thing in both Mark 13:31 and Luke 21:33, which is quite unusual. Both scriptures read, *"Heaven and earth will pass away, but my words will never pass away."* It is extremely obvious that the Bible, His words, are the most important *"matter"* that we could possibly *"search out."*

We've all heard people say in jest that as long as they get to heaven they don't care if they just squeeze in the door; but a thousand years may be a long time to be the city administrator of the real town of Lizard Lick, North Carolina, when all the time you are aware that more time spent in God's Word now could have resulted in being royalty in Monaco or Australia or Brazil. It may well be a thought worth considering.

As an aside, the study of God's Word can be the most exciting pastime we could have. It definitely is not boring.

You may be surprised to know that so far in this book you have already "searched out a matter" in one thousand eighteen verses from the Bible. That may be astonishing to you, but if we counted correctly, just by reading this book to this point you have actually read 1,018 verses, and the vast majority were prophetic. So with the thought of searching out the scriptures being a possible criteria for kingship, the idea of reading your Bible being a rewarding experience takes on a whole new meaning. It is just a thought to ponder.

As we said, although we will be witnessing from heaven the orchestration of the events that will be happening on earth during the tribulation, we will not be going into detail with all of the plagues, disasters, etc. There is one interesting point that is very relative, though, to something that is occurring today that we are sure you will find fascinating. It is a natural phenomenon that is strangely happening today that may well have gigantic spiritual implications.

In the chapter we read above, God foretold that we would witness the Lamb of God, Jesus, being given the scroll to open that had the seven seals. The next chapter is kind of familiar even to non believers because it prophesies what is talked about today as the four horsemen of the apocalypse.

"I watched as the Lamb opened the first of the seven seals. ... I looked and there before me was a white horse! Its rider held a bow, and he was given a crown, and he rode out as a conqueror bent on conquest." Revelation 6:1-2. This is the antichrist sent by God to the earth. Remember, other than the free will that men will have to choose to either continue to reject Him or accept Him as their Lord, God will be totally in control of what happens during the tribulation.

"When the Lamb opened the second seal, ... Then another horse came out, a fiery red one. Its rider was given power to take peace from the earth and to make men slay each other. To him was given a large sword." Revelation 6:3-4. This horse and rider represent war.

"When the Lamb opened the third seal, ... I looked, and there before me was a black horse! Its rider was holding a pair of scales in his hand. Then I heard ... 'A quart of wheat for a day's wages, and three quarts of barley for a days wages, and do not damage the oil and the wine!" Revelation 6:5-6. This represents famine and in a moment we will look more closely at these two verses because of something specific that is happening today.

"When the Lamb opened the fourth seal, ... I looked and there before me was a pale horse! Its rider was named Death, and Hades was following close behind him. They were given power over a fourth of the earth to kill by sword, famine and plague, and by the wild beasts of the earth." Revelation 6:7-8.

This obviously is death.

Let's go back, though, to the red horse and the prophecy about the coming famine, *"A quart of wheat for a day's wages, and three quarts of barley for a day's wages, and do not damage the oil and wine!"* Revelation 6:6. Imagine a person having to pay everything he can earn in an entire day just to pay for food for that one day. That is what is being described. There will be such a shortage of food that the price will have skyrocketed for it. Additionally, we are later told that money won't be the only stumbling block, because we read of the false prophet, *"He also forced everyone, small or great, rich or poor, free and slave, to receive a mark on his right hand or forehead, so that no one could buy or sell unless he had the mark, which is the name of the beast or the number of his name."* Revelation 13:16-17.

Ok, so we know that a famine of epic proportion is coming. What does that have to do with events of today? Lest we forget, Jesus told us that to interpret end times we need to be aware of what is going on in nature, and a strange phenomenon happening this very moment is something called Colony Collapse Disorder. Bees are dying in unprecedented numbers. And their demise might have not only natural but spiritual implications.

Bill Cloud, founder of Shoreshim Ministries and an authority on Hebraic Biblical study may be the first person to have noticed the spiritual implications of this strange occurrence. Please be very alert as you slowly read what we are going to say, because it may well be one of the most astounding things you will ever read.

First, let's look at the natural. In 2007 an extremely alarming event took place. About 80% of all bee colonies mysteriously died or disappeared in the areas of the world that produce most of the worlds food supply. These areas include, the United States, Canada, Australia, England and Western Europe. The phenomenon has even occurred in places like Thailand. Of note, as we shall see, is the fact that colonies not manipulated by chemicals for increased production have not been affected.

This could have serious consequences because fully thirty percent of the things we eat are directly related to pollination by bees. Over ninety fruits and vegetables would disappear without bee pollination. In the natural then, it is not beyond the realm of possibility that this highly unusual Colony Collapse Disorder could very well be a harbinger of a coming famine.

Interestingly, however, olive trees and grape vines are not dependent on bee pollination for their survival. They are self sustaining and increase by scattering by wind. Let's reread the last phrase of verse 6. *"And do not damage the oil or the wine."* Here we can begin to *"search out a matter."*

Both the olive tree and the grape vines are used by God to describe those who will be His betrothed. God talks about the olive tree as being His chosen people, but says, *"If some of the branches have been broken off, and you* (Gentile believer), *though a wild olive shoot, have been grafted in among the others and now share in the nourishing sap from the olive root, do not boast over those branches. If you do, consider this: You do not support the root, but the root supports you."* Hebrews 11:17-18.

Jesus himself then said, *"I am the true vine, and my Father is the gardener. He cuts off every branch in me that bears no fruit, while every branch that does bear fruit he prunes so that it will be even more fruitful. You are already clean because of the word I have spoken to you. Remain in me, and I will remain in you. No branch can bear fruit by itself; it must remain in the vine. Neither can you bear fruit unless you remain in me.*

I am the vine; you are the branches. If a man remains in me and I in him, he will bear much fruit; apart from me you can do nothing. If anyone does not remain in me, he is like a branch that is thrown away and withers, such branches are picked up, thrown into the fire and burned" John 15:1-7.

Now this is really going to send chills up your spine. Olive trees and grape vines need the wind for their survival, not bee pollination. In the Bible the wind always refers to the Holy spirit.

You and I need the Holy Spirit. But what do bees have to do with a spiritual matter like that? Here come the chills. The Hebrew word for "bee" is *"d'vorah,"* which derives from the root word, *"d'var,"* which means in Hebrew, "Word."

To *"search out the matter"* even further, we'll be astonished to look in God's Word, *"The days are coming,' declares the Sovereign Lord, 'when I will send a famine through the land - not a famine of food or water, but a famine for hearing the words of the Lord. Men will stagger from sea to sea and wander from north to east, searching for the word of the Lord, but they will not find it."* Amos 8:11-12.

We need to understand that the predicted famine of food will literally happen; however, God follows the natural with the spiritual. *"The spiritual did not come first, but the natural, and after that the spiritual."* 1 Corinthians 15:46.

Yes, there will be a food famine during the tribulation, and it may be partially caused by the current, very strange, Colony Collapse Disorder; but there will also be a famine for hearing the Word of God. And just as the beginnings of the food famine may have started with the bee demise, the "hearing of the Word" famine has already begun as well, even inside our Church of Laodicia. We've already mentioned that entire sermons being preached on a minister's personal agenda are common place, using the manipulation of one small verse. Go to the nearest church to you and you will probably see it first hand. One verse will be read and thirty minutes will be preached about some point that the minister wants to make.

God said, *"I warn everyone who hears the words of the prophecy of this book: If anyone adds anything to them, God will add to him the plagues described in this book. And if anyone takes words away from this book of prophecy, God will take away from him his share in the tree of life and in the holy city, which are described in this book."* Revelation 22:18-19.

To manipulate the bee, the *d'vrah*, obviously leads to it's death. We are seeing it dramatically today. Let the bee do its work, as it was meant to, and it lives and gives life to others.

To manipulate God's Word, the *d'var*, also brings death, as we see in the words of Jesus to our church, *"I am about to spit you out of my mouth."* Revelation 3:16. But the Word, as it was given by God Himself, brings life everlasting.

"He humbled you, causing you to hunger (famine) *and then feeding you with manna, ... to teach you that man does not live by bread alone but on every word that comes from the mouth of the Lord."* Deuteronomy 8:3.

The Bible, God's communication to us, may well be the most astounding of all His creations. In it He told us that a spiritual event would be preceded by a natural event. In the natural, God allows bees to disappear, which could bring natural famine. Then, by orchestrating the Hebrew word for "bee" to stem from the root word for "Word," He lovingly shows us that the elimination of his Word will likewise bring spiritual famine. Both famines result in death, but the spiritual death is eternal.

Not only can "searching out a matter" possibly be the criteria for later royalty, it also can result in eternal life itself.

"In the beginning was the Word, and the Word was with God, and the Word was God. He was with God in the beginning.

Through him all things were made; without Him nothing was made that has been made. In Him was life, and that life was the light of men. The light shines in the darkness, but the darkness has not understood it." John 1;1-5.

CHAPTER THIRTY-SEVEN

During the seven year tribulation on earth things will be going from bad to worse almost daily. Amid it all, however, God will still be wooing those who will listen. Although it will be the time of His wrath, God's great mercy will continue to be shown to all who will respond.

As we saw earlier, due to God's love for His creation, He will send forth 144,000 witnesses to spread the true gospel. This vast army of evangelists will be made up of 12,000 from each of the original twelve tribes of Israel. You and I will be in heaven and will be overjoyed, as John was in his vision, when we see their results:

"After this I looked and there before me was a great multitude that no one could count, from every nation, tribe people and language, standing before the throne and in front of the Lamb. They were wearing white robes ..." Revelation 7:9.

"Then one of the elders asked me, 'These in white robes - who are they, and where did they come from?"

I answered, 'Sir, you know.'

And he said, 'These are they who have come out of the great tribulation; they have washed their robes and made them white in the blood of the Lamb. Therefore, they are before the throne of God and serve Him day and night in His temple; and He who sits on the throne will spread His tent over them. Never again will they hunger; never again will they thirst. The sun will not beat upon them, nor any scorching heat. For the Lamb at the center of the throne will be their shepherd; He will lead them to springs of living water. And God will wipe away every tear from their eyes." Revelation 7:13-17.

Can we possibly imagine the jubilation we will all feel when we see the sight of these multitudes who have been saved out of the tribulation? Heaven will be abuzz. You and I will be the old hands by then. We will be the welcoming committee for these new saints. By then, we will be able to show these new friends the ropes.

Our eyes will have already been opened to the things that are now mysteries to us. Fortunately, one of those mysteries for me was settled some time ago by a dream recounted by one of my favorite authors, the wonderful Catherine Marshall. Often I had pondered the lesson Jesus taught the Sadducees one day.

As an aside, it is easy to distinguish the Sadducees and the Pharisees. The Pharisees worshiped such things as angels and the like, so we can remember them as "fairies, see"; whereas the Sadducees did not believe in the resurrection of the dead, so they were always "sad, you see."

At any rate, the Bible tells us how they tried to lay a mental trap for Jesus:

"That same day the Sadducees, who say there is no resurrection, came to Him with a question. 'Teacher,' they said, 'Moses told us that if a man dies without having children, his brother must marry the widow and have children for him. Now there were seven brothers among us. The first one married and died, and since he had no children, he left his wife to his brother. The same thing happened to the second and third brother, right on down to the seventh. Finally the woman died. Now then, at the resurrection, whose wife will she be of the seven, since all of them were married to her?'

Jesus replied, 'You are in error because you do not know the Scriptures or the power of God. At the resurrection people will neither marry nor be given in marriage; they will be like the angels in heaven." Matthew 22:23-30

Notice first of all that Jesus said that we will be <u>like</u> the angels. He did not say that we would be angels. Those who "pistevo" Jesus become saints, which is very different from angels.

The answer Jesus gave still seemed puzzling to me. In other words, will our wife be our wife in heaven? As we said, we got our answer from a dream Catherine Marshall had. You may recall that Catherine Marshall was the wife of Peter Marshall, the extraordinarily gifted Presbyterian minister from Scotland who became the Chaplain of the U.S. Senate during World War II. Peter died in 1949 while still only in his forties, leaving behind a distraught Catherine and a young son.

In November of that year Catherine compiled many of Peter Marshall's best sermons in a fabulous book called Mr. Jones, Meet the Master. We encourage you heartily to read it. Catherine then wrote A Man Called Peter, which was made into the movie of the same name that won the Oscar for Movie of the Year in 1952. It is a classic. She went on to become one of the most prolific Christian authors of the Twentieth Century, and even wrote the novel, Christy, which became a TV series after the turn of the Twenty First Century. Her wonderful book, Something More, should be required reading for any Christian.

As would be the case with any young widow who was madly in love, Catherine tells in her book, To Live Again, that: "I began pleading with God for some glimpse of Peter, for some knowledge of his new setting, of what he was doing.

The response came in a vivid dream. It was a dream with a self-authenticating quality. Now years later, every detail is still clear. Of no other single dream in my life can I say that. I also learned from it some of the details of the life we are to lead after death that have rung true with the testing of time.

In the dream I was allowed to visit Peter in his new setting. First I searched for him in a large rambling house with many rooms and airy porches. There were crowds of people about, but Peter was not among them.

Then I sought him in the yard. Finally, at some distance, I saw him. 'I'd recognize that characteristic gesture - that certain toss of the head any time,' I thought, as I began running toward him. I found myself able to run with a freedom I had not known since childhood. As I drew nearer, I saw that Peter was working in a rose garden. He saw me coming and stood leaning on the spade, waiting for me.

I rushed into his arms. Laughing, he pulled me close and rubbed his nose on mine.

'I knew it was you,' I said breathlessly, 'by the way you tossed your head. I've come home to you.'

Then, resting there in his arms, I felt something strange. Mixed with the tenderness of Peter's love was a certain restraint. He was not holding me as a lover." From To Live Again

In many, many books of the Bible, God used dreams not only to give prophecy, but also to give the dreamer a full understanding of something important. In this dream God gave Catherine Marshall, and us, an understanding of the mystery Jesus had touched on. Catherine goes on to explain in her book:

"Precisely what the new relationship was to be I did not then understand. I did not know what being *like the angels in heaven* would be like. ... Yet I guess that part of what this meant was that the one who has stepped over into the next life still remembers every tender moment on earth, still cares what happens to those left behind, ... but that the emotion of his love is intensified and purified. With this purification, as in a refiner's fire, all selfishness and self-seeking, the usual possessiveness that comes with love, ... all this is consumed, gone forever."

From Catherine Marshall's, To Live Again.

The great nineteenth century evangelist and writer, Charles Finney, in his book of sermons, Experiencing the Presence of God, said that "the root of all sin is selfishness." We can be certain that Finney was totally correct. One might possibly say that the exception to that could be in marriage and the family, the institution under fire today throughout the world by Satan, with such diabolical schemes as the "same sex marriage" movement. But even marriage, if built on an "agape" kind of love that God has, does not require selfishness to hold it together.

What Catherine Marshall learned in her vivid dream mercifully sent by God, was that in heaven our love will be much more perfect than it is here on earth. It will be a love that does not require possessiveness. It will be "intensified and purified." It will be a Godly kind of love. It will be the kind of love befitting the bride of Christ.

We can be sure that much of our short time spent in heaven while the tribulation is occurring on earth will be occupied in personal preparation for our millennial duties. As we learned, each of us will be assigned jobs to assist in ruling during the millennial reign of Christ. Some of us will be assigned kingdom positions and some of us will receive priestly assignments. We read about Jesus that He, *"hast made us unto our God kings and priests, and we shall reign on the earth."* Revelation 5:10 KJV. Obviously we will need some time to prepare for our upcoming millennial obligations, but we can be sure that the excitement level will remain so high that the time will literally fly by.

At the end of our seven plus years time spent in heaven will come the time we have longed for during our current days on earth as well as the time spent in heaven during the earthly tribulation. Throughout God's Word we find references to the marriage feast of the Lamb, and our part in it. Paul was inspired by the Holy Spirit in 2 Corinthians 11:2 to write to those who pistevo the Lord, *"I promised you to one husband, to Christ,"* and we will finally sit down to enjoy the wedding feast with Him. What a phenomenal event!

Jesus had talked about it often Himself. In Matthew 22:2, He said, *"The kingdom of heaven is like a king who prepared a wedding banquet for his son,"* so we can surmise that He has been longingly looking forward to the day of it's arrival. And what a day it will be! "I can only imagine!"

The beloved Apostle John saw this fantastic day in his revelation vision on the Isle of Patmos, and foretold us of it:

"Then I heard what sounded like a great multitude, like the roar of rushing waters and like loud peels of thunder, shouting:

'Hallelujah! For our Lord God almighty reigns.

Let us rejoice and be glad and give Him glory!

For the wedding of the lamb has come,

and his bride has made herself ready.

Fine linen, bright and clean, was given her to wear.'

(Fine linen stands for the righteous acts of the saints.)

Then the angel said to me, 'Write: "Blessed are those who are invited to the wedding supper of the Lamb!" And he added, 'These are the true words of God." Revelation 19:6-9.

Chapter Thirty-Eight

This may sound totally foreign to anything anyone has ever penned in a book or preached about on a Sunday morning, but it might be entirely possible that the next big event in our lives, following the glorious wedding feast of the Lamb, may be somewhat bittersweet for us. Let's be honest about it and realize that the next big step in our eternal lives will entail doing what Jesus had to do two thousand years ago, which is to leave the purity and majesty and glory of heaven and return to earth.

While you and I would have been in heaven, with no sin at all to be found anywhere around us, the world that we had left behind will have been concurrently falling deeper into depravity, as it was led by the total opposite of goodness, the antichrist. We have not looked in detail at the seven years of tribulation that is to come on earth because, as we have said, for those of us who "pistevo" Jesus now, those devastating years will be irrelevant.

At least half of the earth's inhabitants at the beginning of those seven years would have died during it, many in horrible agony. Granted, quite a few would have paid heed to the 144,000 Jewish ministers for Christ, and you and I would have excitedly welcomed them with open arms into heaven. But looking at population figures of today, that still means that at least three to four billion people would have died. Imagine, three or four billion people on earth dying in a seven year period. That amounts to between forty and fifty five million deaths per month.

When we consider the total collapse of society that would have been occurring simultaneously, with continuous natural disasters, famines, nuclear wars, riots, lack of civil order, etc., etc., etc., the world that we will be returning to will be a chaotic disaster. Fortunately, the King of kings and Lord of lords will be leading the rescue force. And that is what it will be. What's more, you and I will be a part of that force. And one of our first assignments probably will be to organize the clean up campaigns in the specific areas that we will each be responsible for.

Lest we forget, there will be many still alive who will have not taken the mark of the beast. This return trip will be a mission of mercy for those new Christians. Jesus himself told us. *"For then there will be great distress, unequaled from the beginning of the world until now - and never to be equaled again. If those days had not been cut short, no one would survive, but for the sake of the elect those days will be shortened."* Matthew 24:21-22.

We know quite a lot about the second coming of Christ. Tim LaHaye, prophecy scholar and co-author of the Left Behind series of books, stated in <u>Charting The End Times</u> that there are 325 Biblical prophecies pertaining to Christ's second coming. This coming event is foretold in every book of the Bible. You and I will have the unique perspective of seeing the return from both a heavenly vantage and an earthly one.

Let's start exploring some of the things God has told us about this phenomenal day by reading what John wrote, directly following his account of the wedding feast that we attended:

"I saw heaven standing open and there before me was a white horse, whose rider is called Faithful and True. With justice He judges and makes war." Revelation 19:11.

This is not the same white horse the antichrist rode. This is Jesus. When John mentions that He makes war, it is not much of a war. As we will see, Jesus will speak and the war starting to rage on earth known as Armageddon will immediately be over. John goes on:

"His eyes are like blazing fire, and on His head are many crowns. He has a name written on him that no one knows but He Himself. He is dressed in a robe dipped in blood, and His name is the Word of God. The armies of heaven were following Him, riding on white horses and dressed in fine linen, white and clean." Revelation 19:12-14. In that *"army"*, dear reader, is you.

In the book dictated by the Holy Spirit to Jude, the earthly half brother of Jesus, we read, *"See, the Lord is coming with thousands upon thousands of His holy ones."* Jude 14. You and I are *"holy ones"* only because of what Jesus did for us on the cross. As we studied earlier, the blood of Christ made those of us who "pistevo" him now, *"holy ones."* How thankful we should always be.

John's recounting of this future day continues.

"Out of His mouth comes a sharp sword (His Word) *with which to strike down the nations. He will rule them with an iron scepter. He treads the fury of the wrath of God almighty. On His robe and on His thigh He has this name written: KING OF KINGS AND LORD OF LORDS"* Revelation 19:15-16.

You and I will be a part of the army, but it will be an army in name only. The fight will be over before it begins.

"Then I saw the beast and the kings of the earth and their armies gathered together to make war on the rider on the horse and his army. But the beast was captured, and with him the false prophet who had performed the miraculous signs on his behalf. With these signs he had deluded those who had received the mark of the beast and worshiped his image. The two of them were thrown alive into the fiery lake of burning sulfur. The rest of them were killed with the sword that came out of the mouth of the rider on the horse, and all the birds gorged themselves on their flesh." Revelation 19:19-21.

Let's remember, those of us who died "in Christ," or were in the rapture, will be coming back with our resurrection bodies, the ones like Jesus has. Remember, we will have already spent at least seven years in heaven. Because of that, we will not only witness what was just described that occurs in what we now know of as the physical realm, but we will also be able to see the events outlined next that will happen in the spiritual world.

"And I saw an angel coming down out of heaven, having the key to the Abyss and holding in his hand a great chain. He seized the dragon, that ancient serpent, who was the devil, or Satan, and bound him for a thousand years. He threw him into the Abyss, and locked and sealed it over him, to keep him from deceiving the nations anymore until the thousand years were ended. After that, he must be set free for a short time." Revelation 20:1-3.

God will turn Satan loose one more time at the end of the millennial reign in order to make sure that those who had just begun the engagement period will stay true to Him. Many won't.

It is of interest to see how Jesus himself described the glorious day of His return:

"For as the lightning that comes from the east is visible even in the west, so will be the coming of the Son of Man." Matthew 24:27. Jesus goes on to say that everyone in the world will actually witness it, much to the chagrin of most of them:

"At that time the sign of the Son of Man will appear in the sky, and all the nations of the earth will mourn. They will see the son of Man coming on the clouds of the sky, with power and great glory. And He will send his angels with a loud trumpet call, and they will gather His elect from the four winds, from one end of the heavens to another." Matthew 24:30-31.

The gathering of His *"elect from one end of the heavens to the other"* is a reference to Jesus calling you and I from our heavenly places to join in His *"army"* that will return with Him. As we mentioned, it might be somewhat bittersweet because we will temporarily be leaving heaven's paradise, but it will also be one of the most exciting days of our lives. We will have been preparing for this day in heaven for several years. Our adrenalin will be flowing.

Evidently the first order of business will be to judge those who unfortunately took the mark of the beast. We can be sure that most of them didn't fully understand the consequences of that mark, but as we know, God said, *"My people are destroyed from lack of knowledge."* Hosea 4:6.

Let's read the entirety of the Jude 14-15 that we looked at,

"See, the Lord is coming with thousands and thousands of His holy ones to judge everyone, and to convict all the ungodly of all the ungodly acts they have done in the ungodly way, and of all the harsh words ungodly sinners have spoken against Him."

Remember, after Jesus throws the antichrist and false prophet into the lake of fire, we read, *"The rest of them were killed with the sword that came out of the mouth of the rider on the horse, and all the birds of the air gorged themselves on their flesh."* Revelation 19:21. The sword, of course, is the Word of God. Obviously, Jesus will speak and all those still alive at the end of the tribulation who rejected Him and took the mark of the antichrist, will simply die. This is made even more emphatic by the prophecy of the birds eating their flesh. They will not be resurrected again until the end of the millennial reign when they will be judged for eternity at what we will learn will be the Great White Throne Judgment.

Speaking of judging, it is interesting to note that God's Word foretells that you and I will at some point actually judge angels. The prophecy is given through Paul that reads, *"Do you not know that we will judge angels."* 1 Corinthians 6:3. Obviously the angels referred to are the third of the angelic host that originally rebelled with Lucifer.

This judgment of the angels of darkness may occur at this same time because none of the dark angels or demons will be around earth during the millennial reign of Christ. The only beings on earth during the next thousand year reign will be the Old Testament saints, those who died "in Christ", those raptured, the people who survived the tribulation without taking the mark of the beast, and possibly some of the angels of light. All who died apart from God during Old Testament times, and those who died from the time of His earthly resurrection until the last day of the tribulation who did not "pistevo" Jesus, plus those who were judged and killed the day of his second coming, will all remain dead until the "second resurrection" at the end of the thousand year reign. And remember, Satan will be gone during the thousand years, too. We can read the cast of participants:

" I saw the thrones on which were seated those who had been given authority to judge. And I saw the souls of those who had been beheaded because of their testimony for Jesus and because of the Word of God. They had not worshiped the beast or his image and had not received his mark on their foreheads or hands. They came to life and reigned with Christ a thousand years. (The rest of the dead did not come to life until the thousand years were ended.) This is the first resurrection. Blessed and holy are those who have part in the first resurrection. The second death has no power over them, but they will be priests of God and of Christ and will reign with Him for a thousand years." Revelation 20:4-6.

To make sure no one misses the gigantic point at the end, those who are a part of the first resurrection, including those raptured, will be totally secure from then on. The second death referred to, which will happen a thousand years later at the Great White Throne Judgment, will not affect them one tiny bit.

To be a hundred per cent crystal clear, if we truly "pistevo" Jesus Christ right now, we are assured that we will be a part of the first resurrection. No ifs, ands or buts about it. Additionally, our place in heaven for eternity is a complete certainty. What more reason could a person need to fully give his or her life to Jesus today? This is the "Blessed Assurance" Fanny Crosby wrote about in her wonderful hymn.

With eyes wide open, the only other choice, for anyone who now knows the truth contained in the pages of this book, is way too ludicrous to even conceive of. But what about everyone else who does not have the knowledge we now have? And what about those who died in the centuries before Jesus first came two thousand years ago? Or what about those who died in their sins since then, maybe never having heard the truth of the Gospel? Isn't it unfair that they will miss out on eternity with God? Is God being just to eliminate them? Not at all.

Scholars have called the book of Romans the crown in the Bible. In Romans 11:18, the answer to these questions was discussed. God said, *"But I ask: Did they not hear? Of course they did."* He then refers back to Psalm 19:1-4:

"The heavens declare the glory of God; the skies proclaim the work of His hands. Day after day they pour forth speech; night after night they display knowledge. There is no speech or language where their voice is not heard. Their voice goes out into all the earth, the words to the end of the world."

Why do we think God created the magnificent universe? If the earth was to be the home of his created "other", and His heavenly spiritual home was to be parallel to us, what reason could He possibly have had to also create the fabulous expanse we see in the night sky? We just read it. For all of history *"The heavens declare the glory of God, the skies proclaim the work of His hands. ... night after night they display knowledge."*

Beyond that also, the entire Old Testament is testimony to God's attempt to lovingly woo mankind, only to be rejected over and over and over again. He used such things as the prophets, His Word, nature, and everything imaginable; but for many, to no avail. Some, of course, did pay attention and chose Him.

After that, *"For God so loved the world that He gave His only be-gotten son."* John 3:16 (KJV). Once again, some responded to that incredible love. Many haven't.

During the seven year tribulation God showed that He existed and was the one and only true God, by use of His wrath, cer-tainly; but also by continuing the love call through His Word, the Bible, the 144,000 witnesses, the two prophets, and angels in the heavenlies giving mankind messages. But once again, the major-ity chose Satan.

The meaning of life we looked at earlier has been exactly the same for every single person beyond the age of innocence since Adam. Every individual has had free will, and each one has had a clear and obvious choice. Most made the wrong de-cision. Jesus Himself said, *"For wide is the gate and broad is the road that leads to destruction, and many enter through it. But small is the gate and narrow the road that leads to life, and only a few find it."* Matthew 7:13-14.

We must remember, God is totally holy. He cannot be in the presence of unholiness. Heaven would not be heaven if unholi-ness were allowed in. When we are there we will be glad that is the case. And unholiness can only be made holy through the acceptance by faith in the purification through the shed blood of Jesus. God is also a totally just God. And on the day of His Glori-ous Appearing, His justice will be played out.

You and I, and every person who has ever reached the age of accountability has been able to make choices. Some may say, though, that many in the past and still today are deceived by Satan, so it isn't their fault. The blame really rests with God since He made Satan. That reasoning is as old as Adam.

Adam knew he had disobeyed God when he ate of the forbid-den fruit. The story is well known, but the blaming of God is normally overlooked. Let's read it:

"The Lord called to the man , 'Where are you?'

He answered, 'I heard you in the garden, and I was afraid because I was naked; so I hid.'

And He said, 'Who told you that you were naked? Have you eaten from the tree that I commanded you not to eat from?'

The man said, 'The woman you put here with me - she gave me some of the fruit from the tree, and I ate it." Genesis 3:9-12

Did you catch it. Yes, Adam blamed Eve, but he went even further. He called her, *"The woman you put here with me."*

In other words, "since you put her here it must have been OK, so I ate it. It was all your fault, God. If you hadn't put her here I would have never ever sinned. I'm innocent. You are the real one who tempted me. I had to do what you wanted me to do."

Doesn't that sound exactly like mankind through the ages? But God's Word tells the unwanted truth:

"When tempted, no one should say, 'God is tempting me.' For God cannot be tempted by evil, nor does He tempt anyone; but each one is tempted when by his own evil desire, he is dragged away and enticed. Then, after desire has conceived, it gives birth to sin; and sin, when it is full-grown, gives birth to death." James 1:13-15.

The choices we all make have to do with our own desires. Satan hatches the evolution hoax, but it is man's own desire to not have to be responsible to God, so he jumps at the lie. Satan comes up with "once saved, always saved" for our modern church of Laodicia, and since man's desire is to think he can get to heaven through an easy salvation, he jumps at it. That way he can remain a homosexual or a drunk or a liar or an adulterer or a petty thief stealing office supplies, or whatever, and everything will still be fine. He can still make money his god. He doesn't even have to read God's Word or take his precious time to pray and get to know Jesus. He mainly doesn't have to obey the commandment Jesus said was the most important, *"Love the Lord your God with all your heart and with all your soul and with all your mind. This is the first and greatest commandment."* Matthew 22:37.

Jesus followed what he said was the most important commandment by saying, *"And the second is like it: Love your neighbor as yourself."* Matthew 22:39. A part of that command obviously deals with something most people do not really desire to do in many, many cases, and therefore, they just don't do it.

We are referring to forgiveness. It is extremely dangerous but even Christians who read God's Word don't take Jesus seriously when they read that He specifically said, *"If you forgive men when they sin against you, your heavenly Father will also forgive you. But if you do not forgive men their sins, your Father will not forgive your sins."* Matthew 6:14-15.

Wow! Does Jesus really and truly mean that? We can bet our eternal life on the fact that He did not say it just to hear Himself talk. And we do bet our eternal life on it whenever we stubbornly refuse to forgive others. We are given a commandment by the God who created everything, and are told exactly what will happen if we disobey, but we sluff it off and continue to not forgive. And we need to understand this also, it doesn't matter what the offense was, we are to forgive and let it go. Period. Whether the other person asks to be forgiven or not, we must forgive, or our sins will not be forgiven. This is a part of that vastly important word, "pistevo."

Our personal favorite person in the New Testament, other than Jesus, is Stephen. He started his ministry as a lowly food delivery person for widows, but ended his ministry by giving one of the very best sermons ever given in recorded history. Read the speech for yourself in Acts 7. For his oratory efforts, Stephen was stoned to death, as Saul, later to become Paul, watched over the coats of those who stoned him. Let's read the account;

"At this they covered their ears and, yelling at the top of their voices, they all rushed at him, dragged him out of the city and began to stone him. Meanwhile, the witnesses laid their clothes at the feet of a young man named Saul.

While they were stoning him, Stephen prayed, 'Lord Jesus, receive my spirit.' Then he fell on his knees and cried out, 'Lord, do not hold this sin against them.' When he had said this, he fell asleep." Acts 7:57-60.

This was a man who understood what it means to "pistevo" Jesus: to not only believe in Him, but to commit one's entire being to Him, which entails following His commands, even to the point of forgiving someone who is killing you. For such an "other", Jesus did something for Stephen that is not recorded elsewhere. He left His throne and stood up for him,

"But Stephen, full of the Holy Spirit, looked up to heaven and saw the glory of God, and Jesus standing at the right hand of God. 'Look,' he said, 'I see heaven open and the Son of Man standing at the right hand of God." Acts 7:55-56

Yes, God is just. He gave us commandments. Because we have a sin nature, we break them occasionally and truthfully repent, and because of the work of the cross, God forgives us. But unlike the teaching many "desire" to buy into, the cross did not do away with the commandments. Yes, we are saved by grace, but it is not the cheap grace our modern church teaches.

Jesus said, *"Do not think that I have come to abolish the Law and the Prophets; I have not come to abolish them but to fulfill them."* Matthew 5:17. Yes, as we have seen over and over, Jesus fulfilled the prophecies made about Him, but as He Himself said, in doing so He did not abolish the commandments. Everyone now has, and has had, the choice to obey His Word or not. God's judgment will be a just one.

"Those who live according to the sinful nature have their minds set on what that nature desires; but those who live in accordance with the Spirit have their minds set on what the spirit desires. The mind of sinful man is death, but the mind controlled by the Spirit is life and peace; the sinful mind is hostile to God." Romans 8:5-7.

At the second coming of Christ, He will judge those who are alive but rejected Him, and it will be a just judgment.

As we said, we are told a lot about the day Jesus will return. For instance, we are told, *"On that day His feet will stand on the Mount of Olives, east of Jerusalem, and the Mount of Olives will split in two from east to west, forming a great valley, with half of the mountain moving north and half moving south."* Zechariah 14:3-4.

Anyone reading these things for the first time, without the knowledge you and I have gained about the inerrant fulfillment of God's prophecies, might think such scriptures as that one to be quite fanciful. We have seen, however, that God's prophecies always come to pass. An earthquake causing a mountain to split is nothing compared to Jesus arising from the dead. God even makes sure that man doesn't disrupt His prophecies.

An interesting case in point has to do with where Jesus will walk from the time he reappears on the Mount of Olives. We know that He will walk across the Kidron Valley from the Mount of Olives to the eastern gate of the city, the exact route He walked on Palm Sunday two thousand years ago. We learn that from a vision Ezekiel had twenty five hundred years ago:

"Then the man brought me to the gate facing east, and I saw the glory of the God of Israel coming from the east. His voice was like the roar of rushing waters, and the land was radiant with His glory. ... The glory of the Lord entered the temple through the gate facing east. Then the Spirit lifted me up and brought me into the inner court, and the glory of the Lord filled the temple." Ezekiel 43:1-2, 3-4.

What is so interesting for us today is that Ezekiel saw another vision concerning that particular gate:

"Then the man brought me back to the outer gate of the sanctuary, the one facing east, and it was shut. The Lord said to me, 'This gate is to remain shut. It must not be opened; no one may enter through it." Ezekiel 44:1-2.

The eastern gate in fact is shut, and has been for over four hundred years. At that time, the Moslem leader Suleiman the Magnificent was in control of Jerusalem, and knowing about Ezekiel's prophecy of the Jewish Messiah entering through the eastern gate, ordered it to be sealed. They also built a graveyard in front of it, thinking that to also be a deterrent, because in their religion a holy man would be defiled if he walked through a graveyard. To make it even more secure in their opinion, they put gravestones of children within a few inches from the foundation.

Since then, men have attempted to open the Eastern Gate. An Arabian leader, the Grand Muffti, ordered that it be opened in 1917. On December 9 of that year his workmen took sledgehammers to do just that. "Coincidently," on that same day England's General Lord Allenby, commander of the Allied Expeditionary Army, flew a biplane over the city telling the Arabs to "Flee Jerusalem." Chaos reined that day. The Arabian army heeded Allenby's warning and fled Jerusalem, and the workers dropped their equipment and ran. The gate remained shut.

Fifty years later God again made sure that His prophecy of the shut up Eastern Gate until the Second Coming would eventually come true. The date was June 5, 1967, and King Hussein of Jordan was in control of the Old City of Jerusalem. He, too, wanted the gate opened and ordered it to be done. That morning the workers showed up ready to obey their king.

"Coincidently" again, that morning The Israeli air force flew out of Israel for a preemptive strike that totally demolished both the Jordanian and Egyptian air forces, while their planes were still on the ground. In the excitement of the hour the workers dropped their tools and fled. The defeat of several larger enemies bent on the destruction of tiny Israel in only six days has been looked at as the miracle of the Six Day War; however, the lesser known miracle is the fact that the Eastern Gate remained sealed, awaiting the glorious day that you and I will watch, up close, as Jesus enters Jerusalem through the Eastern Gate, exactly as God foretold that he would. Could it be possible that the earthquake that splits the Mount of Olives that day will also cause the opening of this prophetic gate?

"I am God, and there is no other. I am God and there is none like me. I make known the end from the beginning, from ancient times, what is still to come." Isaiah 46:9-10.

CHAPTER THIRTY-NINE

Had we spent several chapters studying in detail the prophecies God has given us about the seven years of tribulation immediately leading up to Christ's second coming and His thousand year reign on earth, we would have read about the devastating things that would have occurred, which quite obviously will include several nuclear explosions among other diverse natural disasters. It is quite possible that there will even be meteors hitting the earth. Obviously, therefore, the world will be a shambles when we come back.

Historians tell us that the form of government that can accomplish things the fastest is a kingdom government. Endless days and months of bureaucratic meetings don't facilitate quick solutions. Often times, any solutions they do come up with are fraught with compromise and political survivorship in mind.

The Millennial Kingdom will be exactly that. It will be a kingdom headed up by Jesus as the supreme and sovereign King. Under Him will be many nations headed up by lesser kings, appointed from our ranks, with localized governments, also headed up by those who opted to "pestivo" Jesus during their first earthly lives.

Actually, God was the creator of this form of government. When leading the Israelites across the desert, positioned as we saw as a cross, Moses, a type of Jesus, when concerned about the vast number of people under his command, said,

"But how can I bear your problems and your burdens and your disputes all by myself?" Deuteronomy 1:12.

God informed him what to do, and we read Moses saying,

"So I took the leading men of your tribes, wise and respected men, and appointed them to have authority over you - as commanders of thousands, of hundreds, of fifties, and of tens and as tribal officials. And I charged your judges at that time: Hear the disputes between your brothers and judge fairly, whether the case is between a brother Israelite or between one of them and an alien. Do not show partiality in judging; hear both small

and great alike. Do not be afraid of any man, for judgment belongs to God. Bring me any case too hard for you, and I will hear it. And at that time I told you everything you were to do." Deuteronomy 1:15-19.

You may want to reread that passage a few times now, because you can be sure that those words will be our marching orders prior to leaving heaven and returning to earth with Christ. There will be a plan in place, *"For God is not a God of disorder."* 1 Corinthians 14:33.

We will have each been given our assignments before we touched down on earth for "our own second coming." We can assume that much of our seven years in heaven will have been in preparation for this day. And as we saw above, we will be given some autonomy and latitude in carrying out our individual duties. To a certain extent, some of the assigned positions will be based on rewards for what we had done during our earthly lives, *"For we must all appear before the judgment seat of Christ, that each one may receive what is due him for the things done while in the body, whether good or bad."* 2 Corinthians 5:10.

A few of us will be coming back, having just barely made it into this kingdom government at all, for we read about each of us, *"his work will be shown for what it is, because the Day will bring it to light. It will be revealed with fire, and the fire will test the quality of each man's work. If what he has built survives, he will receive his reward. If it is burned up, he will suffer loss; he himself will be saved, but only as one escaping through the flames."* 1 Corinthians 3:13-15.

Obviously it will be better to at least escape *"through the flames"* than not at all, but it should make each of us want to try a little harder to accomplish the tasks God gives us in this life, one of which we will examine in the final chapter.

We can be certain also, that in addition to the reward system, our future positions will somehow be based on the talents and desires we were born with in this world. It would make sense that someone whose entire desire in this life is to be involved with music, might well have a job that will somehow be related to music during the millennial kingdom. And there will obviously be a need for people that love and have talents in architecture to be involved in the rebuilding of the demolished cities. Additionally, a person who loves and is good at teaching would naturally fit nicely into the future educational system. Your current secret goal may have been implanted in your soul by our Father for a very specific reason. Our millennial lives will definitely not be boring. They will be challenging and exciting.

Let us stress that the earth will be basically the same as when we left it. There probably will still be the golden arches of Mc-Donalds restaurants scattered around the world. There will be cars and trains and planes. There will be houses, trees, and animals. Virtually everything will be the same as when we left it, other than the results of seven years of God's wrath and man's destructive forces. It may be kind of like returning to Germany after World War II. In some places it might be like Hiroshima.

One of the big differences will be that intermingled with normal people will be those of us who have already received our resurrection bodies. That may take a little getting used to for those who live through the tribulation and enter the next thousand years as regular folks, but our bodies will also be a constant reminder for them of the hope they themselves have for their own futures beyond the millennial reign.

You and I will have our point of return in Jerusalem, just like Jesus. And we will probably remain there long enough to witness the anointing of Jesus as King of kings, but soon after that we will head to the areas where we will *reign with Christ a thousand years.* Revelation 20:4.

Interestingly, if we can imagine it, if our assigned position happens to be Bermuda (wouldn't that be nice duty?), we won't have to wait around the Jerusalem air terminal to catch a flight. Remember, we will have a body that will allow us to "translate" ourselves there by just thinking. Jesus, of course, did it often during His forty day stay after His resurrection. We even saw Philip do it after his encounter with the Ethiopian eunuch who was reading Isaiah in his chariot. If you recall, Philip baptized him and then instantly was translated from there to Azotus.

One of the truly fantastic differences between the world today and the millennial kingdom will be that Satan and his legions of demons will be gone. We can be sure that there will be no pornographic internet sites nor raunchy movies. The production of alcohol that destroys marriages, etc., will cease. Abortion clinics will be closed. Casinos that addict people to gambling will be used for other things. Gun shops and bomb factories will be refurbished for positive needs. Schools will no longer teach evolution but will teach God's Word along with other necessary disciplines. That's right, the Bible will be studied in depth, and the worship of God will become the priority that it should be today,

"The mountain of the Lord's temple will be established as chief among the mountains; it will be raised above the hills, and the nations will stream to it.

Many people will come and say, 'Come let us go up to the mountain of the Lord, to the house of the God of Jacob. He will teach us His ways, so that we may walk in His paths.' The law will go out from Zion, the word of the Lord from Jerusalem.

He will judge between the nations and will settle disputes for many peoples. They will beat their swords into plowshares and their spears into pruning hooks. Nation will not take up sword against nation, nor will they train for war anymore." Isaiah 2:2-4.

One of the extremely interesting things that we will watch will be the animal population. Many of them will actually change their characteristics during the millennial kingdom, for we read, *"The wolf will live with the lamb, the leopard will lie down with the goat, the calf and the lion and the yearling together, and a little child will lead them. The cow will feed with the bear, their young will lie down together, and the lion will eat straw like the ox. The infant will play near the hole of the cobra, and the young child put his hand into the viper's nest. They will neither harm nor destroy ..., for the earth will be full of the knowledge of the Lord as the waters covers the sea."* Isaiah 11:6-9.

Although death will still occur, we will also definitely witness sickness and disease become a rarity,

"Never again will there be in it an infant who lives but a few days, or an old man who does not live out his years; he who dies at a hundred will be thought a mere youth; he who fails to reach a hundred will be considered accursed." Isaiah 65:20.

(Some consider these verses in Isaiah to describe heaven, but they could not because death will not exist at all in heaven.)

Times will be much less stressful than today. People won't work in vain. Life as a whole will be much more just,

"They will build houses and dwell in them; they will plant vineyards and eat their fruit. No longer will they build houses and others live in them, or plant and others eat. For as the days of a tree, so will be the days of my people; my chosen ones will long enjoy the works of their hands. They will not toil in vain or bear children doomed to misfortune; for they will be a people blessed by the Lord, they and their descendants with them." Isaiah 65:21-23.

Unfortunately, however, even though Satan and his demons will be gone, the people who live through the tribulation will still have their sin nature. They will be regular folks just like you and I are today. Although all would have rejected Satan by not taking the mark of the beast, many would be brand new Christians, baby Christians, if you will. They will still need to be taught how to live as people who "pistevo" Christ. They will need to be taught the commands of Jesus. Such things as forgiveness that we mentioned in the last chapter will not come naturally for them. And as we will see, some will never truly "pistevo" Jesus.

Is it any wonder why it is so imperative that you and I must learn to follow Christ's commands right now, during this life, since these baby Christians in the millennium will be under our care and instruction? Whether they make it into the next step, the eternal heaven, will partially rest on our teaching and impartation. Christ expects and commands that we prepare ourselves now. That may be why Jesus was clear when He said,

"For many are invited, but few are chosen." Matthew 22:14.

The concept that we need to get hold of now is the fact that every single one of the commandments we are to follow are not only good for the kingdom of God, but are good for us as well. Let's look at a few. We mentioned forgiveness, which in many cases seems so hard to us. It actually is a gift for us. How often have each of us been hurt by someone else, maybe deeply, and tossed and turned in bed night after sleepless night thinking about the offense. We mentally plan revenge, or at least wish we had said thus and so to the offending party. Our stomachs sometimes ache from the stress. We may even get ulcers over it.

But is the person who wronged us so badly going through the same terrible sleepless nights? Are they expending the same fruitless energy? Not at all. They probably haven't given the situation a second thought. They have gone on with their lives. They are sleeping like babies.

The cure is really a simple one, forgiveness. The offending party doesn't have to ask for it, deserve it, or even know about it. But when we tell our Father that we forgive them, and then turn the situation over to Him and let it go, we are the ones released from the bondage. Nothing says we have to trust that person again, because trust and forgiveness are two totally different things, but by forgiving we free ourselves to get on with our own lives. Andy Andrews, in his wonderful novel, Island of Saints, says, "Forgiveness frees the forgiver," and he is one hundred percent correct. Andy may have said it even more poetically when he wrote in the same book, "When we forgive we set the prisoner free and discover the prisoner was us."

When we abide in Christ and truly obey His commands we always find that whatever He told us to do makes our lives so very much better. And after we make a habit of doing them, we find them to be easy. Remember, Jesus said, *"Take my yoke upon you and learn from me, for I am gentile and humble in heart, and you will find rest for your souls. For my yoke is easy and my burden is light."* Matthew 11:29-30.

Before we leave this train of thought and get back to the millennial kingdom, it might be wise to briefly discuss another command that very few obey and is even denied to be a command of Jesus by literally hundreds of thousands of ministers today who have unconsciously bought into the "people friendly church" concept that is afraid of running congregational members away. In so doing they have unknowingly robbed their people of one of the most important spiritual truths in God's Word, and have, through *"lack of knowledge,"* made the lives harder of those they are suppose to lead, by causing them to not obey Jesus. We need to perk up for this truth because it is extremely important, both to God, and to us.

The spiritual law we are talking about is the tithe. In today's world it refers to ten per cent of any money we receive. Literally hundreds of thousands of ministers will preach from their pulpits, and probably actually believe, that the tithe is an Old Testament commandment and is not relevant since Jesus died on the cross. As God said in Hosea 4:6, though, *"My people are destroyed from lack of knowledge."* This is definitely the case with the modern church's thinking in this matter. We can clearly see it in Jesus's own teaching,

"Woe to you, teachers of the law and Pharisees, you hypocrites! You give a tenth of your spices - mint, dill and cummin. But you have neglected the more important matters of the law - justice, mercy and faithfulness. You should have practiced the latter, without neglecting the former." Matthew 23:23.

Only a blind man can't see that Jesus is saying that the believers should practice justice, mercy, faithfulness, <u>and</u> tithing. He did not say that it was an obsolete law. But that is what our modern Church of Laodicia is currently teaching. If they mention tithing at all they normally change the meaning to "giving in general," and say that the amount is left up to the giver, or at least that the giver can listen to his heart and figure out the amount God wants. Hogwash. The amount is ten per cent, and there are definite spiritual principles in play with that specific amount. Please pay very close attention to the following discussion because it is extremely critical. We will show that although the tithe involves money in our society, it has nothing at all to do with money.

The very first time the tithe is mentioned is during the meeting we looked at earlier between Abram and Melchizedek, the epitome of the type of Jesus,

"Then Melchizedek king of Salem brought out bread and wine (communion). *He was priest of God Most High, and he blessed Abram, ... Then Abram gave him a tenth of everything." Genesis 14:18-20.*

The act of the offering to God, however, goes back to Cain and Abel, and it is crucial throughout the entire Word of God. Let's look at one of the earliest instructions God gave,

"You are to give over to the Lord the first offspring of every womb. All firstborn males of your livestock belong to the Lord. Redeem with a lamb every firstborn donkey, but if you do not redeem it break its neck." Exodus 13:12-13.

We need to *"search out a matter"* in these verses. The first part is easy, the firstborn male belongs to God. The second part is a little trickier. We need to understand that there were "clean" and "unclean" animals. Sheep, cattle and goats were clean, while donkeys were unclean. Only clean animals were accepted as sacrifices. So, if a firstborn donkey was born, a "clean" lamb was to be sacrificed. God said that would "redeem" the donkey. But if a lamb was not available, God instructed them to break the donkey's neck. Why in the world would God want them to do something so absurd? In the first place, it should be obvious to us now, since we have studied types and shadows, that this scripture is a shadow. Jesus became the "clean" lamb who was to redeem unclean man. Without Him and His sacrifice on the cross, unclean mankind had to die. It was the very first prophecy, *"You will surely die."* Genesis 2:17.

In addition to the profound shadow in these verses, though, is a truth that may even be more important for you and I today; and the modern church has missed it. The secret lies in the gigantic word "trust." Part of the reason for this entire Godly instruction, and every instruction that was to follow concerning the giving or sacrificing of the first born, or later, the first tenth of income, was to show trust, or faith. By giving the first born of a flock, a person was trusting God to replace it, to provide.

Let's paint a picture: you and I want to start a herd and we have a ram and a ewe. The ewe gives birth to a lamb. How certain are we that this lamb might not be the very last one born? Now, God asks us to sacrifice it, knowing that by doing so we are trusting Him to replace that lamb. It is an absolute act of trust. It is a concrete, material show of true faith. That is what God desires, our complete faith in Him. Wouldn't any person who is engaged to an "other" want proof of their complete faith?

"And without faith it is impossible to please God." Hebrews 11:6.

Allow that statement to really and truly sink in, *"without faith it is impossible to please God."*

You and I can say or do anything imaginable that we might think would be pleasing to our heavenly Father, but *"without faith it is <u>impossible</u> to please God."* That is heavy.

And if we ponder it hard, the only two possible ways to show in a concrete way that we really have faith in God are to either be martyred for Him, or to do the much easier thing and give Him our tithe. Everything else is just empty words. The old saying, "put your money where your mouth is," definitely applies in pleasing God.

We must realize that the money part of it is immaterial. God doesn't need our money. God made that clear,

"I have no need for a bull from your stall or of goats from your pens, for every animal of the forest is mine, and the cattle on a thousand hills." Psalm 50:9-10.

"The silver is mine and the gold is mine,' declares the Lord Almighty." Haggai 2:8.

"Everything under heaven belongs to me." Job 41:11

No, God has no need of our money, or anything. In fact,

"Don't be deceived, my brothers. Every good and perfect gift is from above, coming down from the Father of heavenly lights." James 1:16.

Instead of needing money from us, God is our provider. The tithe acknowledges that spiritual truth and gives God concrete proof that we understand that truth and trust Him to fulfill it. God wants us to grasp this principle so much that the only time in the entire Bible that God not only gives us permission to test Him, but encourages it, deals with the tithe. Let's read God's following words very slowly,

"Will a man rob God? Yet you rob Me.

But you ask, 'How do we rob You?'

In tithes and offerings. You are under a curse - the whole nation of you - because you are robbing Me. Bring the whole tithe into the storehouse, that there may be food in my house. **Test** *me in this,' says the Lord Almighty, 'and see if I will not throw open the floodgates of heaven and pour out so much blessing that you will not have room enough for it."* Malachi 3:8-10.

God knows that the only way we can really show that we trust Him in a practical manner is by tithing the first ten per cent of every dollar we get. All the pious and righteous sounding words that we may whisper or shout are meaningless beside the one true act of faith, the tithe.

"Abraham believed God and it was credited to him as righteousness."
Romans 4:3.

The way we prove we believe God is by tithing ten per cent.
The number ten, by the way, stands for redemption. When we
give God our <u>first</u> ten per cent, the other ninety per cent is redeemed. That means that we find in practical experience that it
becomes enough.

An interesting poll was taken by a New York church during the
great depression. While thousands were standing in soup lines,
members walked down the lines asking a simple question, "Are
you a tither?" Out of the many thousands of people asked, not
one said that they were a tither. Not one. Where were the tithers?
Obviously God had somehow provided for them. They may not
have been wealthy, but they were not in soup lines.

As an aside, however, a profound statement worth contemplat-
ing is that "true wealth is the poverty of desire." Think about it.

We are taking a lot of time on this subject of tithing because it
may well be one of the most important lessons in this entire book.
Someone may say, though, "I donate money to a church." Unless
they tithe first, no, they don't. Any donation made without tithing first is only a partial payback of the money that God says is
His. It is not an offering or donation at all.

Imagine we own a house and a man is supposed to give us a
thousand dollars a month. Let's say he doesn't ever pay his rent
but occasionally gives us ten dollars and feels like he is donat-
ing money to us. Sorry, but as they say in the South, that dog
won't hunt.

In God's case, we don't just owe Him some rent money. Everything we have, everything we are, everything in our world
is His, and He is only asking us to give back a small ten per cent
to show that we trust him to keep His Word, to be faithful in
return. No wonder that, *"Without faith it is impossible to please
God."* Hebrews 11:6.

Before we leave this extremely spiritual subject of tithing and
get back to the millennial kingdom, let's answer a few very practical questions. The first one is, where should I give my tithe? Does
it have to be given to a church? The answer is no. God's house

is any place that is spreading the gospel and saving souls. There are many good places for you to choose. A church may be a great one, if they are actually saving souls. If they are just building big buildings and gymnasiums and the like, maybe not. Otherwise, there are wonderful places such as Gospel for Asia (www.gfa.org) and Youth with a Mission (www.ywam.org) that are excellent. You may want to give to a smaller ministry, such as Keith Wheeler, (www.kw.org) who literally carries a cross around the globe and wins thousands of souls to Christ on every continent. There are numerous choices you can make, but be sure the organization is really saving souls and teaching people how to truly "pistevo" Christ. Be a good steward with God's money. But once it leaves your hands, it is in God's hands.

Another question one might pose has to do with giving to organizations that feed the poor, or orphanages, or organizations like the cancer fund. These may be all fantastic organizations to donate money to, but unless they are bringing people to Jesus, they are not places for your tithe. They are places for the giving of your own money, which we should all be doing as well, but just feeding or caring for people is not leading souls into an eternity with God. Even Hindu, Moslem and atheistic organizations feed and care for people.

A word of caution might be in order. Ministries and churches that are constantly asking for money could and should be questioned. If they actually have the faith God wants, why are they asking man instead of asking their God to provide for their needs? There are many, many instances through the years of Godly people and ministries who never once asked man for anything, but only prayed, and were provided for by God. If God truly guides, God provides. You can read exciting biographies of people such as George Mueller, George N. Patterson and Mother Teresa who followed this principle and God always answered their prayers. Even today, Godly people like Keith Wheeler and Dr. Michael Guido, the Sower, receive their financial needs in this exact manner. If you pray about it, God will lead you to these types of ministries where He may want His tithe sent. Don't let emotions direct God's tithe.

We can be sure that part of our priorities in our assigned positions in the millennial kingdom will be to make sure that the new believers under our care understand these kingdom principles. Among other things, King Jesus will still expect His subjects to forgive and to tithe, and the reasons will remain the same. As to tithing, it will continue to be a matter of showing faith and trust. And they will learn, as we do today, that when they tithe, God truly does provide. Giving is not a key to wealth, as many prosperity preachers on earth today try to teach, but the tithe is a key to pleasing God, which somehow always results in needed provision. *"Test me in this,' says the Lord Almighty."* Malachi 3:10.

In the next chapter we will not only learn more about our future lives in the millennial kingdom, but we will also find out what God foretells will happen to us after that thousand year reign of Christ on earth is over. Our lives today can't hold a candle to what is in store for us in our future.

CHAPTER FORTY

Dr. Gene Scott was one of the better Bible scholars of the twentieth century. In much of his teaching he put forth the idea that God, the Father, had to box Himself away from his beloved creation, man, when He created in us a sin nature. It is obvious that since sin is totally abhorrent to the Father, it cannot be in the presence of God and survive. That is why the original tabernacle was built. The inner sanctum, the Holy of Holies, gave God a place to be with His people, but at the same time be cut off from them, allowing them with their inbuilt sin nature to survive.

Christ's death on the cross rent the dividing curtain from top to bottom, which allowed mankind to communicate directly with the Father, but since then His residence has remained in the heavenlies. The Holy Spirit has resided on earth with mankind, but the Father Himself has remained in heaven.

When Jesus returns to set up His millennial kingdom on earth, one of the first things He will do is build a gigantic temple with a new Holy of Holies for the Father to reside in until the thousand years is completed. The sin nature would have been eliminated in you and me when we received our resurrection bodies, otherwise we would not have been able to stand in front of the throne of the Father in heaven, but the new Christians who lived through the tribulation will continue to carry the sin nature inside them. The Father, therefore, must still be temporarily "boxed off" from His creation.

Our heavenly Father "abided" with man in the past in four distinct settings. First, of course, He was with Adam in the Garden of Eden before the manifestation of sin. We know this because we read, *"The man and his wife heard the sound of the Lord God as He was walking in the garden in the cool of the day."* Genesis 3:8.

God's second abode on earth was in the tabernacle Moses built, which lasted from roughly 1,500 BC to 1,000 BC. We read of that tabernacle, *"Then the cloud covered the Tent of meeting, and the glory of the Lord filled the tabernacle."* Exodus 40:34.

Then Solomon built his temple about 1,000 BC and that lasted until about 500 BC. We read of that structure after the ark of the covenant was placed in it, *"When the priests withdrew from the Holy Place, the cloud filled the temple of the Lord. And the priests could not perform their services because of the cloud, for the glory of the Lord filled the temple."* 1 Kings 8:10-11.

The fourth and final abode of God the Father with man has its roots in the person we looked at in the very first prophecy we studied in this book, Cyrus. If you recall, God had written Cyrus a letter over a hundred years before he was even born and outlined what would happen in his life, saying that he was going to be the person to free the Israelites from their Babylonian bondage. About this very same Cyrus we read in Ezra 1:2-3, *"This is what Cyrus king of Persia says: 'The Lord, the God of heaven, has given me all the kingdoms of the earth and He has appointed me to build a temple for Him at Jerusalem in Judah. Any one of His people among you - may his God be with him, and let him go up to Jerusalem in Judah and build the temple of the Lord, the God of Israel, the God who is in Jerusalem."*

We learned earlier that Solomon's temple was destroyed by Nebuchadnezzar's army when they took the Israelites into captivity. That was the reason for Cyrus's decree to have it rebuilt. Ezra, Nehemiah and Zerrubabel oversaw the rebuilding of it, and it was later expanded by King Herod in 19 BC. This was the temple that was standing in the days Jesus was first on earth, and the one He prophesied about, *"As for what you see here, the time will come when not one stone will be left on another, every one of them will be thrown down."* Luke 21:6.

Of course, as in every one of the other fulfilled prophecies we have looked at, this one came to pass exactly as Jesus had said that it would. In 70 AD four Roman legions under the command of Titus burned it, and since gold melted and ran into the cracks of the walls, the conquerors literally removed every stone to find the treasure. One item that most people overlook but we find very interesting is that both Solomon's Temple and Herod's Temple were destroyed on the exact same day, the tenth of Av. Coincidence?

As we know, another temple will be rebuilt either prior to or during the tribulation. It will be completed before the three and a half year midpoint because that is when the antichrist will enter it and declare himself god, the *"abomination that causes desolation."* God, our Father, will not inhabit this new temple, the tribulation temple, because of the defiling by the antichrist, thus the reason for the building of a new temple at the beginning of the millennial reign of Christ.

God takes an incredible fourteen full pages in His Word to describe in the minutest of detail the Millennial Temple. You can read it all yourself in Ezekiel 40-47. All of the dimensions are given for every part of it, including the furniture. Obviously, since it will be His dwelling place, this temple is understandably of importance to Him. It will be huge, with the outer walls being 750 feet square. To put that in perspective, each side will be as long as two and a half football fields.

And lest we gloss over all of this as somehow just fanciful, please remember and be assured that all of God's prophecies do come to pass. You and I will one day stand inside this structure as we will definitely occasionally go there to worship during the thousand years of the millennial kingdom. There is nothing "way out" about this at all. You and I personally will walk into this phenomenal temple. Count on it. It will be an exciting experience, for while Jesus, God the Son, will be literally reigning from the throne of David in Jerusalem, God the Father will be dwelling in the Holy of Holies within the Millennial Temple that you and I will actually enter to worship. Talk about church chills going up your spine. Wow!

One thing we as Gentiles need to remember is that the Jewish people have always been, and will continue to be, God's chosen people. God tells us,

"I do not want you to be ignorant of this mystery, brothers, so that you may not be conceited: Israel has experienced a hardening in part until the full number of the Gentiles has come in. And so all Israel will be saved, as it is written:

'The deliverer will come from Zion; He will turn godlessness away from Jacob (Israel). And this is my covenant with them when I take away their sins.'

As far as the gospel is concerned, they are enemies on your account; but as far as election is concerned, they are loved on account of the patriarchs, for God's gifts and His call are irrevocable. Just as you who were one time disobedient to God have now received mercy as a result of their disobedience, so they too have now become disobedient in order that they too may now receive mercy as a result of God's mercy to you. For God has bound all men over to disobedience so that He may have mercy on them all." Romans 11:25-32.

Yes, throughout Biblical history, the Israelites disobeyed, repented, and disobeyed again. They did this over and over and over. But God had made promises to the patriarchs, Abraham, Isaac and Jacob, that their decedents would always be His people, and God is a God of His word. He did, though, blind their eyes for the last two thousand years in order that you and I could be saved. In the end, however, they will still be His people. And this is rightfully so, for we read, *"Theirs is the adoption as sons; theirs the divine glory, the covenants, the receiving of the law, the temple worship and the promises. Theirs are the patriarchs, and from them is traced the human ancestry of Christ, who is God all over, forever praised! Amen."* Romans 9:3-5.

Because of this, Israel will still be Israel, and it will still be Jewish during the Millennium, even more than it is today. Ezekiel 48 describes in detail exactly what will happen to the geography that is now Israel. The nation that we know as Israel today will be divided into thirteen parallel sections with boundary lines running from east to west, and will include the nations we today know as Syria and Lebanon. The western border, of course, will be the Mediterranean Sea. The eastern border will go up through the dead Sea and the Jordan River and then move more easterly through what is now Damascus and northward. Each division of at least eighty square miles will be for each of the twelve original tribes, starting with a section for the tribe of Dan at the top and going down to Asher, Naphtali, Manasseh, Ephraim, Rueben and Judah. Next will be an area known as the Holy Portion in which Jerusalem now sits, which will be the location of the new Millennial Temple. Below that will be the areas for the tribes of Benjamin, Simeon, Issachar, Zebulon and Gad at the southernmost end by Egypt.

It probably would be good to remember that God told Abram in Genesis 12:2-3 with what is known as the Abrahamic Covenant, *"I will make you into a great nation and I will bless you; I will make your name great and you will be a blessing, I will bless those who bless you, and whoever curses you I will curse; and all peoples on earth will be blessed through you."*

All the people on earth have been blessed by Israel, for as we read, *"from them is traced the human ancestry of Christ."*

As far as the blessings and curses part, an entire history book can be written showing how they have always come to pass. For example, many of us who are older can remember when "the sun never set on the British Empire." It was everywhere. Within an extremely short fifty year period after the official English stance on the Jewish people and Israel as a nation changed from positive to negative, the British Empire was dramatically reduced almost beyond belief. Could it be that the United states is the power they are today because of their continual blessing of Israel and its people? If so, a word of caution might be made concerning any drastic shift in that position.

And we as individuals would do well to remember that God gave the command, *"Pray for the peace of Jerusalem: May those who love you be secure."* Psalm 122:6. Yes, Israel will remain God's people. We should consider that as we watch the news.

Getting back to the Millennial Kingdom, as we have seen, life will be much better then than it is today. Disease will be a rarity if at all, babies will not die, people will live longer, there will be no more wars, prosperity will be everywhere, and Satan and his cronies will be gone. The quality of life will far exceed anything we could imagine today. Jesus will actually be on His earthly throne in Jerusalem, and the Father will be in the Holy of Holies. What more could anybody want? What will happen next is in many ways very startling,

"When the thousand years are over, Satan will be released from his prison and will go out to deceive the nations in the four corners of the earth." Revelation 20:7-8.

The reason for this should be clear to us now. God still wants an "other" who truly has had the choice to love Him.

Up until this point, although these people who came out of the tribulation had a sin nature within them, they had no other choice but to choose God. Satan had been kept away so there would have been no other suitor for them to choose, therefore they truly had not had free will. As is the case now, God will want to make sure their love for Him is genuine. And His wisdom will prove to be born out, for,

"In number they are like the sand on the seashore. They march across the breadth of the earth and surround the camp of God's people, the city He loves." Revelation 20:8-9.

This, to us, may seem like one of the oddest predictions, that people who have lived under the earthly Reign of Jesus Christ Himself could be deceived enough by Satan to join forces with him, to choose to be engaged to Satan over the God of love. Remember, all of those people who survive the tribulation and enter and live in the millennial kingdom will have professed to be followers of Jesus. Obviously the "once saved always saved" doctrine of Calvin will break down yet again. Granted, these people would not have had experience with Satan's cunning, but their commitment to Jesus will prove to be superficial at best.

How will Satan deceive them? We can bet that it will be in the same old tired ways , such as appealing to some form of their selfishness. You and I will witness this event, probably with a sense of utter disbelief and sadness that these people could allow themselves to be so destructively deceived. We can be sure that God is likewise totally saddened as he watches our fellow man being similarly deceived.

The rebellion will be short lived, however, for, *"But fire came down from heaven and devoured them.*

And the devil, who deceived them, was thrown into the lake of burning sulfur, where the beast and the false prophet had been thrown. They will be tormented day and night for ever and ever." Revelation 20:9-10.

At this point in His story, God's "other" will have been completed. It will now be time for all those who have died in the history of the world who had rejected God to be raised from the dead. The next event is the second resurrection. You and I will thankfully not be a part of it. Our positions will be secure.

"Then I saw a great white throne and Him who was seated on it. Earth and sky fled away from His presence, and there was no place for them." Revelation 20:11.

From that statement we can know that what is to now occur will be totally in the spiritual realm. The dead who will be raised in the second resurrection will not receive resurrection bodies.

"And I saw dead, great and small, standing before the throne, and books were opened. Another book was opened , which is the book of life. The dead were judged according to what they had done as recorded in the books. The sea gave up the dead that were in it, and death and Hades gave up the dead that were in them, and each person was judged according to what he had done. Then death and Hades were thrown into the lake of fire. The lake of fire is the second death. If anyone's name was not found in the book of life, he was thrown into the lake of fire." Revelation 20:12-15.

As we now know, God sadly told us in His Word,

"My people are destroyed for lack of knowledge." Hosea 4:6.

But fabulous news is ahead, for we learn from His Word,

"No eye has seen, no ear has heard, no mind has conceived what God has prepared for those who love Him. But God has revealed it to us by His spirit." 1 Corinthians 2:9-10.

Although you and I have not yet been caught up into paradise to witness first hand the wonders of heaven in the same manner Paul and John were, we can get a fascinating view of what will happen next in the detailed recording of John's vision,

"Then I saw a new heaven and a new earth, for the first heaven and the first earth had passed away, and there was no longer any sea." Revelation 21:1.

Not only did the earth we now live on have remnants of sin, but since we know that Satan had been in heaven, it had been contaminated as well. God will cleanse both realms with fire, not destroying them, but making them new. And interestingly, there will no longer be oceans, giving us three times as much inhabitable area on earth as we currently have. As we shall see, there will still be rivers, and probably lakes as well.

"I saw the Holy City, the new Jerusalem, coming down out of heaven from God, prepared as a bride beautifully dressed for her husband."

Revelation 21:2. As we will see, this new city will be stunning to say the least. Actually, it will be magnificent.

"And I heard a loud voice from the throne saying, 'Now the dwelling of God is with men, and He will live with them. They will be His people, and God Himself will be with them and be their God." Revelation 21:3. Sin will have been completely removed, so God will not have to be "boxed in" any longer.

He will live with us, just like originally in the garden. Wow!

"He will wipe every tear from their eyes. There will be no more death or mourning or crying or pain, for the old order of things has passed away." Revelation 21:4. This is the real heaven, the hope of our lives now and the millennium to come. Ponder it for a moment, a world with never any sadness or pain or death. As the song says, "I can only imagine," yet like every prophecy from God, it will one day be reality.

John goes on to describe the new Jerusalem, the new capital of the earth, *"And he carried me away in the Spirit to a mountain great and high, and showed me the Holy City, Jerusalem, coming down out of heaven from God. It shown with the glory of God, and its brilliance was like that of a very precious jewel, like a jasper, clear and crystal. It had a great high wall with twelve gates and with twelve angels at the gates. On the gates were written the twelve tribes of Israel. ... The wall of the city had twelve foundations, and on them were the names of the twelve apostles of the Lamb."* Revelation 21:10-14.

John then is given a measuring rod to measure the city,

"The city was laid out like a square, as long as it was wide." Revelation 21:16. We then find out that the city measures over fourteen hundred miles long and fourteen hundred miles wide. Interestingly, John tells us that it is also fourteen hundred miles high. Whether the city is a cube or a pyramid we are not told, but we personally think it will be a pyramid.

Another interesting thing is the probable location. We are told in Genesis 2:11-14 that the original Garden of Eden was bordered by four rivers, the Pishon, Gihon, Tigris and Euphrates. That would make the Garden of Eden about fourteen hundred miles square, and encompassing what is now Israel. It seems logical that the New Jerusalem will be in the exact same place.

The description of the city continues,

"The wall was made of jasper, and the city of pure gold, as pure as glass. The foundations of the city walls were decorated with every kind of precious stone,...jasper,...sapphire,... chalcedony,...carnelian,...chrysolite,...beryl,...topaz,... chrysoprase,...jacinth,...and the twelfth amethyst. The twelve gates were twelve pearls, each gate made of a single pearl. The great street of the city was of pure gold, like transparent glass.

I did not see a temple in the city, because the Lord God Almighty and the Lamb are its temple. The city does not need the sun or the moon for the glory of God gives it light, and the Lamb is its lamp. The nations will walk by its light and the kings of the earth will bring their splendor into it. On no day will its gates ever be shut, for there will be no night there. The glory and honor of the nations will be brought into it." Rev. 21:18-26.

Notice that there will evidently be nations of saints around the world in addition to those saints who will actually reside in the Holy City.

"Then the angel showed me the river of the water of life, as clear as crystal, flowing from the throne of God and of the Lamb down the middle of the great street of the city. On each side of the river stood the tree of life, bearing twelve crops of fruit, yielding its fruit every month." Revelation 22:1-2.

Did you notice the word month? Obviously eternity will not be an absence of time. Instead it will be unlimited time. That in itself conjures up pleasant thoughts. Think of never being in a hurry. We will be able to chat with friends, old and new, for hours if we want, because we will have an endless supply of time. Speaking of that, we will surely be able to meet and chat with people like, Moses, and Daniel, and George Washington, and Augustine. What a fantastic life, a fantastic eternal life.

Just as Jesus spoke at the beginning of the book of Revelation when He dictated the seven letters to the seven churches and seven church ages, Jesus speaks again in this final chapter of Revelation, the final chapter of God's Word,

"Behold, I am coming soon! My reward is with me, and I will give to everyone according to what he has done. I am the Alpha and the Omega, the First and the Last, the Beginning and the End.

Blessed are those who wash their robes, that they may have the right to the tree of life and may go through the gates into the city." Revelation 22:12-14.

PART EIGHT

CHAPTER FORTY-ONE

Years ago we heard an interview with an elder theologian who had studied God's Word for hours on end for over fifty years. His Biblical knowledge was incredible. The questioner ended the interview with probably the best question possible for such a learned scholar, "After all of these years of intense study, what is the most profound thing you have learned about God?"

The white haired theologian didn't hesitate a moment with his answer, "That God loves us so much."

"God loves us so much." Then why didn't He make it easier to know that He was there? Why didn't He do more dramatic things to show us that He existed, and that He loved us? Why didn't He make it completely impossible for any person to not know about Him and race to His open arms? And why in the world did He allow some people to make the wrong choice and totally miss out on heaven?

We can be sure that in many ways He wanted to do all those things, however, that would have eradicated the idea of free will. Yes, God could have made His existence a no brainer. He could have written messages to us daily in the heavens that no one could miss. God is obviously that powerful. But once again, that would have taken away our choice to choose Him over the evil one. And that ability to choose is an eternal necessity.

On the other hand, God did provide us with so much proof that once we "searched out a matter," the debate would be over. You and I have explored that proof. We have looked at about twelve hundred and fifty verses from God's own communication to us, most of them being prophetic verses that have already been fulfilled. It was *"the glory of God to hide a matter,"* because He <u>had</u> to hide it, and it was to our everlasting glory to search it out.

You and I are now in an extremely unique position. We have seen the truth, as very few of our contemporaries have.

In fact, the vast majority of the world doesn't even have a clue as to where to look. Obviously, logic should tell them that God exists because of the unbelievable complexity of everything in nature, from the expansive universe to the intricacy of the sense of sight. But the one proof God alerted man to examine, His fulfilled prophecies, have been hidden from man by his own worst enemy, himself. The funny but deep line from the Pogo comic strip, "we have met the enemy and he is us," has never been as true of anything as it is of man's quest for spiritual truth. Mankind's selfishness and pride have done more to blind his eyes than even Satan and his horde of demons could do. All demons have had to do is occasionally fan the flames of man's own desire to be his own god. Looking at the self destruction from the outside must be a very ludicrous and sad sight indeed.

You and I, however, saw God prophesy the date Jesus would ride into Jerusalem on a donkey, and have it fulfilled. We witnessed his incredible foretelling of another date, that of the creation of Israel as a nation, twenty five hundred years in advance. And we saw God correctly give the date of the ends of both the Egyptian and Babylonian captivities. We read, as if reading a newspaper account, the detailed events following Alexander the Great's death. Virtually none of our neighbors on planet earth have seen these things. What a shame.

God gave us these prophecies, and thousands more, not to brag. He is the creator of everything. He is God. He doesn't need to brag. No, he wrote these prophecies because He loved us so much. His Word is called the ultimate love letter because through it He was giving us glaring clues that would lead us to His loving arms.

He also told us startling truths, such as the fact that the earth was round, thousands of years before man would figure it out for himself. He even threw in countless other things that could open our eyes, such as the need for sterilization and occasionally quarantine. We looked at several similar things, but we only scratched the surface in this book.

God created us, and He wanted us to love Him and be His bride for eternity. He brilliantly gave us another choice in the form of Satan and even put in us the sin nature to make that choice a possibility, but His desire was that we would choose Him, and so He conceived of and personally gave us the remedy in the form of Jesus, so that once we did choose Him we could be holy enough to live in His presence forever.

Additionally, after God started all of this phenomenal plan into motion and put all the clues in His Word for us to find, He didn't leave us on our own. He sent the Holy Spirit to help us in life and to be a guide to lead us to His outstretched arms.

In return, all He asks is that once we know the truth we will choose to love Him, and then remain faithful to Him. Those two things we can easily accomplish by giving our lives to Him and following His commandments, which as we saw were all given for our ultimate good anyway.

With the knowledge you and I now possess we can easily see that everything God has ever done literally screams "I love you" into our ears.

But the courtship and wooing process obviously can't go on forever. There comes a time when any engaged person wants to actually live with his "other." That time is now here for us. It is time for God to go to the final phase, which will be the millennial kingdom, to bring in the last remnants of the bride.

God told us to watch for the signs that would bring the courtship to a conclusion. Thousands of end time prophecies were put in God's Word to make sure we would all be ready. We have seen scores of them, and most are already fulfilled. On top of the Biblical prophecies, God has also continued to give us clues of the timing through post Biblical prophets.

Many teachers in our modern church tell us that once the Bible was written God stopped giving prophecies to His loved one, His creation, but that is not the case. He told us very plainly,

"Your sons and daughters will prophesy, your old men will dream dreams, your young men will see visions." Joel 2:28.

Through these things God has continued to give us clues. We will say here and now, however, that the normal "thus saith the Lord" stuff that is almost an every Sunday morning occurrence in many Charismatic churches, that seem to happen right on cue, is not what we are talking about. Much of that is a nice ego boost for the speaker, and maybe the recipient, but that is about it. It is definitely not the kind of thing about which we are referring. We won't elaborate further on such "utterances."

What we are concerned with here are actual foretellings made by God to His true servants. They do exist, and many are quite detailed. I will tell you that although one of these prophecies came to mind several times in the past few days of writing this book, through several different avenues, I was extremely hesitant to share it because you and I had been looking at only Biblical prophecies up until now. Without going into scores of examples, though, I will say that God has been extremely faithful in guiding the writing of this book in supernatural ways, so, since the nudge to include the following was so strong, I naturally went to God in prayer about it last night. As I was praying a scripture popped into my head that I hadn't thought about in years.

After the prayer I thought that I would try to find the verse, but since my Bible was not in the room I was in at the time, I decided to look something else up in my library first. I picked a book from the shelf that looked like it might contain the unrelated topic, and opened the book to the middle to start browsing. I looked down at the first page I turned to and was astonished to see that the scripture that had come to mind while I was praying was right in front of me. I am relating this event solely to let you know that I feel God wanted me to share these prophecies, even though they are not in His Word. The scripture that jumped out at me from the very unlikely source is,

"Surely the Sovereign Lord does nothing without revealing His plan to His servants the prophets." Amos 3:7.

With that as a starting point let's examine a few very intriguing prophecies.

The first comes from a very Godly Irish priest who became the Archbishop of Armage in 1132 AD. Sainthood was conferred on him following his death and he is known today as Saint Malachy. Many miracles were attributed to him because of specific prayers he prayed, and he was known to have the gift of prophecy, even predicting the hour and date of his own death.

In 1139 Malachy had a vision in which he was given a long list of Popes that would head the Catholic Church until the end of time.

Malachy wrote down the list and in the following year personally gave it to Pope Innocent II. It remained in the Vatican until 1590 when it was printed by the church historian, Arnold Wion.

The 1913 edition of the Catholic Encyclopedia says of these prophecies, "These short prophetic announcements ... indicate some noticeable trait of all future popes from Celestine II, who was elected in the year 1130, until the end of the world. They are enunciated under mystical titles. Those who have undertaken to interpret and explain these symbolic prophecies have succeeded in discovering some trait, allusion, point or similitude in their application to the individual popes, either as to their country, their name, their coat of arms or insignia, their birthplace, talent or learning, the title of their cardinalate, or the dignities which they held. There is something more than coincidence in the designations given to ... popes so many hundreds of years before their time."

Malachy listed 112 popes in the list he said God gave him in his vision, and the list has proven to be extremely accurate. We won't take the time to go through all 112 of them here, but let's at least look at Malachy's designations and the actual popes of the past fifty years by Malachy's pope number:

105 - *"Pastor and Marine"* - Pope John XXII was from Venice, a marine city.

106 - *"Flower of Flowers"* - Pope Paul VI's coat of arms was three lilies.

108, plus 109, & 110 were then lumped together and designated - *"The year of three popes."* - In 1978 we saw three popes in the same year, Popes Paul VI, John Paul I and John Paul II.

109 -*"of the half of the moon"* - Pope John Paul I died a month after he was elected. He was elected during a half moon and died during a half moon.

110 - *"of the eclipse of the sun"* - Pope John Paul II was born may 18, 1920, during a solar eclipse, and was buried April 8, 2005, also during solar eclipse.

111 - *"the glory of the olive"* - Joseph Ratzinger, the current Pope Benedict XVI came from the order known as Olivetans.

112 - *"Peter the Roman"* - According to Malachy this would be the last pope in world history. Interesting is the fact that since the

apostle Peter was the first pope, no other pope has had the audacity to call himself Peter. This seems to lend credence to our previously mentioned thought that the False Prophet in Revelation might turn out to be an apostate pope who combines the apostate church and Islam into the prophesied one world religion. A point to consider also is that if the current Pope Benedict XVI were to be raptured, another pope would obviously be elected who would not "pistevo" Jesus.

Again we will make the point as clearly as we can that this is not a prophecy from God's Word that we know for a certainty will come true. However, when a Godly man like Saint Malachy has a vision that seems to never err in its accuracy through 111 predictions, over hundreds of years, it is worth considering as being a clue from God that the current pope could be the last one before the tribulation. It is just a point to ponder.

The next non Biblical prophecy is the one I had been thinking about that caused me to pray, asking God if it should indeed be included in this book. As I said, while praying, the following scripture popped into my mind, and then in less than a minute of the prayer, I opened a book at random and was uncannily looking down at the exact same scripture, *"Surely the Sovereign Lord does nothing without revealing His plan to his servants the prophets."* Amos 3:7

The prophecy itself was given to William Branham, an extremely controversial evangelist in the 40's, 50's and 60's. We do not for a moment question Branham's love for Jesus, although many do find his healing ministry questionable, and his latter doctrines stray pretty far afield from God's Word in some areas.

It may be, however, that those later areas of question should not cause us to totally discount the seven vision prophecy that was given to Branham on the morning in June, 1933, as he was preparing a Sunday School lesson that he was to teach. Branham maintained the visions came from God in rapid succession. Perry Stone describes the visions in the third volume of his book series entitled, <u>Unusual Prophecies Being Fulfilled</u>. Let's read Perry Stone's description of the 1933 seven visions,

"First, Branham saw, and publicly predicted, that Benito Mussolini, the Italian dictator, would establish a fascist state in Italy and invade Ethiopia. Thirty months later the vision came to pass. Branham said the dictator would die a horrible death and his people would spit upon his corpse. This was fulfilled on April 28,1945. ...

In the second vision he saw the Siegfried line two years before it was built. He saw an Australian named Hitler rising in Germany, and saw numerous lives lost with Germany. He predicted Roosevelt would declare war on Germany and would be elected for a fourth term. All of this happened.

The third vision revealed three major isms: fascism, Nazism and Communism. The first two would come to naught but the third, communism, would flourish. A voice told him to keep his eye on Russia, because fascism and Nazism would end up in Communism.

The fourth vision predicted advancement in technology right after the war. He saw automobiles shaped like eggs.

The fifth vision he saw involved women. He witnessed the moral decay of America entering into 'worldly affairs, bobbing (cutting) their hair and adapting the clothing of men.' He then saw women who were stripped nearly naked, covering themselves only with tiny aprons about the size of a fig leaf.

This was 1933, before bikinis. ...

Branham's sixth vision involved a woman rising to power in the United States. Branham was quoted as saying,

'... There will be a powerful woman raised up, either to be president or dictator or some great powerful woman in the United States, and America will sink under the influence of women.'

On July 26, 1964, many years later, Branham preached a sermon in which he remarked:

'... I saw a woman stand in the United states like a great queen or something. And she was beautiful to look at, but wicked in her heart. She made America's step go with her step." By Perry Stone.

Obviously such a prediction in 1933 would have sounded foolish. No woman had ever even been thought of to be a possible president. In fact, women had just recently been given the vote.

As I write these words, however, Nancy Pelosi is second only to the vice president in succession to the president, should anything happen to him. Additionally, Hillary Clinton is the first serious female contender for the office of US president. Neither one of those two women may become the first female US president, but this prophecy could soon be fulfilled as the others were.

The seventh and final vision that Branham had immediately followed his vision of a woman in power in the United States.

In that final vision Branham saw a gigantic explosion in the United States and the country was left in total ruins. His description seems to describe a nationwide nuclear holocaust.

As we noted, Branham did go off the deep end with some of his doctrines in his final years, but we have no reason to believe that he did not love and "pistevo" Jesus until his very last breath. Saint Malachy obviously did "pistevo" Jesus as well. And both men were definitely used by Christ during their lives. It is not beyond reason, then, that their visions were from the Master.

We obviously cannot give the same credence to their visions as we can to the direct prophecies given by God in His Word, but taken along with His fulfilled end time prophecies, as well as everything we see in current events and the changing nature, it does seem plausible that we may well be living in the days when those who "pistevo" our Lord Jesus could hear the trumpet sound that will bring about the rapture of His bride.

All others will face the tribulation, or worse.

As these words are being written, there is no way to predict who will read them. It is possible that someone may read this page who will breathe his or her last breath the very next day. Whether the rapture or our own personal death occurs tomorrow, the result will be the same. The Bible says of God's Word,

"For everything that was written in the past was written to teach us, so that through endurance and the encouragement of the scriptures we might have hope." Romans 15:4.

The twelve hundred and fifty or so scriptures we have looked at do give us hope, the hope of an eternity spent as the bride of the only living God. All anyone must do to have this hope realized is accept God's gift of salvation through Jesus Christ, repent of their sins, which means a turning away from them, obey His commands to the best of their ability, and begin the exciting love affair through communion in prayer with the most loving person there is, and remain committed to Jesus and faithful to the end.

It may not always be a bed of roses. You may actually encounter persecution along the way. If you live in America you will probably learn quickly that to be fully committed to Jesus is not politically correct. In many circles you may be tolerated as a follower of Christ, but only so long as you keep your beliefs to yourself. And even if tolerated you may be ridiculed by those who don't know the truths that you have learned. As darkness descends on America, as the Bible says it will throughout the entire world, you may find that following Jesus will result in actual hardships.

If you live in another nation you may be ostracized completely from your family and friends. You may forfeit you job. You may even have to flee the country or risk imprisonment or death, but it will be worth it. Jesus did not mince words when He told us.

"If anyone would come after me, he must deny himself and take up his cross and follow me. For whoever wants to save his life will lose it, but whoever loses his life for me and for the gospel will save it. What good is it for a man to gain the whole world, yet forfeit his soul? Or what can man give in exchange for his soul? If anyone is ashamed of me and my words in this adulterous and sinful generation, the Son of Man will be ashamed of him when he comes in His Father's glory with the holy angels." Mark 8:34-38.

No matter what, though, Jesus will be right by your side.

He doesn't promise untold wealth or a life without trouble or sickness. In fact, in John 16:33, He said very plainly, *"In this world you will have trouble. But take heart! I have overcome the world."* Don't listen to the prosperity teachings that would have you believe that if you have enough faith everything in this life will be fantastic. That isn't from God. But Jesus does promise, *"I will never leave you, never will I forsake you."* Hebrews 13:5. Knowing that the loving and powerful God of all creation will never leave you nor forsake you should be plenty for anyone.

It sure is for me.

On the other hand, there is only one other alternative, and that is eternal hell. We don't have the option to be neutral. Neutrality is rejection of Jesus just as much as outright Satan worship is. Quite plainly, we are either totally for Jesus, or we are against Him. There is no middle ground. We can't just decide to ignore Jesus and live a really good life and get into heaven. And we can't join any religion that can help us. In John 14:6, Jesus said, *"I am the way and the truth and the life. **No one** comes to the Father except through me."* And when Jesus said no one, He literally meant no one. There is <u>not</u> a heaven for Muslims, Hindus, Buddhists, or just good people.

"As surely as I live,' says the Lord, 'every knee will bow before me; every tongue will confess to God.'

So then, each of us will give an account of himself to God." Romans 14:11.

If you haven't already made the decision to make Jesus the Lord of your life, please do not put it off one more minute. It is critical. The very next moment may be too late. It isn't at all complicated. Just sincerely tell Jesus that you want to give your life to Him, that you repent of your sins. Tell Him that you accept His gift of eternal life, and that you want to trust Him for every aspect of your earthly and eternal life. <u>Any</u> words that are heartfelt will do, but time is of the essence.

CHAPTER FORTY-TWO

A humorous episode happened in my life recently that I pray, through you, will turn out to be meaningful to many souls. As I mentioned some time back, I type with my one right index finger. Old habits die hard.

Several weeks ago I had decided that since I had been working on this book for several months, and was getting eager to have it completed, I would not read a single book until the last word was typed, even though I am a truly avid reader. The next day after making that declaration to myself, I stupidly cut my finger with electric hedge trimmers. How I did such a dumb thing, to this day I cannot fathom. It seems to me now that it would almost take planning to somehow get my right finger from the normal position on the trigger to the blade, but inexplicably I managed to do it.

The cut wasn't very long but since I couldn't stop the bleeding I ended up at the emergency room having it sewn tightly shut. All I could think of while it was being sewn up was that I would not be able to type this book for several days. I was as useless for this book as a runner with blisters on his feet.

However, when I got back home from the hospital I had an incredible urge to pray and thank God for the injury. I suppose I need to tell you that, like Hannah Whitall Smith, I believe that God only allows trials to come for reasons to those who have surrendered to Him. Yes, God allowed Satan to mess with Job's life, but there were ulterior reasons. I also believe God when He says in His Word, *"In all things God works for good for those who love Him, ..."* Romans 8:28. The results for Job were great.

At any rate, as I prayed I did thank Him for the injury and told Him that I knew it was for a good reason and trusted that it would be used for His kingdom and His glory. Never, though, did I imagine that He would allow me to see the reason in just a few short hours, if ever at all.

Not being able to type, my declaration not to read until this book was completed went out the window. My wife had recently picked up two old books for me while rummaging through her favorite antique (junk) shops. By the time I was into the second chapter of the first book I knew that I knew that I knew that the message being presented in it absolutely needed to be shared with you. Had the finger not been cut, you would not have had the meaningful experience of reading what you are about to read. My declaration to not read would have injured a lot of people, for eternity. It had to be cancelled. God is an incredible God!

The first book I read that day was an eighty year old, well worn and discolored copy of a book of sermons by R.A. Torrey, an evangelist right out of the letter to the Church of Philadelphia in Revelation, the Age of Missions Church that Jesus had not a single unkind word for. Born in 1856, Torrey's work was primarily during the Age of Missions that ended about 1900. A point should be reiterated that we all would do well to read more of the wise teachings of the Godly saints of that era. The book I held was printed the year Torrey died, 1927, and was entitled <u>The Holy Spirit, Who He Is and What He Does.</u>

Knowing that trying to summarize the thoughts Torrey laid out could cause you and others to miss out on something extremely important, I will instead give you direct excerpts from his timeless book. The scriptures he quotes will, of course, be from the King James Version of God's Word. We will start with Torrey's quote from Jesus found in John 16:7-11,

*"Nevertheless I tell you the truth: It is expedient for you that I go away: for if I go not away, the Comforter will not come unto you; but if I go, I will send Him unto you. And **He, when He is come, will convict the world in respect of sin,** and **of righteousness,** and **of judgment:** of sin, **because they believe not on Me;** of righteousness, **because I go to the Father,** and ye behold me no more; of judgment, **because the prince of this world hath been judged.'**

In these verses we are told that, it is the work of the Holy spirit to **'Convict the world in respect of sin, and righteousness, and of judgment.'**

First of all, It is the work of the Holy Spirit to convict men of sin.

Now you will notice just what sin it is of which the Holy Spirit convicts men. Let me read it to you again. *'And He, when He is come, will convict the world in respect of sin ... of sin, **because they believe not on Me.'** * The sin of which the Holy Spirit convicts men and women is the sin of unbelief in Jesus Christ: not the sin of drunkenness, not the sin of stealing, not the sin of adultery, not the sin of murder, nor any other immorality or crime, but just the sin of not believing on the Son Of God, not believing on Jesus Christ.

To sum it all up then; it is the work of the Holy Spirit to convict men of sin, and of righteousness, and of judgment. It is not our work, but His. But please notice carefully that, WHILE IT IS THE HOLY SPIRIT WHO CONVICTS MEN OF SIN, AND OF RIGHTEOUSNESS, AND OF JUDGMENT, HE DOES IT THROUGH US, i.e, THROUGH THOSE WHO ALREADY BELIEVE ON JESUS CHRIST. This thought comes out in the seventh and eighth verses: *'Nevertheless I tell you the truth: It is expedient that I go away; for if I go not away, the Comforter will not come **unto you**; but if I go, I will send him **unto you*** (that is, to believers). *And He, when He is come* (that is, come unto you, come unto believers), *will **convict the world** in respect of sin, and of righteousness, and of judgment.'* That is to say, the Holy Spirit comes to the believer, and through the believer to whom He comes convinces the unsaved.

As far as we are told in the Bible, the Holy Spirit has no way of getting at the unsaved except through the channel of those who are already saved; He comes to the believer and through the believer convinces the unsaved of sin. What a solemn thought that is. If we realized that the Holy Spirit could only reach the unbeliever through us, us who are already saved, would we not be more careful to present the Holy Spirit an unchoked channel for the Holy Spirit to work through?

Every conversion recorded in the Acts of the Apostles was through human instrumentality, not one single conversion is recorded there that was not through human instrumentality. Take, for example, the conversion of Cornelius. If there was ever a miraculous conversion it was that! Why, we are told in the tenth chapter of the Acts of the Apostles that an angel appeared to Cor-

nelius and spoke to him, but the angel did not tell Cornelius what
to do to be saved. On the contrary, the angel said, 'Send men to
Joppa, and call for one Simon, whose surname is Peter; who shall
tell thee words whereby thou and all thy house shall be saved'
(Acts 11:13-14). In other words, not even an angel could show
him the way of life, it must be a saved fellow-man, and a Spirit-
filled fellow man, who did it.

Take the conversion of Saul of Tarsus. If ever there was a miraculous conversion it was certainly that, when the risen and ascended
Lord Jesus Himself appeared to him, he actually saw Jesus in the
glory, but the Lord Jesus did not tell him what to do to be saved.
Paul cried, ' What shall I do, Lord?' (Acts 22:10). And the Lord
said unto him, 'Arise and go unto Damascus, and *there it shall be
told thee* of all things which are appointed for thee to do.' The Lord
did not tell him what to do to be saved, 'a certain' man 'named
Ananias' had to be brought upon the scene, and Ananias told him
what to do, saying, 'Arise, and be baptized, and wash away thy
sins, calling on the name of the Lord.' (Acts 9:10; 22:16).

As far as God tells us in His Word, the HOLY GHOST HAS
NO WAY OF GETTING AT THE UNSAVED WORLD EXCEPT
THROUGH US WHO ARE ALREADY SAVED. This is exceed-
ingly solemn. ... Do take that in! Does it mean you? ...

But then again there are many of us who will not even offer
ourselves at all to the Holy Spirit as an instrument for Him to
work through. Oh, how many there are here in this audience today whose lips the Holy Spirit is trying to get to use, but you will
not give Him the use of your lips. He is trying to reach someone
through you, but you will not allow Him to.

I once read of a young lady who died in New York City. A Presbyterian minister was invited to conduct the funeral services; he
was not her own pastor; I do not know why her own pastor was
not invited. This minister who was to conduct the services went
first to her own pastor and asked him, 'Was Mary a Christian?'
Her pastor replied, 'I do not know. Three weeks ago I had a very
solemn impression that I ought to speak to Mary about Her soul,
but I put it off. I said, "Mary is in my congregation every Sunday
and I can speak to her when I will," and I put it off and now Mary

is dead and I do not know whether Mary was a Christian or not.' He next went to her Sunday School teacher, 'Was Mary a Christian?' The Sunday School teacher replied, 'I do not know. Two weeks ago I had a profound impression that I ought to speak to Mary about her soul, but I put it off. I said, "Mary is in my class every Sunday and I can speak to her when I will." and I put it off. And now Mary is dead and I don't know whether Mary was a Christian or not.' He next went to her own mother and said to her, 'Was Mary a Christian?' 'I do not know. A week ago I had a deep impression that I ought to speak to Mary about her soul, but I put it off. I said, "Here is Mary in the house with me all the time. I meet her three times a day at the table. I can speak to her when I will," and I put it off, and now Mary is dead and I do not know whether Mary was a Christian or not.' Three pair of lips that the Holy Spirit was trying to get the use of, the three pair of lips that one would naturally think would be most easily at His disposal, her minister's, her Sunday School teacher's and her mother's, and not one of the three would let the Holy Spirit have the use of their lips, and so Mary died unsaved. When I got back from going around the world and spent a month with my church in Chicago, I related this incident one Sunday morning. There was in my audience a young woman who had a class of girls from about fourteen years of age up. What I said made a deep impression upon her, and when she went to her class that Sunday afternoon she spoke to every member of her class about accepting Christ. Among those girls who did accept Christ was a girl fourteen years of age, if I remember correctly, apparently perfectly well and strong. Before the next Sunday came round that girl's body was lying out in a cemetery. Oh, how fortunate that young woman that morning gave her lips to Jesus Christ to use. Have you given yours?

Let me beseech you, every one of you that professes to be a Christian, to put your lips today at the Holy Spirit's disposal for Him through you to convict whomever He will of sin, and of righteousness, and of judgment.

When Mr. Alexander and I were holding meetings in Brighton, England, in the great Dome, one afternoon one of our workers went away from the afternoon meeting and went to a restaurant for tea before coming back to the night meeting. While he was sitting at the table he had a deep impression that he ought to speak to the waiter about his soul, but he put it off. It seemed to him as if it would be a strange thing to speak to a man who was waiting on him about accepting Christ. He finished his meal and went outside, but his impression that he should have spoken to that waiter was so deep that he waited outside for the waiter to come out, intending to talk to him then. When he had waited there for some time, the proprietor of the restaurant came out and began to put up the shutters, and asked him what he was waiting for. He replied. 'I am waiting to speak to that man that waited upon my table.' The proprietor said, 'You will never speak to that man again. Immediately after serving you he went up to his room and blew his brains out.' Oh, men and women, we live in a solemn world, and we need to be very careful how we walk. We need to be ready for God to use us any moment, and to respond to His call. THE HOLY SPIRIT ALONE CONVINCES MEN OF SIN, AND OF RIGHTEOUSNESS, AND OF JUDGMENT; BUT HE DOES IT THROUGH US - never forget that."

From Torrey's The Holy Spirit, Who He Is and What He Does.

There is something to deeply ponder in the idea that the all powerful Holy Spirit can't or won't draw souls to Christ without a believer's involvement. We can easily eliminate the word "can't' from the possibility because the Holy Spirit is the power of God, so he can do anything. He was the power Who raised Jesus from the dead, so His ability is not in question.

That leaves us with the word, "won't." But why won't He? The extremely interesting thinker and Bahamian minister, speaker and author, Dr. Myles Monroe, put forth an intriguing concept in his book, Prayer, which may be at the heart of not only a question posed by the evident necessity of prayer before God will involve Himself in man's affairs, but also this unexplained need for the Holy Spirit to rely on man in the salvation process as well.

Dr. Monroe examined the actions of God throughout the entire Bible and discovered that God never once acted without man being somehow involved in the beginning of the action. This led him back to the beginning, *"Then God said, 'Let us make man in our image, in our likeness, and let them rule ..."* Genesis 1:26. The king James Version uses the words *"have dominion over"* in the place of *"rule."* Dr. Monroe's contention was that since God gave man dominion over the earth, and since God is a God who abides by the rules He puts forth, God will not interfere with man's domain unless He is invited to. Therefore, we <u>must</u> pray before God will move in a situation. It may well be that Dr. Monroe's thoughts in this matter are totally correct. There may be more to the old saying that "prayer moves the hand of God" than we ever realized.

In the same manner, it could be reasonable that although the Holy Spirit is all powerful, He waits to use believers as His instrument for salvation for the very same reason, because of man's gift of dominion on the earth.

As an aside, however, we must understand that Satan and his host of demons do not play by the rules. They don't care if they have earthly license or not. They have no sense of guilt about anything, least of all their interference in man's domain.

At any rate, according to what we saw in the powerful R.A. Torrey pages, the Holy Spirit requires our availability to bring souls to Christ. Remember, though, that it is our availability, not our ability, that is the pivotal word. You and I can say things that will be a complete hodgepodge and mess, and the Holy Spirit can still bring the listener under conviction of the only true deadly sin, the sin of rejecting Jesus. We can say words that don't even make sense to us when we are talking, but the other person will hear exactly what the Holy Spirit wants him to hear. Our main part in the exercise is to be open to allow the precious Holy Spirit to use us.

Whether the dominion issue is in fact the underlying reason or not, we cannot be certain. What is undeniable is that each and every person who does "pistevo" Jesus Christ as their Lord has been given the awesome responsibility of telling others about the true way to eternal salvation. There are no exceptions. Every true Christian, including you and me, is commanded by Jesus Himself to speak out. The very last commandment of Jesus, known as the Great Commission, was given to you and to me just as surely as if we had been standing there with Him before He ascended to heaven, and He meant for us to obey it, *"Therefore go and make disciples of all nations, baptizing them in the name of the Father and of the Son and of the Holy Spirit, and teaching them to obey everything I have commanded you. And surely I am with you always, to the very end of the age."* Matthew 28:19-20. This was not a suggestion; this was a direct order from the King of kings, and it was to you and to me. We are to make disciples of all, which means we are to tell all people, then baptize or see that those new believers are baptized, and then you and I are <u>ordered</u> to teach them to obey all the other commandments Jesus gave us. Notice that He didn't tell us to tell them that once they believed and were baptized they didn't have to be concerned about any commandments anymore because "once saved always saved." No, we were ordered to teach them to obey His commands, every single one of them. But as we carry out that order Jesus promised that He would be right there with us.

We hear people say that they will let their lives be their testimony, but that is not good enough. There are wonderful people who truly believe in Islam, or Hinduism, or atheism, or whateverism who lead exemplary lives, but whose near perfect lives can in no way result in a person who is closely watching them receiving salvation. A totally righteous Christian life without words can be just as useless to an observer. In fact, the observer might come away with the strong belief that being a good person is the key to eternal life, and such a belief only leads to eternal death. We heard Jesus say in John 14:6, *"I am the way and the truth and the life. No one comes to the Father except through Me."* Showing people a good life does not give them understanding about Jesus and the spiritual truths we have looked at. That takes words, either spoken or written.

Even if it weren't a direct command from Jesus, however, the reasons to speak up are plentiful. Let's pretend that you got a call tomorrow from someone in the White House. The person told you that you had been selected at random to represent "everyday" people in the world at a gigantic banquet, which would include the top person in government from the forty most influential nations. Additionally, the caller then read down the list of others who were going to attend and each person was someone you would dearly love to meet, including movie and TV stars, sports heros, and world business billionaires. A private jet was going to be sent to pick you up and you could bring along up to fifty of your friends and relatives. The jet would even pick them up if they lived elsewhere. You were all going to be treated like royalty. An adventure of a lifetime.

Do you think you would be burning up the phone lines calling everybody you could think of to invite them to this once in a lifetime feast? You know you would. So would I. Now compare that one night earthly gathering to the heavenly wedding feast of the Lamb you are already invited to. There is no comparison, and it is an eternal invitation, not for just a one night dinner. To know that someone would be almost crazed with excitement and immediately tell everyone on their list about the White House dinner, but yet be reluctant to say anything to anyone about His wedding feast and the rest of the fabulous eternal life He has offered, must make Jesus totally embarrassed and completely disgusted. Wouldn't you be if you were Him? Would you feel like taking back the invitation? I sure would.

In fact, there is a part of a parable that Jesus taught that should be examined very closely. Unfortunately, it never is in our Church of Laodicia. In fact, the entire parable is normally taught to mean altogether something different from what Jesus was actually teaching us about, which was our responsibility to talk to others about the way to salvation. We are referring to His parable of the talents.

We all know the story Jesus taught in Matthew 25. In it a master left on a trip and entrusted three servants with different amounts of talents. To one he gave five, to another he gave two, and to the third he gave one talent. Since a talent was worth a little over a thousand dollars, many ministers today use this parable to try to persuade their congregations that they should be giving more money, "investing in the kingdom." It's an especially powerful parable to preach about when a building program is initiated and big dollars are needed.

The truth is that the parable had nothing whatsoever to do with money. Everyone realizes that the master in the parable represents God. Are we to think that money is an important commodity to God? Of course not. As we have seen, even in the command to tithe the important thing is the trust in Him that the tithe represents. Tithing is not about money to God.

In the final analysis, what is important to God is souls. The parable really teaches that the result the master expected from His three servants was souls brought into eternal life. Yes, they were each given different amounts of ability or forgiveness, or placed in different situations that should result in bringing more or less souls to God, but they were each expected to do their part.

In the story the ones who got five and two talents each, got results. They were responsible for lost souls being saved, and they were rewarded handsomely. To each of them the master said, *"Well done, good and faithful servant! You have been faithful with a few things; I will put you in charge of many things. Come and share your master's happiness."* Matt. 25:21.

The third servant, however, did nothing. His reply was, *"I was afraid and went out and hid your talent in the ground."* Matthew 25:25. Although he had been given a very valuable thing, salvation, he hid it. Does that sound like the average Christian of today to you? Next, let's pay extremely close attention to what the master says at the end of the parable in response to the slacker's admission.

"Take the talent from him ... And throw that worthless servant outside, into the darkness, where there will be weeping and gnashing of teeth." Matthew 25:28,30.

Did you catch the plain as day inference? Obviously our modern church doesn't, because that statement is never ever expounded on, if even read at all. Please remember a statement we quoted some chapters back from Saint Augustine, "If you believe what you like in the gospels, and reject what you don't like, it is not the gospel you believe, but yourself."

Am I stating that if you don't tell those who are lost what you now know, that you won't get into heaven? I'm not stating anything. I am just putting down in black and white the exact, verbatim words of Jesus Christ Himself, Lord of lords and King of kings. I am stating that Jesus did not have words recorded in God's Word unless He meant them. Of that, I am sure.

The other old book that my thoughtful wife, Barb, had "happened" to pick up for me in a dusty corner of one of her favorite junk stores was a long forgotten book by another minister of a past generation from Greenville, S.C, by the name of Oliver B. Greene. The book was <u>The Gospel Of Grace</u>. Was it "coincidence" that it, along with the R.A. Torrey book, hammered this same theme home to me while my typing finger was on the mend and I was forced to read and not write? I don't think so. A short excerpt from Oliver Greene's book will tell you what I am talking about,

"It is a grand and glorious privilege to be called a child of God and bear the name "Christian." But just so grand and glorious the privilege, so great and weighty the responsibility.

In the sense of evangelism, we are our brothers keeper. The tragedy of tragedies is for the believer to live and work beside unbelievers, rub shoulders with them, but never try to lead them to Christ. **This is the most cruel sin man can commit against his fellow man.**

It is our responsibility to tell others about the Savior who saved us. All unbelievers are blind, they are bound in the shackles of sin, they are led about by the devil; and we should attempt to rescue them through the message of salvation:

' ... *If our gospel be hid, it is hid to them that are lost: In whom the god of this world hath blinded the minds of them which believe not, lest the light of the glorious Gospel of Christ, who is the image of God, should shine unto them.'* II Cor. 4:3-4.

Paul declared, 'As much as in me is, I am ready to preach the Gospel. ... For I am not ashamed of the Gospel of Christ; for it is the power of God unto salvation to every one that believeth." Romans 1:15-16." (KJV) From Greene's, <u>The Gospel Of Grace</u>.

We put in bold Greene's words that should jump up and grab us, that not telling the unbelievers we are in contact with the truth "is the most cruel sin man can commit against his fellow man." That says it in a nutshell. And Greene is so right.

The idea of Near Death Experience (NDE) is a controversial one, primarily because there is no scientific way to know for a certainty if the person involved actually went to the spiritual realm. I, for one, though, have studied hundreds and hundreds of them and quite frankly am a believer that they are real, other realm experiences. One that stands out in my mind was of a man who saw things that happened here on earth that he could not possibly have seen while he was lying on his back clinically dead for many minutes. In relating his experience he told of these things which were later verified as true.

This man's experience was unlike most NDE's in what happened next. Normally the experience that people tell about NDE's is one that is so glorious that it makes them not want to return to earth. In this instance it was completely opposite. The man stood at the entrance to hell itself. What he saw was so indescribably horrible that he came back from the dead ready to completely "pistevo" Christ from then on. Interestingly, he had been a devout atheist prior to his death. The dramatic change occurred <u>during</u> the NDE.

What was really germane to this discussion, though, was the remarks he made about his Christian friends. Disappointment in them would not describe it. In fact, his exact words were, "They should have crawled over broken glass if necessary" to get him to see where he was going to spend eternity if he didn't turn from his ways and accept Jesus as his Lord and Savior. His rebuke of his friends is a haunting one. We should remember it always and let it guide us.

We learned that the meaning of life consists of three parts: the wooing of us by our two totally opposite suitors, our decision as to our choice, and the engagement period. If we choose Jesus, the engagement period is a time to "pistevo" Him, which means that we love Him with everything we are and have, we develop a deep relationship through time spent in His Word and in prayer, we repent of sin and surrender our lives fully to Him, we trust Him implicitly for our lives both here on earth and eternally, and we totally commit ourselves to obey His commands. Probably the most important of those commands by Jesus were the ones He gave to us in the Great Commission, because those were the commands He emphasized as he was ascending to the Father.

Even the thief on the cross who decided to "pistevo" Christ in his last hours, and is now in paradise with Him, took the time to rebuke the third thief and praise and lift up Jesus while he was dying in agony. Those words of that thief were put in God's Word for a reason. *"All scripture is God breathed and is useful for teaching, rebuking, correcting and training in righteousness, so that the man of God may be thoroughly equipped for every good work."* 2 Timothy 3:16.

Once we have made our decision for Jesus, we are not then to just go about our normal lives as we did in the past. The Christian life is not suppose to be lived one hour on Sunday morning for Christ, even if we do get emotional and cry a few tears for Him, and then live the other 167 hours of the week just like we did before we became engaged to Him. That seems to be acceptable with the average church leader of our day, but it isn't acceptable to Jesus.

If you think we are attacking our current Christian leaders, you are absolutely correct. They are the ones who brought Christian thinking and lifestyle from the Church of Philadelphia Age of Missions, which received nothing but praise from our Lord, into the modern Church of Laodicia, the church which Jesus said He was going to spit out of His mouth. They have been the ones who were called to shout against Satan's hoax of evolution that gave people a reason to deny God's existence, but for the most part, comfortable silence was all that was heard. They shrank from their duty to teach their flocks the true message of Jesus, that sin still is sin and that God still abhors it. Their refusal to teach their congregations the hard truths about sin, so that they could make people feel good about themselves and want to keep occupying the pews, resulted in a society that passively sat silent as the most horrendous of all human crimes ever perpetrated in the history of the world flourished right under their noses, the mass murder of over a billion babies worldwide, including well over fifty million innocent babies in America alone.

The baby killings are still going on every single day while ministers continue to just give the syrupy messages that "God loves you," and "nothing can keep you from heaven so long as you believe in Jesus," and "if you only believe, your life will be wonderful and full of peace unspeakable." They continue to teach a selfish religion that turns a blind eye to others, choosing instead to allow the bake sale and building drive to consume their energies and remain their priorities, instead of the gross daily unimaginable slaughter of unborn babies.

Many church leaders have even bought into the idea that babies in the womb are not really people, even though, as we saw in Genesis 25:23, Jacob and Esau were distinct individuals in Rebecca's womb. And when we *"search out the matter"* in Jeremiah 1:5 and Galatians 1:15, Jeremiah and Paul both acknowledged that God formed them in their mothers' wombs, and He even knew them by name. These are just a few of the proofs that the church leaders should still be screaming, but they are not. As a crowning point, when the pregnant Mary visited her cousin, Elizabeth, when Mary was still in her first trimester, Elizabeth said of her son, John the Baptist, *"the baby in my womb leaped for joy."* Luke 1:44. He recognized the Messiah.

But the modern Laodician church leaders continue to conveniently ignore the atrocity, and allow their followers to defile themselves in God's eyes. We can state that because God's always accurate Word says, *"They shed innocent blood, the blood of their sons and daughters ... and the land was desecrated by their blood. They defiled themselves by what they did."* Psalm 106:38-39.

Former Surgeon General, Dr. C. Everett Koop, says that the majority of abortions are solely for convenience. Only 4% are for reasons of rape, incest, the possibility of deformation, or any threat to the mother's life. You can know for a certainty that God is watching closely. I shudder to think of His coming response.

When we see that according to Newsweek about twenty per cent of those involved consider themselves to be evangelical Christians, it is obvious that the church leadership must be held accountable for lack of the honest teaching of God's Word. Of course, it is understandable when we study a recent poll taken by Christian pollster George Barna that found that less than half of America's Protestant pastors have a biblical worldview, which is defined as believing that absolute moral truth exists, and that it is based on the Bible. This same majority group of church leaders also did not affirm the accuracy of the Bible, the sinless nature of Jesus, the literal existence of Satan, salvation by grace alone, nor the personal responsibility to evangelize unbelievers. They would be well advised to read James 3:1, in which God says,

"Not many of you should presume to be teachers, because you know that we who teach will be judged more strictly."

(By writing this book I understand that I, too, have accepted that awesome responsibility, and stricter judgment, and I take it extremely seriously.)

The church leaders we have been referring to, by the way, also refuse to stand up against the political correctness of homosexuality that God calls "detestable." They as a group sit silently by as the family structure is torn so apart that the divorce rate within the church is now as high as it is in the secular world.

The list goes on and on. Yes, there are many, many who have fought the fight of Christ, but for the most part, current leaders condoned the concept of the "people friendly church" in order to not offend anyone, which keeps the coffers full. They preached a "cheap grace" and "once saved always saved" so that the converts wouldn't feel uneasy about anything and get scared away. They allowed the precious blood of Christ and the mention of the sins which God cannot abide, to be taken out of their vocabulary, and political correctness was then put in their place.

They replaced the true Gospel of Christ with a feel good "I'm Ok, you're OK" message, and labeled it Christianity.

Yes, we attack them, because without their leading, either by commission or worse, omission of leadership action, the average person today who innocently sits in a church on Sunday morning, thinking that he or she will spend eternity in heaven, will in fact be spit out of the mouth of Christ and unbelievably told by Jesus, *"I never knew you, away from me."* Matthew 7:23.

Since the majority of the ones who were suppose to fight the good fight have instead become what Jesus referred to in Matthew 23:24 as, *"blind guides,"* it falls to each one of us individually who do not want to be spit out of Christ's mouth to *"search out the matter"* for ourselves. The outcome is way too important to be left up to a fellow human for guidance, especially a fallible person who paints the Christian walk as one taken solely on a path of roses and daffodils.

So what does this tirade against the leadership of the Christian church as a whole have to do with the theme of this chapter, which is our responsibility to tell lost souls the way to eternal life? Obviously, the individual Christian is not being taught that he was <u>ordered</u> by Christ to personally evangelize. Many of the churches don't even do it, so naturally they don't feel it is important for their individual members to do it, and with this attitude they are leading their congregation astray. There are churches with million dollar budgets that don't save a soul all year. Jesus would be better served if they would close their doors and turn off their lights and send the money they collect to an organization that does still bear the responsibility for lost souls.

Let's read a little bit more of the thoughts of an honest leader from a past generation, Oliver B. Greene, "There are those who think the Christian life is one for little folk, sick folk, and old folk who are ready to depart this life - but nothing could be further from the truth. *Anyone* can yield to temptation, serve sin, be led about by the devil, and at the end of life's journey die and go to hell; but it takes a person of character, with determined will and 'strong backbone' to say 'no.' One needs no will power in order to yield to the world, the flesh, and the devil.

The Christian life is a battlefield - not a picnic. Christians are on a pilgrimage - not a vacation. We are commanded to 'fight the good fight of faith.' Hear what Paul has to say about it in I Corinthians 4:9-16:

'I think that God hath set forth us the apostles last, as it were appointed to death: for we are made a spectacle unto the world, and to angels, and to men. ... Even unto this present hour we both hunger, and thirst, and are naked, and are buffeted, and have no certain dwelling place; and labor, working with our own hands: being reviled, we bless; being persecuted, we suffer it; being defamed, we entreat: we are made as filth of the world, and are the offscouring of all things unto this day. I write not these things to shame you. But as my beloved sons I warn you. For though ye have ten thousand instructors in Christ, yet have ye not many fathers: for in Christ Jesus I have begotten you through the Gospel. Wherefore I beseech you, be ye followers of me." (KJV) from Oliver B. Greene's, <u>The Gospel Of Grace</u>.

Yes, this life with Christ may be filled with troubles and high expectations from the Master, but there is nothing else so wonderful in the world. We are not promised a garden of rest in this life, or even in the next chapter of our lives in the Millennial Kingdom. Granted, Satan will not be there to cause us grief, but we will still have jobs to do, and Christ will still have high expectations for us. After that, however, comes the true paradise.

Our other option, rejection of Christ, may appear easier in this life, but that option brings eternal death. And once we truly "pistevo" Jesus, life without Him is absolutely unthinkable. He is that wonderful.

When we solemnly repent of our sins, no matter what we have done in the past, they are forgiven. The slate is wiped totally clean and we are a new creation in Christ. When we lay our sins at the foot of the cross, there is not one sin that is not completely forgiven by our loving and merciful God.

If we have anything in our past that we know has displeased Jesus, He will not only forgive us, but He will also forget it and never bring it up to us again. It will be forgotten. And that includes <u>anything</u>. If we have been a parent of an aborted child, Jesus will forgive and make us new when we solemnly repent. And since Jesus forgives us, we then need to forgive ourselves.

If we have been on the other side as a medical professional, we, too, can receive the same mercy by turning away from any future involvement in it, repenting of our past, and asking forgiveness.

If you are one of the church leaders that we so harshly criticized in this chapter, and if you deep down truly agree that you may have been part of the problem and not the solution, all you need to do is get on your face and repent. This same Jesus will make you a brand new creation, again. Earnestly seek His guidance as to what needs to be done to correct the situation. You will probably find that He will lead you directly to His Word. Preach it as He wrote it and you will again bring a smile to His lips. You can then make a difference.

The wisest man who ever lived, Solomon, ended his writings in Ecclesiastes by saying, *"Now all has been heard; here is the conclusion of the matter: fear God and keep his commandments, for this is the whole duty of man. For God will bring every deed into judgment, including every hidden thing, whether it is good or evil."* Ecclesiastes 12:13-14.

That statement is still true today, the fortunate thing is that since those lines were written, Jesus came into the world and died on the cross, shedding His blood for us. Now our past deeds can be forgiven and forgotten if only we sincerely repent and ask his forgiveness, turning away from them in the future. If we do our best but in our humanity stumble and fall and sin again, Jesus is so merciful that he will forgive again. He is that wonderful.

"This is the message we have heard from Him and declare to you: God is light; in Him there is no darkness at all. If we claim we have fellowship with Him yet walk in darkness, we lie and do not live by the truth. But if we walk in the light, as He is in the light, we have fellowship with one another, and the blood of Jesus his Son, purifies us from all sin.

If we claim to be without sin, we deceive ourselves and the truth is not in us. If we confess our sins, He is faithful and just and will forgive us our sins and purify us from all unrighteousness. If we claim we have not sinned, we make Him out to be a liar and His word has no place in our lives.

My dear children, I write this to you so that you will not sin. But if anybody does sin, we have one who speaks to the Father in our defense - Jesus Christ, the Righteous One. He is the atoning sacrifice for our sins ...

We know that we have come to know Him if we obey His commands. The man who says, 'I know Him,' but does not do what He commands is a liar, and the truth is not in him. But if anyone obeys His word, God's love is truly made complete in him. This is how we know we are in Him: Whoever claims to live in Him must walk as Jesus did." 1John 1:5-2:6.

Chapter Forty-Three

We started this book talking about the debate we had watched in which the Christian debaters hung their hat on the idea that the existence of God must be taken on faith. As we now have seen, that is not the case at all. God proved conclusively that He exists through His fulfilled prophecies. Faith, however, is of gigantic importance in the Christian life.

The modern Christian church has taken quite a beating in this book, and partly because the leadership as a whole has so dramatically lost that necessary faith in such a short period of time. And with that loss, much of the excitement of the Christian walk is being missed. This generation's grandfathers had it, and every day was an adventure.

For example, shortly after the Dallas Seminary was founded in 1924, it almost folded. Bankruptcy was knocking at the door. In fact, the movie High Noon seemed the appropriate title for the situation it was in because a day arrived when all of the creditors were going to foreclose on the school at exactly high noon if the needed sum to pay them off could not be collected.

That morning the founders of the school met in the president's office to pray. Almost no money had been forthcoming, so, as Christian's often mistakenly do, they had decided to pray together as a last ditch hope. Henry Ironside, one of the founders, got up and prayed a simple prayer, "Lord, we know that the cattle on a thousand hills are Thine. Please sell some of them and send us the money."

A few minutes later, a tall Texan, as if scripted by a movie director, strolled into the business office with a great big "Howdy." He looked at the secretary and said, "I just sold two carloads of cattle over in Fort Worth. I've been trying to close another business deal but it just won't go through. I feel God wants me to give this money to the seminary. I don't know if you need it or not, but here's the check."

Thinking this might be important the secretary timidly tapped on the door to the president's office as someone else was about to pray. The president, Dr. Lewis Sperry Chafer, opened the door and was handed the check. It was for the exact amount the school needed to pay off its debts and remain in operation. Recognizing the name on the check as a cattleman, Dr. Chafer turned to Mr. Ironside and said, "Harry, God sold the cattle."

True stories like that abound. If you search for them you will find them by the thousands. The closer we get in our personal relationship to Jesus through prayer, the more we see such wonders in our own lives. Often they are even more dramatic than that.

God told us in James 5:16, " *The prayer of a righteous man is powerful and effective.*" Jesus also told us in Matthew 21:22, "*If you believe you will receive whatever you ask for in prayer.*" Faith obviously is the key. That is why God instituted the tithe, to teach us to have faith in Him. It works. The prayer of faith also tends to build our faith because it, too, brings results. And with each result our faith grows stronger. But like our muscles, faith must be exercised daily or it atrophies. Exercise it, though, and it grows and grows.

The one big stumbling block to faith is doubt. God tells us, "*If any one of you lacks wisdom, he should ask God, who gives generously to all without finding fault, and it will be given to him. But when he asks, he must believe and not doubt, because he who doubts is like a wave of the sea, blown and tossed by the wind. That man should not think he will receive anything from the Lord; he is a double-minded man, unstable in all he does.*" James 1:5-8.

Does that mean that anything we pray for will come to pass? Not hardly, although some churches grow in leaps and bounds by teaching such things. But we are admonished to learn from all of the scriptures, and we are also told, "*When you ask, you do not receive, because you ask with wrong motives, that you may spend what you get on your pleasures.*" James 4:3.

Interestingly, however, we do find in Psalm 37:4, "*Delight yourself in the Lord and He will give you the desires of your heart.*" What happens, though, is that the more we delight in the Lord, the more we find that the desires of our own hearts take on the form of His desires. Our longings for material things seem to disappear and become replaced by spiritual things, the same spiritual things that are attuned to God. When that occurs the following scripture comes alive for us,

"This is the confidence we have in approaching God: that if we ask anything according to His will, he hears us. And if we know that He hears us - whatever we ask - we know that we have what we have asked of Him." 1 john 5:14-15

We've seen that the Bible is utterly phenomenal. One of the things we learn the more time we spend in it is the heart of God. Study God's Word and know His will. Then He listens.

We learned that Jesus said of today's church in Revelation, *"Because you are lukewarm - neither hot nor cold - I am about to spit you out of my mouth."* And a visit to most churches can certainly give us that lukewarm feeling. They definitely are predictable: open with two songs, give some announcements, pray about giving and collect money while the choir or praise team sings their rehearsed number, the pastor says a prayer and reads a short scripture, both programmed to be lead ins to his talk, a sermon about what his agenda is for the week that ends in something warm and fuzzy, and then end with one or two more songs. The only difference between traditional and contemporary services is the age of the music. Some churches, though, do call down the Holy spirit during the second song. Find something different and you can write home to mother about it. Of course, non Protestant churches will be even more structured with prayers right out of a book. In either case, the congregational member's Christian duties are fulfilled for the week in that hour or so. They can now resume there normal "non spiritual" life.

There are, however, many, many wonderful churches that don't fit that lukewarm mold. They teach that Christianity is a full time life. They believe in a very active, living God, and they aren't disappointed. They also stress to their members all that is required to fully "pistevo" Christ, including telling others the good news of Jesus whenever they can throughout the week. Their "normal" lives are surrendered to their Lord and each day brings exciting opportunities to serve Him, and miracles happen because of it.

Such a body of believers can be found in Redding, California, at Bethel Church, pastored by Bill Johnson. The members look at church service as a refreshing time to bring back the fascinating stories of how God is working through them throughout the week. Several of those stories were reported by Paul Strand of CBN News. Let's read just one of them,

"Chad Dedmon was going to a Redding grocery store to buy donuts, and decided to pray for a lady with hearing aids at a checkout stand. She was instantly healed.

'She was 90 percent deaf in one ear and about 85 percent in the other,' Dedmon said. 'So she had her hearing totally restored. She started crying ... the checkout girl started crying.'

Then Chad announced on the checkout girl's intercom, 'Attention, all shoppers, God is here and He wants to release his presence and His healing.'

A crippled lady rolled up to Chad for prayer and was healed right away.

'She stands up,' Dedmon recalled. 'She begins to run around the checkout aisles, screaming, "Jesus has just healed me. Jesus has just healed me."

Still there in the store, Chad then prayed for a man with a horrible pain in his wrists.

Dedmon said, 'And he starts screaming, "They're on fire, they're on fire." I'm saying, "this is good heat ... this is good." And he's like, "Oh, my gosh," and he starts crying and says, "the pain is all gone."

'He gave his heart to the Lord,' Dedmon said, 'and that's when I realized the Kingdom just showed up and it would probably be a good idea to introduce the King.'

Chad led seven people to the Lord.

He said, 'I was so excited that when I got home, I realized that I had left my donuts at the grocery store!'

'This is really what God wants to do,' Dedmon said, ' and this is what's available for every Christian.'

Bethel people are always looking for crutches, wheelchairs, hearing aids - any sign that God's moved them next to a person they can pray for.

If the Kingdom of God is going to invade the streets, the businesses, the homes of the world, it's going to take the body of Christ waking up to the fact that God means for them to be His ministers, His witnesses, His hands extended." P. Strand, CBN.

What a fantastic true story. Bethel Church members see miracles every week. Should you expect to see something like that happen if you pray for someone? Why not? It may not happen, but it won't happen if you don't expect it. But what if you never have an exciting day of seeing healings like Chad did? It doesn't matter. Healings are only temporary. The people eventually always die someday anyway. What is important is the greatest miracle of all, the eternal miracle, salvation. If you obey God and tell others about Him, things will happen. The Holy Spirit will do his part. Maybe not every person will be saved for the Lord, but if only one is, you will have done more in your life than any earthly thing you could ever imagine doing.

Additionally, God gave all of us this awesome responsibility when He said, *"When I say to a wicked man, 'You will surely die,' and you do not warn him or speak out to dissuade him from his evil ways in order to save his life, that wicked man will die for his sin, and I will hold you accountable for his blood. But if you do warn the wicked man and he does not turn from his wickedness or from his evil ways, he will die for his sin; but you will have saved yourself."* Ezekiel 3:18-19.

We repeat, God does not say things in His Word just to hear himself speak. He means what He says. And He said very plainly that if a wicked man, defined as any non believer, is not warned by us, God will hold us accountable. That is a sobering thought. How many people in your family, work place, school, or social life, who do not know the truth, will you be accountable to God for if they die without your telling them? You and I definitely have heavy responsibilities both in this life and the Millennial Kingdom to come. But the precious and powerful Holy Spirit will be right beside us, helping us each step of the way.

The challenge facing you and me that past believers did not have is the fact that so many people, because of Satan's theory of evolution, do not even believe in God to begin with. In the past, that part was a given. But that is why we wrote this book in the manner we did. We started with the irrefutable facts of God's fulfilled prophecies in order to drive home His undeniable existence first, and we suggest you reread the first part of this book and make some notes about your favorite ones. They do make an impression. They will open any skeptic's eyes.

God instructed us, *"In your hearts set apart Christ as Lord. Always be prepared to give an answer to everyone who asks you to give the reason for the hope that you have. But do this with gentleness and respect."* 1 Peter 3:15.

Let's break this important instruction down into some very simple and easy and practical things we can do in real life. First, of course, we must make Jesus the Lord of our lives. Until He is, nothing we can say or do means anything. In fact, until He is our Lord, the Holy Spirit will not even be in us to take charge of the situation. We need to believe Jesus when he said, *"Apart from me you can do nothing."* John 15:5. We make Christ the Lord of our lives by surrendering our entire being to Him, trusting him in prayer with every aspect of our lives. And the more time we spend in prayer, the more we grow to love and adore Him. In this manner we *"in our hearts set apart Christ as Lord."*

Once that is done, we are to *"be prepared to give an answer."* This requires actual preparation. It will take some time on your part, but it is now the most important part of your life. And think about it, McDonald's even has its Hamburger University, so doesn't this deserve at least that much effort in preparation. A person's eternal soul is at stake. Take it to heart.

As we will momentarily discuss, my personal experience is that in today's society most people don't really believe there is a God, or obviously that He wrote the Bible; so it is smart to learn things that unquestionably prove those two facts. Once again, we suggest strongly that you reread the first parts of this book and make some notes about fulfilled prophecies. It will astonish you at the results you will see by telling them to people.

The last part says that we are to present the reasons for our hope with *"gentleness and respect."* When we go over some suggestions in a moment you will see that nothing is ever done in an argumentative or heated fashion. Our job is to *"warn"* the person.

It is the Holy Spirit who will convict. Although the other person may be someone we love dearly, they do have free will. We can't force them to make a choice. We can only present the truth and pray that the Holy Spirit will be successful in convincing them of that truth.

My own personal situation for the past eleven years has been in the business world of insurance. I talked to brand new people daily, all over the United States, who primarily were insurance agents. Almost all of it was done by phone. Much of it was in a recruiting position and as such I was able to work with many of them for years after our initial conversation, and many eventually became very good friends and family members in Christ. Obviously I am not a great evangelist like Billy Graham or you would have heard of me, but I have been amazed at the results God has allowed me to witness first hand, so I will tell you what types of things I said that the Holy Spirit used.

The first important thing, I think, has been my attitude. Jesus is the most wonderful person in my life and I love him passionately. I also have a heartfelt desire for everyone to know and love Him, too. Additionally, I cringe at the thought of anyone not going to heaven. We all should. With those two things on my mind, my very first thought in talking to anyone is to eventually and gently steer the conversation in that direction.

Secondly, since my experience is that very few people I meet in the business world even believe in God, much less that the Bible came from him, that subject needs to be gently broached first. I normally bring up something to get the conversation on that track. A suggestion for easily opening the conversation might be to say something like,

"By the way, I read something very interesting the other day that has really started me thinking about things. It seems that there are over eight thousand prophecies in the Bible and most of them have already been fulfilled. But there's not a single other holy book from any other religion that has a single fulfilled prophecy. And some of those Bible prophecies are really dramatic. For instance, the Bible predicted the exact day Israel would become a nation in 1948, over twenty five hundred years in advance."

That is an easy, simple and practical opening that I guarantee will get a response. The worst that can happen is that the person will say, "I don't believe in any of that stuff." My response would be a very gentle and respectful,

"I understand. I didn't use to either, but some of it is really phenomenal. For instance, there was one prophecy that not only told all about the life of Alexander the Great long before there was even a nation of Greece, but it even told step by step what would happen to his empire after he died. The prophecy was written like a history book, but hundreds of years in advance. You should see it. It is mind boggling."

I won't go on and on, but you can see what I am doing. Sometimes it takes more conversations than one, and I might need to send him or her a copy of something, but in most cases, by not pushing hard but just trying to make it interesting, the person comes around. Once the person really believes there is a God, and that He communicated with man through the Bible, the rest seems to be a cake walk. Once they believe that God is real and that He created everything, the meaning of life we have discussed makes sense. He or she then wants to "pistevo" Jesus.

Normally I hear things like "really" and "wow" throughout the conversations. That is understandable when we realize that so very few people have ever heard about the things you and I have examined in this book. Even people who have gone to church for years have seldom been taught these things. It is sad but true. Unfortunately, that even can be said about many ministers.

Occasionally, but I will say rarely, the person will totally shut me out. I hate it when that happens, for his sake, but I know that my responsibility has been handled in the eyes of God; and remember that God said, *"He will die for his sins, but you will have saved yourself."* Ezekiel 3:19. More importantly, my prayer then becomes a request that the seeds I planted will be watered by someone else, or maybe his or her own conscience, and it will eventually sprout into full salvation.

Another thing that I have found useful is a little personal testimony that I wrote out. You can do the same if you want. If you have been a believer for any length of time you should be able to write some things Christ has done for you or meant to you. If you are brand new, you might want to invest in a book of someone else's testimony to give to your friend or loved one. There are hundreds of them. On the last page of this book we will list some books for recommended reading, and some of those will be listed there. Of course, we also see nothing wrong with buying the person a copy of this book. You could do worse.

At any rate, I do like to give follow up material for the new person to go over. The main thing, of course, is a Bible. If they don't have one, or if you don't, we recommend getting a large print, red letter (of words of Jesus), New International Version, known as the NIV. Purists believe the old King James Version, written in 1610, is the only version, but quite frankly I find that new believers have trouble understanding it, and the NIV seems the closest to the KJV, except it is in normal every day language. And every believer, brand new or old, must talk to God constantly. Remember, Brother Lawrence taught us that "the practice of the presence of God" should be our profession.

What about church attendance. If there is still a minister reading this book who I have not thoroughly offended by now, I am sure he will be ready to string me up for the next statement. A person can truly "pistevo" Jesus and not have a denominational church that he attends. Please hear me out. Yes, we are instructed to meet together with other brothers and sisters in Christ, for God's Word says,

"Let us not give up meeting together, as some are in the habit of doing, but let us encourage one another - and all the more as you see the Day approaching." Hebrews 10:25.

A church can be a fantastic part of your Christian life, and we do encourage you to look for one to attend regularly. Don't be concerned about the denomination. There are excellent ones in every denomination, including non denominational. The key is the leadership. If there are several churches near you, visit them all. Do not, however, get stuck in a lukewarm, church of Laodicia. That could actually be more harmful than beneficial.

You don't want to form the habits of those people who Jesus will spit out of His mouth. Make sure any church you choose to attend believes that every word in the Bible came directly from God, because it did, and that the church teaches that. Also, be sure they love Jesus with their entire lives, not just their words. And make sure they understand and teach that to "pistevo" Jesus is a full time occupation, not just a Sunday morning one, and that it includes the responsibility of each believer to tell others the good news, which is a direct command from Christ.

If you are reading this in a country in which a church is not available, or you can find only lukewarm or cold churches where you live, you can start your own group. Even if you are brand new yourself, there are organizations such as Chuck Missler's Koinonia House that will supply you with information as to how to get started and study materials to guide you. They can be contacted at www.khouse.org or phone 800 KHOUSE1.

Remember, Jesus told us, *"For where two or three come together in my name, there am I with them."* Matthew 18:20. Some of the most phenomenal Christian assemblies are house churches in China and other areas of Christian persecution.

The main thing to believe with all your heart is that if you earnestly pray for God's guidance in the matter, the precious Holy Spirit will lead you, either to a local church, or to a Bible study group, or to a mentor, or to actually start your own group, with as few as one other believer if necessary. The Holy Spirit is as real as your best friend, and as close as the tears on your pillow. He will lead you. Depend on Him and trust him implicitly. He may work quickly or slowly, but He <u>will</u> work on your behalf. He will lead you if you trust Him. And he won't lead you by way of emotionalism or weird stuff. He won't have you handling snakes. The Holy Spirit does not panic; He may surprise you, and often will, but His leading is normally orderly and deliberate. If you think He has led you but are not totally sure, ask for confirmation. If it is from Him, He will give it. He is on your side. He is unbelievably wonderful.

Hopefully this book, if nothing else, has sparked an intense hunger in you to learn more about God. I can remember when I was a baby in Christ and was sitting in my living room thinking about what God must be like, I had a strange thought. I imagined myself in a one room, box like structure. I imagined that I knew that God, the Creator of everything, with intelligence beyond comprehension and more power than could be fathomed, was outside my box, and there were peep holes for me to look out.

I knew that I would strain with everything I had to get a glimpse of Him. It was then I realized that the Bible was that peep hole. In fact, it was an entire picture window. And I could spend as much time as I wanted to learn about this God of all majesty.

The Bible is the most phenomenal communication the world has ever seen because the author is the most phenomenal being in the world. The more you delve into His Word, the more amazed you will be. The smallest details defy anything any human has ever conceived of. Take the very central verse of the Bible for example. It is Psalm 118:8. Everything about that verse is incredible. In the first place, when a number is used twice, it is like Jesus saying "verily, verily," in that it gives that number added emphasis. In Psalm 118:8 we have the number one emphasized, the number for God or creation, along with the number eight given twice as well, the number for Jesus.

Next, when we count the chapters before and after this chapter, we find there are 594 before and 594 after, which again adds up to 1188. Don't just skim over that thought. It is totally awesome. Only God could do that. Speaking of chapters, the one directly before Psalm 118 is the very shortest in the Bible, whereas number 119, the one immediately following it, is the very longest. Could that give reference to the length of our lives before we "pistevo" Jesus versus the eternal life after that moment? So, what does the very central verse of the Bible tell us? *"It is better to take refuge in the Lord than to trust in man."* Psalm 118:8. That, of course, is the central message of God's Word. Give those facts to anyone with the sense of awe that they deserve and spiritual eyes will open.

In this book you have *"searched out the matter"* in about thirteen hundred verses of God's Word, but since there are 31,174, there are still so many exciting verses for you to dig into.

The more time you spend in it, the more you will find that not only will you be blessed, but others you talk to about your discoveries will be blessed as well. By sharing what you learn with others, souls will have eternal life that otherwise would not. This will bring a smile to the lips of our Lord. He will not ever forget it, for His Word teaches us,

"Those who are wise will shine like the brightness of the heavens, and those who lead many to righteousness, like the stars for ever and ever." Daniel 12:3

That verse begins by mentioning those who are wise and continues with those who help lead those to the righteousness which comes from Jesus. To become wise we learn,

"The fear of the Lord is the beginning of wisdom, and knowledge of the Holy One is understanding." Proverbs 9:10.

To get knowledge of the Holy One, Jesus, what better place to start than by *"searching out the matter"* in the 332 fulfilled prophecies that manifested in His life? With that in mind, we will include after this chapter the listing of all 332 of them for you to use as a guide. We have listed them for you in chronological order to make it easy for you to read them for yourself, or in a small Bible study group, and we strongly encourage you to do it. Even though it will only take a few minutes to look up each one, you may only want to read one or two or five a day.

As you do, please remember the astronomical odds we looked at of any one person fulfilling just eight of them in a lifetime. In fact, to put it in perspective, we are told that the odds of fulfilling just ten of them would be like covering all of North America with silver dollars and randomly picking up a particular one that had a small red dot painted on it.

The listing we are providing does not even include my personal favorite, the foretelling of the exact day the Messiah would ride into Jerusalem on a donkey and present Himself as the King of kings and Lord or lords. By gaining a working knowledge of these fulfilled prophecies you will be increasing your knowledge and wisdom, which is needed, for Jesus said,

"Behold, I send you forth as sheep in the midst of wolves: be ye therefore wise as serpents, and harmless as doves." Matthew 10:16.

Continue to *"search out a matter"* every day for the rest of your life, and diligently search out even the smallest details. The results will bless you, and others. For example, John 20 tells the story of the day it was discovered that Jesus had arisen from the grave. Mary Magdalene found out about it first and hurried to tell the disciples. Peter and John then ran to the tomb. John got there first, but did not go in. We then read,

"Then cometh Simon Peter following him, and went into the sepulchre, and seeth the linen clothes lie, and the napkin, that was about His head, not lying with the linen clothes, but wrapped together in a place by itself." John 20:6-7.

Two thousand years ago a wadded up napkin tossed on a table after a meal meant, "I'm done," but a folded up napkin told anyone paying attention, "I am coming back."

THREE HUNDRED
THIRTY-TWO PROPHECIES
"The testimony of Jesus is the spirit of prophecy" Revelation 19:10

Prophecy	Foretold	Fulfilled
1. Woman's (virgin birth)	Gen. 3:15	Luke 1:35
		Matt. 1:18-20
2. He will bruise Satan's head	Gen. 3:15	Heb. 2:14
		1 John 3:18
3. Bodily ascension to heaven	Gen. 5:24	Mark 6:19
4. Son of Shem	Gen. 9:26-27	Luke 3:36
5. From Adam's seed	Gen. 12:3	Acts 3:25-26
6. Promised to Abraham's seed	Gen. 12:7	Gal. 3:16
7. A priest after Melchizedek	Gen. 14:18	Heb. 6:20
8. A King also	Gen. 14:18	Heb. 7:2
9. Last Supper foreshadowed	Gen. 14:18	Matt. 26:26-29
10. Seed of Isaac	Gen. 17:19	Rom. 9:7
11. Lamb of god promised	Gen. 22:8	John 1:29
12. Isaac's seed to bless nations	Gen. 22:18	Gal. 3:16
13. Redeemer from Isaac's seed	Gen. 26:2-5	Heb. 11:18
14. Time of His appearing	Gen. 49:10	Luke 2:1-7
		Gal. 4:4
15. Seed of Judah	Gen. 49:10	Luke 3:33
16. Called Shiloh or "One Sent"	Gen. 49:10	John 17:3
17. Before Judah loses identity	Gen. 49:10	John 11:47-52
18. Obedience to Him	Gen. 49:10	John 10:16
19. The Great I AM	Exod. 3:13-14	John 4:26
20. Lamb without blemish	Exod. 12:5	1 Pet. 1:19
21. Lamb's blood- no wrath	Exod. 12:13	Rom. 5:8
22. Christ our Passover	Exod. 12:21-27	1 Cor. 5:7
23. No bone of Lamb broken	Exod. 12:46	John 19:31-36
24. Exaltation as Yeshua	Exod. 15:2	Acts 7:55-56
25. Holiness His character	Exod. 15:11	Luke 1:35
		Acts 4:27
26. Spiritual Rock of Israel	Exod. 17:6	1 Cor. 10:4
27. Merciful	Exod. 33:19	Luke 1:72
28. Leper clean; priesthood sign	Lev. 14:11	Luke 5:12-14
		Matt. 8:2
29. Christ's death once for all	Lev. 16:15-17	Heb. 9:7-14
30. Suffering outside the camp	Lev. 16:27	Matt. 27:33
		Heb. 13:11-12
31. Blood-life of the flesh	Lev. 17:11	Matt. 26:28
		Mark 10:45

32. Blood makes atonement	Lev. 17:11	John 3:14-18
33. "If any man thirst" offering	Lev. 23:36-37	John 19:31-36
34. Not a bone broken	Num. 9:12	John 19:31-36
35. Christ lifted up on cross	Num. 21:9	John 3:14-18
36. Time:"see him but not now"	Num. 24:17	Gal. 4:4
37. A prophet would come	Deut. 18:15	John 6:14
38. Believed Moses, believe me	Deut. 18:15-16	John 5:45-47
39. Sent to speak Father's word	Deut. 18:18	John 8:28-29
40. Bear sin if you will not hear	Deut. 18:19	John 12:15
41. Cursed, hangs on tree	Deut. 21:23	Gal. 3:10-13
42. Christ redeemed us	Ruth 4:4-9	Ep. 1:3-7
43. Anointed King to the Lord	1 Sam. 2:10	Matt. 28:18
		John 12:15
44. David's seed	2 Sam. 7:12	Matt. 1:1
45. Son of God	2 Sam. 7:14	Luke 1:32
46. Establish David's house forever	2 Sam. 7:16	Luke 3:31
		Rev. 22:16
47. Bodily ascension to heaven	2 Kings 2:11	Luke 24:51
48. David's seed	1 Chr. 17:11	Matt. 1:1;9:27
49. Reign on David's throne forever	1 Chr. 17:12-13	Luke 1:32-33
50. I will be his Father, and he...my Son	1 Chr. 17:13	Heb. 1:5
51. Resurrection predicted	Job 19:23-27	John 5:24-29
52. Became lowly among men	Job 25:6	Matt. 27:30-31
53. Enmity of kings foreordained	Ps. 2:1-3	Acts 4:25-28
54. To own the title "Anointed"	Ps. 2:2	Acts 2:36
55. His character: holiness	Ps. 2:6	Rev. 3:7
56. To own the title "King"	Ps. 2:6	Matt. 2:2
57. Declared the Beloved Son	Ps. 2:7	Matt. 3:17
58. Crucifixion & Resurrection	Ps. 2:7-8	Acts 13:29-33
59. Life through faith in Him	Ps. 2:12	John 20:31
60. Babes perfect His praise	Ps. 8:2	Matt. 21:16
61. His humiliation/exaltation	Ps. 8:5-6	Luke 24:50-53
		1 Cor. 15:27
62. Was not to see corruption	Ps. 16:10	Acts 2:31
63. Was to arise from the dead	Ps 16:9-11	John 20:9
64. Resurrection predicted	Ps. 17:15	Luke 24:6
65. Forsaken for sins of others	Ps. 22:1	2 Cor. 5:21
66. Calvary words, "My God..."	Ps. 22:1	Mark 15:34
67. Darkness upon Calvary	Ps. 22:2	Matt. 27:45
68. They shake the head	Ps. 22:7	Matt. 27:39
69. Trusted God, let God help	Ps. 22:;8	Matt. 27:43
70. Born the Savior	Ps. 22:9	Luke 2:7
71. Died of a broken heart	Ps. 22:14	John 19:34
72. Suffered agony on Calvary	Ps. 22:14-15	Mark 15:34-47
73. He thirsted	Ps. 22:15	John 19:28
74. Pierced His hands and feet	Ps. 22:16	John 19:34-37, 20:27
75. Stripped Him before men	Ps. 22:17-18	Luke 23:34-35

76. They parted His garments	Ps. 22:18	John 19:23-24
77. Committed Himself to God	Ps. 22:20-21	Luke 23:46
78. Satan bruised His heel	Ps. 22:20-21	Heb. 2:14
79. His resurrection declared	Ps. 22:22	John 20:17
80. Governor of the nations	Ps. 22:27-28	Col. 1:16
81. "It is finished"	Ps. 22:31	John 19:30
82. "I am the Good Shepherd"	Ps. 23:1	John 10:11
83. His exaltation predicted	Ps. 24:3	Acts 1:11 Phil. 2:9
84. His ascension	Ps. 24-7-10	John 7:33
85. His resurrection predicted	Ps. 30:3	Acts 2:32
86. "Into they hands I commend my spirit"	Ps. 31:5	Luke 23:46
87. His friends fled from Him	Ps. 31:11	Mark 14:50
88. Counsel put Him to death	Ps. 31:13	John 11:53
89. Trusted God- let Him deliver	Ps. 31:14-15	Matt. 27:43
90. Not a bone of Him broken	Ps. 34:20	John 19:31-36
91. False witnesses against Him	Ps. 35:11	Matt. 26:59
92. He was hated without cause	Ps. 35:19	John 15:25
93. His friends stood afar off	Ps. 38:11	Luke 23:49
94. Predicted joy of resurrection	Ps. 40:2-5	John 20:20
95. His delight, will of Father	Ps. 40:6-8	John 4:34
96. Righteousness told in Israel	Ps. 40:9	Matt. 4:17
97. Confronted in the garden	Ps. 40:14	John 18:1
98. Betrayed by familiar friend	Ps. 41:9	John 13:18
99. Grace came from His lips	Ps. 45:2	Luke 4:22
100. To own title God or Elohim	Ps. 45:6	Heb. 1:8
101. Anointed by Holy Spirit	Ps. 45:7	Matt. 3:16 Heb. 1:9
102. Christ (Messiah, Anointed)	Ps. 45:7-8	Luke 2:11
103. Worthy of our worship	Ps. 45:11	Matt. 2:2
104. Friend betrayed, not enemy	Ps. 55:12-14	John 13:18
105. Betrayer's unrepented death	Ps. 55:15	Matt. 27:3-5 Acts 1:16-19
106. To give gifts to men	Ps. 68:18	Eph. 4:7-16
107. Ascended into heaven	Ps. 68:18	Luke 24:51
108. Hated without cause	Ps. 69:4	John 15:25
109. Stranger to own brethren	Ps. 69:8	Luke 8:20-21
110. Zealous for Lord's house	Ps. 69:9	John 2:17
111. Messiah's anguish on cross	Ps. 69:14-20	Matt. 26:36-45
112. My soul is exceeding sorrowful	Ps. 69:20	Matt. 26:38
113. Given vinegar in thirst	Ps. 69:21	Matt. 27:34
114. Savior given and smitten	Ps. 69:26	John 17:4, 18:11
115. Great persons visit Him	Ps. 72:10-11	Matt. 2:1-11
116. Corn of wheat fall to ground	Ps. 72:16	John 12:24
117. Name, Yinon, produce offspring	Ps. 72:17	John 1:12-13
118. All nations blessed by Him	Ps. 72:17	Act 2:11-12,41
119. He would teach in parables	Ps. 78:1-2	Matt. 13:34-35

120. Spoke wisdom w/authority	Ps. 78:2	Matt. 7:29
121. From tribe of Judah	Ps. 78:67-68	Luke 3:33
122. He would have compassion	Ps. 86:15	Matt. 9:36
123. They stood afar and watched	Ps. 88:8	Luke 23:49
124. Higher than earthly kings	Ps. 89:27	Luke 1:32-33
125. David's seed endures forever	Ps. 89:35-37	Luke 1:32-33
126. His character: faithfulness	Ps. 89:36-37	Rev. 1:5
127. He is from everlasting	Ps. 90:2	Mic. 5:2
		John 1:1
128. Identified as messianic	Ps. 91:11-12	Luke 4:10-11
129. His exaltation predicted	Ps. 97:9	Acts 1:11
		Eph. 1:20
130. His character goodness	Ps. 100:5	Matt. 19:16-17
131. Suffer, reproach of Calvary	Ps. 102:1-11	John 19:16-18
132. Messiah is preexistent Son	Ps. 102:25-27	Heb. 1:10-12
133. Ridiculed	Ps. 109:25	Matt. 27:39
134. Son of David	Ps. 110:1	Matt. 22:43
135. Ascend to right hand of Father	Ps. 110:1	Mark 16:19
136. David's son called Lord	Ps. 110:1	Matt. 22:44-45
137. Priest- Melchizedek's order	Ps. 110:4	Heb. 6:20
138. His character: compassionate	Ps. 112:4	Matt. 9:36
139. Resurrection assured	Ps. 118:17-18	Luke 24:5-7
		1 Cor. 15:20
140. Rejected stone: corner head	Ps. 118:22-23	Matt. 21:42
141. Blessed One given to Israel	Ps. 118:26	Matt. 21:9
142. To come while temple stands	Ps. 118:26	Matt. 21:12-15
143. Seed of David (fruit of His body)	Ps. 132:11	Luke 1:32
144. David's seed amazes kings	Ps. 138:1-6	Matt. 2:2-6
145. Christ's earthly ministry	Ps. 147:3, 6	Luke 4:18
146. He will send Spirit of God	Ps. 147:18	John 16:7
147. A friend of sinners	Prov. 18:24	Matt. 11:19
148. The altogether lovely One	S of Sol. 5:16	John 1:17
149. Judge among nations	Isa. 2:4	Luke 11:22
150. Beautiful branch- true vine	Isa. 4:2	John 15:1
151. When Isaiah saw His glory	Isa. 6:1	John 12:40-41
152. Parables fall on deaf ears	Isa. 6:9-10	Matt. 13:13-15
153. Blind to Christ, deaf to His words	Isa. 6:9-12	Acts 28:23-29
154. To be born a virgin	Isa. 7:14	Luke 1:35
155. To be Emmanuel, God with us	Isa. 7:14	Matt. 1:18-23
156. Called Emmanuel	Isa. 8:8	Matt. 28:20
157. Stumbling stone, rock of offense	Isa. 8:14	1 Pet. 2:8
158. His ministry begins- Galilee	Isa. 9:1-2	Matt. 4:12-17
159. A child born, humanity	Isa. 9:6	Luke 1:31
160. A son given, deity	Isa. 9:6	Luke 1:32
		John 1:14
		1 Tim. 3:16
161. Son of God with power	Isa. 9:6	Rom. 1:3-4
162. The Wonderful One, Peleh	Isa. 9:6	Luke 4:22

163. The Counselor, Yaatz	Isa. 9:6	Matt. 13:54
164. The Mighty God, El Gibor	Isa. 9:6	Matt. 11:20
165. Everlasting Father, Avi Adth	Isa. 9:6	John 8:58
166. The Prince of Peace, Sar Shalom	Isa. 9:6	John 16:33
167. Establish lasting kingdom	Isa. 9:7	Luke 1:32-33
168. His character: just	Isa. 9:7	John 5:30
169. No end government/throne/peace	Isa. 9:7	Luke 1:32-33
170. Called a Nazarene	Isa. 11:1	Matt. 2:23
171. Rod of Jesse, Son of Jesse	Isa. 11:1	Luke 3:23, 32
172. Anointed One by the Spirit	Isa. 11:2	Matt. 3:16-17
173. His character: wisdom	Isa. 11:2	John 4:4-26
174. His character: truth	Isa. 11:4	John 14:6
175. Gentiles seek Him	Isa. 11:10	John 12:18-21
176. Jesus, Yeshua (salvation)	Isa. 12:2	Matt. 1:21
177. Resurrection predicted	Isa. 25:8	1 Cor. 15:54
178. Power of resurrection predicted	Isa. 26:19	John 11:43-44
179. Precious cornerstone	Isa. 28:16	Acts 4:11-12
180. Hypocritical obedience	Isa. 29:13	Matt. 15:7-9
181. Wise confounded by Word	Isa. 29:14	1 Cor. 1:18-31
182. A refuge, hiding place	Isa. 32:2	Matt. 23:37
183. He will come and save you	Isa. 35:4	Matt. 1:21
184. Have a ministry of miracles	Isa. 35:5	Matt. 11:4-6
185. Preceded by forerunner	Isa. 40:3-4	John 1:23
186. "Behold your God"	Isa. 40:9	John 1:36, 19:14
187. Shepherd, compassionate life-giver	Isa. 40:11	John 10:10-18
188. Faithful, patient redeemer	Isa. 42:1-4	Matt. 12:18-21
189. Meek and lowly	Isa. 42:2	Matt. 11:28-30
190. He brings hope for hopeless	Isa. 42:3	John 4:1-26
191. Nations await His teachings	Isa. 42:4	John 12:20-26
192. Light, salvation of Gentiles	Isa. 42:6	Luke 2:32
193. His is a world of compassion	Isa. 42:1, 6	Matt. 28:19-20
194. Blind eyes opened	Isa. 42:7	John 9:25-38
195. He is the only Savior	Isa. 43:11	Acts 4:12
196. He will send Spirit of God	Isa. 44:3	John 16:7, 13
197. He will be the Judge	Isa. 45:23	John 5:22 Rom. 14:11
198. The first and the last	Isa. 48:12	John 1:30 Rev. 1:18, 17
199. He came as Teacher	Isa. 48:17	John 3:2
200. Called from the womb	Isa. 49:1	Matt. 1:18
201. Servant from the womb	Isa. 49:5	Luke 1:3 Phil. 2:7
202. He is salvation for Israel	Isa. 49:6	Luke 2:29-32
203. He is Light of the Gentiles	Isa. 49:6	Acts 13:47
204. Salvation to ends of earth	Isa. 49:6	Acts 15:7-18
205. He is despised of the nation	Isa. 49:7	John 8:48-49
206. Heaven black at His humiliation	Isa. 50:3	Luke 23:44-45

207. Learned counselor for weary	Isa. 50:4	Matt. 11:28-29
208. Servant willingly obeys	Isa. 50:5	Matt. 26:39
209. "I gave my back to the smiters"	Isa. 50:6	Matt. 27:26
210. He was smitten on cheeks	Isa. 50:6	Matt. 26:67
211. He was spat upon	Isa. 50:6	Matt. 27:30
212. Publish tidings of peace	Isa. 52:7	Luke 4:14-15
213. The Servant exalted	Isa. 52:13	Acts 1:8-11
		Eph. 1:19-22
214. "Behold, my servant"	Isa. 52:13	Phil. 2:5-8
215. Servant shockingly abused	Isa. 52:14	Luke 18:31-34
		Matt. 26-67-68
216. All startled by His message	Isa. 52:15	Rom. 15:18-21
217. His blood shed- atonement	Isa. 52:15	Rev. 1:5
218. People wouldn't believe Him	Isa. 53:1	John 12:37-38
219. He grew up in poor family	Isa. 53:2	Luke 2:7
220. Appearance of ordinary man	Isa. 53:2	Phil. 2:7-8
221. Despised	Isa. 53:3	Luke 4:28-29
222. Rejected	Isa. 53:3	Matt. 27:21-23
223. Great sorrow and grief	Isa. 53:3	Luke 19:41-42
224. Men hide from Him	Isa. 53:3	Mark 14:50-52
225. His healing ministry	Isa. 53:4	Luke 6:17-19
226. Bear sins of the world	Isa. 53:4	1 Pet. 2:24
227. Thought to be cursed by God	Isa. 53:4	Matt. 27:41-43
228. Bears penalty for man's sin	Isa. 53:5	Luke 23:33
229. Peace between man and God	Isa. 53:5	Col. 1:20
230. His back would be whipped	Isa. 53:5	Matt. 27:26
231. Sin-bearer for all mankind	Isa. 53:6	Gal. 1:4
232. God's will to bear man's sin	Isa. 53:6	1 John 4:10
233. Oppressed and afflicted	Isa. 53:7	Matt. 27:27-31
234. Silent before His accusers	Isa. 53:7	Matt. 27:12-14
235. Sacrificial Lamb	Isa. 53:7	John 1:29
236. Confined and persecuted	Isa. 53:8	Matt. 26:47, 27:31
237. He would be judged	Isa. 53:8	John 18:13-22
238. Stricken and crucified	Isa. 53:8	Matt. 27:35
239. Dies for sins of the world	Isa. 53:8	1 John 2:2
240. Buried in rich man's grave	Isa. 53:9	Matt. 27:57
241. Innocent, done no violence	Isa. 53:9	Mark 15:3
242. No deceit in His mouth	Isa. 53:9	John 18:38
243. God's will- He die for man	Isa. 53:10	John 18:11
244. An offering for sin	Isa. 53:10	Matt. 20:28
245. Resurrected and lives forever	Isa. 53:10	Mark 16:16
246. He would prosper	Isa. 53:10	John 17:1-5
247. God satisfied with His suffering	Isa. 53:11	John 12:27
248. God's Servant	Isa. 53:11	Rom. 5:18-19
249. Would justify man to God	Isa. 53:11	Rom. 5:8-9
250. Sin-bearer for all mankind	Isa. 53:11	Heb. 9:28
251. Exalted by God for His sacrifice	Isa. 53:12	Matt. 28:18

252. Gave His life to save man	Isa. 53:12	Luke 23:46
253. Grouped with criminals	Isa. 53:12	Luke 23:32
254. Sin-bearer for all mankind	Isa. 53:12	2 Cor. 5:21
255. Intercedes on man's behalf	Isa. 53:12	Luke 23:34
256. Resurrected by God	Isa. 55:3	Acts 13:34
257. A Witness	Isa. 55:4	John 18:37
258. Inhabits eternity, lives in heart	Isa. 57:15	Rom. 10:10
259. His ministry set captives free	Isa. 58:6	Luke 4:17-18
260. Came to provide salvation	Isa. 59:1-16	John 6:40
261. Intercedes- man and God	Isa. 59:15-16	Matt. 10:32
262. Came to Zion as Redeemer	Isa. 59:20	Luke 2:38
263. Spirit of God upon Him	Isa. 61:1-2	Matt. 3:16-17
264. Preached the good news	Isa. 61:1-2	Luke 4:17-21
265. Gave freedom from bondage	Isa. 61:1-2	John 8:31-32
266. Proclaim a period of grace	Isa. 61:1-2	John 5:24
267. Power to save	Isa. 61:3	Matt. 9-6
268. Giving joy for mourning	Isa. 63:1	John 17:13
269. Descendant of David	Jer. 23:5-6	Luke 3:23-31
270. Messiah would be God	Jer. 23:5-6	John 13:13
271. Messiah both God and man	Jer. 23:5-6	1 Tim. 3:16
272. Born of a virgin	Jer. 32:22	Matt. 1:18-20
273. Messiah was new covenant	Jer. 31:31	Matt. 26:28
274. Descendant of David	Jer. 33:14-15	Luke 3:23-31
275. Spoke words of God	Ezek. 2:1	John 17:8
276. Descendant of David	Ezek. 17:22-24	Luke 3:23-31
277. Men marvel amazed	Ezek. 32:10	Mark 5:20
278. Descendant of David	Ezek. 34:23-24	Matt. 1:1
279. He would ascend into heaven	Dan. 7:13-14	Acts 1:9-11
280. Highly exalted	Dan. 7:13-14	Eph. 1:20-22
281. His dominion everlasting	Dan. 7:13-14	Luke 1:31-33
282. To make an end to sins	Dan. 9:24	Gal. 1:3-5
283. He would be holy	Dan. 9:24	Luke 1:35
284. Decree to rebuild Jerusalem	Dan. 9:25	John 12:12-13
285. Messiah cut off	Dan. 9:26	Matt. 27:35
286. Die for sins of the world	Dan. 9:26	Heb. 2:9
287. Killed before temple's destruction	Dan. 9:26	Matt. 27:50-51
288. Messiah in a glorified state	Dan. 10:5-6	Rev. 1:13-16
289. The personification of love	Hosea 11:4	2 Cor. 5:14
290. He would defeat death	Hosea 13:14	1 Cor. 15:55-57
291. His Spirit poured out	Joel 2:28	Acts 2:17-18
292. Offer salvation to mankind	Joel 2:32	Rom 10:12-13
293. Preexistence of Christ	Mic. 5:2	Heb. 1:8
294. Born in Bethlehem	Mic. 5:2	Matt. 2:1-2
295. God's Servant	Mic. 5:2	John 15:10
296. From everlasting	Mic. 5:2	John 8:58
297. Would visit second temple	Hag. 2:6-9	Luke 2:27-32
298. Descendant of Zerubbabel	Hag. 2:23	Luke 3:23-27
299. God's Servant	Zech. 3:8	John 17:4

300. Priest and King	Zech .6:12-13	Heb. 8:1
301. Greeted with rejoicing in Jerusalem	Zech. 9:9	Matt. 2:8-10
302. Beheld as King	Zech. 9:9	John 12:12-13
303. Messiah would be just	Zech. 9:9	John 5:30
304. Messiah brought salvation	Zech. 9:9	Luke 19:10
305. Messiah would be humble	Zech. 9:9	Matt. 11:29
306. Rode donkey into Jerusalem	Zech. 9:9	Matt. 21:6-9
307. The cornerstone	Zech. 10:4	Eph. 2:20
308. Unfit leaders in Israel	Zech. 11:4-6	Matt. 23:1-4
309. Protection removed at rejection	Zech. 11:4-6	Luke 19:41-44
310. Rejected for another king	Zech. 11:4-6	John 19:13-15
311. Ministry to poor	Zech. 11:7	Matt. 9:35-36
312. Unbelief forces rejection	Zech. 11:8	Matt. 23:13-36
313. Despised and abhorred	Zech. 11:8	Matt. 27:20
314. Ceases ministry to His rejectors	Zech. 11:9	Matt. 3:10-11
315. Protection removed at rejection	Zech. 11:10-11	Luke 19:41-44
316. Messiah would be God	Zech. 11:10-11	John 14:7
317. Betrayed for 30 pieces of silver	Zech. 11:12-13	Matt. 26:14-15
318. Rejected	Zech. 11:12-13	Matt. 26:14-15
319. Silver thrown into house of Lord	Zech. 11:12-13	Matt. 27:3-5
320. Messiah would be God	Zech. 11:12-13	John 12:45
321. Messiah's body would be pierced	Zech. 12:10	John 19:34-37
322. Messiah both God and man	Zech. 12:10	John 10:30
323. Messiah would be rejected	Zech. 12:10	John 1:11
324. His will to die for mankind	Zech. 13:7	John 18:11
325. A violent death	Zech. 13:7	Matt. 27:35
326. Both God and man	Zech. 13:7	John 14:9
327. Israel scattered for rejecting Him	Zech. 13:7	Matt. 26:31-56
328. Messenger prepared the way	Mal. 3:1	Matt. 11:10
329. Sudden appearance at temple	Mal. 3:1	Mark 11:15-16
330. Messenger of the New Covenant	Mal. 3:1	Luke 4:43
331. Forerunner in the spirit of Elijah	Mal. 4:5	Matt. 3:1-2
332. Turn many to righteousness	Mal. 4:6	Luke 1:16-17

Please note that the above prophecies do not include the more complicated ones such as the foretelling of the exact date Jesus would ride into Jerusalem on a donkey and allow the people to declare Him the King of the Jews.

They also do not include the myriad of types and shadows that also foretold His coming, such as the fabulous one in which God positioned the several million Hebrew population into the shape of a cross as they crossed the desert, with the four characters of Jesus being an ox, an eagle, a lion, and a face of a man on the outside four banners of the human cross.

CHRIST'S PRAYER FOR YOU

The night Jesus was arrested to be crucified he prayed a three part prayer. The first part was for Himself, the second part was for His disciples, but the third part of the prayer was for you. It was an amazing prayer and one that we should all intently read and understand. Below is that wonderful prayer. I have taken the liberty to omit the word "them" and leave it blank. Please insert your own name in every blank spot as you read it, because this prayer by Jesus is personally for you:

"I pray also for _____ who will believe in me through their message, that all of them may be one, Father, just as you are in me and I am in you. May _____ also be in us so the world may believe that you sent me. I have given the glory that you gave me, that they may be one as we are one. I in _____ and you in me. May they be brought to complete unity to let the world know that you sent me and have loved _____ even as you have loved me.

Father, I want _____ who you have given me to be with me where I am, and to see my glory, the glory you have given me because you loved me before the creation of the world.

Righteous Father, though the world does not know you, I know you, and _____ knows that you have sent me. I have made you known to _____, and will continue to make you known in order that the love you have for me may be in _____ and that I myself may be in _____." John 17:20-26.

Exceptional Recommended Reading

Book	Author
The Practice of the Presence of God	Brother Lawrence
The God of All Comfort	Hannah Whitall Smith
The Christian's Secret of a Happy Life	Hannah Whitall Smith
The Signature of God	Grant R. Jeffrey
Cosmic Codes	Chuck Missler
Unleashing the Beast	Perry Stone
The Science of God	Gerald l. Schroeder
Something More	Catherine Marshall
The Case for Christ	Lee Strobel
Is That Really you, God	Loren Cunningham
Making Jesus Lord	Loren Cunningham
The Screwtape Letters	C.S. Lewis
Ruthless Trust	Brennan Manning
God's Fool	George N. Patterson
The Divine Romance	Gene Edwards
Release of Power	George Mueller
Loving God	Charles Colson
Rebel With a Cause	Franklin Graham
Experiencing God Through Prayer	Madame Guyon
Fresh Wind, Fresh Fire	Jim Cymbala
Even Greater	Reinhard Bonke
Heaven, Here I Come	Jean Darnall
Brush Of An Angel's Wing	Charlie W. Shedd

Many of the above can be ordered as used books very inexpensively by doing a Google search. The above books are not in any order and we hope you will read them all.

About The Author

Although Bob Morley's educational background at the University of North Carolina was in psychology, his overriding passion is the study of all things pertaining to God. Unlocking God's Secrets is the culmination of over 13,000 hours of intensive research and study into that passion.

Mr. Morley is also the president and founder of Christian Insurance Marketing , a nationwide personal lines insurance marketing company with agents in 32 states. The company's web address is www.christianinsurancemarketing.com.

Bob currently resides in South Carolina with his wife, Barbara. They have four daughters and twelve grandchildren. He can be reached for speaking, information, or personal dialogue by email at morley120@juno.com. Bob would love to hear from you with any comments.